THE ADEODATUS HANDBOOK ON CATHOLIC EDUCATION & CULTURE

THE ADEODATUS SERIES ON CATHOLIC EDUCATION & CULTURE

General Editors: Alex E. Lessard & R. Jared Staudt

The Adeodatus Series on Catholic Education & Culture offers books and essay collections dedicated to the retrieval, renewal, and refinement of the Catholic educational tradition. In covering Catholic educational figures, principles, themes, pedagogies, curricula, and culture, this series provides rich, practical resources to support Catholic leaders, teachers, and laity.

THE ADEODATUS HANDBOOK ON CATHOLIC EDUCATION & CULTURE

Volume 1: From Jesus the Teacher to St. John Henry Newman

EDITED BY *Alex E. Lessard and R. Jared Staudt*

FOREWORD BY *Most Rev. James D. Conley*

Catholic Education Press
Washington, D.C.

Catholic Education Press,
The Catholic University of America

The paper used in this publication meets the minimum requirements of American National Standards for Information Science—Permanence of Paper for Printed Library Materials, ANSI Z39.48-1992.

∞

Cataloging-in-Publication Data is available at the Library of Congress
ISBN (paperback): 978-1-949822-54-0
ISBN (ebook): 978-1-949822-55-7

TABLE OF CONTENTS

Introduction to The Adeodatus Series on Catholic Education & Culture

Alex E. Lessard

"Educating the mind without educating the heart is no education at all." This saying, often misattributed to Aristotle, captures a key insight into the nature and purpose of learning. In his prescient work *The Abolition of Man* (1943), C. S. Lewis diagnoses the central malady of modern education with this vivid analogy: "The task of the modern educator is not to cut down jungles but to irrigate deserts" (14). For Lewis, the defining feature of the deserted soul is not an excess of rational thought but a dearth of rightly ordered loves. Our students suffer not because they think too much but because they desire too little; the disease is not atrophy of intellect but a withering of the chest, the seat of magnanimity and courage: "We make men without chests and expect of them virtue and enterprise. We laugh at honour and are shocked to find traitors in our midst" (37).

Over a century before Lewis, St. John Henry Newman foresaw the spiritual hole at the core of an emerging industrial-educational complex. In a celebrated and controversial passage of *The Idea of a University* (1873), Newman asserts that if he was forced to choose between a "so-called University" that "dispensed with residence and tutorial" guidance but conferred degrees to all who pass a comprehensive examination, and a University that "merely" gathered students together for their undergraduate years with "no professors or examinations at all," he would without hesitation choose the latter. Such is the indispensable value Newman placed on the personal influence in the formation of heart and mind. Against the "indigestible knowledge stones" Nietzsche heard rattling around in modern man, and against the utilitarian cognitional schema of Bentham and Mill, with its aggregate of discrete, quantifiable, eminently useful facts, Newman upheld an older ideal of education as the cultivation of philosophic and moral virtue within a community of friends. A university in the fullest sense, he insists, "is not a foundry, or a mint, or a treadmill"; rather, it is an alma mater, a nourishing mother, "knowing her children one by one" (145).

In this spirit, Adeodatus was founded by teachers dedicated to the integral formation of our students because we were formed thus through the personal influence of great mentors. We are merely the latest links in a long chain of hearts speaking to hearts (*cor ad cor loquitur* multiplied eternally in the Sacred Heart). Each recipient of such a great gift is naturally inspired to share it—becoming, in Newman's words, "a link in a chain, a bond of connection between persons" (*Meditations and Devotions*, March 7, 1848, no. 2).

In early 2018, we lost three giant links in the chain within forty days: Roy Rohter, founding donor of several Catholic academies; Father Matthew Lamb, beloved teacher at Boston College and Ave Maria University; and Don Briel, the founder of the Catholic Studies movement. They left behind rich legacies to preserve, as well as works to be carried forward. It is in their honor that Adeodatus supports the ongoing renewal of Catholic education and culture.

Adeodatus takes its name from St. Augustine's beloved son—a figure whose life illuminates the intimate connection between learning and love that lies at the heart of authentic education. Born out of sin but transformed by grace, Adeodatus became not only Augustine's student but his interlocutor in *De Magistro* (*On the Teacher*), a philosophical dialogue that explores the deepest mysteries of teaching and learning. Augustine writes in Book IX of *The Confessions* that the boy's remarkable intellectual gifts "filled me with awe," yet it was the formation of his heart through the witness of his father's own conversion that proved most significant for him. When both were baptized by St. Ambrose in Milan, their relationship was transfigured from a merely natural bond into a spiritual fellowship oriented toward eternal wisdom. Like that intimate conversation between father and son, this series seeks to foster the integration of mind and heart, wisdom and love, that characterizes authentic Catholic education.

These insights, though they have taken on a new urgency in the light of our postmodern discontents, are perennial truths as old as Western civilization itself. From Plato and Aristotle through Augustine and Aquinas down to the recent past, the classical and Christian traditions have consistently stressed the essential unity of intellectual and moral formation, the necessary bond between training the mind and tempering the passions. Whether our present cultural moment feels dire or hopeful, we should take solace in the realization that thoughtful souls in every age have grappled with crises that must have seemed to them no less imposing. Even a figure as outwardly serene as Socrates had to defend his vision of liberal learning against the skeptical pragmatism of the Sophists and the violent anti-intellectualism of the Athenian mob. On his deathbed in 430 AD, St. Augustine wept copious and continuous tears while praying the penitential psalms as the Vandals advanced, a memento that civilization is always a fragile achievement, ever vulnerable to the forces of barbarism. At critical junctures like these, the way forward requires a reappropriation of first principles, a return to the sources of wisdom.

Today, Adeodatus pursues its mission through three complementary paths. First, it gathers the finest resources from the Catholic educational tradition, bringing together leading contemporary scholars to share their insights in conference and forum talks. This also helps sustain and expand the community of friends in Catholic education. Second, it seeks to bring practically-oriented educational resources to Catholic laity of all ages and stages of life, publishing videos, books, courses, and curricula that make lifelong education accessible. Third, it actively supports Catholic culture through commissioning new art and reviving traditional forms, recognizing that education is part of an integral communal life.

This mission is actualized through several key initiatives. The organization hosts biennial national conferences on Catholic Education & Culture, along with single-author and single-themed forums. It has established this book series with Catholic University of America Press, producing works dedicated to retrieving, renewing, and refining Catholic education. The Adeodatus Series on Catholic Education & Culture will include comprehensive handbooks covering all aspects of Catholic educational principles, pedagogy, curriculum, and culture, as well as works focused on topics such as the sacramental mission of Catholic education, cultivating good students, and the sociological study of American Catholic education.

The organization's educational programs span multiple levels and formats. Its lifelong learning courses bring together Catholics of various ages and backgrounds to study foundational texts and topics under expert guidance, with the goal of fostering intellectual community and ongoing formation. For Santiago Catholic Trade School students, Adeodatus provides intellectual formation that complements their technical training. At the graduate level, members teach courses on the foundations of Western education and the history, philosophy, and mission of Catholic schools, helping to form the next generation of educational leaders.

At its core, Adeodatus believes that education should awaken wonder for the pursuit of wisdom. The organization works to retrieve the wisdom of the past and reformulate it for today's world, promoting authentic renewal in Catholic education and culture through an integrated approach that touches all aspects of intellectual, moral, and spiritual life. Through these various initiatives, Adeodatus strives to fulfill Cardinal Newman's vision of an intelligent, well-instructed laity who deeply understand and can give an account of their faith.

For those of us who stand in the Judeo-Christian current of the great tradition, the ultimate source and end of all our seeking is the creative and redemptive intelligence disclosed in Scripture and the incarnation. The Catholic vision of education flows from a profound understanding of reality as sacramental, of truth as unified, and of the human person as made for communion with God. This is not merely a theoretical framework but a living wisdom that shapes how we teach, what we teach, and why we teach. At its heart lies a radical claim: that all authentic education is fundamentally a participation in the divine pedagogy, in God's own patient work of forming souls for eternal life.

This vision stands in stark contrast to both ancient and modern reductionisms. Against the materialist view that sees education as mere skill acquisition or career preparation, it insists that learning is ordered to wisdom, not just knowledge. Against the rationalist tradition that would divorce reason from faith, it maintains their essential unity and complementarity. Against the relativism that denies objective truth, it upholds the mind's capacity to know reality and to grow in understanding of God's creation. And against the individualism that fragments community, it emphasizes education as a fundamentally relational activity, rooted in love and oriented toward communion.

The Original Great Command and Original Sin

As the first verse of Genesis declares, "In the beginning, God created the heavens and the earth"; and as the Prologue of John's Gospel proclaims, that same eternal Logos who is with God and is God became flesh and dwelt among us, the light shining in the darkness. Seen in this radiance, the story of humanity's engagement with the mystery of being begins not with Socratic questioning but with our first parents in the Garden of Eden. It is there that we must look to discern the fundamental lineaments of our nature and destiny, the origin of our errant desires, and the path to their divinely ordained fulfillment.

In the primordial paradise vividly depicted in Genesis, we find man and woman abiding in a state at once resplendent and delicate, marked by original innocence and preternatural gifts, yet charged with a challenging vocation. Created in the *imago Dei* and placed in a garden of delight, Adam and Eve are called to be fruitful and multiply, to fill the earth and subdue it, to cultivate the soil and exercise benevolent dominion over every living thing that moves upon the earth. As the medieval exegetes loved to point out, the first man is fashioned from the *adamah*, the humble humus, and appointed to serve as the keeper of the garden, the prototypical *georgos* or tiller of the earth. Adam's work of "dressing and keeping" (Gn 2:15), the Hebrew *shamar*, is no mere horticultural hobby but a high priestly calling, a consecrated custodianship of the sanctuary of creation.

Interwoven with this mission of stewardship is the equally exalted task of contemplation, enshrined in the primal act of naming the animals. In bestowing names on the various creatures, Adam penetrates their God-given natures, perceiving their inherent forms and purposes. Here we find the archetypal pattern of all true education: the intimate connection between careful tending and deep understanding, between loving custody and contemplative insight. For the unfallen Adam, endowed with preternatural clarity of intellect, this metaphysical transparency of creation is the rule rather than the exception. The book of nature is an open and inexhaustible text, yielding its deepest secrets to the innocent eye and attentive heart.

In this original state of integrity, our first parents enjoyed an immediate intimacy with God and each other, an effortless alignment of nature and grace, knowledge and love, that theologians call the *donum superadditum* or superadded gift. Their nakedness is at once corporeal and spiritual, an unselfconscious openness to the gaze of the beloved, untainted by shame or fear: "And the man and his wife were both naked, and were not ashamed" (Gn 2:25). In Eden, Adam and Eve enjoyed a blessed state, their bodies undamaged by death, their souls untroubled by disordered desires. Their vision—both physical and spiritual—was clear and unimpeded, allowing them to perceive the goodness of creation, including themselves, as a reflection of God's love. In their preternatural innocence, they delighted in God both directly in his presence and also through the splendor of his works.

Yet even in this paradisal state, the life of our first parents was neither static nor complete. The presence of the tree of life alongside the tree of the knowledge of good and evil suggests a probationary period, a divinely appointed curriculum of growth in wisdom and love. By abstaining from the forbidden fruit, by freely subordinating their own wills to the will of their Creator, Adam and Eve would have been led progressively deeper into participation in the inner life of the Trinity. They would have advanced from the natural knowledge of God gleaned from the created order to an ever more direct and unmediated contemplation of the divine essence. Here we glimpse the original pattern of human learning: not a grasping after autonomous knowledge, but a patient receptivity to truth bestowed as gift.

Tragically, this upward ascent was cut short by the primal act of disobedience, the fateful choice of the first couple to assert their own autonomy and become "like God, knowing good and evil" (Gn 3:5). In reaching for the fruit of the forbidden tree, in transgressing the divine commandment, Adam and Eve ruptured the delicate harmony of nature and grace, setting in motion a ripple effect of disorder that would extend to the farthest reaches of the cosmos. The immediate consequences of the fall are cataclysmic: the loss of sanctifying grace and preternatural gifts, the darkening of the intellect, the weakening of the will, the malicious rebellion of the passions. Where once they enjoyed the gift of integrity, our first parents now experience the sting of concupiscence, the interior division of the soul against itself. Where once they walked in easy fellowship with their Maker, they now feel the need to hide from his presence, to cover their shame with fig leaves.

This primordial rupture shapes all subsequent human learning. Knowledge becomes both remedy and temptation—a means of healing our wounded nature and a potential source of pride that can drive us further from wisdom. Yet even in this fallen state, the *imago Dei* remains fundamentally intact, indelibly impressed on the human soul as a seal of its high calling and ultimate destiny. The glory of creation, though obscured by the smoke of sin, continues to declare the eternal power and divinity of the Creator, accessible to the natural light of reason. In St. Augustine's telling phrase, the restless heart of man remains an abiding reminder of its origin and end in God, a personal and collective craving for the infinite that no finite reality can satisfy: "For Thou hast made us for Thyself and our hearts are restless till they rest in Thee" (*Confessions* bk. I, ch. 1).

In this light, the successive covenants and divine pedagogy of the Old Testament may be seen as a gradual preparation for the definitive theophany of the incarnation. From the initial promise to Abraham that his descendants will outnumber the stars, through the giving of the Law to Moses on Sinai, down to the messianic yearnings of the later prophets, Israel is progressively inducted into the mind and heart of God, educated in holiness as no other nation has been. Yet even this intimate knowledge of the divine will remains partial and veiled, an oblique anticipation of the Advent. It is only when the eternal Son takes flesh and dwells among us, bearing the human likeness and embracing the human lot, that the face of the Father is finally revealed in its fullness. In the opening words of the Letter to the Hebrews, "In the past, God spoke to our ancestors through the prophets at many times and in various ways, but in these last days he has spoken to us by his Son."

Incarnate Love

With the incarnation, the eternal Word through whom all things were made descends into human flesh, assuming a human nature in order to restore and elevate it. In Christ, the New Adam and gardener of the new creation, the divine image shines forth in a perfect and definitive epiphany. His life, death, and resurrection recapitulate and bring to triumphant conclusion the entire narrative arc of salvation history, inscribing the names of the redeemed in the Book of Life of the Lamb. For each disciple, as for the whole pilgrim people of God, the task is to take up this divinely authored story and make it our own, allowing it to shape our identity and guide our actions. Education becomes participation in this drama of redemption, a means by which we are gradually conformed to the image of the Son.

And because Jesus reveals God as Love, if we distill the essence of education down to a single element, it must be love. As Pope Benedict XVI reminded Catholic educators in an address at The Catholic University of America during his historic visit to the United States in April 2008:

> Education is integral to the mission of the Church to proclaim the Good News. First and foremost every Catholic educational institution is a place to encounter the living God who in Jesus Christ reveals his transforming love and truth. This relationship elicits a desire to grow in the knowledge and understanding of Christ and his teaching. In this way those who meet him are drawn by the very power of the Gospel to lead a new life characterized by all that is beautiful, good, and true; a life of Christian witness nurtured and strengthened within the community of our Lord's disciples, the Church.

This primacy of love is inscribed in our very nature as relational beings, made in the image and likeness of a Trinitarian God. Long before we are capable of rational thought or deliberate choice, we are already enmeshed in a web of relationships, dependent on others for our physical, emotional, and spiritual sustenance. From the first moments of life, when we gaze into the face of our mother and see there a reflection of our own dignity and worth, we are learning what it means to be loved into wholeness. The sacrificial love of parents, the unconditional acceptance of family, the formative matrix of a stable home—these are the indispensable preconditions for the emergence of a healthy sense of self.

As we grow and mature, our circle of loves naturally expands to include friends, mentors, teachers, and the larger community of learning. Yet in all of these human loves, however noble and enriching, there remains an unquenchable thirst for a deeper meaning, a yearning for the infinite that points beyond itself to the divine. Again we think of our restless hearts. Only in the absolute and unconditional love of God do we find the true fulfillment of our deepest desires, the answer to the question that we are to ourselves.

For Christians, this revelation of divine love finds its definitive expression in the person of Jesus Christ, the incarnate Word who becomes man in order to redeem and divinize our fallen humanity. "In this the love of God was made manifest among us, that God sent his only-begotten Son into the world, so that we might live through him" (1 Jn 4:9). In the self-emptying love of Christ, poured out on the cross for the salvation of the world, we discover the true measure of our worth, the depths of a mercy that knows no bounds. "Greater love has no man than this, that a man lay down his life for his friends" (Jn 15:13).

To believe in the Gospel, then, is to be seized by a Love that surpasses all understanding, to be drawn into the very heart of a Mystery that embraces the whole of reality. This is also the supreme invitation and challenge of Christian education: to be a living sacrament of God's love in the midst of a wounded and broken world. For it is not mere knowledge that will transform our lives and communities, but rather a knowledge that is born of love, a wisdom that purifies the heart and illumines the mind. In the words of St. Paul, "If I speak in the tongues of men and of angels, but have not love, I am a noisy gong or a clanging cymbal" (1 Cor 13:1).

At the heart of this transformative love is a spirit of reverence, a profound attentiveness to the mystery of the other. To love in truth is to honor the unique dignity of each person, to see in every human face an image of the living God, and to be present to each other in an attitude of receptivity and humility, recognizing that we are all beggars before the threshold of grace. In the context of education, this ethos of encounter finds its most powerful embodiment in the witness of the teacher, whose love for God, for truth, and for his or her students can awaken in them a desire for the good, the true, and the beautiful.

This understanding of education as an act of love transforms our entire approach to teaching and learning. Like Augustine with his son Adeodatus, the Catholic educator engages students in a dialogue that transcends mere academic exchange. Each subject becomes an occasion for encounter—not just with facts or concepts, but with truth that bears the imprint of divine love. Mathematics reveals not just abstract patterns but the loving intelligence that orders the cosmos; literature opens not just windows into human experience but into the divine drama of salvation; history traces not just the sequence of events but the patient work of Providence drawing all things to their proper end.

In the Catholic school, love must permeate not just individual relationships but the entire culture of learning. When parents entrust their children to such a school, they are not abdicating their responsibility as primary educators but enlisting the help of a wider community in the formation of mind, heart, and spirit. The bond of trust between parent and teacher, rooted in their shared love for the integral development of the child, becomes the foundation for authentic education in wisdom and virtue. Through this network of relationships—between teachers and students, among students themselves, between school and family—love creates the conditions where true learning can flourish.

This is why, in the Catholic tradition, the witness of holy teachers has always been held up as the supreme model of educational excellence. From the early Benedictine monasteries through the medieval universities to the teaching orders of more recent times, the Church has understood that education flows most powerfully through the channel of personal influence animated by love. Such teachers are not merely transmitters of information but living embodiments of the truth they teach, witnesses to the integration of faith and reason, nature and grace, that they seek to foster in their students.

Sacramental and Integrated

This primacy of love leads us naturally to understand education in sacramental terms. For if all reality bears the imprint of divine love, then every aspect of learning can become a means of encounter with the living God. This sacramental worldview, nurtured by the Church's liturgy and devotional life, is essential to the formation of a Catholic imagination. By faith we understand that the world was created by the word of God, that the visible realm is charged with the grandeur of its invisible Source. The book of nature and the book of Scripture are complementary revelations of the divine mystery, each shedding light on the other. The teacher's task is to help students read both books aright, to see creation as a sacrament of God's presence, a finite participation in his infinite light, truth, goodness, and beauty.

Indeed, this sacramental understanding of reality transforms every aspect of Catholic education. It shapes not only what we teach but how we teach, for if all creation bears the divine imprint, then every subject becomes a potential path to wisdom. Mathematics reveals the intelligible order woven into the fabric of being; literature opens windows into the depths of the human heart; history traces Providence's subtle thread through time; the sciences unveil the rational structure of the material world. Each discipline, properly understood, leads the mind toward contemplation of eternal truth.

Yet this integration demands more than mere intellectual assent. As Newman understood, the formation of a genuinely Catholic mind requires a particular habit of thought, what he called an "illative sense"—the capacity to see connections, to grasp the unity of truth across different domains of knowledge. This habit is best cultivated through personal influence within a community of learning. The relationship between teacher and student becomes not merely the transmission of information but an initiation into a way of seeing and being in the world.

Here we touch upon the heart of Catholic education: the formation of persons capable of recognizing and responding to truth in all its manifestations. This formation engages the whole person—intellect, will, imagination, and affections. Through encounter with beauty in art and literature, students develop the spiritual sensibility needed to recognize and love what is truly good. Through rigorous training in logic and rhetoric, they acquire the tools to distinguish truth from falsehood. Through immersion in history and tradition, they gain the wisdom to judge present challenges in light of timeless principles.

The Catholic educator's task is thus both humble and exalted. We are called to be witnesses as well as instructors, modeling in our own lives the integration of faith and reason, nature and grace. Our work participates in the divine pedagogy, in God's patient drawing of souls toward himself. Again, as with Augustine and Adeodatus, we engage in a dialogue of love that transcends mere academic exchange, touching the deepest springs of human formation.

This vision has deep implications for how we structure and conduct Catholic education at every level. The curriculum must reflect the inherent unity of knowledge, not as an artificial construct but as an organic whole, oriented toward wisdom. The classical liberal arts provide a tested framework for this integration: grammar trains precision in thought and expression; logic develops rigorous reasoning; rhetoric cultivates persuasive communication; while the quadrivium of arithmetic, geometry, astronomy, and music reveals the mathematical harmonies underlying creation. These arts are "liberal" precisely because they free the mind for contemplation of truth.

Yet this classical heritage must engage contemporary needs. Modern disciplines, from the natural sciences to social studies, have their proper place when oriented toward genuine understanding rather than mere utility. The challenge is not to choose between ancient and modern, but to maintain the unity of knowledge while respecting the legitimate autonomy of each field. This requires teachers who grasp both the distinct methods of their disciplines and their ultimate orientation toward wisdom.

The incarnational principle suggests that teaching methods must respect both natural development and supernatural calling. Like the divine pedagogy revealed in Scripture, Catholic education proceeds gradually, meeting students where they are while drawing them toward what they are called to become. Wonder precedes analysis; experience grounds abstraction; imagination prepares the way for conceptual understanding. The teacher guides students through these stages not mechanically but organically, attentive to both universal patterns of development and individual paths of growth.

The school itself must become a living community that embodies the truths it teaches. Its culture should foster the habits of mind and heart essential to genuine learning: reverence before mystery, patience in pursuing truth, charity in dialogue, humility in receiving wisdom. Regular rhythms of prayer and worship, shared meals and celebrations, common readings and discussions—all these create an environment where faith and reason, nature and grace, can flourish together.

The object of a liberal education is the cultivation of a particular habit of mind, an intellectual virtue that cannot be reduced to the mastery of any specialized technique. Newman aptly describes this intellectual enlargement as a capacity "to see things as they are, to go right to the point, to disentangle a skein of thought, to detect what is sophistical, and to discard what is irrelevant" (*The Idea of a University*, 178). To achieve this well-rounded judgment, he argues, it is essential to perceive the relations between the various branches of knowledge, to locate each part within the whole. Only in this way can the student transcend the narrow bounds of his own experience and achieve an impartial view of reality.

At the heart of Newman's educational philosophy is a vision of the unity of truth. Against the fragmentation and specialization of knowledge, he contends that the disciplines exist in dynamic interrelation, each shedding light on all the others. In his words, "all branches of knowledge are connected together, because the subject-matter of knowledge is intimately united in itself, as being the acts and the work of the Creator. Hence it is that the Sciences, into which our knowledge may be said to be cast, have multiplied bearings one on another, and an internal sympathy, and admit, or rather demand, comparison and adjustment. They complete, correct, balance each other" (*Idea*, 99).

In this respect, we may say that the branches of knowledge are each a finite participation in God's infinite knowledge of himself and of all things in relation to himself. The created intellect, made in the image of the divine intellect, reaches its perfection when it attains the beatific vision, that eternal face-to-face encounter in which God is known even as we are fully known. The integral curriculum of a Christian liberal arts education is an anticipation of that supremely fulfilling act in which all our desires are brought to rest in the contemplation of Uncreated Truth, Goodness, and Beauty.

The ordered unity of knowledge should inform the life of Catholic schools. For it suggests that the ultimate aim of our institutions is not to transmit discrete bodies of information but to form students capable of seeing the connections among all things in God. Such formation requires both breadth and depth—broad enough exposure to recognize the unity of truth across different domains, and deep enough engagement in particular disciplines to appreciate their distinct methods and insights. The curriculum becomes not a mere collection of subjects but an ordered path to wisdom.

The notion of a "liberal" education thus takes on deeper meaning. For the authentic freedom of the mind is not a mere liberty of indifference, a rootless and arbitrary freedom of choice, but the freedom of a creature made in the image of God, called to share in the inner life of the Creator. It is the freedom of the soul that recognizes in the truth its own origin and destiny, its birthright and inheritance as a child of God. As Jesus declares in the Gospel of John, "If you continue in my word, you are truly my disciples, and you will know the truth, and the truth will make you free" (Jn 8:31–32).

This integration extends to the relationship between faith and reason. Faith seeks understanding through reason, while reason finds its completion and transcendent purpose through faith. Neither faculty abolishes the other; rather, they work together in harmony, like two wings on which the human spirit rises to contemplation of truth. This means Catholic schools must maintain high academic standards while orienting all learning toward ultimate questions of meaning and purpose. Every discipline becomes a potential path to wisdom when understood in its proper relationship to divine truth.

Here, too, we see the nobility of the Catholic teacher's vocation. Rather than a mere specialist in one field, the teacher becomes a guide to the unity of truth itself. Whether teaching mathematics or literature, science or history, the Catholic educator helps students discover how each discipline opens onto the infinite, how each way of knowing contributes to the great symphony of truth. This requires teachers who are themselves lifelong learners, constantly seeking to deepen their understanding not only of their particular subject but of its connections to other fields and ultimately to divine wisdom.

This approach transforms everyday classroom practice. A lesson in geometry becomes an exploration of the eternal forms that structure reality; the study of poetry reveals the analogical nature of being itself; scientific investigation unveils the rational order impressed by the divine Logos on creation. Even seemingly practical subjects like grammar and rhetoric take on deeper significance as tools for approaching truth and communicating it to others. The goal is not to impose artificial connections but to help students discover the real unity that undergirds all authentic knowledge.

The student's journey likewise becomes a gradual initiation into this unified vision of reality. Beginning with the natural wonder of childhood, proceeding through the disciplined study of particular subjects, and culminating in the capacity for synthetic understanding, education follows the mind's natural movement from the particular to the universal, from the visible to the invisible, from the temporal to the eternal. At each stage, students need both the security of clear guidance and the freedom to make discoveries for themselves, both the transmission of tradition and the space for creative appropriation.

This is why the Catholic intellectual tradition has always prized both structure and spontaneity in education. The ordered progression of the trivium and quadrivium provides the necessary foundation, while the spirit of open inquiry and contemplative leisure creates room for genuine insight. Memory work and careful analysis prepare the way for imaginative synthesis; mastery of fundamental skills enables creative expression; disciplined study strengthens the intellect for contemplative wisdom.

This Catholic educational vision, with its emphasis on the unity of truth and the development of the whole person, stands in stark contrast to the fragmentation and information overload of the modern world. In an age where knowledge is rapidly expanding but wisdom seems increasingly elusive, the role of the Catholic teacher becomes even more vital. Rather than simply transmitting facts or training narrow specialists, the Catholic educator is called to guide students on a journey of intellectual and spiritual integration. The classroom becomes a place not just for the mastery of particular subjects, but for the cultivation of the capacity to perceive the deeper connections that link all authentic knowledge to divine wisdom.

This holistic approach prepares students not merely for professional success, but for the lifelong pursuit of truth, goodness and beauty—an essential task in an era when the very meaning of these transcendental ideals is under assault. Thus, the Catholic teacher's vocation takes on a particular nobility, as an ever more crucial counterweight to the fragmenting forces of our time.

These fragmenting forces, these very challenges, properly understood, render its wisdom more urgent and precious. In his *Choruses from "The Rock"* (1934), T. S. Eliot distilled the essence of our modern predicament: "Where is the wisdom we have lost in knowledge? Where is the knowledge we have lost in information?" (7) The digital revolution has intensified this crisis, transforming not just how we access information but how we encounter reality itself. Deep reading gives way to superficial scanning; sustained attention fragments into constant distraction; memory atrophies through outsourced recall; direct experience yields to mediated interaction; contemplation surrenders to constant stimulation. The "shallows" of the perpetual "ping" is a hostile environment for the cultivation of wisdom.

The dangers are especially acute for the young. As mounting clinical evidence attests, smartphones and screen-based technologies pose serious risks to children's cognitive, social, and emotional development. The spike in adolescent depression, anxiety, and loneliness signals a profound crisis of human formation. The "i" in iPhone, as it were, refers more to an atomized, anomic, autonomously expressive self than to a whole person flourishing in the nourishing relationships of family, friendship, and flesh-and-blood community.

Yet rather than either reject or uncritically embrace technology, Catholic education must develop what we might call a sacramental approach to the digital age. This means creating intentional practices that preserve and nurture essential human capacities: regular periods of "digital fasting" that restore the ability to be fully present; sustained training in deep reading that develops powers of attention;

emphasis on handwriting and memory work that maintains direct neural engagement; priority given to face-to-face discussion that cultivates genuine dialogue; integration of physical books and materials that ground learning in tactile reality.

Above all, Catholic schools must establish and explain healthy technological boundaries within a rich communal life. When students experience the joy of shared meals and conversations, the satisfaction of athletic and artistic endeavor, the wonder of scientific observation and mathematical discovery, the beauty of liturgical prayer and sacred music, they develop an experiential counterweight to digital distraction. Technology finds its proper place as servant rather than master of human formation.

More fundamental than the technological challenge is the increasing fragmentation of knowledge into isolated specialties lacking any unified vision. When disciplines no longer communicate with each other, when facts are divorced from meaning, when skills are separated from wisdom, education loses its power to transform the soul. This fragmentation manifests not just in curriculum but in the very structure of learning: departmental silos replace interdisciplinary dialogue; standardized testing substitutes for authentic assessment; career preparation overshadows character formation.

The Catholic response must begin with recovery of the unity inherent in reality itself. Through carefully chosen core texts that span disciplinary boundaries, through thematic units that reveal hidden connections, through team teaching that models intellectual dialogue, we can help students discover the organic relationships among all truths. A lesson in mathematics becomes an exploration of divine order; historical study reveals patterns of providence; scientific observation awakens metaphysical wonder. The goal is not to impose artificial connections but to unveil the unity already present in creation.

This integration extends to the relationship between faith and reason, nature and grace. In Catholic education, theology is not merely one subject among many but the light that illuminates all fields of study. Yet this illumination respects the proper autonomy of each discipline. The science teacher need not become a theologian, nor the literature professor an apologist. Rather, each discipline contributes its unique perspective to our understanding of reality, while the Catholic intellectual tradition provides the architectural framework that shows how these perspectives cohere.

The Aims of The Adeodatus Series on Catholic Education & Culture

The contemporary crisis of authority and tradition perhaps poses the most fundamental challenge to authentic education. When received wisdom is reflexively rejected, when institutional authority is systematically distrusted, when objective truth itself is called into question, how can genuine learning take place? Yet here, too, the Catholic vision offers not just critique but constructive response. Authority in Catholic education is always understood as service, oriented toward the student's genuine good. Teachers exercise their authority not through imposition but through witness, modeling both mastery of their subject and docility before truth.

This understanding transforms how tradition is handed on. Rather than a dead deposit to be memorized, tradition becomes a living conversation in which students are invited to participate. Through Socratic seminars that engage perennial questions, through writing assignments that demand personal appropriation of ideas, through artistic projects that encourage creative interpretation, students discover themselves as active receivers of wisdom rather than passive consumers of information. The goal is not mere preservation of the past but its fruitful engagement with present challenges.

Meeting these challenges requires more than individual effort, however dedicated. It demands communities of educators formed in Catholic wisdom and committed to mutual support and ongoing development. The Adeodatus Series on Catholic Education & Culture aims to nurture such communities by providing both theoretical foundation and practical guidance. Drawing from Scripture, tradition, and the great masters of Catholic education, from the Church Fathers through medieval masters to modern renewers, these works will offer not antiquarian interest or the nostalgic repristination of old forms but living wisdom for our time.

Each series volume will approach the task of educational renewal from a different angle within a unified vision. Some will explore the philosophical and theological foundations that ground Catholic education; others will examine successful historical models that demonstrate how principles take flesh in particular communities. Some volumes focus on specific aspects of school life—curriculum design, character formation, leadership development—while others address the broader cultural formation essential to Catholic education. Throughout, the goal is to show how perennial principles can engage contemporary challenges while maintaining their essential truth.

The work ahead is both demanding and exciting. Catholic educators must be deeply formed in their tradition while remaining keenly attuned to the signs of the times. They must master their specific disciplines while understanding how each field of study leads towards wisdom. They must exercise authority with gentle firmness while fostering students' growth in genuine freedom. Above all, they must be witnesses to the joy of learning, showing in their own lives how faith and reason, nature and grace, work together in harmony.

This is why ongoing formation of teachers stands at the heart of educational renewal. Through study of Catholic intellectual tradition, through training in classical and contemporary pedagogy, through spiritual development and community building, teachers grow in their capacity to serve as true mentors. The volumes in the Adeodatus series aim to nurture such communities of educators, providing both theoretical foundation and practical guidance, again drawn from Scripture, tradition, and the great masters of Catholic education.

Theory must always serve practice. The ultimate measure of Catholic education is not the sophistication of its philosophy but the transformation of souls—the degree to which students grow in wisdom and virtue, in knowledge and love of God. This requires attention to the concrete reality of classroom life, to the day-to-day work of forming habits of mind and heart. This series will therefore include guidance for creating and sustaining authentic Catholic school culture, for crafting curricula that integrate faith and learning, for implementing pedagogical methods that engage the whole person.

In the end, Catholic education is nothing less than participation in the divine pedagogy, the eternal dialogue of love between God and his creatures. It calls for courage and creativity, wisdom and patience, knowledge and love. Above all, it requires hope—not mere optimism about outcomes, but the theological virtue grounded in God's faithfulness. Our culture increasingly fragments knowledge, relativizes truth, and reduces education to technical training. These increasingly transparent truncations serve to make the renewal of authentic Catholic education more urgent and its paths more obvious.

What we offer is not simply skills or information, but an invitation into the great circle of God's friends—that communion of saints and scholars who have sought the face of truth in every age. Through study of the liberal arts, contemplation of beauty, and practice of virtue, we initiate students into a way of seeing and being that transcends any particular epoch. We invite them to discover their place in God's story, to recognize their role in the drama of salvation history.

At the heart of this educational vision stands Christ himself, the Logos through whom all things were made and in whom all things hold together. He is the master Teacher who continues to draw all people to himself, the living Water that alone can quench our deepest thirst. To encounter him in the pursuit of learning is to discover both the source and end of all our intellectual striving. In his light, we see light; in his truth, we find freedom; in his love, we discover the meaning and purpose of our existence.

We take up this noble task with courage and hope, knowing that he who calls us is faithful. In the midst of modern labyrinths, may we be bearers of the light that never fails, witnesses to the truth that sets us free. And may Our Lady, Seat of Wisdom, guide us and our students ever deeper into the heart of her Son, until that day when faith gives way to sight and we behold him face to face in the eternal friendship of heaven.

This is the great adventure and high calling of Catholic education: to form a new generation who will be poets and prophets of a world transfigured by grace, with minds and hearts expanded by encounter with divine wisdom. In this noble mission lies our deepest joy and surest hope, for we know that the light shines in the darkness, and the darkness has not overcome it.

Foreword

History matters. The effects of historical ignorance become clearer every day as fundamental elements of our culture continue to erode. We do not know who we are or where we are going because we have broken continuity with the great achievements of our civilization—we have forgotten our family history. As Cicero warned the Romans: "To be ignorant of what occurred before you were born is to remain always a child. For what is the worth of human life, unless it is woven into the life of our ancestors by the records of history?" (*Orator* 120, LCL 342, pg. 395) Each generation cannot carry the burden of figuring out fundamental problems on its own, which only leads to existential confusion and anxiety.

The great tradition of Catholic education stands ready and poised to repair this breach. No institution, apart from the Church, straddles two millennia, integrating the great achievements of classical civilizations and drawing together the contributions of peoples throughout the entire globe. Only the Church has proven that every culture and each generation can take up its place in the great story of salvation history through the power of the Gospel that has proven unrivaled in its ability to educate, heal, and bring forth great cultural fruits.

The life of St. John Henry Newman, in particular, represents the power of rediscovering lost history. Through his arduous and prayerful study of the Church Fathers, Newman came to find himself situated outside of the organic continuity of the Apostolic Church, leading to his momentous conversion to the Catholic faith. His passion for truth, which he discovered through the inherited wisdom of the Church, has inspired countless others, myself included, to become "deep in history," as he famously put it. The Catholic Church is a historical reality, the communion of believers that stretches across generations, preserving and handing on the deposit of faith entrusted to us by Our Lord himself.

I know from experience that, like Newman, we can continue to discover the power of faith through immersion into our cultural heritage. Arriving at the University of Kansas in the early 1970s, I, like so many of my peers, had not grown up experiencing the riches of that great tradition in public school. Through the workings of God's providence, I enrolled in the Integrated Humanities Program (IHP), founded by Dennis Quinn, Frank Nelick, and John Senior as a two-year freshman/sophomore program that walked through the Great Books from the Greeks to the modern age. But it did not teach history for its own sake. We did not just learn about old texts, but entered into an ongoing conversation about the things that matter most. Our professors instilled a sense of wonder into our minds and hearts, helping us to experience for ourselves truth, goodness, and beauty through songs, poems, gazing at the stars, dancing, and trips to Europe. A whole community was formed around the adventure of learning, vocations of every kind were discovered and embraced, and lifelong friendships were forged.

IHP did not teach the truth of the Catholic faith directly. Simply restoring contact with the lost tradition of education did enough to open our minds to seek the truth. We sought out our professors outside of class to continue pursuing questions raised from our reading and in our formal courses. We, as a group of students and friends, began talking about faith and influencing one another, and some of us even ventured off to a French Benedictine monastery to seek God in earnest. The great voices of Western education, transmitted through conversations and the living witness of our professors, were embodied in these powerful experiences and led over three hundred of us into the Catholic Church over a fifteen-year span.

This is why history matters, and how Catholic education can harness its power.

Young people today deserve to receive "the best which has been thought and said," as Matthew Arnold expressed it (*Culture and Anarchy*, xi). They should not be deprived of the inheritance that has largely been withheld from them. As Catholics, however, they can go further, encountering the fullness of truth in Christ. The Church acts as the great transmitter not only of the Catholic faith but also of the legacy of Western civilization focused on the truth of human nature. As we teach about divine grace, we must also teach the cardinal virtues and the natural law, drawing from the literature and philosophy of the ancients. The Church esteems and upholds all that is truly human and represents the genuine longing of the person for truth and happiness. We cannot separate the effective teaching of faith from the most important achievements of the great tradition, which continues to teach us about our humanity both in its fallenness and its unbroken transcendence.

The first volume of *The Adeodatus Handbook on Catholic Education and Culture* offers a brilliant starting point for those beginning to explore the story of the Church's efforts to teach the Gospel to every nation. Beginning with the Bible and the Greeks, it explores the essential meeting of faith and reason that has remained a hallmark of Catholic education in every age. In our secular age, this is precisely what we need to recover, looking to reason as a means of recovering our sanity, and faith as a font for ascending to the highest truths. They need one another, as St. John Paul II so emphatically reminded us in his great encyclical, *Fides et Ratio*. For faith to flourish, the mind must awaken to truth and goodness, and reason, too, needs faith so that it does not become trapped in the mundane demands of efficiency.

This volume assembles the lives and legacies of the greatest Christian educators, produced by many of the most competent teachers of our own day. Educators, who may not have been able to study the original sources, can discover great theologians such as Augustine, Bonaventure, and Aquinas, as well as those who have shaped our pedagogical approach in modern times, such as St. Ignatius, Newman, and Don Bosco. Other overlooked figures like Boethius, Alcuin, and Hugh of St. Victor await discovery. As I experienced in college, these luminaries can continue to shine light into the minds of our students, bringing them to the one who is Truth.

I urge Catholic educators to rediscover our educational heritage anew, embracing its wisdom so as to effectively transmit it to the next generation of young people. As the Gospel awakens their minds to the truth, they will be prepared to transform our culture and to continue this great legacy after us.

Most Rev. James D. Conley, DD, STL
Bishop of Lincoln, Nebraska

Introduction: A Ressourcement for Catholic Education

R. Jared Staudt

For a tree to grow, it must retain vital contact with its roots. Modern education, however, spurred on by movements of rationalism and romanticism, has attempted to make a new start, a remaking of humanity in revolutionary fashion. The future, not the past, would dictate pedagogy, with the student construed as an individual who must follow his own instincts more than outside authority to reach subjective personal fulfillment within the democratic community. Fragmentation, banal utilitarianism, and existential confusion now prevail in schools, with more insidious currents gaining force to encourage students to completely remake their own identity, not after the image of God but through personless technocratic potential.

"To be deep in history is to cease to be Protestant," St. John Henry Newman remarked polemically as he discerned his way into the Catholic Church while writing his *Essay on the Development of Christian Doctrine*. Protestantism sought something new, cutting through the alleged accretions of history to reach the reality of faith directly, without the need for authority or any intermediaries. Contemporary education likewise seeks direct access to the reality of human experience without the meditation of the past or any authoritative direction to the truth. The self has become an end in itself, orphaned from the spiritual and intellectual heritage bequeathed by the development of culture. To be deep in history today is to cease to be an orphan by allowing the past to guide and direct in the search for abandoned wisdom.

In our reckless abandon, we have discarded much of the great treasury of human culture. This trend has impacted Catholic education as well, divorcing it from its roots. Immersed primarily in contemporary methods and sensibilities, it becomes mute, unable to answer the pressing needs of our time. The urgent need for a *ressourcement*, a return to the sources, in Catholic education, therefore, should not surprise us. In this work of renewal, nothing good should be rejected, whether, like the master bringing forth his treasures, it proceeds from what is new or old (Matthew 13:52). In the case of Catholic schools, they have received a charter in the Great Commission and an inheritance of overwhelming beauty and wisdom. We must, therefore, return to the sources of Catholic education to inform the things that are new, bringing within them the deepest source of light and life.

The Foundation of Catholic Education

Christian education first took shape in the catechetical schools of the Church's leading cities: Alexandria, Antioch, and Rome. These nascent schools formed catechists and clergy by teaching the classical liberal arts, including pagan literature and mathematics, as well as Sacred Scripture. It was not possible to teach sacred science alone apart from the liberal arts. Without grammar, logic, rhetoric, and philosophy, we could not receive the message of God's revelation with understanding and hand it on clearly and coherently to others. We must penetrate the working of words to comprehend the meaning of the Word of God.

The Church from its earliest moments, therefore, recognized the necessity of profane learning to support her own transmission of the faith. Yet, tensions remained in using pagan classics to learn the art of language. St. Augustine, for instance, relates the irony of a teacher proposing the allure of learning while offering it through corrupting expressions:

> "This is the place to learn words! This is the place to acquire the eloquence that is so essential for persuasion and argument!" So then do you mean that we would not know the words "golden rain," "lap," "trick," and "heavenly temples," and the other words that appear in that passage, if Terence had not used them to tell of a wicked young man who took Jupiter as a model for his own fornication?[1]

As an accomplished rhetor, Augustine certainly put his studies to good use, but he hesitated on the best means to accomplish the aims of education. Surely the classics provided an ample storehouse of learning, but their legacy must be reconciled with the true aims of education: union with God. St. Basil likewise advised caution in reading the works of pagan antiquity:

> Now, then, altogether after the manner of bees must we use these writings, for the bees do not visit all the flowers without discrimination, nor indeed do they seek to carry away entire those upon which they light, but rather, having taken so much as is adapted to their needs, they let the rest go. So we, if wise, shall take from heathen books whatever befits us and is allied to the truth, and shall pass over the rest. And just as in culling roses we avoid the thorns, from such writings as these we will gather everything useful, and guard against the noxious.[2]

Though Christians must select their sources prudently, there was honey to be found in classical authors. Despite their hesitations regarding the limits of liberal education, and even its possible harm, both saints drew heavily from their own classical studies in their eloquent and powerful teaching, providing a model for future generations.

---

1. Augustine, *Confessions*, trans. Thomas Williams (Hackett Publications, 2019), bk I, 16.26.

2. Basil of Caesaria, "Address to Young Men on the Right Use of Greek Literature," in *Essays on the Study and Use of Poetry by Plutarch and Basil the Great*, ed. Frederick Morgan Padelford (Henry Holt and Company, 1902), 105.

The study of the Bible depends upon the liberal arts, relying on its study of language, history, and philosophy for its interpretation and the formation of theological studies. If God revealed himself by employing human language and culture, then we must enter into these realities to understand his message. We even see biblical precedence for this approach in the prophet Daniel's study of Chaldean literature and Sirach's synthesis of secular and sacred learning. On the other hand, the Bible also transforms the study of the liberal arts, for, in this Christian context, the arts no longer find their culmination in the human search for wisdom but as a response to the wisdom revealed from on high.

For a Christian, classical studies could never suffice, for they would miss the "one thing necessary," the speech of the Word of God, articulated first from the Father's bosom that reverberates through history in the Incarnation. Yet, classical authors should be studied, for their attention to the *ratio* of the cosmos and the order latent within the human person resonates with revelation of the Logos, the one who created the cosmos and perfected humanity by drawing it to himself. Pope Benedict XVI recognizes a providential encounter between biblical wisdom and Greek learning that stands at the very foundation of Christian education: "This inner rapprochement between Biblical faith and Greek philosophical inquiry was an event of decisive importance not only from the standpoint of the history of religions, but also from that of world history—it is an event which concerns us even today."[3]

What we now refer to as "classical education" was created by the Catholic Church in late antiquity as classical culture crumbled in the face of barbarian invasions. Boethius and Cassiodorus, both in the service of the Ostrogoth King, Theodoric, discerned the need to transmit the legacy of classical civilization to a new age. Boethius undertook

3. Pope Benedict XVI, "Faith, Reason and the University: Memories and Reflections," University of Regensburg, September 12, 2006.

to translate the Greek philosophers into Latin, particularly Plato and Aristotle, and to create a series of textbooks on the trivium and quadrivium, which became fundamental for medieval education. Cassiodorus, for his part, established a significant monastic library when he retired from public service to his estate, known as Vivarium, and wrote a comprehensive overview of the fusion of profane and sacred learning in his *Institutes*. He advocated placing the Bible at the forefront of Christian study, as the true font of wisdom, leading to heaven like Jacob's ladder, but also recognized that "the holy Fathers have not decreed that the study of secular letters should be rejected either; since to a considerable degree it is by this that our minds are equipped to understand Sacred Scripture."[4] Through the effort of these two men, enough fragments of classical culture survived to lay the foundation for a new springtime of learning.

The Medieval Synthesis

The vision of a Christian liberal education planted by Boethius and Cassiodorus took root in medieval Christendom, with the monastery and later the university serving as the centers of Christian learning. Jerome and Augustine formed the Patristic pillars of the Church's teaching. Jerome served as a kind of Christian Cicero with his Vulgate as the key text studied, taught, and prayed. Augustine provided the theological vision that encompassed both the Church's doctrinal teaching and its philosophical vision of the human person and society. In addition, two other great pillars emerged from the early medieval period. The last of the great Western Fathers, Gregory the Great, organized the liturgy and its chant as the foundations of the Church's liturgical life that shaped the rhythm of time within the Church. We can also credit him for inspiring the great monastic

4. Cassiodorus, *Institutes of Divine and Secular Learning and On the Soul*, trans. James W. Halporn (Liverpool University Press, 2004), 160.

tradition of missions into pagan territory, sending St. Augustine of Canterbury to the Kingdom of Kent. Finally, St. Benedict of Nursia provided the key organizational and social program for the establishment of Christian culture in the West through his *Rule* for monks. The monastery would become the center not only of prayer and evangelization for Christendom but also of agriculture, learning (including the copying of books), the arts, and medicine.

The legacy of these figures fused into a coherent vision within the Carolingian Empire, which brought forth a rebirth of learning and culture in the ninth century. Alcuin, a Northumbrian monk, served as Charlemagne's key advisor in establishing monasteries and schools throughout his realm, conveying a renewed vision of the liberal arts. The cathedral and monastery schools that flourished following this renewal laid the foundation for the medieval universities as the faculty and students organized into coherent guilds. Hugh of St. Victor relates the educational vision of this time period in his *Didascalicon*, rearticulating the central contentions of Cassiodorus on divine and human learning for a new age. In one passage, he lays forth the scope of study, demonstrating the extent of medieval learning drawing upon the ancients:

> Philosophy is divided into the theoretical, the practical, the mechanical, and the logical. The theoretical is divided into theology, physics, and mathematics; mathematics is divided into arithmetic, music, geometry, and astronomy. The practical is divided into solitary, private, and public. The mechanical is divided into fabric making, armament, commerce, agriculture, hunting, medicine, and theatrics. Logic is divided into grammar and argument: argument is divided into demonstration, probable argument, and sophistic: probable argument is divided into dialectic and rhetoric.[5]

5. Hugh of St. Victor, *Didascalicon*, trans. Jerome Taylor (Columbia University Press, 1961), 61.

The reintroduction of Aristotle's corpus, beyond his few works on logic previously in circulation, caused a serious stir in scholastic circles. Traditional Augustinian thinkers, of a more Platonic bent, resisted the errors of Aristotle on creation and human knowledge, while radical Aristotelians pushed back and sought to pursue philosophy on its own terms. They were accused of Averroism, of following the Islamic commentator on Aristotle on the unity of the mind and "two truth" principle that divided philosophy and theology into separate and untouching realms of knowledge. St. Bonaventure and St. Thomas Aquinas pursued their own solutions to the problem, with the former drawing upon Aristotle with more hesitation and the latter creating a great synthesis of Augustinian and Aristotelian thought. Both doctors of the Church embodied the great synthesis of faith and reason that represented the enduring achievement of scholastic learning. At the beginning of his *Summa Contra Gentiles*, we see Aquinas's crucial principle for Catholic education that truths we learn properly from nature cannot stand in opposition to faith:

> Now, although the truth of the Christian faith which we have discussed surpasses the capacity of the reason, nevertheless that truth that the human reason is naturally endowed to know cannot be opposed to the truth of the Christian faith. For that with which the human reason is naturally endowed is clearly most true; so much so, that it is impossible for us to think of such truths as false. Nor is it permissible to believe as false that which we hold by faith, since this is confirmed in a way that is so clearly divine. Since, therefore, only the false is opposed to the true, as is clearly evident from an examination of their definitions, it is impossible that the truth of faith should be opposed to those principles that the human reason knows naturally.[6]

6. Thomas Aquinas, *Summa Contra Gentiles*, trans. Anton C. Pegis (University of Notre Dame Press, 1975), bk 1, ch. 7.

The harmony of faith and reason continues to stand as a cornerstone of a Catholic approach to the liberal arts.

The Divorce of Faith and Reason

During the rise of the modern period in the sixteenth century, the authority of the Church was rejected during the Protestant Reformation in favor of *sola scriptura*. The role of philosophy in theology was largely rejected, fracturing the unity of the Catholic liberal arts. The Scientific Revolution rejected Aristotle's approach, casting out formal and final causality along with him, while making empiricism the center of learning and even social organization. Although the Greco-Roman classics continued to be taught in the original languages into the twentieth century, nonetheless a "battle of the classics" broke out that continues to this day. At the center of this dispute stands the question: Do we pursue education for humane purposes, directed toward the inner formation of the person, or should it be rooted in the material sciences and directed toward utility?[7]

The last five hundred years have witnessed the continual and growing marginalization of the Church in society. Yet, despite even violent persecution in secular revolutions, Catholics have remained the largest group of educators and providers of healthcare in the world, continuing the great legacy of the monasteries. In fact, some of the greatest educational accomplishments in the Church's history have occurred in this time period. The Church has continued to found schools, opening up the first free schools to the poor in the world, staffed by religious orders dedicated to education. Catholic universities have remained centers for advanced teaching and research throughout the world. And great saintly educators have emerged as models of charity to the young and impoverished.

---

7. See Eric Adler, *The Battle of the Classics: How a Nineteenth-Century Debate Can Save the Humanities Today* (Oxford University Press, 2020).

The Jesuits were not the first teaching order to be established, as St. Angela Merici founded the Ursuline Sisters in 1535. The Jesuits, arising only five years later, were not established as a teaching order at all, but the founders placed themselves at the service of the Church, and of the Holy Father in particular, and found themselves establishing their first school in Messina, Sicily in 1548. From there, their schools spread throughout the world, even sought after by Protestants and Orthodox Christians, due to their tremendous success in intellectual and personal formation. The *Ratio Studiorum* represented the continued unfolding of the Catholic approach to the liberal arts more than any other document in the early modern period. It emphasized Aristotelian philosophy, Thomistic theology, mathematics, writing, speaking, and drama, among other subjects, for a complete formation. Jesuits would produce some of the greatest mathematicians and scientists of the modern period, both from within the order and among their students.

St. Jean Baptiste de La Salle founded the first academy for the training of teachers, called a "normal school," and dedicated his life to the education of the poor, founding the Brothers of Christian Instruction. He broke ground in his organization of the day's schedule, division of the students into distinct classes by age, and his charitable disciplinary methods. All of this would prove foundational for modern education and would be followed by other key Catholic educators, such as St. John Bosco with his Preventative System. These two saints demonstrate that a liberal arts education geared toward intellectual formation cannot suffice for the formation of the child, who needs, also, to be formed in the will through love and mentorship in order to live the Christian life within the difficult circumstances of the modern world.

Our volume's final figure, St. John Henry Newman, offers a powerful defense of the unity of knowledge and the role of theology in the university. After his pivotal conversion while serving as Vicar of St. Mary's in Oxford, which spurred many to follow him into the

Church, Newman was asked by the bishops of Ireland to found the Catholic University of Ireland in Dublin. The lectures he delivered to the faculty provide one of the most important articulations of the essence of a liberal arts education as the formation of the intellect in truth. Newman makes clear that if we fragment the truth, deliberately cutting off one part from the whole, we are left only with a distortion of it.

> I say then, if the various branches of knowledge, which are the matter of teaching in a University, so hang together, that none can be neglected without prejudice to the perfection of the rest, and if Theology be a branch of knowledge, of wide reception, of philosophical structure, of unutterable importance, and of supreme influence, to what conclusion are we brought from these two premisses but this? that to withdraw Theology from the public schools is to impair the completeness and to invalidate the trustworthiness of all that is actually taught in them.[8]

We see too clearly today the consequence of ignoring Newman's warning, with technological breakthroughs accompanying ever-greater deficiencies in the interior life of thought and prayer. Despite claims of confidence in modern science, certainty concerning the most basic of human realities has been undermined, and society hinges on the verge of chaos due to moral and spiritual confusion.

For this reason, the Church has increasingly been addressing the importance of education in her magisterial teaching. Pope Pius XI wrote the first encyclical on education in 1929, *Divini Illius Magistri,* which emphasized the right of parents to choose Catholic education. The Second Vatican Council also took up the topic, insisting that parents are the primary educators of their children, cooperating with the Church in bringing children to their full potential in Christ.

8. John Henry Newman, *Idea of a University* (Longmans, Green & Co., 1907), 69, Discourse 3, no. 10.

Following the Council, the Congregation for Education wrote a number of documents, including "The Catholic School" in 1979, that offered a vision for uniting faith, education, and life in light of modern fragmentation. Pope John Paul II and Pope Benedict XVI both offered strong defenses of the unity of faith and reason in an age of relativism, encouraging Catholic schools to rediscover their heritage and identity.

Our Goal: Continuing a Saintly Heritage

Returning to the sources of Catholic education cannot be dismissed as an antiquarian study. We cannot face the novel challenges of our day apart from the inherited wisdom we have received from the great voices of the past. Despite enormous advances in science and technology, we remain even more in need of what the past possessed: clarity and conviction in the truth of God's revelation and its implication for human life. The classics do not have ready-made answers to the challenges of our day, but their wisdom will enable us to face these challenges with the right frame of mind and disposition of the heart. For instance, no thoughtful response to transhumanism can arise without a genuine understanding of the nature of the human person. Likewise, how can a young student resist the allure of drugs, or even the distraction of technology, without a love that impels them to the heights?

Catholic education stands in need of renewal, for it, too, has experienced the consequences of the rupture of faith and reason in the modern period. Secularism affects Catholic schools as well as public ones when faith remains confined solely to a religion class or the celebration of the Mass. Our past provides a model of integration: the unity of divine revelation and the liberal arts and a life of wisdom that pursues what is truly highest. Modern people too often settle for less—little comforts and distractions—while the theologians, philosophers, and educators of the past spur us on to stop at nothing less than God's invitation to enter his divine life.

This first volume of *The Adeodatus Handbook* seeks to provide inspiration to return to the central vision of Catholic education: an integrated approach to the liberal arts that flows from God's initiative toward us and is ordered toward eternal union with him. The essays of this volume unfold the narrative offered in this introduction in more detail. We consider the subjects of these essays to be the most essential figures who have established the Catholic approach to education. Two of them, Plato and Aristotle, were pagan authors who formed the philosophical basis of the Catholic approach. The others, flowing from the incarnation of the Son of God, appropriated the truths of the natural world contemplated by philosophy and drew them into a synthesis with the truths of divine revelation. Any genuine Christian education must help the student to contemplate the whole of reality and to live a life of wisdom rooted in the virtues that perfect human nature while becoming receptive of the supernatural gifts and fruits of the Holy Spirit.

Most of the figures addressed in this volume are canonized saints, a fact that points us to the priority of holiness in Catholic education. Education must serve the ultimate goal of human life: our perfect happiness in the beatific vision. To reach this ultimate vocation, we need the support of mentors and friends, which requires the concrete embodiment of Christian community within the home and school. But this connection within the Body of Christ also binds us to the great sainted educators of our heritage, who continue to guide us with their teaching and example. We have inherited their legacy, and with their prayers and support, we have been tasked with continuing their work in our own age. We may not be able to replicate their efforts, but with the grace and inspiration of the Holy Spirit, we can make our contribution to educating the youth, young adults, seminarians, and lay people of the Church of God today.

1 The Bible

R. Jared Staudt

Not all educational sources bear the same level of importance. We can identify the authors who shaped civilization, calling their works the Great Books in acknowledgement of how they guided education through the centuries. Above and beyond this human canon, we also must recognize a divine one, *the* Book that transcends human wisdom through the speech of God, drawing us into his eternal Word and the consuming fire of his most Holy Spirit.[1] This singular book does not compete with our own limited reflections of the eternal, but enables them to enter into an even greater conversation. Human literature serves as preparation for study of the Sacred Page and then helps us to formulate a response to it, applying its wisdom in the world.[2] The divine Scriptures elicit from human words a greater depth by situating them in relation to God's speech and a conversation that takes on eternal import.

Jesus, the Logos, the Word made flesh, is *the* source of Catholic education. He speaks the Father and reveals God's plan of salvation, which he accomplishes through the paschal mystery. We find the key written source within the Bible precisely because its words pro-

1. Although we refer to the Bible in the singular, *biblia* in Greek and Latin originally referred to a collection or library of inspired books. And in terms of the singularity of the Bible, in speaking of *sacra doctrina,* which flows from divine revelation, Thomas Aquinas states, "This doctrine is wisdom above all human wisdom; not merely in any one order, but absolutely." *Summa Theologiae* I, q. 1, a. 6, corpus, trans. Fathers of the English Dominican Province, 1920.

2. Jean Leclercq's monumental study of Benedictine education comes to mind as a prime example of this, as the monks diligently studied classical authors, especially Virgil, to attune their minds to language precisely out of love for the Sacred Page. See his *The Love of Learning and the Desire for God* (Fordham University, 1961).

vide access to the Word of God, spoken forth into the world. We simply could not imagine Catholic education without it. Just as the Second Vatican Council's dogmatic constitution, *Dei Verbum*, called Scripture the soul of theology, so we could say the same about education itself, which finds its inner life in God's revelation of himself.[3] St. John Henry Newman spoke of theology as necessary to complete the circle of knowledge within the university by providing access to the highest and most important truths known to humanity, seeing it even as a condition for knowledge of the Truth as a whole, and, likewise, no education would be complete without sustained attention to the revealed Word.[4] For without it, human formation could not reach its ultimate destination within the everlasting life and happiness of God.

Education in the Bible

Formal education has been rare throughout history, even though everyone received preparation of some sort to enter into maturity.

---

3. "For the Sacred Scriptures contain the word of God and since they are inspired, really are the word of God; and so the study of the sacred page is, as it were, the soul of sacred theology. By the same word of Scripture the ministry of the word also, that is, pastoral preaching, catechetics and all Christian instruction, in which the liturgical homily must hold the foremost place, is nourished in a healthy way and flourishes in a holy way." Second Vatican Council, *Dei Verbum* [Dogmatic Constitution on Divine Revelation] (November 18, 1965), §24.

4. For instance, Newman argues, "I say, then, that the systematic omission of any one science from the catalogue prejudices the accuracy and completeness of our knowledge altogether, and that, in proportion to its importance. Not even Theology itself, {52} though it comes from heaven, though its truths were given once for all at the first, though they are more certain on account of the Giver than those of mathematics, not even Theology, so far as it is relative to us, or is the Science of Religion, do I exclude from the law to which every mental exercise is subject, viz., from that imperfection, which ever must attend the abstract, when it would determine the concrete." *Idea of a University* (Longmans, Green & Co., 1907), discourse 3, no. 4.

Education is necessary for human beings, who, unlike animals, must learn how to live within a particular culture, all of which have included religious initiation until recently. Although the Bible may have little to say about formal education, it has much to say about learning, focused on becoming a human being in the fullest sense. Through it, we are taught by God himself, first in covenants mediated by the patriarchs and prophets and then by his Son coming in the flesh. The Bible could even be seen as a fundamentally educational text in its essence as the instruction of humanity by God. Through God's teaching, we can understand the nature of education more deeply as a communication of truth that calls forth a response from the student, in this case Israel, as the embodiment of humanity itself.

The Bible leads us through a process of education on what matters most. Coming to know the one, true God, learning the discipline of living in a covenant relationship with him, and growing to the full stature of our humanity that he intends for us: a share in his own divine life. The progression of salvation history from creation to the coming of the Holy Spirit captures the progression that he intends for each human being. St. Basil tells us that "the Holy Scriptures lead us into eternal life," which he recognizes as our supreme good, "teaching us through divine words."[5] Because humanity has been by marked by a supernatural end, eternal life with God in heaven, education could not be complete without God's revelation, making this end known to us and guiding us in the way to enter it. Even in regard to the natural elements of human life, the Bible manifests how we should situate everything else in light of the end, offering the wisdom by which we can organize our understanding of human life into a coherent whole. This vision of life, the broadest perspective of what is true and how

---

5. Basil of Caesaria, "Address to Young Men on the Right Use of Greek Learning," in *Essays on the Study and Use of Poetry by Plutarch and Basil the Great*, ed. Frederick Morgan Padelford (Henry Holt and Company, 1902), 103. I altered the order of the sentence translation.

to live in light of it, gives shape to Catholic education, providing an inexhaustible source of inspiration for learning and life. Just as the Eucharist is the source and summit of the Christian life, so the Bible must take its place as the source and summit of Christian education, providing the strongest stimulant for education in fulfilling the human desire to know the truth of life and the summit in revealing our eternal union with God. The Church founded schools to bring about the encounter with God that flows from the divine Scriptures, keeping its knowledge alive within the community of the Church and passing it down through each generation.

Literacy for the Bible and Biblical Literacy

God made us in his own image and likeness as beings who can hear the Word and perceive its meaning. From all eternity, God has spoken his divine Word and the rationality of human beings enables them to participate in his trinitarian communion by receiving and responding to the Word. Walking with him in the garden, God began by teaching Adam directly, but after the Fall it became necessary for God to reveal himself through intermediaries: patriarchs and prophets using human words to convey the teaching of God both orally and in writing. The origins of human literacy are bound up with this revelation. The cultures of the Ancient Near East developed written means of communication through symbols, whether geometric in Mesopotamia or pictorial in Egypt, while the first alphabet appears to have arisen from the Semites, the ethnic and linguistic group from which Israel sprung, dating to the mid-nineteenth century BC in Egypt using a script called Proto-Sinaitic.[6] From a Christian perspective, this first alphabet, using morphed

6. Although it was first discovered on the Sinai Peninsula, its Egyptian origin is attested by inscriptions discovered at Wadi el-Hol. For more on this ancient script's connection to Hebrew, see Douglas Petrovich, *The World's Oldest Alphabet: Hebrew as the Language of the Proto-Consonantal Script* (Hendrickson Academic, 2017).

hieroglyphs, appears to have arisen providentially at the service of the revelation that God would bestow upon enslaved Israel through the mediation of Moses.

Although we generally accept that the revelation given to Israel began through oral tradition (in part because a later date for the rise of the alphabet has been commonly accepted), we see within the Bible itself that Moses was commanded to write the Law (Ex 34:27), presupposing his own literacy, developed in pharaoh's own household, and also an audience who would be able to receive it. Before his death, he entrusted the written Law to the priests, commanding them to read it to the people every seven years: "Assemble the people, men, women, and little ones, and the sojourner within your towns, that they may hear and learn to fear the Lord your God, and be careful to do all the words of this law, and that their children, who have not known it, may hear and learn to fear the Lord your God, as long as you live in the land that you are going over the Jordan to possess" (Dt 31:12–13, RSVCE). God invites his people to know him through the reading of the Law and to assent to the covenant through it, as we see at the base of Mount Sinai in Exodus 24, where the Israelites affirm, "All the words which the Lord has spoken we will do" (v. 3), an event that must be repeated every sabbath of years, through the mediation of a literate class of priests. In ensuring the continuity of the covenant, Moses also foresees a role for the civil ruler of Israel, the king, who especially must learn the Law and use it as a basis for his own rule:

> And when he sits on the throne of his kingdom, he shall write for himself in a book a copy of this law, approved by the Levitical priests. And it shall be with him, and he shall read in it all the days of his life, that he may learn to fear the Lord his God by keeping all the words of this law and these statutes, and doing them, that his heart may not be lifted up above his brothers, and that he may not turn aside from the commandment, either to the right hand or to the left, so that he may continue long in his kingdom, he and his children, in Israel. (Dt 17:18–20)

There can be no doubt that God established a literate culture in Israel. Even if God did not command literacy for all the people, we do find that, unlike other cultures who preserved literacy only within a small class, that all Israelites must in some way receive the Law and respond to it.

The central text of Israelite education can be found in the Shema, which commands every Israelite to know the commands of the Lord and to do them. The Shema is both a summary of the Law itself and a command to parents to prioritize the education of their children:

> Hear, O Israel: The Lord our God, the Lord is one. You shall love the Lord your God with all your heart and with all your soul and with all your might. And these words that I command you today shall be on your heart. You shall teach them diligently to your children, and shall talk of them when you sit in your house, and when you walk by the way, and when you lie down, and when you rise. You shall bind them as a sign on your hand, and they shall be as frontlets between your eyes. You shall write them on the doorposts of your house and on your gates. (Dt 6:4–9)

Although priests are given the command to preserve the Law and read it to the entire assembly of Israel, parents are given a short catechism for their children, helping them to recall the Lord each day and to write these words where they can serve as a constant reminder. It should not surprise us, therefore, that Israel did have a higher rate of literacy than other ancient cultures, and over time, began to establish synagogue schools to teach boys how to read the Torah in Hebrew (especially when Aramaic became its daily language).[7] The task of teaching within these synagogue schools, which

7. James Crenshaw notes that Jewish "tradition ascribes the beginning of compulsory education to the high priest Joshua ben Gamala (63–65 CE) or to Simeon ben Shetah (second century BCE). To be sure, some sort of mass education was envisioned in the time of Ezra (fifth century BCE)." *Education in Ancient Israel: Across the Deadening Silence* (Doubleday, 1998), 5–6.

came to prominence in the centuries immediately before the time of Jesus, was entrusted to the Scribes, a class of scholars who came to prominence after the Exile and would copy and interpret the Law.[8] Israel was given an educational mission by God to receive his Law, preserve it, pass it down to each generation, conform to it, instantiate it within the Kingdom of Israel and Judah, and return to it in times of laxity. The mission of the prophets largely focused on calling Israel back to the Law, to remember God and his commands, and to embrace the teaching of the Lord.

The Role of Memory

The constant falling away and returning to the Lord reveals a fundamental dynamic of education in the Bible. The oral instruction in the Law aimed at forming memory so that the Law would remain present constantly to the mind to shape action, not as an end in itself, but to make the Lord himself present to his people, shaping the consciousness of their identity in relation to him. This requires a constant reading and rereading, along with regular proclamation and teaching, so that God's people do not fall into forgetfulness of

---

William F. Albright held the opinion that literacy was evident "even among the peasants by the 10th cent. BC, i.e. during the early monarchy; thus it has been suggested that though literacy was not universal (Is 29:11) it was widespread (see Dt 6:9; 17:18, 19; 27:2–8; Jo 18:4, 8, 9; Jgs 8:14; Is 10:19)." "Education in Biblical Times," in *Encyclopedia of the Bible*, https://www.biblegateway.com/resources/encyclopedia-of-the-bible/toc, accessed June 12, 2023.

The foundation for the synagogue schools were laid earlier, as "the prophets seem to presuppose that all priests shared in the teaching office (Mal 2:6, 7). At least some Levites were also instructed to teach (Dt 33:10; 2 Chr 35:3). Priests were not to be paid for their instruction (Mi 3:11). Instruction was carried out by the priest visiting a town (2 Chr 17:8, 9), gathering the people together and expounding the Torah (Dt 31:10–13; 2 Chr 17:8, 9). This practice continued after the return from the Exile (Ezr 8:15–20; Neh 8:7–9)."

8. Ezra, for instance, is described in the Bible as a scribe "skilled in the law of Moses which the Lord God of Israel had given" (Ezr 7:6).

who he is and how to live out the covenant with him, a falling away that seemed to happen all too often in Israel's history. The annual festivals, for instance, stimulated memory to make the great saving deeds and blessings of the Lord present and new to each generation.

Events, therefore, serve an educational purpose of teaching about God and his saving deeds.[9] In instructing Israel to observe it annually, God prescribed the Passover as "a memorial day, and you shall keep it as a feast to the Lord; throughout your generations, as a statute forever, you shall keep it as a feast" (Ex 24:14). The actions are accompanied by instructions: "And when your children say to you, 'What do you mean by this service?' you shall say, 'It is the sacrifice of the Lord's Passover, for he passed over the houses of the people of Israel in Egypt, when he struck the Egyptians but spared our houses'" (Ex 24:26–27). Here we see that deeds accompany words to reinforce and embody them. The Israelites saw that they were spared from the angel of death in the Passover, and now each generation must experience this by learning of those events and experiencing them ritually through the blood of the lamb, showing that they too have received the salvation of this event. They must discover the continuity between their own lives and the great deeds of salvation history.

In the task of forming memory, we see yet another connection between literacy and the Bible. The words of revelation are written precisely to maintain memory of God and of the covenant enacted by him and through repeated reading to recall the Law and the saving deeds of God. St. Thomas Aquinas lays out a similar dynamic at the very heart of the nature of religion itself, drawing up St. Isidore's engagement of Cicero, which he backs up with a reference from Proverbs:

9. As Paul teaches the Corinthians about Israel's rebellion and punishment in the desert, he states that these past events continue to instruct: "Now these things are warnings for us, not to desire evil as they did" (1 Cor 10:6).

> I answer that, as Isidore says (*Etymologies*, x), "according to Cicero, a man is said to be religious from 'religio,' because he often ponders over, and, as it were, reads again [*relegit*], the things which pertain to the worship of God," so that religion would seem to take its name from reading over those things which belong to Divine worship because we ought frequently to ponder over such things in our hearts, according to Proverbs 3:6, "In all thy ways think on Him."[10]

Reading and rereading the Bible enables one to meditate upon him often to the point that this thinking shapes the mind as a whole with God at the center. This recall becomes even stronger when passages are memorized so that they could be brought to mind readily.[11]

This rereading also leads to the possibility of rediscovery. In a way, each Israelite must discover God's law, accept the obligation and blessing of the covenant, and follow it as a path through life. Josiah, King of Judah, may embody this renewal most vividly in his rediscovery of the Law in the Temple, where it was kept as a record, but also in how this led to a rereading and recommitment for the entire people:

> Then the king sent, and all the elders of Judah and Jerusalem were gathered to him. And the king went up to the house of the Lord, and with him all the men of Judah and all the inhabitants of Jerusalem and the priests and the prophets, all the people, both small

---

10. *ST* II-II, q. 81, a. 1. c.

11. The Psalms were the most important text to be memorized within the Church, as it was even a requirement for ordination in some periods of history. In advising Laeta and Gaudens on the instruction of their daughter, St. Jerome suggested memorizing verses in Greek and then learning them in her own language: "Let her every day repeat a lesson culled from the flowers of Scripture, learning a number of verses in Greek, and immediately afterward being instructed in Latin." "Letter 107," in *Nicene and Post-Nicene Fathers, Second Series*, vol. 6. ed. Philip Schaff and Henry Wace, trans. W. H. Fremantle, G. Lewis, and W. G. Martley (Buffalo, NY: Christian Literature Publishing Co., 1893).

> and great. And he read in their hearing all the words of the Book of the Covenant that had been found in the house of the Lord. And the king stood by the pillar and made a covenant before the Lord, to walk after the Lord and to keep his commandments and his testimonies and his statutes with all his heart and all his soul, to perform the words of this covenant that were written in this book. And all the people joined in the covenant." (2 Kgs 23:1–3)

It is not enough to know of the existence of this Law, even if it must be presented to someone as a first step in discovery, because God's teaching requires a commitment of life, calling forth a response of heart and soul. The education of the Bible always moves from knowledge to action, shaping the entirety of life in accordance with the will of God. The same kind of communal rediscovery occurred after the Exile through the scribe Ezra, who "brought the Law before the assembly, both men and women and all who could understand what they heard" (Neh 8:2).[12] Ezra was assisted by the Levites, who also gave instruction: "They read from the book, from the Law of God, clearly, and they gave the sense, so that the people understood the reading" (Neh 8:8). The people demonstrated attentiveness and reverence to the word, while also responding to it, initially through repentance, when they saw the distance of their lives from it, but later through celebration, as Ezra teaches them to show gratitude for this instruction.

Initiation into the People of God

In the unending process of rediscovery, God's self-revelation requires a response of faith from each person. That said, we could never understand the biblical vision of education as an individual discovery of God and his Law. God does not provide isolated information for

12. "For Ezra had set his heart to study the Law of the Lord, and to do it and to teach his statutes and rules in Israel" (Ezr 7:10).

our own private salvation because he teaches us within the context of a community. God did not simply give Israel a book in order to come to know about him. He formed a people with all the details of a shared life, or culture, so that the daily life of his people would be immersed in a covenant relationship with him and one another as his chosen people, Israel. The daily worship of sacrifice shaped the heart of this life, which taught people the primacy of God over material things, with moral instruction and judicial precepts rounding out this embodied instruction. God taught Israel in a fully human way, engaging the material and communal dimensions of our nature.

God taught Israel as a people, and each generation required initiation into the covenant and the relationship with God that it entailed. This builds upon the very nature of education, which can be seen as an initiation into a community and its culture, as Christopher Dawson explains: "Taken in its widest sense education is simply the process by which the new members of a community are initiated into its way of life and thought from the simplest elements of behavior up to the highest tradition of spiritual wisdom."[13] In order for God's revelation and his chosen people to continue in the world, the inheritance of Israel must be passed down successfully through every generation. This entailed more than simply religious instruction, as Dawson has pointed out, noting that Israel was a "pure religious culture in which all the aspects of culture—sociological, political, legal, moral, ritual, and theological—are united in one all-embracing sacred order."[14] This complete culture was not unique to Israel, as every ancient culture similarly was constituted as an integrated whole with religion at the center. In response to revelation, however, both in a Jewish and Christian context, education

13. Christopher Dawson, *Understanding Europe* (The Catholic University of America Press, 2009), 198–99.

14. Christopher Dawson, "The Study of Christian Culture," *Thought: Fordham University Quarterly* 35, no. 4 (1960): 485–93. This article is available online at www.catholicculture.org/culture/library/view.cfm?id=650.

became more than an "initiation into the . . . community," because, as Dawson relates, "it was an initiation into another world; the unveiling of spiritual realities of which the natural man was unaware and which changed the meaning of existence."[15] The two, communities rooted in this life and the next, cannot really be separated, because this supernatural revelation, which transcends reason, was imparted to and preserved within the cultural life of God's people.[16]

Israel embodied God's revelation, because he constituted it as a nation, providing his people with his teaching, worship, laws, and even daily customs pertaining to eating and dress. Returning to the book of Deuteronomy, we see how God describes his role in forming Israel in both the past and future tense, implying that this constitutive action continued to unfold through generations. On one level, the people of Israel must always look back, because God presents himself as the God of their fathers, even as he revealed himself to Moses as the God of Abraham, Isaac, and Jacob at the burning bush (Ex 3:6). Moses, therefore, teaches Israel in Deuteronomy, that they

> are a people holy to the Lord your God; the Lord your God has chosen you to be a people for his own possession, out of all the peoples that are on the face of the earth. It was not because you were more in number than any other people that the Lord set his love upon you and chose you, for you were the fewest of all peoples; but it is because the Lord loves you, and is keeping the oath which he swore to your fathers." (Dt 7:6–8)

15. Dawson, *Understanding Europe*, 197.

16. Albright explains plausibly that "children were trained in their everyday duties (1 Sm 16:11; 2 Kgs 4:18), and artistic training was given in some cases, at least (Jgs 21:21; 1 Sm 16:15–18; Ps 137; Lam 5:14). Girls learned household crafts presumably from their mothers (Ex 35:25, 26; 2 Sm 13:8). During the second commonwealth, the schools were intended only for boys. Girls learned their household skills at home (Prv 31:13–31). If there were no sons girls did the work of the sons (Gn 29:6; Ex 2:16)."

On the other hand, Moses tells them later, "The Lord will establish you as a people holy to himself, as he has sworn to you, if you keep the commandments of the Lord your God, and walk in his ways. And all the peoples of the earth shall see that you are called by the name of the Lord" (Dt 28:9–10). He both established Israel through the events of the Exile, to fulfill his promises to Abraham, and *will* establish Israel in the land *if* they walk in his ways. This ongoing establishment entails an educational mission to make the Law of the Lord known so that God would continue to bless and establish his people, enabling Israel to serve him as a witness to the nations. Each generation received initiation through circumcision, intending to form a disposition of faith akin to that of the great Patriarch, and experienced ritually the liberation of the Passover in the annual observance. All Israelites must abide by the cycle of festivals to mark the turning of the seasons and to learn a way of life shaped and guided by divine worship. The God of Israel's fathers must also become Lord of each successive generation, which embraces and in turn passes on the covenant with God.

A Way of Wisdom

To complement the context of cultural and covenantal initiation, we must also attend to the Bible's educational vision as providing a sure path for all those called into communion with God. We see that Israel often failed to learn what God wanted to teach his people, leading him to remind them, "For my thoughts are not your thoughts, neither are your ways my ways" (Is 55:8). The Psalms respond to this chastisement correctly, "Teach me your ways, O Lord that I may walk in your truth" (Ps 86:11). The Law of the Lord presents those initiated into the covenant with a personal choice: will I conform my thoughts and ways to the Lord? Psalm 1 presents an image of this choice by contrasting the wicked with the blessed man, whose "delight is in the law of the Lord, and on his law he meditates day and night" (Ps 1:2). There are two paths, and the education of life given by God leads those whom he calls to accept, assimilate, and apply the truth offered within his law.

The wisdom books, in particular, focus on interiorizing God's Law through virtue, the foundation for a blessed life.[17] The wisdom books offer this teaching to Israel as a form of discipline from a father to a son, instruction from a teacher to a disciple, love from a husband to his wife, and guidance for a king's rule. All these metaphors express the believer's reception of truth, learning from God how to live and to achieve the true *telos* of human life. This requires walking along a path of wisdom, which follows the Word as if it were a lamp for the feet (Ps 119:105). Wisdom presents each person with a choice to follow the Lord's way or to wander in the dark

---

17. Mark Giszczak provides a helpful, succinct overview of these books at the beginning of his commentary of the Wisdom of Solomon:

> While these books collect everyday advice on self-discipline, daily work, and personal relationships, they are fundamentally oriented toward God. The path of wisdom begins with 'fear of the Lord' (Prv 9:10) and ultimately 'leads upward to life' (Prv 15:24). Wisdom itself is hard to define. A nonbiblical Jewish text that is contemporaneous with Wisdom of Solomon, *4 Maccabees*, offers the following: 'Wisdom, I submit, is knowledge of things divine and human, and of their causes.' Similarly, St. Thomas Aquinas will name wisdom as the highest of intellectual virtues 'because wisdom considers the Supreme Cause, which is God.' In its essence, wisdom has three distinct yet related meanings: (1) God's perfect knowledge, (2) the knowledge of causes that human beings can come to possess, and (3) the habitual seeking of knowledge with integrity of heart. The Wisdom of Solomon proposes a way of knowing God that begins with honest seeking after truth, leads to embracing what is found on this path, and eventually arrives at union with wisdom itself in God.

Wisdom of Solomon, Catholic Commentary on Sacred Scripture (Baker Academic, 2024), 17–18.

For a succinct overview of these books, within what may be the best Catholic single-volume introduction to the Old Testament, see John Bergsma and Brant Pitre, *A Catholic Introduction to the Bible*, vol. 1, *The Old Testament* (Ignatius Press, 2018).

according to "what seems right" to oneself, ultimately offering a choice between life and death (Dt 30:19).

The Psalms contain a frequent request that God would "teach us" (Ps 90:12). Psalm 119 alone contains eleven such requests, requesting the Lord to teach his Law so that it may be kept diligently: "Teach me, O Lord, the way of your statutes; and I will keep it to the end" (Ps 119:3), and asking that this teaching would provide "good judgment and knowledge" (119:66). The Law itself can be read and understood, although the Psalmist requests a deeper understanding that would lead to a more perfect life according to the Lord's own ways, receiving his "steadfast love" and the radiance of his own "face" (Ps 119:124, 135). God himself must act for a true enlightenment and to provide the ability to follow his own path in perfection. We see this dependence expressed in Psalm 25: "Make me to know your ways, O Lord; teach me your paths. Lead me in your truth and teach me, for you are the God of my salvation" (Ps 25:4–5).[18]

Proverbs approaches teaching from the viewpoint of a father giving instruction to his son: "Hear, my son, your father's instruction" (Prv 1:8). This instruction stems from piety, as we see in the famous line, "The fear of the Lord is the beginning of knowledge" (Prv 1:7).[19] The entire book is presented as a hidden instruction that must be teased out through docility: "To know wisdom and instruction, to understand words of insight, to receive instruction in wise dealing, in righteousness, justice, and equity; to give prudence to the simple, knowledge and discretion to the youth—Let the wise hear and increase in learning, and the one who understands obtain guidance, to understand a proverb and a saying, the words of the wise and their riddles" (Prv 1:2–6). This wisdom will come from the

18. See also Psalm 32:8 and Psalm 143:10.

19. We also find in Proverbs the famous line: "Train up a child in the way he should go, and when he is old he will not depart from it" (22:6).

guidance of a father, who steers his son away from the allurements of the world, particularly expressed through an adulterous woman, and instructs in understanding the hidden sense of the proverbs, as if learning to find the ways of the Lord hidden in each moment and difficulty. The teaching of the Lord will face opposition from the enticement of sinners, who seek to profit from violence (Prv 1:10). Wisdom stands against this worldly way, calling out and offering counsel, although most refuse to listen (Prv 1:24). God's wisdom helps his sons to see more clearly, to perceive what is truly good and worth pursuing and how to avoid the pitfalls of sin, judging life's action from a higher and more heavenly standard.

The Book of Wisdom addresses itself to rulers of the earth as its intended audience. Nonetheless, its message, like Proverbs, comes forth equally as guidance offered by the heavenly Father for all his children. Throughout the wisdom literature, the fool stands in contrast to the wise man, and the Book of Wisdom opens with a description of how a fool sees the world: a product of mere chance, to be enjoyed in a passing moment, with no thought to the need of others. God sees things differently, judging the heart and soul, and accounting good deeds as a lasting testament, enduring even beyond death. It is wisdom that should be sought before all else: "The beginning of wisdom is the most sincere desire for instruction, and concern for instruction is love of her, and love of her is the keeping of her laws, and giving heed to her laws is assurance of immortality, and immortality brings one near to God; so the desire for wisdom leads to a kingdom" (Ws 6:17–20).[20] A key part of education entails eliciting this desire in the young: "I loved her and sought her from my youth, and I desired to take her for my bride, and I became

20. Wisdom 7:22–23 provides a description of God's wisdom: "For in her there is a spirit that is intelligent, holy, unique, manifold, subtle, mobile, clear, unpolluted, distinct, invulnerable, loving the good, keen, irresistible, beneficent, humane, steadfast, sure, free from anxiety, all-powerful, overseeing all, and penetrating through all spirits that are intelligent and pure and most subtle."

enamored of her beauty" (Ws 8:2). A life of wisdom transcends the desires and fears of this world, firmly rooted in God's thoughts and ways, which endure forever. Through it, one can judge the things of the earth rightly and order them well.

Life should consist in its essence in learning God's wisdom and abiding within it. This entails recognizing him as the source of true wisdom in humility, knowing that on our own we cannot arrive at its secrets. The Book of Wisdom affirms this: "But I perceived that I would not possess wisdom unless God gave her to me" (Ws 8: 21). This receptivity is affirmed even more strongly in Sirach, written to appeal to Gentiles, instructing them that true wisdom comes only from God. It must be received from him, and cannot be grasped on one's own: "All wisdom comes from the Lord and is with him for ever. . . . The height of heaven, the breadth of the earth, the abyss, and wisdom—who can search them out?" (Sir 1:1, 3). Chapter 3 contains an admonition not to seek wisdom on one's own: "Seek not what is too difficult for you, nor investigate what is beyond your power. Reflect upon what has been assigned to you, for you do not need what is hidden. Do not meddle in what is beyond your tasks, for matters too great for human understanding have been shown you" (Sir 3:21–23). Worldly wisdom seeks after the secrets of the world, revealing an inner pride in wanting to obtain and control what is beyond our ability and calling, although God reveals what is necessary as a gift for those who are willing to receive it from him. In the following chapter, Ben Sira explains that "Wisdom exalts her sons and gives help to those who seek her," although she must also discipline her sons so that they learn to trust her (Sir 4:17). Wisdom clearly stems from a graced purification and elevation of mind through God's teaching, rather than human efforts.

Having received what is hidden from the Lord, the wise man must, in turn, instruct others. It is a mark of wisdom to listen and attend (Prv 12:15), because the wise man knows the limits of his own ability, enabling him to counsel others with a prudence rooted in the Lord rather than his own opinions. St. Thomas Aquinas, in speaking about how the boy Jesus grew in wisdom, relates that "four things are necessary for man in order to advance in wisdom: that he listens open-heartedly, inquires diligently, answers prudently, and meditates attentively."[21] In this way, we can see how a life of wisdom emerges from unceasing listening, inquiring, and meditating, always engaging the mind and heart in receiving the Lord's own wisdom and passing it on through answering when necessary. The teacher, therefore, must always point to the Lord, with Ben Sira advising that when the wise man gives "education through the words of the tongue" that he should "never speak against the truth." Rather, he exhorts: "Be mindful of your ignorance. Do not be ashamed to confess your sins" (Sir 4:24–26). Those who are wise point to a truth above and beyond human understanding, helping others to grow in humility by witnessing to their own ignorance and sin before the perfection of God.

God the Teacher: Our Model

The biblical vision of wisdom points us directly to God as the one who teaches his people (Is 30:20), initiating them into a covenant and instructing them to walk in his ways while also interiorly illuminating them with supernatural wisdom. God stands as the true teacher of Israel and of each of his children, instructing both through the written words of the Bible, which provides the content to be learned, and through the hidden workings of grace in the mind and heart, enabling this message to take root and come alive within us. As the perfect teacher, God models how we should teach, but, like the Law itself, we serve more as a pedagogue, a tutor who can help others to find the true source of wisdom in the one teacher.

21. St. Thomas Aquinas, "Sermon 08: Puer Jesus," in *Academic Sermons* (The Catholic University of America Press, 2012), 100.

God's teaching throughout the Old Testament maintains its relevance for Christians, for within it, we see how God educates us through a transformative process: by making himself known, calling his people out of their former ways, drawing them into a covenant relationship with him, teaching them to worship him and serve him through a life of faithfulness to the commandments, entering into a life of true wisdom, and correcting them by calling them back to faithfulness. The many centuries of slow unveiling unfolding throughout the old covenant had a goal. The teaching and practices of the Law were fulfilled and perfected by Christ, the true teacher and master, who came to embody God's wisdom, making the Father known, enabling us to share in his own sonship, and pouring out the Holy Spirit to enflame the heart and enlighten the mind.

The pedagogy of the Bible finds its fulfillment and goal in Jesus Christ, who is the wisdom we seek and the righteousness that enables us to fulfill the law. He is what God teaches us, and in coming to know him we come to know the truth and the way in which we come to life (Jn 14:6). Although it finds its fulfillment in Christ, the great story of salvation history, narrated by the Bible, has not ended. The story still looks toward its final act, to the time when Christ will be "all in all" (1 Cor 15:28), bringing his great work to completion through its full fruit in us. We too, therefore, have been drawn into this story, and we are being taught by God as members of his own people and family, being made ever more into the image of his Son, "full of grace and truth," which is the goal of his teaching (Jn 1:14). The Church's education, therefore, stems from God's own teaching of humanity, which we call the divine pedagogy, translating it into a pedagogy of faith.[22] This pedagogy, which we generally call catechesis, seeks to make the movement of God to his people, as

22. See Caroline Farey, Waltraud Linnig, and Sr. M. Johannah Paruch, FSGM, eds., *The Pedagogy of God: Its Centrality in Catechesis and Catechist Formation* (Emmaus Road, 2011).

narrated by Scripture, accessible within the life of the Church, taking an all-encompassing form through the sacraments, doctrinal and moral teaching, community life, and mission. This catechetical teaching expresses the movement of Christ from the Father in emptying himself for our salvation, his manifestation of the Father to us, and the movement back to the Father in the Holy Spirit. As the *General Directory for Catechesis* explains, "Thus catechesis takes the form of a process or a journey of following the Christ of the Gospel in the Spirit towards the Father" (*GDC*, §143).

The Church lays out the divine pedagogy as the great model for her own educational efforts, instantiated within the baptismal catechumenate, which in turn serves as a model for all catechesis. We see the divine pedagogy flowing from God's revelation of himself throughout salvation history, with the following characteristics, which can guide our own teaching. God uses accessible signs to communicate his truth to us in ways that we can understand. He adapts himself to us, first using human words and then, most fully, by taking on human flesh. He uses concrete events to embody what he teaches so that it can be seen and even experienced, providing tangible ways to encounter him in divine worship and the sacraments. He unfolds his teaching gradually and sequentially, building to a greater maturity and understanding. He teaches in a relational way, with his teaching ultimately meant to draw us to him in love and to guide us in knowing how to relate to him as our God and Father.[23] This takes the form of a dialogue that stems from receiving his word and responding to it in faith and prayer. This relational dimension

23. Augustine recognizes growth in love as a primary response to the study of Scripture: "It is necessary, then, that each man should first of all find in the Scriptures that he, through being entangled in the love of this world—i.e., of temporal things—has been drawn far away from such a love for God and such a love for his neighbor as Scripture enjoins." *On Christian Doctrine*, in *Nicene and Post-Nicene Fathers, First Series*, vol. 2, trans. James Shaw, ed. Philip Schaff (Buffalo, NY: Christian Literature Publishing Co., 1887), 2.7.

also entails using messengers to speak on his behalf and to serve as witnesses to his truth. His pedagogy also takes root within a community that should embody what has been entrusted to it and to pass it down to each generation. God uses story as a central way of manifesting himself, not only particular stories, such as the life of Abraham, but also in providing an overarching narrative that presents the great movement of history from creation to the end and fulfillment of creation.[24] This forms the basis of a distinctively Christian worldview that informs how believers view reality as a whole. Finally, his teaching is efficacious, ordered toward conversion and union, making the written word powerful through the presence of the Holy Spirit within us, who enables past events and seemingly abstract truths to come to life as a present and living reality.

The Essential Lesson

God is the one and only teacher who provides education on how to live well on this earth so that we can reach eternal happiness with him.[25] Any other education pales in comparison with this greatest and most consequential lesson. Yet human beings are so slow to learn, as we see through God's central student, Israel, who

---

24. Augustine said to begin catechesis with the narrative of salvation history in his work *De Catechizandis Rudibus*.

25. In the *De veritate*, Aquinas clarifies that although God is the ultimate teacher, he does not prohibit us absolutely from calling others teachers who help draw us to the truth that God has implanted within nature and revealed to us: "Since our Lord had ordered the disciples not to be called teachers, the Gloss explains how this prohibition is to be understood, lest it be taken absolutely. For we are forbidden to call man a teacher in this sense, that we attribute to him the pre-eminence of teaching, which belongs to God. It would be as if we put our hope in the wisdom of men, and did not rather consult divine truth about those things which we hear from man. And this divine truth speaks in us through the impression of its likeness, by means of which we can judge of all things." Thomas Aquinas, *De Veritate*, vol. 2, Questions 10–20, trans. James V. McGlynn, SJ (Henry Regnery Company, 1953), q. 11, ad 1.

seemed constantly to fail, to follow after other gods and to fall away from the duties of the covenant, instructing us about our own difficulties in receiving God's teaching. After coming into the promised land, an angel appeared to the people saying, "But you have not obeyed my command. What is this you have done?" (Jgs 2:2), setting off a repeated cycle of punishment, prophetic chastisement, and repentance, only for the people to return once again to laxity. Each generation must receive the word and respond to it anew, rejecting the temptation of the world, repenting for sin, and conforming to the will of the Lord. Each human life must go through a similar cycle of continual repentance and renewal in response to God's movements.

God's teaching forms an arc from the disobedience of Eve to the obedience of the New Eve, from walking with Adam in the Garden to the new Adam being laid in the Garden beneath Calvary to remake humanity from within. Mary receives the lesson given to Israel; she hears it in silence, meditates upon it, pondering it within her heart, and speaks as a true expression of wisdom: *Fiat!* This is the response that God seeks from all his disciples, his students and sons. Jesus, who himself is the Word of God, emptied himself in order to learn with us, growing in wisdom (Lk 2:52) and seeing the things he had created with human eyes so that he could teach us as one of us. The teacher has come down to the level of the student, not just teaching with his voice but associating so closely with his students that they could receive the fullness of all that God wants to give them through him, both exterior and interior supports: knowledge of the Father, a perfect example, the divine nourishment of his own flesh, a communion of fellow disciples in his body, and an outpouring of his own Spirit to "lead them to all truth" (Jn 16:13).

God is a patient teacher, giving us our entire lives to learn his ways. He disciplines us through the many events of our lives, helping us to recognize the movements of his providence within them. He respects our freedom, given to us as a gift, and will not impose himself upon us. He invites us, eliciting a desire for his wisdom within us, slowly enabling us to grow in conformity with the great model he has provided us. He works out his pedagogy in us so that the great story of salvation history can become our story, worked out within us, leading us ever to awaken to the true lesson of life. This story lays out a blueprint, moving from the disobedience of Eve to the *fiat* of Our Lady, the model of perfect conformity to Christ. The teaching of God has as its end that we become Christ in the world, transformed as members of his Body and living as temples of his Holy Spirit.

Conclusion

There can be no Christian education without the Bible, in which God himself teaches us. As teachers, therefore, we must remain rooted within it, in our own prayer and study, and share it often with our students. We have received the gift to be able to proclaim its message to our students on God's behalf, becoming fellow workers with Christ. As St. Paul reminds us, "All scripture is inspired by God and profitable for teaching, for reproof, for correction, and for training in righteousness, that the man of God may be complete, equipped for every good work" (2 Tim 3:16). God knows infinitely better than we do what we should think and how we should live within this world. The Bible invites us into his vision and the wisdom of his most holy will. If our students do not have a strong grasp of biblical revelation in its general outlines and key themes, are not familiar with how to access and understand it, and cannot find in it a daily source for prayer and inspiration, we have truly failed in our educational mission.

The Bible has the same goal as education as a whole: to learn the meaning and purpose of life and to achieve it. Its vision should anchor Catholic education, providing the broadest context and even condition for understanding and thinking properly about life in all its dimensions. We must study it, as well as live it, for its teaching cannot remain words on a page. In fact, it communicates its power most fully in worship, eliciting a response of prayer from our hearts.[26] As we come before God in prayer, the Bible manifests our deepest identity and calls us to enter into the community of his holy people and to be adopted into the divine life itself. God is our teacher, with many pedagogues assisting us along the way. He teaches us not simply through the Book of his revelation but also in its embodiment within the Tradition, life, and worship of the Church, the mystical body of Christ in the world.

Within the life of this community, the Bible maintains an indispensable role in education, prayer, and shared experience. Every generation must receive its message, turn toward God in conversion, live out the life it prescribes, and enter into the covenant anew. The world needs God's instruction, and he offers his wisdom to us freely, although, like the fool narrated in the Old Testament, we too often follow this adulterous world for the immediate gratification it offers. In response, the Word revealed to us in the Bible himself comes to us and calls out: "Take my yoke upon you, and learn from me; for I am gentle and lowly in heart, and you will find rest for your souls" (Mt 11:29). It is here that our restless hearts find their peace in the truth and love of the Word made flesh.

We end where we began. God the Creator, the origin of our lives, calls us to him as our final end. The Word, *the* source of Catholic education, speaks, and we must respond. As we receive the Word of the divine teacher, our own minds should conform to him, becoming ever more like him. "We have the mind of Christ," Paul

26. Within the psalms God provides us the words to respond to him. Students can learn to attend to the word and respond through the practice of lectio divina, which Pope Benedict XVI predicted would lead to a "new springtime of the spiritual life" in the Church. Pope Benedict XVI, "Address to Commemorate the 40th Anniversary of the Dogmatic Constitution of Divine Revelation, *Dei Verbum*," September 16, 2005, https://www.vatican.va/content/benedict-xvi/en/speeches/2005/september/documents/hf_ben-xvi_spe_20050916_40-dei-verbum.html.

reminds us, but, even with this gift, he also teaches that we must grow to the "full stature of Christ." Our education on earth largely focuses on this growth, with its goal not simply to imitate Christ but to become him: "it is now no longer I who live but Christ who lives in me" (Gal 2:20). The conformity to the Word entails a posture of sonship, to receive all that the Father gives, to speak "only what the Father tells" us, and to do only "what the Father commands" (Jn 12:49, 14:31). Within this conformity to Christ, the task of the believer becomes to continue to share what has been received, spreading his Word throughout the world. This will entail passing on the message of salvation, but also increasing literacy, so that others can access the Word through the human words it employs.[27] Catholic education must maintain this essential focus, preparing for and responding to the Word of God given through the one essential book, which will not be superseded until we see the Father face to face.

---

27. Adrian Hinkle speaks of the necessity of preserving literacy within a religious community: "Religious literacy is only maintained when one generation accepts the responsibility of training the next. The ethos that defines a community of believers permeates daily behaviors and purposeful activity for presenting and passing on one's core religious insight to other fellow believers." *Pedagogical Theory of the Hebrew Bible: An Application of Educational Theory to Biblical Texts* (Wipf & Stock, 2016), xi.

2 Jesus the Teacher

Michael Waldstein

Jesus is the *teacher* in a unique way. "Do not let yourselves be called teacher (*rabbi*), because one is your teacher (*didaskalos*). You by contrast are brothers" (Mt 23:8). He is the *teacher* in this unique way because he is "the *savior*" (Jn 4:42). By his cross and resurrection "the love of God has been poured out into our hearts through the Holy Spirit who has been given to us" (Rom 5:5). Jesus, *the Teacher* and The Holy Spirit, *the Advocate*—these two belong inseparably together.

It is easy to be confused about the order between *teacher* and *savior*: as if Jesus were savior because he is teacher; as if he saved us by merely showing us the right way through word and example; as if we were then able to follow the right way and save ourselves. This is the Pelagian heresy.

> The hidden and horrendous poison [*virus*] of your heresy is this, that you want the grace of Christ to consist in his example, not in the gift [*donum*], by saying that one becomes just by imitating him rather than by the help of the Holy Spirit . . . whom he poured out in great richness on his own.[1]

How can one learn from this unique teacher, who speaks not only by word and example from the outside but from "more inside than my innermost, *interior intimo meo*" (Augustine, *Confessions* 3.6.11)? I will address this question by examining the experience of encounter with Jesus in the Gospel of John. My understanding of this experience has been shaped by Luigi Giussani, founder of the movement Communion and Liberation, of which I have been a

1. Augustine, *Contra Julianum opus imperfectum* 2.146; PL 145:1202.

member for more than thirty years. It is well expressed in these words of Pope Benedict XVI: "Being Christian is not the result of an ethical choice or a lofty idea, but the *encounter* with an event, a person, which gives life a new horizon and a decisive direction."[2] The English word "encounter" (like the Italian *incontro*) combines two Latin prepositions, *in* with the accusative, which means *into*, and *contra*, which means *against*. Both prepositions have a dynamic meaning, often dramatically so, either negative or positive.

"Alas, poor Romeo," Mercutio says in *Romeo and Juliet*, "he is already dead. . . . Is he a man to *encounter* Tybalt?" (act 2, scene 4). The word "encounter" reappears in a positive sense two scenes later, when Romeo and Juliet meet in Friar Lawrence's cell to exchange their marriage vows.

> ROMEO:
> Ah! Juliet, if the measure of thy joy
> be heap'd like mine and that thy skill be more
> to blazon it, then sweeten with thy breath
> this neighbor air, and let rich music's tongue
> unfold the imagin'd happiness that both
> receive in either by *this dear encounter*.
> JULIET:
> Conceit, more rich in matter than in words,
> brags of his substance, not of ornament.
> They are but beggars that can count their worth;
> but my true love is grown to such excess
> I cannot sum up half my sum of wealth.
> (*Romeo and Juliet*, act 2, scene 6)

Juliet's response highlights the connotation of rich promise that often accompanies positive uses of the word "encounter." In Shake-

2. Benedict XVI, *Deus caritas est* [Encyclical Letter], The Holy See, December 25, 2005, 1, https://www.vatican.va/ content/benedict-xvi/en/encyclicals/documents/ hf_ben-xvi_enc_20051225_ deus-caritas-est.html.

speare's *Tempest,* Prospero observes his daughter Miranda and Ferdinand declare their love for each other.

> PROSPERO (aside):
> *Fair encounter*
> of two most rare affections!
> Heavens rain grace
> on that which breeds between them!
> FERDINAND:
> Wherefore weep you?
> MIRANDA:
> At mine unworthiness, that dare not offer
> what I desire to give; and much less take
> what I shall die to want.
> (act 3, scene 1)

Newman uses "encounter" in similar negative and positive senses. "God bade them [Israel] *encounter* their enemies and so gain Canaan" (*Parochial and Plain Sermons,* vol. 4, p. 77). Like Shakespeare, Newman emphasizes the connotation of deep promise in the positive use of the word. "The outward exhibition of infinitude is mystery; and the mysteries of nature and of grace are nothing but the mode in which His infinitude *encounters* us and is *brought home* to our minds" (Newman, *Discourses to Mixed Congregations,* 231). God is the one who *encounters* us to *bring home* to us his infinity so that we come to grasp his ungraspability.

Giussani closely links *experience* with *encounter.* Popular culture prizes *experience* in many senses, not all of them helpful for understanding the *experience of encounter* with Jesus in John. Our age tends to hold up individual *experiences* as ultimate measures and goals. It regards abstract thought and dogmas with suspicion. Computer software and smart phones compete to deliver the best user *experiences. Experiences,* more than things, or rather, *experiences* by means of things, are what consumers are interested in.

Nevertheless, there is a sense of *experience* that is useful for understanding the encounter with Jesus in John. My daughter Monica has been a pediatrician for several years. To say that she has gained experience as a doctor is not to say that she has had her feelings tickled, shocked, fascinated, and intoxicated, even less that she experienced "likes" on Facebook. It means that many particular experiences of rationally examining and treating children have produced cumulative experience, which enables her to make medical judgments quickly, accurately, and firmly.

The depth of promise in an event, by which that event can be recognized as a true encounter, is *brought home* to us (as Newman puts it) by experience, both particular and cumulative. Aristotle uses a word close to Newman's *brought home*, namely, *enoikeo*, living in (*en-*) the same house (*oikos*) in an important text on experience.

> Lack of experience makes us less able to see the recognized facts together as a whole. For this reason, those who dwell [*enoikeo*, lit. "live in the house"] more among natural things are better able to grasp beginnings that can speak about many facts together as a whole, while those whom many words have kept from looking at the existing things are quick to proclaim their opinions by looking at a few.[3]

The Encounter with Jesus in the Gospel of John

Encounter and Desire

> John [the Baptist] was standing with two of his disciples,
> and he looked at Jesus as he walked, and said,
> "Look, the Lamb of God!"
> The two disciples heard him say this and followed Jesus.
> Jesus turned, and saw them following,
> and said to them, "What are you *seeking?*"

3. Aristotle, *On Generation and Corruption*, 1.2.

> And they said to him, "Rabbi," which means teacher,
> "Where are you *remaining* [verb *meno*]?"
> He said to them, "Come and see."
> They came and saw where he was *remaining.*
> And they *remained with* him that day.
> It was about the tenth hour. (Jn 1:35–39)

The trigger in this encounter with Jesus is the mysterious pronouncement by John the Baptist, "Look, the Lamb of God," which carries many echoes of the hope of Israel for atonement and salvation. Mystery, attraction, and depth of promise are forcefully brought together in, "Look, the Lamb of God."

"What are you *seeking?*" Jesus addresses the inner energy of *desire* stirred up in them by the mysterious words "the Lamb of God." Jesus turns his attention to the desire stirred up by a mysterious promise. Fail to seek, and you will not find. Without desire, an initial impact cannot unfold into an experience of encounter.

Remaining With

The answer of the two disciples is surprising. They address him as teacher but do not ask, "What does Lamb of God mean?" Instead, they ask, "Where are you *remaining?*" Where are you staying? Perhaps their question is due to the custom that the learners at that time lived with their teacher. Shared life with a teacher shapes the whole person—intelligence, sentiment, affection, and decision.

In answer, Jesus invites them to come and see. For those who know that the true place in which the Son *remains* is the Mystery par excellence, the mystery of the Father, the question, "Where are you *remaining?*" opens into a great depth.

> In my Father's house there are many *places to remain.*
> If not, would I have told you
> that I am going to prepare a *place* for you?
> And if I go and prepare a *place* for you,

> I will return and take you to myself
> so that *where I am* you also may be. (Jn 14:2–3)

The Greek word behind "places to remain" is *monai,* a noun derived from the verb *meno,* "remain." It is usually translated as "mansions" or "dwelling places," which loses the connection with *meno,* remain.

The way of learning from Jesus the teacher is to *remain* with him from the beginning, whatever poor place he may be *remaining* in, in order eventually to *remain* with him in the spacious house he *remains in,* namely, the Father.

In order for the event of seeing where Jesus remains to become an encounter in the full sense, the two disciples must remain with him on a long path that leads to a still unattained end of remaining with him in the Father's house.

The Tenth Hour

At the end of the scene, John uses "remain" twice, with great emphasis. "They came and saw where he was *remaining.* And they *remained* with him that day. It was about the tenth hour" (Jn 1:39). The precise hour in which this seeing and remaining began is fixed in retrospect as the decisive moment of encounter.

Married couples often say, "It was love at first sight." Some people dismiss this statement as false, as projecting a later result back into the beginning. Yet, there is a deep truth in remembering an acorn as *the oak* it has grown into. The acorn is truly the oak at its beginning. An initial impact, which might disappear in the stream of the many impacts that fill our daily lives, becomes the experience of an encounter when it unfolds under the guidance of emotion and judgment.

"The Word became flesh and has pitched his tent among us, and we have seen his glory" (Jn 1:14). It was a glimpse of this glory, the first dawn of its light, that stirred up the desire of the two learners in the word of John the Baptist about "the Lamb of God." The end-point is still far away in the future, but it is essentially the same, "Father, what you have given me, I will that where I am they too may be with me, that they may see my glory, which you have given me because you loved me before the foundation of the world" (17:24). The encounter begins in concrete circumstances, that may seem poor and insignificant. Its power becomes evident on a path of verifying, of judging whether its promise is true. Without sustained verification, the original encounter with Jesus would suffocate in its finiteness.

Communion

The word "remain" reappears in Jesus's Eucharistic discourse. "The one who eats my flesh and drinks my blood *remains in* me and I *in* him" (Jn 6:56). The disciples have come a long way from asking where Jesus was *remaining*. The wording Jesus uses is no longer "remain with" but "remain in." Mutual *remaining in* suggests communion, an interior presence of persons to each other, which is the fruit of love, of giving oneself to another. Through the Eucharist, the one *with whom* they *remained* as a teacher has the power to *remain in* them and to make them *remain in* himself.

Jesus unfolds the nature of this communion in the image of the vine in John 15, where he uses "remain" seven times.

> I am the true vine... (1) *remain in* me and I in you. As the branch cannot bear fruit by itself if it does not (2) *remain in* the vine, neither can you if you do not (3) *remain in* me. I am the vine, you are the branches. The one who (4) *remains in* me and I *in* him bears much fruit, because apart from me you can do nothing. Whoever does not (5) *remain in* me is thrown outside like a branch and withers. and they will gather them and throw them into the fire, and burn them. If you (6) *remain in* me, and my words (7) *remain in* you, ask for whatever you wish, and it will be done for you. My Father is glorified by this, that you bear much fruit and become my disciples. (Jn 15:1, 4–8)

The number seven is deeply rooted in nature, both human and cosmic. Our head has seven openings through which much of our life takes place: two ears, two eyes, two nostrils, and the mouth. Without the help of a telescope, we can see seven heavenly bodies that have a movement of their own in addition to the daily movement around the earth: the sun, the moon, and the five visible planets.

The experience of encounter with Jesus begins in external circumstances but reaches into the innermost depth of the learner. It draws the disciple into the inner life of Jesus the teacher.

Root of Communion in the Trinity

Immediately after illustrating *remaining in* by the image of the vine, Jesus points to the root of communion in the Trinity. The apparently inconspicuous word AS plays a key role in his argument.

> **AS** the Father has loved me, so I have loved you.
> *Remain in* my love.
> If you keep my commandments,
> you will *remain in* my love,
> **AS** I have kept my Father's commandments
> and *remain in* his love.
> I have said these things to you so that my joy may *be in* you,
> and that your joy may be complete.
> This is my commandment, that you love one another
> **AS** I have loved you.
> No one has greater love than this
> that he lays down his life for his friends. (Jn 15:9–13)

The first and the third clauses with AS combine to form a golden chain descending from the Father to the commandment of love.

> AS the Father has loved me,
> so have I loved you (15:9).
> Love one another
> AS I have loved you. (15:12)

The chain does not begin as a commandment but as the reality of communion between the Father and the Son. As the Father has loved me, eternally, as a fact, in the gift of the whole divine nature, so have I loved you, in laying down my life and giving myself to you in the communion of the Eucharist. It is from these facts that the commandment arises: love one another.

Between these two instances of AS, which form the golden chain, there is a passage that places the commandment and its meaning squarely within Trinitarian *remaining*.

> *Remain in* my **love**.
>   If you keep my COMMANDMENTS,
> you will *remain in* my **love**,
>   **AS** I have kept my Father's COMMANDMENTS
> and *remain in* his love.

The three instances of *remain in my/his love* surround the two instances of *keeping my/his commandments*. The word AS connects the Trinity and human morality. Remaining in Jesus's love as he remains in the Father's love—this is the point of the commandment of love. Communion as participation in the Trinity, this is the place to which the encounter has led the disciples. Communion was implicit in the repetition of *remain*. "Where are you *remaining*? . . . They saw where he *remained*. And they *remained* with him that day" (Jn 1:38–39).

The beginnings of the encounter with Jesus as well as its end lie in the communion of the Father and the Son in the Spirit.

The Cross

When some Greeks approach Jesus, he makes a mysterious pronouncement.

> The hour has come for the Son of Man to be glorified.
> Amen, Amen, I say to you,
> unless the grain of wheat falling into the earth dies,
> it itself remains alone;
> but if it dies, it brings much fruit. (Jn 12:23–24)

The image of the grain of wheat interprets the glorification of the Son of Man. As the grain of wheat does not remain alone but becomes fruitful through its death, so also the Son of Man: through his death he no longer remains alone but constructs the community of his own. His glory appears in the power of his suffering and death to "bear or carry away the sin of the world" (Jn 1:29) and build communion through the Eucharistic flow of blood and water from his side (Jn 19:34).

Just as Jesus the teacher accepted the cross, so must those who learn from him. The grain of wheat must die to produce the fruit of communion.

Ecclesial Communion as Sign

Table 2-1

Not Yet: Jn 17:20–21	Already: 17:22–23	Morality: 13:34–35
I do not **ask you** for them alone, but for those who believe in me through their word,	And the glory you have given me **I have given** to them,	I give you a new **commandment**,
THAT all may be one	**THAT** they may be one	**THAT** you love one another
AS you, Father, are in me and I in you,	**AS** we are one, I in them and you in me,	**AS** I have loved you
THAT they too may be in us,	**THAT** they may be completed into one,	**THAT** you too may love one another.
THAT the world **may believe** that you sent me.	**THAT** the world **may know** that you sent me and that you loved them as you loved me.	In this all **will know** that you are my disciples, if you have love for one another.

The three texts set next to each other in this table follow the same literary structure. An introductory statement is followed by two "that" clauses that sandwich an AS clause. Another "that" clause follows, which indicates the overall purpose (in 13:35 a separate main clause that indicates the result).

The introductory sentences distinguish the three texts from each other. In the first text, Jesus prays to the Father for a future desired result. In the second, he states an accomplished fact, "The glory you have given me I have given to them." In the third, he announces the new commandment. These are the three basic dimensions of Christian life. The first two belong to the order of being: what will be and what already is. The third belongs to the order of moral norms: what ought to be. One and the same reality, communion in the Trinity, is presented in these three basic modes. They complete the Johannine reflection about "remaining in" in the form of "being one" and "being in."

All three texts end by pointing to communion among the disciples of Christ as a perceptible sign for the world. Communion is the persuasive sign that brings others to communion.

The encounter, which began with Jesus at "about the tenth hour," is continued by the community that flows from the death and resurrection of Jesus. Jesus is not only remembered as a figure in the distant past, but he is present in the communion of his disciples, which has the power of a missionary sign.

Over-View of the Seven Points

(1) The inner motor of the experience of encounter with Jesus is *desire* stirred up by a mysterious promise. Unless one seeks and asks, the impact of an event cannot unfold into a true encounter.

(2) One must *remain* with Jesus the teacher to allow the encounter to unfold. A lifelong path of verification is needed. The goal is to remain with him in the Father's house.

(3) The encounter begins in *concrete circumstances* that may seem poor and insignificant. Yet, they contain a power that becomes

evident on a journey of verification. Experience in the full sense requires verification. Without verification, the original encounter with Jesus would suffocate in its finiteness.

(4) The encounter with Jesus begins in external circumstances but reaches into the innermost depth of persons. It draws the disciple into communion with the teacher.

(5) The beginning and end of the encounter is the communion between the Father and the Son in the Spirit.

(6) Encounter with Jesus inevitably leads to the cross. Unless the grain of wheat dies, it remains alone, without the fruit of communion.

(7) The experience of encounter with Jesus is made possible today by the visible sign of ecclesial communion.

Jesus the Teacher in an Age of Science

The dominant scientific-technological culture of the West sees reason and religious faith as opposites. Natural science—this and only this is the domain of reason. The most influential New Testament scholar of the twentieth century, Rudolf Bultmann, argues that Christian faith as understood for two millennia cannot be maintained any more.

> All of this is mythological talk. . . . Insofar as it is mythological talk *it is not believable to men and women today* because for them the mythical world picture is a thing of the past. Therefore, contemporary Christian proclamation is faced with the question whether, when it demands faith of men and women, it expects them to acknowledge this mythical world picture of the past. If this is impossible, it then has to face the question whether the New Testament proclamation has a truth that is independent of the mythical world picture, in which case it would be the task of theology to demythologize the Christian proclamation. . . . We cannot use electric lights and radios and, in the event of illness avail ourselves of modern medical and clinical means and at the

> same time believe in the spirit and wonder world of the New Testament. And if we suppose that we can do so ourselves, we must be clear that we can represent this as the attitude of Christian faith only by making the Christian proclamation unintelligible and impossible for our contemporaries.[4]

Voluntarism in Islam and the Medieval West

In his Regensburg Lecture, Benedict XVI challenges the self-limitation of reason presupposed by Bultmann. He begins his argument by quoting the Byzantine emperor's critique of Mohammed's practice of conversion by the sword.

> Not to act with reason, *syn logo*, is contrary to the essence of God. Faith is a fruit of the soul, not the body. To lead someone to faith one needs the ability to speak well and think rightly, not violence and threats.[5]

"In the beginning was the Logos . . . and the Logos was God" (Jn 1:1). This text, Benedict XVI argues, is the concluding Christian word about the relation between reason (*logos*) and God.

> *Logos* is both reason and word—a creative reason that can communicate itself precisely as reason. John thereby gave us the concluding word of the biblical concept of God, in which all the often toilsome and tortuous paths of biblical faith reach their goal and find their synthesis.[6]

---

4. Rudolf Bultmann, *New Testament and Mythology and Other Basic Writings* (Fortress Press, 1984), 2–5. Emphasis original.

5. Benedict XVI, "Faith, Reason and the University: Memories and Reflections" (hereinafter, *Regensburg Address*), lecture delivered at the University of Regensburg, September 12, 2006, §3, https://www.vatican.va/content/benedict-xvi/en/speeches/2006/september/documents/ hf_ben-xvi_spe_20060912_university-regensburg.html.

6. Benedict XVI, *Regensburg Address*, §5.

Conversion by the sword is an affirmation of the primacy of will and power *on the level of practice. On the level of theory* radical voluntarism is affirmed by Islamic thinkers such as Ibn Hazm (994–1064). "God is not bound to keep his own word nor under any obligation to reveal the truth to us. If he willed it, we would have to practice idolatry."[7] Radical voluntarism also arose in the medieval West. Benedict XVI sees Duns Scotus (c. 1265–1308) as the beginning of a voluntarist trend.

> In contrast with the so-called intellectualism of Augustine and Thomas, there arose with Duns Scotus a voluntarism which, in its later developments, led to the claim that we can only know God's *voluntas ordinata* [actually decided will]. Beyond the realm of *voluntas ordinata* lies the realm of God's freedom, in virtue of which he could have done the opposite of everything he has done.[8]

While Scotus still affirms the primacy of God's wisdom, which he sees reflected in the natural law, William of Ockham (1287–1347) abandons this primacy and affirms the absolute primacy of will and power. "God can command the created will to hate him."[9] "God cannot be bound to any act, and therefore by the very fact that God wills this, it is right for it to be done."[10]

Voluntarist Self-Limitation of Reason

Ockham's voluntarism deeply shaped the beginnings of the scientific revolution. Descartes, one of the seminal figures of the revolution, proposes that a new practical philosophy should replace the theoretical philosophy taught in schools and universities.

---

7. Benedict XVI, *Regensburg Address*, §4.
8. Benedict XVI, *Regensburg Address*, §7.
9. Ockham, *Opera Theologica*, 10 vols. (St. Bonaventure Press, 1967–86), 7:352.
10. Ockham, *Opera Theologica*, 7:198.

> It is possible to reach knowledge that will be powerfully useful to life and instead of the theoretical philosophy which is now taught in the schools, we can find a practical one by which, knowing the force and the actions of fire, water, air, stars, the heavens, and all the other bodies that surround us as distinctly as we know the various skills of our workmen, we can employ them in the same way for all the uses for which they are fit, and so make ourselves masters and possessors of nature.[11]

Descartes understood that the choice of power as the goal of knowledge implies the choice of mechanics, later called mathematical physics, as the master science of nature. Mechanics gives a precise mathematical account of how force needs to be applied to control the behavior of bodies. Since its method is mathematical, mechanics shares the limits of mathematics. Mathematics deals only with quantity and with more abstract items that can be set in quantitative relations. Goodness, beauty, life, consciousness, knowledge, love, male, and female—none of these can be grasped mathematically. In the degree to which mathematical physics becomes the master science of nature, what cannot be grasped mathematically tends to fade away as merely subjective. What can be grasped mathematically stands out as rationally significant.

One can see the force of this self-limitation of reason in Stephen Hawking, one of Newton's successors in the chair of mathematics at Cambridge.

> It is Laplace who is usually credited with first clearly postulating scientific determinism: Given the state of the universe at one time, a complete set of laws fully determines both the future and the past. This would exclude the possibility of miracles or an active role for God. The scientific determinism that Laplace formulated . . . is, in fact, the basis of all modern science. A scientific

11. Descartes, *Discourse on Method* (1637), part 6, §2.

> law is not a scientific law if it holds only when some supernatural being decides not to intervene. Recognizing this, Napoleon is said to have asked Laplace how God fit into this picture. Laplace replied: "Sire, I have not needed that hypothesis."[12]

It is curious that Hawking bases his determinism not on observations about the allegedly infallible causal power with which real causes determine real effects, but on the governing power of mathematical laws themselves.

> M-theory predicts that a great many universes were created out of nothing. Their creation does not require the intervention of some supernatural being or god. Rather, these multiple universes arise naturally from physical law. They are a prediction of science.[13]

In Hawking's way of understanding them, mathematical laws are more than quantitative descriptions gathered from observing real causes. Multiple universes naturally arise from them.

What relation to being and non-being do these laws have? Do they themselves work effectively as laws before the existence of anything, at least in the logical and nontemporal sense of *before*? Are they a non-physical cosmos of Platonic ideas hovering over nothingness to cause the emergence of physical universes from nothing? Why should one call such laws "predictions of science" if they exist before a universe inhabited by scientists who discover laws that allow them to make predictions?

Hawking believes that one needs to look no further than mathematical laws to account for the emergence of being from nothing. He overlooks that mathematics does not consider being as a whole but abstracts quantitative relations to focus on them alone. The distinction between real being and non-being cannot be expressed in

12. Stephen Hawking, *The Grand Design* (Bantam, 2010), 33.
13. Hawking, 8.

quantitative terms. To limit the breadth of reason to mathematical physics suppresses the question of being instead of answering it. Hawking seems to have forgotten Hamlet's words, "To be or not to be. That is the question."

Ratzinger observes that responses to the question of God are not shaped on the level of theory alone, not even if reason extends itself beyond self-imposed boundaries. Responses are shaped by the habit of reliance on technological power and—still more deeply—by fundamental experiences and decisions about love and communion.

> Human beings have all the power over the world. They see right through its functions and know the laws that determine its course. They can disassemble the mechanism, as it were, and reassemble it. It is a functioning assembly they can use and force to serve them. If one can see right through the world, then it has no room any more for God to intervene. Help can come to humanity only from humanity itself, because power over the world lies with humanity alone. A God without power, however, is not God. When power lies with humanity alone, God no longer exists. . . .
>
> It becomes clear that knowing God is in the end not only a question of theory but in the first place of the praxis of life. It depends on the relation established by human beings between themselves and the world, between themselves and their own life.
>
> Yet, the problem of power is only one side. Prior to it, deeper decisions are made in the relation to one's own *I*, to *You*, and *We*—in the experience of being loved or rejected. The fundamental experiences and decisions in this mutual orientation of *I*, *You*, and *We* determine whether one sees being accompanied and preceded by the Wholly-Other as competition, as danger, or as a basis for trust.[14]

---

14. Joseph Ratzinger, "Gott hat Namen," in *Joseph Ratzinger Gesammelte Schriften* (JRGS) (Herder, 2020), 3/1:130–31.

Engaging the Full Breadth of Reason

The Regensburg lecture reconfigures the conventional geography of cultural debate by focusing on the contrast between the primacy of reason (intellectualism) and the primacy of will and power (voluntarism). According to the conventional geography, two cultural continents face each other, separated by the ocean of opposition between religious faith and reason.

> **RELIGIOUS FAITH** is represented by Islam and Christianity. It favors conservative politics of repression.
> **REASON** is represented by natural science. It favors liberal politics of emancipation.

By focusing on the contrast between intellectualism and voluntarism, the Regensburg lecture draws the boundaries of the continents in a different way.

> **THE PRIMACY OF WILL AND POWER** is represented by Islam, medieval voluntarism, and the ideology of scientism. It favors the voluntarism of individualist liberal democracy or the voluntarism of statist dictatorship.
> **THE PRIMACY OF REASON** is represented by Greek (Socratic) philosophy as well as Christianity. It favors the communion of persons.

This reconfiguration of the geography of cultural debate explains why Benedict XVI concludes the Regensburg lecture with an appeal to engage the full breadth of reason.

> Courage to engage the whole breadth of reason, not the denial of its grandeur—this is the program with which a theology grounded in Biblical faith enters the debates of our time. "Not to act reasonably, not to act with *logos*, is contrary to the nature of God," said Manuel II, according to his Christian understanding of God, in response to his Persian interlocutor. It is to this great

> *logos*, to this breadth of reason, that we invite our partners in the dialogue of cultures. To rediscover it constantly is the great task of the university.[15]

Conclusion

Encounter with Jesus is possible today because remembering him is to remember a present reality (Giussani). This statement seems paradoxical. How can one remember something *past* as a *present* reality? While the act of remembering may take place in the present, what one remembers is *past, not present.*

The encounter with Jesus as portrayed in John resolves this paradox. As the eternal Son of God made flesh, Jesus is actively present now in his Church. The Eucharistic words of institution exactly display this paradoxical structure of memory. "Do this in memory of me" (Lk 22:19; 1 Cor 11:24). "Do this" refers to a present doing of Jesus's past deed of giving his body. In memory of him, his body is given as a present and living reality. Scripture joins the past and the present in a similar way.

> It is a great danger . . . in our reading of Scripture that we stop at the human words, words from the past, past history, and do not discover the present in the past, the Holy Spirit who speaks to us today in the words of the past. In this way we do not enter the interior movement of the Word, which in human words conceals and reveals divine words. Therefore, there is always a need for seeking. We must always look for the Word within the words. . . . With his incarnation he said: I am yours. And in baptism he said to me: I am yours. In the Holy Eucharist, he says ever anew: I am yours, so that we may respond: Lord, I am yours. In the way of the Word, entering the mystery of his incarnation, of his being among us, we want to appropriate his being, we want to expropriate our existence, giving ourselves to him who gave himself to

15. Benedict XVI, *Regensburg Lecture* §16.

us. I am yours. Let us ask the Lord that we may learn to say this word with our whole being. Thus we will be in the heart of the Word. Thus we will be saved.[16]

16. Benedict XVI, Opening Discourse for the Synod of Bishops on Scripture, October 6, 2008, https://www.vatican.va/content/benedict-xvi/en/speeches/2008/october/documents/hf_ben-xvi_spe_20081006_sinodo.html.

3 Plato

James Matthew Wilson

Oscar Wilde, whose words are always true so long as one takes them to mean just the opposite of what the author actually intended, once praised the ancient Greek philosopher Plato in rapturous terms. In *The Picture of Dorian Gray*, Wilde's Lord Henry Wotton celebrates him as "that artist in thought, who had first analyzed" the way "the mere shapes and patterns of things" become "themselves patterns of some other and more perfect form whose shadow they made real."[1] There is scarcely a page in Wilde's writing that does not demonstrate his perverted but profound debt to Plato; it is almost as though the entirety of the modern artist's work were itself a mere commentary on that of the ancient philosopher, who is above all an artist in thought. Wilde was known as the consummate aesthete, but it was Plato who taught him to dwell aesthetically. For Wilde, this entailed living for beauty alone, to the exclusion of everything else. In this he misunderstood Plato. For Plato also tells us to live in the light of eternal beauty, but in doing so we enter into truth, into goodness, into reality as a whole. For Wilde, playing the aesthete was a road to perdition, but dwelling aesthetically as Plato actually teaches us is the way to become properly human, to fulfill our natures, and to enter on the path of the proper formation of the soul.

Wilde's debt should not surprise us, even if his distortions of Plato still have the power to shock. The philosopher Alfred North Whitehead once observed that the "safest general characterization of the European philosophical tradition is that it consists of a series of footnotes to Plato." What more need be said? What

1. Oscar Wilde, *Complete Works* (HarperCollins, 1989), 41.

further argument could we make in favor of the study of Plato? His dialogues are the source text for the whole philosophical tradition. But, as the example of Wilde indicates, he is also one of the great source texts of our culture more generally. Western civilization has been so shaped by his thought that I have argued in the past that the western intellectual tradition is best described as the Christian-Platonic tradition.[2]

I will not repeat such a historical argument. If Plato is as foundational as I propose, then each of us will be influenced by him, just as Wilde was, even if we never read his works or even learn his name. If, as it were, the philosophical tradition of footnotes becomes extensive enough, then we may do as many historians do to develop an argument in their research: we may ignore the text of the book and simply follow the string of references. As I have already indicated, my argument here will be of a different kind. I propose that the direct encounter with Plato's dialogues is the best possible initiation into the intellectual, and beyond that, the spiritual, life to be found outside of our sacred texts. And, in contrast with scripture, Plato's works teach us the proper way to read them. They are therefore the ideal first texts to encounter in one's liberal education.

Let us first appreciate together Plato's historical significance, but do so only in passing, as we attend at greater length to two central aspects of Plato's importance, both of which help explain the kind of "initiation" I have just mentioned. Second, we shall consider Plato's dialogues under the aspect of what they have to teach all of us, at any stage of life, about how we ought to address ourselves to the world. This we shall consider under the rubric, dwelling aesthetically. And third, we shall consider the privileged role the dialogues can and ought to play in education as introduction to it. Plato's dialogues provide the ideal initiation into how our intellectual vocation

2. James Matthew Wilson, *The Vision of the Soul: Truth, Goodness, and Beauty in the Western Tradition* (The Catholic University of America Press, 2017).

and life ought to be practiced. Specifically, I want to propose the dialogues as the proper way to introduce the young to those four great orienting points of liberal education, the transcendental properties of being: Unity, Truth, Goodness, and Beauty.

The first part of my discussion, in sum, will remind us of Plato's historical importance. The second will explain the irreducible and permanent importance of an encounter with Plato's dialogues as formative for all of us. The third part proposes to answer a question that will be of particular importance to educators: In what way could Plato's thought be presented to Catholic, classical, and liberal arts school students so that it serves as a formative introduction to the life of the mind?

Platonic Lives, Homeric Afterlives

Before entering into those two major questions, it is appropriate to offer some comment on who Plato was and where he fits into the western tradition. With good reason, Homer is the first great author of the classical West and in a sense a foundational figure for our culture, second only to Sacred Scripture. Let me remind us of the familiar details of Plato's life and offer a brief, transitional thought on the relationship of Plato to Homer.

Greek philosophy as a way of life and as a kind of inquiry begins with Socrates, who lived in late fifth century BC Athens. He was condemned to death for impiety and died at the beginning of the fourth century. The shape of Socrates's character and the nature of the charges against him were contested in his day and are open to debate still in ours. But the richest, most abundant, and most exciting account of that character is that we find in the dialogues of Plato, where Socrates is generally, though not exclusively, the main speaker and protagonist. Plato was born around 428 BC and so may have spent as many as two decades as a follower of Socrates before the latter's death sentence. Plato lived for another fifty years thereafter, dying around 348 BC, which time must have been largely filled with the composition of his famous dialogues. Thrasyllus, an early editor, attributed thirty-five dialogues to Plato; a more conservative estimate would give us twenty-nine dialogues confidently ascribed to him. He founded the famous Academy, which endured as an institution for two centuries after his death and continues as the paradigm or exemplar of real education to this day. Among his students was Aristotle, whose work and spirit as a philosopher is often—but mostly wrongly—contrasted with that of Plato. In fact, Aristotle's work is best read as a continuous dialectical engagement with Platonic ideas and questions. His are the first footnotes, as it were; they derive from Plato and it is a late and erroneous idea that Aristotle constitutes a separate school of philosophy (although he did establish his own school, the Lyceum). What we call classical philosophy is, for the most part, simply the work of Plato and Aristotle conjoined. The Socrates we know is Plato's Socrates. Other schools of philosophy before Socrates we know also largely through Plato and Aristotle. Aristotle's work is best read in light of Plato. In this sense at least, Plato alone *is* classical philosophy. It will be one of my contentions that in one sense Plato *is* philosophy itself.

This emphatic description of Plato and my judgment that our intellectual tradition, the western intellectual tradition, is a Christian-Platonic one should raise questions among us, if not objections. The term suggests that Sacred Scripture and Christ are foundational to our civilization, as indeed they are—but was not Homer to the city of Athens what Scripture was to Jerusalem? In a sense, yes.

The philosopher Alasdair MacIntyre once observed that Greek society was essentially a Homeric one; its cultural life was an ongoing dialogue with Homeric voices and this constituted its intellectual tradition.[3] For the Athenians, Homer is the great authority and the one foundation. In classical Athens, however, the meaning of that

3. Alasdair MacIntyre, *Whose Justice? Which Rationality?* (University of Notre Dame Press, 1988), 24.

authority, the meaning of Homer, was not settled but subject to ongoing contention. As MacIntyre shows us, for instance, there was the great contest between the historians and advocates of glory and action or effectiveness, on the one hand, and the philosophers on the other. If Athenian society was a Homeric one, where all the arguments were essentially arguments over the meaning of Homer, it was Plato who finally provided the definitive account of Homer to us and thereby shaped how we understand human nature, human action, and the nature of glory.

To demonstrate this claim, let me just offer the one, central point of contention between Plato and the classical historians as interpreters of Homer. Homer's poems are poems of excellence and glory; on this the philosopher and the historians agree. The poems enact the remembering of great actions and induce us to consider what makes those actions worthy of praise or glory, even when other moral questions hang about them with some ambiguity.[4] What makes human action excellent? Under what circumstances does that excellence merit our judgment or recognition as an object of glory?

To read the philosopher Charles Taylor on the origins of Platonic thought is to realize how open these questions once were, even if the answers finally given now seem to us self-evident.[5] One answer, the answer furnished by the classical historians, was that of effectiveness or success. In which case, the actions of the warrior are good in themselves and, the more awesome the warrior and his actions, the more worthy will be our retrospective giving of glory. Athens was a warrior society, and Homer the great poet of war. This response may have seemed beyond question. Plato and Aristotle contended otherwise, however, and in three ways. First, martial actions were indeed forms of excellence, but useful ones subordinate to ends beyond themselves. The end they served was the practice of

4. Cf. MacIntyre, *Whose Justice? Which Rationality?* 35 ff.

5. Charles Taylor, *Sources of the Self* (Harvard University Press, 1989), 115–27.

different kinds of excellent action, which the philosophers called the life of virtue. Second, the highest and most final virtues were those of the life of the mind that culminates in contemplation, but which also reforms and governs, disciplines and refines, the rest of the moral life as it draws the practical realm under its intellectual rule. Third, and finally, the glory a warrior society normally awarded externally and retrospectively on the deeds of the dead was, said the philosophers, more properly to be granted to the practice of the intellectual virtues in the act of contemplation, or the love of wisdom called philosophy. This glory was not something that society could award. The glory, rather, was interior to the life of the philosopher itself, the product of the interior illumination of his own activity.

These three claims are all interpretations of Homer. They transform Homer, yes, by spiritualizing and interiorizing his meaning, but they nevertheless remain interpretations. Moreover, they are the interpretations that won out. The Homer that post-Athenian civilization inherited was Plato's Homer. But Plato's Homer is so radically different from the alternatives that we may well simply call it Plato—and that is what I have done in characterizing our civilization, not as Christian-Homeric, but rather as Christian-Platonic.

We sense how complete was Plato's argumentative victory here in several ways. All that we find in Homer that is irreconcilable with Plato strikes us as alien; merciless warfare we condemn, whereas we see the great mercy and justice of Achilles to Priam, when he returns Hector's body, as a moment of the triumph of rational justice over martial effectiveness. Further, in the modern age, we encounter critics of Plato, such as Friedrich Nietzsche, who would undo the philosopher's influence and take us back to Homer. Truly, for that project to be a success, everything from Plato's Homer onward would have to be stripped away and the figure that emerges from this experiment appears even to Nietzsche as a monster of willfulness. If it is not without its power of attraction for some, it is an attraction to what has long since become alien to us. And finally, in some critiques of Plato, we find points well-articulated and attractive—and we are led to say, such-and-such does seem an important idea for us to affirm, and if Platonism does not affirm it, Platonism must go. But, as I shall propose in just a moment, when we turn from those critics back to Plato, we find that Plato had the resources to furnish us with that idea all along and it was our sloppy reading, not Plato's bad philosophy, that was to blame. As a matter of history, we are all Christian-Platonists. But this, in my view, is to say nothing. Plato himself would have us ask another question: is it good to be a Platonist and why? It is to answering those questions that I will now turn.

Dwelling Aesthetically

The German philosopher Josef Pieper long ago argued that "Man's ability to *see* is in decline." By this he meant "the spiritual capacity to perceive the visible reality that truly is."[6] Pieper's sense of the cause of this decline was at least twofold. Modern life has grown increasingly restless and furtive, and so we no longer can understand the kind of receptive and contemplative activity that would be necessary for proper seeing. But, also, he diagnoses a general impoverishment of what *seeing* is in itself. Seeing has gradually been reduced from a vision of reality to a mere vision of the sensible, and from a vision of the sensible to an abstract measure of the aspects of the sensible which can be quantified.

This modern poverty of sight the Swiss theologian Hans Urs von Balthasar diagnosed at an even more fundamental level. Modern persons may still speak of truth and goodness, but they tend to dismiss beauty as the mere "ornament of a bourgeois past."[7] This, he holds, we must not do. Beauty was the word "without which the

6. Josef Pieper, *Only the Lover Sings: Art and Contemplation* (Ignatius Press, 1990), 31.

7. Hans Urs von Balthasar, *The Glory of the Lord* (Ignatius Press, 1998), vol 1.18.

ancient world refused to understand itself," and without it in our vocabulary, the modern person and reality as a whole soon become unintelligible and undesirable; indeed we even become unintelligible and unlovable to ourselves.[8] Von Balthasar's reasoning here can be explained with two statements. First, he contends that beauty is "the primal phenomenon."[9] Second, to see that phenomenon requires being able "to see the form," that is, to be able to receive being in its wholeness and fullness of depth and richness. Von Balthasar follows Plato and the tradition he inaugurated by speaking of beauty in terms of form and form's splendor: ontological form and what it irradiates and discloses from its interior fullness. In von Balthasar's words, beauty is "the figure and that which shines forth from the figure, making it into a worthy, a love-worthy thing."[10] Whoever is blind to form, dismisses it; whoever thinks he can get behind form to some pure abstraction, or—worse—whoever thinks it can be crumbled or disintegrated into parts and fragments, as if the whole were in some way not more than but even less than the sum of its parts—all this von Balthasar condemns as utterly illegitimate—impossible in fact and disfiguring when attempted. Beauty's disclosure as form and splendor is primordial and though we need not receive it in inert fashion, we may neither dismiss it, nor dissolve it, nor leave it behind. Only thus, as a formal whole, can we receive the gift of being, including the being of divine revelation in Scripture and in the Church. We must learn, insists von Balthasar, to contemplate the form of revelation just as we contemplate the form of a painting.[11]

Elsewhere in von Balthasar's great study of the transcendental of beauty, he shows himself a perceptive and appreciative reader of Plato. In the pages from which I have been quoting, however, von

8. von Balthasar, *The Glory of the Lord*, I.18.
9. von Balthasar, *The Glory of the Lord*, I.20.
10. von Balthasar, *The Glory of the Lord*, I.20.
11. von Balthasar, *The Glory of the Lord*, I.32.

Balthasar accuses Plato of attempting just what the theologian has declared to be impossible. According to von Balthasar, Plato sought to preserve the splendor of beauty, but believed he could do so only by going behind the phenomenon of form. Plato thereby took the intelligible splendor of form, which properly speaking is symbolic or even sacramental, and reduced it to mere allegory.[12] Plato thus is found guilty of being the progenitor of that modern drive towards abstraction which reduces the fullness of form to this or that separated portion that we can find useful or isolate as a truth. Such a drive is a source of our modern restlessness, our incapacity for contemplation, and so our imperceptivity of contemplation's true object which is always beauty whole, form and splendor in unison.

Without contesting that there are aspects of Plato's thought that expose themselves to just such a criticism, I want nonetheless to reject the charge on the whole. If we take Plato in the fullness of his work's form, we find that, far from being a cause of man's decline of vision, Plato's work is the consummate and in some ways unsurpassed exemplar beckoning us to openness to beauty as the primal phenomenon. It is for this reason that I began with Wilde's reference to Plato as an artist in thought. His philosophy is a poetic philosophy specifically in the sense of causing us to dwell on the whole, to see the form without reduction. Plato's work in fact subtly induces us to take things as a whole, playfully insists on our openness to seeing the form of things, and even seduces us to enter upon to the full scope and structure of being. Wilde clearly learned from Plato the appreciation for aesthetic form; he simply failed to see it whole in the fashion Plato demanded.

As I proposed before, Plato is in a literal sense a commentator on the poet, Homer. One of the ways that relationship most reveals itself is that Plato, the philosopher, is also the Plato whom Wilde called—truly—an "artist in thought," a poet who sees the form and

12. von Balthasar, *The Glory of the Lord*, I.20–21.

splendor of intellectual beauty. Plato calls us to dwell aesthetically in the world. His work leads us to see the whole aesthetic form of things and, even as we distinguish between them, to unite them in the harmonious whole that is the Real. There are indeed moments when his writing would seem to indicate we are to leave behind the fullness of reality as a mere oyster shell in order to get at some ethereal, abstract pearl of truth. We can find such moments. But, to prescind those very moments, to allow them to become parts more significant than the whole, is precisely to misread Plato and to miss the unsurpassed value of the dialogues.

Let me explain this bold claim by way of several illustrations. The most obvious basis for it is the dialogue form in which Plato, with certain exceptions, exclusively writes. When we encounter a poem, a play, a novel, at no point do we ever suspect that any one statement here-or-there within the work can be understood in isolation from the whole. The poem is not its message, as it were; the poem is everything that is the poem, and every part is interpretable only within the body and unity of the whole. The whole is the poetic form and to see aesthetically is to see the whole. To recognize this is to see the form. Plato, in composing no mere aphoristic verses of wisdom, as had the philosophers before him, and in composing no lectures or treatises as would the sophists who were his contemporaries and the philosophers who followed him, is not performing some kind of trick.[13] His dialogue form is not a rhetorical strategy, but a poetic act.

The dialogue form in which he writes refuses all reduction. We cannot get behind the form. We cannot take any statement given us within it and read it as a mere gem of wisdom, after the fashion of the pre-Socratics. We cannot take any of the dialectical inquiries that take place in the dialogues and—when we arrive at last at what may be their solution or final answer—simply take the answer and

13. Legend says that Plato began as a poet and several of his verse epigrams survive (Plato, *Complete Works*, 1742–1745).

set aside the inquiry. We cannot even reduce Plato's dialogues to, or explain their dialogical form in terms of, the dialectic of the famous Socratic method! Many of Plato's dialogues contain little or no instances of Socratic questioning and all of them contain much more than that. The dialogues thus operate as dramatic or poetic forms. We do not encounter the full form unless we accept it all as constitutive of the whole. If we pick and choose elements among the whole, we will disfigure the dialogue and misunderstand it.

If we do wish to arrive at understanding of the whole, this will entail determining how we should weigh or value statements or observations made in the dialogue. Not all parts are equal and we cannot read them all the same way. Being sensitive to the various weights of the parts does not entail reducing the whole to any of those parts, however; we never leave the whole behind. My contention, therefore, is twofold. The dramatic structure of the dialogues ensures that Plato is not simply going to offer us truth in the form of a treatise. The form guides understanding but does not reduce it to a pearl or pith. The fleet-footed gymnastics of the dialogue form always keeps us open to the possibility that it may disclose further depths such that even if it leads us to the truth, the possession of that truth does not allow us to leave the dialogue behind. Second, it is the dialogue form taken as a whole that leads us to the truth; there is no distinction in Plato such as the Roman poet Horace made between poetry's capacity sometimes to please and sometimes to instruct. To the contrary, the arrival at truth is to occur only through a taking of the form as a whole. This is not an observation merely about Plato's method of writing; the method of writing is expressive of how Plato wishes to initiate us into the love of wisdom. We are asked to remain in contemplation, in a receptive state continuously open to form and splendor, to beauty, to the dramatic whole of the art-form and also to the ontological whole of reality.

We might explore this in terms of the famous Platonic irony. If a statement cannot be taken at face value, then we are always reliant on context, and so the larger form, if we are to interpret it properly. Consider, to offer a very modest example, Socrates's treatment of Protagoras in the *Theaetetus*. Socrates praises the wisdom of the sophist frequently even as he proceeds to demolish Protagoras' specific claims to wisdom. We find a similar example in the *Meno*, where Socrates laments that the Sophist Gorgias spends all his time giving "bold and grand" answers in Thessaly, while leaving Athens so "poor."[14] Behind his smile, we can deduce, Socrates lives in willing poverty. Or consider Socrates's enthusiasm for speeches in the *Phaedrus*, which we very quickly discover is only his genial wink of an eye to show that he recognizes Phaedrus's love of speeches and also the need to ween Phaedrus away from that love.

The full meaning of the dialogues often conceals itself unless we are able to see the form whole. In the *Meno*, for instance, some would contend that the subject of the dialogue is whether virtue can be taught, while others may highlight its answer to the question of how learning itself is possible. We might also take for theme the possibility of the immortality of the soul and the activity of *anamnesis* by way of which Socrates posits that our learning is but a recollection of what the soul already knows. This third theme includes the famous use of Socratic questioning of a slave boy, by way of which Socrates demonstrates that even the base and ignorant can, if helped, recall what the soul has forgotten and so answer correctly questions about the science of geometry. Maybe the Socratic method is the theme! Early in the dialogue, however, ostensibly in order to establish the immortality of the soul, Socrates quotes the Greek poet Pindar with these words:

> Persephone will return to the sun above in the ninth year
> the souls of those from whom
> she will exact punishment for old miseries,
> and from these comes noble kings,

14. Plato, *Complete Works*, ed. John M. Cooper (Hackett, 1997), *Meno*, 70b.

> mighty in strength and greatest in wisdom,
> and for the rest of time men will call them sacred heroes.[15]

The verse is by no means irrelevant to Socrates's immediate point, but it is not the most obvious support of the claim he uses it to make, which is threefold: a) the soul is immortal; b) it has therefore seen all things; and c) it should live a pious or good life. What the verses more potently suggest is a way of understanding death: death will be a humiliation but not a final one. By submitting to humiliation, we open ourselves to knowledge, and, possessed of this knowledge, we can become wise and attain the immortality of glory. A moment later, Socrates in a sense humiliates himself by taking for his conversation partner a slave boy rather than a fellow aristocrat. The context of the *Meno*, as with so many of the dialogues, is the contrast between the philosopher and the sophist. In such a context, through these verses we learn something that is never directly stated. Plato is telling us that, while the sophists are bold, the philosopher is humble. Humility involves submitting oneself to humiliation, that is, to having one's pride stripped away, not merely in talking to a slave, but in allowing one's dead soul to undergo punishment and misery in the underworld. The initial subject of the dialogue, whether virtue can be taught, receives then a subtle, never properly stated response. We cannot be taught by another; we can only discover the truth for ourselves through the process of *anamnesis*. But the only way we can begin that movement of recollection is first to subject ourselves to humiliation: we must radically strip ourselves bare of pride and open our souls to the order of truth that precedes in existence our own present lives. The *Meno*, taken as a whole, then is a poetic hymn admonishing us to silence ourselves so that, first, we may trust being to instruct us, and, second, that we may quiet our pride and, with all humility, listen to the instruction of being.

---

15. *Meno*, 81b-c.

We find also consequential and subtle aspects of the dialogues that stand outside the dialectical exchanges but which are formative of the meaning of the whole and cannot be set aside. They are not mere dramatic ornaments. Indeed, they often constitute the central underlying theme of the dialogues insofar as they address not a particular philosophical question but the appropriate way for one to dwell aesthetically. I will offer three examples, one each taken from the *Phaedo*, the *Gorgias*, and the *Symposium*.

The *Phaedo* retells the narrative of Socrates's death by suicide after the condemnation recounted in the *Apology*. The dialogue consists of a conversation between Echecrates and Phaedo, which chiefly provides a frame for the story of those last and fatal hours. The central concern of the dialogue is the presentation of the form of Socrates's character as philosopher, which entails being one who is "willing and ready to die."[16] Much of the discussion that follows consists of a philosopher's argument for why he should be prepared for death without actually seeking out death. The foundational principle for such an argument is, of course, that the soul is immortal, such that the soul's condition apart from the body is qualitatively fuller than life in the body, at least for those who have sought wisdom and goodness in life.[17]

Central to the dialogue, however, is not just the merit of this particular argument but also the question of how we ought to respond to it and, really, to philosophical arguments in general. Plato presents all ideas in a dramatic context and asks us to respond to the poetic whole rather than to a mere part. But, if we responded only to a part, the mind could close on truth as if it were a possession: it could grasp a single doctrine, and think no more. This is just what the dialogue form discourages and indeed resists by its poetic structure, which keeps us always open to the meaning of the whole,

16. Plato, *Complete Works*, *Phaedo*, 62d.

17. *Phaedo*, 107c-d.

to the likelihood of an excess that goes beyond answering any single question. In the dialogue, we learn about two imperfect possible responses to this aesthetic openness, which Socrates will describe alternately as misology and pedantic insistence, by which he means, respectively, intellectual despair and what we might call dogmatism.

When we enter into philosophical dialogue, we are bound to encounter premises whose arguments we find faulty or about which we ourselves lack the capacity to argue about competently. On such occasions, it will seem as if reason has failed; and so, we may fall into depression, doubting that reason can ever attain its proper end. In the middle of the *Phaedo*, those who sit in vigil with Socrates fall into sorrow, when he leads them to doubt his own argument for the immortality of the soul. They are filled with grief. Socrates warns that such sorrow can lead one to come to "hate reasonable discourse," presuming either reason's weakness or, worse, its subservience as a mere "rationalization" to motives of the will.[18] This is "misology," which Socrates describes as the error of shifting the blame. Instead of blaming truth and reason, let us blame ourselves, but trust in truth and reason, he admonishes us. This warning was as necessary in Socrates's time as it is in ours, for both Plato's and our society were largely constructed on the misological premise that reason is nothing but a slave of the passions, especially those of lust, vanity, and the thirst for power. Plato enjoins us to remain open to the whole of reality, which only a receptive intellect can apprehend; he urges us to refrain from closing the mind off by settling upon a desire for power and the consequent reduction of reason either to a cynical tool or a futile invalid.

At the end of the *Phaedo*, Socrates proceeds from an argument for the soul's immortality to a different kind of an account, a mythological account, describing the spiritual geography that the soul will encounter in Hades. Although his account is well reasoned and not

18. *Phaedo*, 89d.

in the least arbitrary in its details, Socrates warns us against a pedantic insistence: "No sensible man would insist that these things are as I have described them, but I think it is fitting for a man to risk the belief . . . a noble one . . . that this, or something like this, is true about our souls."[19] Misology is the closure of reasoning that occurs through a blame-shifting disenchantment and cynicism. Pedantic insistence, in contrast, is the closure of reason that occurs through the mind's act of demanding that whatever it may know be certain knowledge or nothing—and, once certain, that it be incapable of further change. But to dwell aesthetically, as Plato would have us do, demands an essential openness of the reason, not in the sense of being unsettled, unconvinced, or even doubtful, but in the sense of remaining receptive to that which transcends the mind's present vision. For Plato as for Saint Paul, to see darkly is still to see, but also to insist that someday we will see more clearly. We must dwell aesthetically, eschewing both misology and the demand for a possessive rationalism, with a reason open to transcendence and grateful for a slender grasp of the highest knowledge. Such a mind will be confident, not because it already grasps the truth with certainty, but because it deeply and abidingly trusts that there is always still more truth to be grasped. The life of the love of wisdom, the life of contemplation, is just the kind of life that entrusts itself even to the truth it does not yet understand.

The *Phaedo* teaches us that philosophy is more a matter of the disposition of the person to keep reason open to being than it is a particular method or set of doctrines ascertained. This becomes clearest in those dialogues where Socrates's antagonists, present or absent, are sophists. No distinction in the person could be more fundamental than that between the philosopher and the sophist. For a philosopher is the one whose reason is open to being even to the point of humiliation and death, while the sophist is one who claims

19. *Phaedo*, 114d.

the power to use the appearance of reason to attain his own desired end, which is itself power.

The *Gorgias* illustrates this more vividly and dramatically than any of the other dialogues. The central subject of discussion is the nature of justice and goodness. Socrates proposes that human beings should seek what is good and, in the pursuit of the good, they should more willingly suffer injustice than the shame of committing an injustice.[20] The sophists seem to have a different conception of justice and goodness. Justice is rule by the strong over the weak, and goodness is the greatest quantity of pleasure.[21] Socrates has no difficulty making a successful argument in favor of his own account of justice and goodness. The poetic genius of the dialogue shows us, however, that a successful argument does not settle the matter. By questioning, Socrates leads his sophist interlocutors to contradict themselves and to agree with everything he says and then fall silent. Socrates is confused. Callicles the sophist speaks aloud what has up to now been kept quiet: the sophists concede Socrates's points not because they believe them, but because they are ashamed to say what they really believe. They believe themselves by nature the strong, but they live in the conventional regime of laws instituted by "the weak and the many."[22]

The shamed silence of the sophists is a shattering one—for Socrates and for us. We cannot presume all people speak within a commitment to reason, honesty, or truth. Reasoning requires that ideas be sincerely proposed and sincerely questioned by means of dialectic; that is our means to truth. The philosopher has to be willing to be humiliated and changed by this act of reasoning. The philosopher must love truth more than his own power. But most of us, most of the time, do not share this commitment. Indeed, we harbor

---

20. Plato, *Complete Works*, *Gorgias*, 469c.

21. *Gorgias*, 491e, ff.

22. *Gorgias*, 483b.

beliefs that we know would be shameful to confess, but around which we organize our lives. We adhere to them even when they are shown to be unreasonable, as the sophist position certainly is: if it is the strong who should rule, and yet the strong are afraid even to speak what they believe, for fear of the weak, then the strong clearly are not *really* the strong.[23] Rather than changing their minds in light of this simple logic, the sophists simply smile and appear to agree with everything Socrates says. They do not care what reason instructs and there is nothing Socrates can do to make them care. Truth is in this sense defenseless, but it nonetheless remains the truth.[24] To adhere to it in justice may entail suffering injustice, of which the sophists' contempt for Socrates' careful arguments is just one instance. In a sense, the most important dimension of the *Gorgias* is what cannot be said, the defiant silence of shame that is akin to the sorrow of misology in the *Phaedo*. What we find in the dialogue is not a philosophical argument but a dramatic demonstration: we have to witness it in the drama of the moment, because it can never be fully comprehended under the dialectic of reason. No argument can convince the sophists to cease being impervious to argument, and yet their stubbornness is a common phenomenon of human life. Some things lie beyond articulate reason that nonetheless constitute part of the form of the real. While we cannot always argue about them, they can be shown to us dramatically and aesthetically.

To dwell aesthetically, as Plato would have us do, requires us to be open to the whole of being, even its sorrow and shame woven into silences that cannot be spoken. We see this not only in individual dialogues, but in the dramatic whole that is Plato's complete works. In the *Republic*, for instance, Socrates speaks of one of several limitations of the poets. Although they produce many imitations,

23. *Gorgias*, 489b-d.

24. See D. C. Schindler, *Plato's Critique of Impure Reason* (The Catholic University of America Press, 2008), 226 ff.

they can only imitate a few things well. The same poet, for instance, cannot write both comedy and tragedy.[25] This provocation of sorts prepares us for the strange, digressive, apparent afterthought that constitutes the conclusion of the *Symposium*. There, we hear Socrates's disciple Aristodemus speak of the long, late-night discussion on love conducted in the house of the tragic poet Agathon. For him the discourse ends only with his falling asleep. When he wakes in the early morning, however, Socrates is still awake and arguing that the same man may write both comedy and tragedy.[26] That, more or less, is the end. Why has the dialogue taken this odd and seemingly pointless turn? We might suspect it has something to do with Socrates, who in the course of the dialogue is shown to be the very image of love and the lover of wisdom. He is philosophy's face. Plato, in contrast, is invisible, concealed behind his own work. He has no image. In that work, however, he depicts both the comic and tragic.[27] Plato thus is the true poet, the one unlimited by form and so capable of dwelling aesthetically, forever open to the whole of being.[28] Wilde himself once remarked that the artist's purpose is to "reveal art" but to "conceal" himself.[29] In this, Plato is the consummate artist: present everywhere but always masked by his characters.

The initiation into the ever-open, never-reductive practice of seeing the form in the dialogues is a good in itself. It is also clear, however, that this discipline of dwelling aesthetically is specifically that to which Plato is attempting to habituate his disciples *as* philosophers. To dwell aesthetically is, in Plato's terms, more properly the

---

25. Plato, *Complete Works*, *Republic*, 345a.

26. Plato, *Complete Works*, *Symposium*, 223d.

27. Plato depicts, for instance, Aristophanes's comical speech on love and shows us also the drunk, plaintive, boorish Alcibiades, who loves Socrates but fails to live like him and thus ends his life a tragic figure.

28. See James Matthew Wilson, *The Vision of the Soul: Truth, Goodness, and Beauty in the Western Tradition* (The Catholic University of America Press, 2017), 291–92.

29. Wilde, *Complete Works*, 17.

life of the philosopher than it is of the poets Plato dramatizes. Those who dwell aesthetically before being are living philosophically. That is what makes them philosophers. But Plato is at pains to show us that not everyone does this, that most people do not, and that the greater number will consent to the death of those who do.

He is further at pains to show us that to be a philosopher is not simply to be a person who stands apart from human life, but rather to be someone who is committed to a particular way of life that is fuller, less partial, than other lives. The life of the philosopher is not something other than someone who lives and acts in the world, but is a more excellent way of so acting. The clues to this are not always obvious and they mostly occur in aspects of the dialogues that, once again, stand outside the dialectical reasoning frequently on display. I shall name just two. To return to the *Symposium* for a moment: we see that this dialogue contains very little of the Socratic questioning that we identify with the dialectic proper to reasoning, whether with oneself or with others.[30] Much of the dialogue is composed of long speeches on the nature of love, all of which are sophistic insofar as they affirm as a universal truth something that is to the particular advantage of the speaker. The speeches by the characters besides Socrates are also all failed but partial accounts that get swept up and partially affirmed in Socrates's speech, which is not a speech at all, but rather a recollection and anecdote of his conversation with Diotima the priestess. Diotima reveals the truth about love and beauty to him in the form of a mystery.

Socrates gives us a speech-within-a-speech. But, then we recall that his speech is recounted by Aristodemus, whose speech is being recalled in turn by Apollodorus, who is reciting to an unnamed person, from an experience he just had the "other day," when another person, Glaucon (who will appear in the *Republic*), asked him to recite the events of the famous dinner at Agathon's house.[31] As Josef

30. Plato, *Complete Works, Theaetetus*, 189e.

31. Plato, *Complete Works, Symposium*, 172a.

Pieper once remarked, it seems plausible that neither Glaucon nor the anonymous friend are interested in the events for worthy intellectual reasons. They come in search of gossip—perhaps regarding the drunken and vainglorious general and "ignored" lover of Socrates, Alcibiades—rather than in hopes of gaining the wisdom that the true philosopher is mad to acquire.[32] Plato provides us characters, then, whose position relative to the narrative that Apollodorus has heard and now retells must be understood, not in terms of their propinquity to it but of their intention in listening in the first place. As such, the core of the *Symposium* does not come to us as an instance of fruitful dialectical reasoning (*logos*) but provocatively as a story (*mythos*) capable of being heard and interpreted in multiple ways, some admirable and some frivolous.

We are thus being shown—with remarkable subtlety!—that the philosopher is one who listens to stories, speeches, and arguments for the sake of wisdom, not out of mere idle gossip or in search of rhetorical advantage. We are being taught to see the whole, but also to look upon it with an openness rightly ordered to the still greater whole of truth and being. To be a philosopher is to address oneself to the world in this manner. This is the way of life to which the philosopher is called. We find here Plato's articulation of what Augustine and Thomas Aquinas will later define as the difference between curiosity and studiousness.[33] Curiosity is a closed and lustful kind of interest; it can quickly be sated. Studiousness is an open address to being for the sake of wisdom and salvation.

We learn more about the way of life of the philosopher in the *Theaetetus*. There, Socrates relates an anecdote that is comic and at the philosophers' expense:

---

32. Josef Pieper, *Leisure, the Basis of Culture* (Ignatius, 2009), 86.

33. Thomas Aquinas, *Summa Theologica*, trans. English Dominican Province (Benzinger Bros., 1948), II-II.167.

> they say Thales was studying the stars . . . and gazing aloft, when he fell into a well; and a witty and amusing Thracian servant-girl made fun of him because, she said, he was wild to know about what was up in the sky but failed to see what was in front of him and under his feet.[34]

Socrates hams up this notion of the philosopher as apparently absentminded and indeed extends the catalogue of the philosopher's oddities to some length. Philosophers are clumsy and fatuous in the eyes of the many, they are unimpressed by large estates, wealth, and noble ancestry. All these things right at their feet seem small compared to the great vistas they study not merely aloft in the heavens, but aloft in the invisible, spiritual heaven of thought. This lack of concern with things before them turns out to be of a threefold origin. Philosophers are concerned with the absolutely real, rather than this or that particular. They are concerned with things in themselves rather than how they can be harnessed for use or power. And, finally, because not driven by the concerns of utility, they are at leisure and capable of idling over questions for their own sake, rather than being driven heedlessly on under the pressure of time and servile necessity.[35] From a typically modern perspective, philosophers seem abstracted and extracted from actual life, and Socrates concedes that this is indeed how the philosopher will appear. The appearance is deceiving, however. The philosopher is the kind of human being who has learned to be humiliated—literally to the point of falling down beneath the surface of the earth!—so as to live in freedom and openness to being. He is not a strange sort of human; he is the image of the properly human.

34. Plato, *Complete Works*, *Theaetetus*, 174a.

35. *Theaetetus*, 175e.

Plato as Introduction to the Transcendentals: Unity, Truth, Goodness, and Beauty

I would now address a related matter. How, within the context of contemporary liberal education, can the work of Plato help initiate students into an authentically philosophical way of dwelling aesthetically? Wilde's *Picture of Dorian Gray* is in part about the evil consequences of bad teaching, which includes a perverse love of beauty that leads to spiritual ugliness and disfigurement. What might authentically good teaching look like with Plato for guide?

I want to propose a curriculum ordered by the transcendental properties of being, those four main aspects under which reality appears: Unity, Truth, Goodness, and Beauty. I propose that while other texts often address these questions more directly or efficiently than the works of Plato, the Socratic ignorance that leads each question to be addressed at its foundations and the dialectical and dramatic procedures of the dialogues as a whole make them the ideal introduction to thinking philosophically about any question. Even when Plato's answers are insufficient—and they often are and must be, or the rest of the history of philosophy would not have furnished us so many footnotes—the dialogues are the optimal way to initiate the young into the life of reason. I propose a course of study that would take Plato as the beginning of inquiry into each of the transcendentals. They would serve as the true beginning, an initiation into the questions. They could then be supplemented with the necessary "footnotes" who take us farther than does Plato toward a vision of reality.

We begin with Unity. When we discuss the transcendental properties of being, the idea of unity does not generally excite much immediate interest. What is there to say about the fact that every being is *a* being, that each thing is one in itself? Quite a lot, actually. In our age, postmodern thought disintegrates human nature into a mere node through which run threads belonging to a multitudinous web of power, while the modern mechanistic approach to physical reality, too often sold as the true doctrine of the physical sciences, disintegrates material being into its parts. It atomizes. The integrity of the person and of the world are both under assault. In the *Apologia,* the integrity of Socrates's character is demonstrated by his showing we are accountable to reality beyond our private desires. In the *Phaedo,* we learn that the integrity of character is rooted in the unity of the soul, and that the unity of all things requires something that stands beneath them, a form in which they participate. The immortality of the soul, the idea of the forms, and the consequent distinction between being and becoming, all convene to help us determine what are the conditions in which being really is *one.*

The second module, on Truth, would begin with the *Theaetetus* and continue with *Republic* VI-VII. The *Theaetetus* takes as its primary question the nature of knowledge and, as its point of departure, Protagoras's axiom that man is the measure of all things. In other words, Plato drops us right into the dictatorship of relativism and leads us through it, toward an understanding of knowledge and truth. The dialogue explores several avenues of defining knowledge, each of them rooted in an understanding of all being as becoming, that is to say, in a state of continuous flux. It marvelously ends in *aporia.* We cannot have an account of knowledge if there is no stable reality to be known. In *Republic* Books VI-VII, we hear of the divided line and the Allegory of the Cave, both of which show us that real knowledge involves not measuring differences among different fluctuating things in the realm of becoming, but in measuring things in flux against the stable reality of the forms which the intellect alone can see. Knowledge is not of becoming but of being; knowledge is not a possession had but a vision beheld, as one stands gazing up into the light of the truth. We find in this journey from becoming to being a further insight on what it means for our souls to have unity or integrity: they must not be entirely subsumed in the realm of becoming; they must journey toward and be rooted in truth's invisible stability.

Socrates's account, in the *Republic*, of conforming our souls to a divine pattern also anticipates our turn to Goodness and Beauty. It may seem that excerpting from a dialogue would violate its poetic integrity, and indeed this is the case. But the dialogues also form a poetic whole, as others have demonstrated.[36] I recommend excerpting the *Republic*, because it answers with memorable poetic clarity the questions that *Theaetetus* raises and also because the theme of its wonderful early books, which explore justice and sophistry, are even more potently dramatized in the *Gorgias*, to which we will turn now.

After Truth, we may explore Goodness. Just as the *Theaetetus* begins us with the problem of relativism and shows that ancient concerns are very much our contemporary concerns, so the *Gorgias* begins with the most dire modern account of the nature of goodness and leads us beyond it. As we saw above, the sophists believed goodness was effectiveness, utility, and power. Socrates shows both the emptiness and the rational impossibility of their account. Furthermore, he demonstrates that though most human beings reject their ordination to the Good, that the cosmos itself demonstrates this ordination and that the soul makes us ineluctably ordered to it. Hence, we must live our lives under the aspect of eternity and the eternal good that will judge us not based on our effectiveness or any other relative terms but in light of what simply is.[37]

In the preceding three modules, we have learned that the soul is one, and that its integrity orders it to truth as its good. These three transcendentals drawn together culminate in Beauty, which is the radiance of all the transcendental united, as Jacques Maritain once put it.[38] In the *Symposium*, Socrates leads us from object of love to

36. Catherine H. Zuckert, *Plato's Philosophers: The Coherence of the Dialogues* (University of Chicago Press, 2012).

37. Plato, *Complete Works*, *Gorgias*, 523a, ff.

38. Jacques Maritain, *Art and Scholasticism and the Frontiers of Poetry*, trans. Joseph W. Evans (University of Notre Dame Press, 1974), 173n66.

object of love, desire to desire, until the soul has ascended a ladder of being that culminates in a vision of the eternal Beauty. This is the dramatic and true Odyssey of every human life: to see eternal beauty and beget good things through its vision. The unified soul that embraces truth as its good will be made beautiful. The splendor of wisdom will be its fruit. The *Symposium* is, as I just indicated, Plato's epic poem about the journey of human life; in the short Palinode of Socrates found in the *Phaedrus*, we are given a vision of how the beautiful soul is destined to assume its place within the beautiful whole of the cosmos, the order of becoming that participates in the splendor of being. Here it is a pity to excerpt, because the whole of the *Phaedrus* is very rich, but by appending the Palinode to the *Symposium*, we gain a fuller sense of what Plato means by the human destiny to engender in beauty: we take our place as participants in a beautiful whole infinitely greater than ourselves. The *Symposium* by itself reminds us of the individual destiny of the soul; the *Phaedrus* reminds us that our dignity is rooted in a whole that transcends us and in which we participate, a whole ordered to a greater whole.

As I say, Plato cannot be the end. The questions raised in these dialogues will find their fuller expression and more satisfactory answers in such places as Aristotle's *Physics*, Aquinas's *de Veritate*, and Augustine's *Confessions*. But, by allowing Plato to lead the way into the life of the mind, he will help the young to learn to enter into such things dialectically and to build upon sure foundations. And, to return to my second argument, the essential initiation of the philosopher to learn how to dwell aesthetically before being, open and in awe, seeing the form, and refusing to dissolve it or overlook it, is the permanent lesson that every last one of us must learn if we are to become properly human. It is in this respect that we must all follow Plato in becoming artists in thought.

4 Aristotle

Edward Feser

Introduction: Education and Politics

The moral and cultural controversies that have ever more deeply riven Western society since the 1960s have in recent years spilled over wholesale into primary and secondary education. Conservatives, whose approach to education has long emphasized vouchers, charter schools, and other private or semi-private solutions, have found that they can no longer stay aloof from the mainstream public school system. Hence their recent attempts to take control of school boards away from progressive ideologues and those who will not resist such ideologues. These conservatives are, perhaps, learning something the ideologues have known all along, which is that education cannot be divorced from politics, and indeed is foundational to the political order. But they should not have had to learn that from progressives, because it is a key theme of the work of the founders of Western political philosophy, Plato and Aristotle.

I hasten to add that I am not talking about what we usually think of today when we hear the word "politics"—about which party to support, whom to vote for in this or that election, whether some policy or law currently being debated should be adopted or resisted, and so on. Indeed, such controversies should in general be kept out of education. What I am talking about is the basic constitutional order of a polity, the framework presupposed by these everyday debates and which all sides generally take for granted. Education cannot be "privatized" in a sense that would leave it neutral about the nature of that fundamental political order. That, in any event, was the view of the classical thinkers I mentioned.

Let's consider, specifically, Aristotle's position on the nature and purposes of education, which is spelled out most systematically in *The Politics*.[1] To understand it, we need to know something about Aristotle's accounts of human nature, of the moral life, and of the nature and purposes of the state. So, let's begin with an overview of those themes.

Rational Social Animals

Aristotle famously takes human beings to be, by nature, *rational social animals*. Each word in this characterization is crucial. First, when I say that he takes us to be this way *by nature*, what that means is that being rational social animals is our very *essence*, it is just *what it is to be human*, rather than some contingent, changeable, or secondary fact about us. That we are rational social animals is true not merely by convention, nor the result of human legislation. It is a bedrock fact about us that all conventions, all legislation, and all contingent and changeable facts about us must presuppose.

We are *animals* insofar as we are embodied living things of the kind which rely on sensory experience to acquire knowledge of the world, move ourselves about so as to interact with the things we thereby come to know, are prompted to action by appetites or inner drives that mediate between sensory experience and behavior, and exhibit also the even more fundamental organic properties of having to take in nutrients, to go through a growth cycle, and to reproduce ourselves. All of this is, again, true of us *by nature*. We are not souls trapped in bodies, as Plato thought. Embodiment, and all of the powers and liabilities that follow upon it, are normal for us.

We are, however, not *mere* animals, because we are, unlike any other animal, also *rational* by nature. What this entails, first, is that

1. All quotes are from Aristotle, *The Politics*, trans. T. A. Sinclair and Trevor J. Saunders (Penguin Books, 1992).

we can form *concepts* or general ideas that represent the natures of things, including our own nature. A dog can recognize a tree or a cat, but it has no concept of what it is to be a tree or a cat, much less more abstract concepts like *plant* or *animal* or *living thing* or *physical substance*. Our capacity to form concepts is reflected in something else we possess and other animals lack, namely language. Concept-possession goes hand in hand with the mastery of general terms, such as the words "cat," "tree," "plant," and "animal."

The second characteristic of rationality is the capacity to put concepts together into judgments or complete thoughts. Hence we can not only grasp the concepts of *being a man* and *being mortal*, but can go on to form the complete thought that *all men are mortal* and judge it to be true. And we can entertain the thought that *some cows are dogs* and judge it to be false. The third characteristic of rationality is the capacity to reason logically from such truths and falsehoods to their implications. For example, we can reason from the fact that *all men are mortal* and that *Socrates is a man* to the conclusion that *Socrates is mortal*. And though we know that it is false that *some cows are dogs*, we can reason from the fact that *all dogs are carnivorous* to the conclusion that some cows would be carnivorous *if* they were dogs. This is an example of what philosophers call a *counterfactual*—a statement about what *would have* been true *had* a certain non-actual state of affairs obtained.

What all of this in turn makes possible for us as rational animals is the capacity to generate a body of knowledge of things very distant from immediate experience. For example, because we can know the natures of things and represent them in language, we can come to know not only what is true of dogs and cats and plants and animals that we have actually seen, but also certain truths about those we have not seen, including those that existed in the distant past and which will exist in the distant future. We can also consider what is at least *possible* for them even if it never in fact happens, and what is strictly impossible for them. These capacities in turn allow us to engage in scientific inquiry and philosophical speculation, to write fictional narratives and portray people and events in dramatic performances, and to represent things in yet more abstract ways in music, dance, poetic descriptions, and so on. They also make it possible for us to alter our physical environment by exploiting our knowledge of the natures of things technologically. Hence we make tools, buildings, works of art, and so on.

In this way our rational nature adds a thick layer of *culture* atop our animal physiological and psychological attributes. But it also transforms those attributes. For example, like other animals, we need to eat and drink in order to survive. But where other animals merely feed, we have *meals*, which involves preparing food in ways that go well beyond the requirements of utility, and observing certain conventions of etiquette. Like other animals, we reproduce ourselves sexually. But unlike other animals, this is in us associated with romance, courtship, marriage and the like. Even pornography and other disordered expressions of sexuality reflect our rational nature. Nothing like them exists among non-human animals, because only rational creatures can represent sexuality to themselves in either a moral or an immoral way.

This brings us finally to our being *social* animals. Needless to say, we come into the world only by way of our parents, and remain dependent on them long after birth. This is true not only with respect to our material needs, but also our moral and spiritual formation, which is the work of many years. Nor is it only our parents on whom we depend in these ways. Siblings and extended family are crucial to normal socialization and the provision of mutual aid. Then there are the needs which can be provided only by yet larger social orders. Our material needs outstrip any one person's skills, which entails the need for a division of labor. Hence the need for the butcher, the baker, the carpenter, the teacher, the soldier, and so on. For more sophisticated social orders to arise, the limitations on any one individual's knowledge entail the need for a division of intellectual labor, with some functioning as scientists, others as lawyers, yet others as theologians, and so forth. As this indicates, our rational and social natures are deeply intertwined. Nor is this merely a reflection of contingent limits on what any one person happens to know. Language is a fundamental and necessary concomitant of our kind of rationality, and is also essentially social in nature.

Now, to flourish as both rational and social animals, we need to acquire the *virtues* and avoid the *vices*. Virtues and vices are habituated patterns of action, virtues being those habits which facilitate our flourishing as rational social animals, and vices being those habits which frustrate it. Aristotle famously analyzes a virtue as a mean between extremes, with each extreme constituting a distinctive vice. For example, *courage* is the virtue of being disposed to do the right thing even in the face of fear of danger. It is the sober middle ground between, on the one hand, the vice of *cowardice* (which involves letting fear prevent one from doing the right thing), and on the other hand, the vice of *rashness* (which involves putting oneself in danger for no good reason). *Temperance* or *moderation* is the virtue of being disposed to enjoy pleasure and avoid pain only when and to the extent that it is reasonable to do so. It is the middle ground between the vice of *licentiousness* (which involves seeking pleasure to excess or in the wrong things), and the vice of *insensibility* (which involves a failure to take pleasure in things when it would be good to do so, or being a "stick in the mud"). And so on.

We acquire the virtues by practice, and especially by following the example of others who possess them and heeding their admonitions and encouragements. In this respect the moral life is social in nature. And again, it is also social in nature insofar as certain virtues are essential to getting on well with the others on whom we depend and who depend on us. To possess virtues such as courage, temperance, wisdom, justice, patience, and the like is both to flourish as an individual rational animal and also to be well-suited to living in community with other rational animals.

Social and Political Order

For Aristotle, the most basic natural social organization is the household that results from man and woman coming together and beginning a family. The function of the household is to provide for our daily material and moral needs—meals and shelter, companionship, the instruction and example of mother and father, and so on. But there are also needs that go beyond this, so that family households tend naturally to unite into villages. The village provides the material and moral preconditions for the family's daily existence—the food purchased from butcher and baker, schools, a sense of belonging to, and being able to call upon the aid of, a larger community. But all of this is in turn made possible within the framework of a state, which naturally arises out of collections of villages. The state, Aristotle argues, is the *perfect* social order in the sense that it alone is *complete*. It is characterized by a common culture and history and provides basic physical infrastructure, law and order, national defense, and other goods that smaller-scale social formations lack the resources to provide.

That the state alone is, for Aristotle, the perfect or complete sort of social order lends itself to an organic conception of society, on which individual citizens and the smaller-scale communities they give rise to relate to the state as a whole in a manner analogous to the way limbs and organs relate to the body of which they are parts. But it is important to emphasize that this by no means entails for Aristotle a totalitarian conception of the state. On the contrary, he is critical of Plato's political philosophy precisely for its tendency in that direction, and notes that this tendency follows from exaggerating the analogy between the state and the individual organism. A household has a lower degree of unity than the individual, and the village and the state have lower degrees of unity still. So, it would be a mistake to model the state exactly on the individual or the household, and to expect its citizens to relate to one another with the same intimacy that members of the same household do. People by nature tend to regard family members and friends with special concern, and to take special care of what belongs to them personally. Hence a state must recognize the legitimacy of the private sphere—of private property, and of the family—and not attempt to make of itself one gigantic household where everything is held in common. Aristotle's conception of society thus amounts to a middle ground position between the individualism of liberalism and libertarianism and the collectivism of communism and other forms of socialism.

Now, how should a state be governed? Aristotle famously distinguishes between three main forms of good government and three main bad forms, which are corruptions of the good ones. The good forms all involve government for the sake of the common interests of all citizens, and differ with respect to who does the governing. In *monarchy* there is a single ruler, in *aristocracy* a small plurality of rulers, and in what he calls *polity* the people as a whole rule. The bad or corrupt versions of these Aristotle calls *tyranny*, *oligarchy*, and *democracy*, and in each case the rulers do not govern for the common interests of all citizens. Tyranny involves rule for the good of the tyrant himself, oligarchy rule for the good of the wealthy alone, and democracy rule for the good of the poor masses alone.

Aristotle thinks that in practice it is likely that the most workable sort of state will combine elements from the idealized good forms of government, that it will have to be dominated by a middle class that curbs the excesses of the rich and the poor, and that it will call upon all citizens to participate in political life. But any good state, however organized, must govern in a manner that best enables the citizens to develop the virtues and, by way of them, to realize the potentials inherent in our nature as rational animals. It cannot be neutral about this, the way modern liberal democracies aim to be (or at least claim to be, however implausibly) neutral about what the best sort of life is.

With this overview of Aristotle's account of human nature and his ethics and political philosophy in hand, we can turn at last to our main concern, which is his account of education. Naturally, since we are rational beings, education involves in part the acquisition of knowledge in various areas of study. What is remarkable, however, is that in treating the subject of education, Aristotle devotes much more attention to its moral and political aspects—to what goes on apart from and prior to book-learning, both in the character of the individual and in his social context. No doubt this is in part because the discussion occurs in the context of a book on political philosophy, and one that appears to be incomplete. But there is more to it than that. Remember, for Aristotle we are not souls trapped in bodies, but rational *animals* and *social* animals. Our rationality is so deeply embedded in our animal and social nature that its exercise does not float free of them and cannot go well if things are not going well for us as animals and social beings. Hence a precondition of the proper formation of the mind is a proper formation of the body and its habits, and a healthy social environment.

Now, that is a comment about what the individual needs from the larger social order if his education is to go well. But when Aristotle begins his treatment of the subject in Book VII of *The Politics*, he actually starts at the other end, that is to say, with what the larger social order needs. And what it needs is sound citizens, citizens of good character and good judgment. Now, as Aristotle observes, "men become sound and good because of three things. These are nature, habit, and reason."[2] Nature is what is simply given to us, namely our essence as rational social animals. But habit is acquired, even if it can become so ingrained as to amount to a kind of second nature. And the knowledge that reason makes possible for us, as well as the capacity to reason well from what we come to know, are also acquired. Aristotle notes that "man . . . needs all three working concertedly," nature, habit, and reason together. Because the latter two have to be acquired, education is necessary. And because their acqui-

2. *Politics*, VII.13, 1332a38, at p. 429.

sition is a precondition of sound citizens, the statesman must be concerned with education. Accordingly, Aristotle's treatment of education approaches the subject from the point of view of the state—the larger political order and those who govern it—and its needs and duties vis-à-vis its citizens.

Before we go any further, let's note how this ties in with a point I made at the beginning, when I said that education is, for Aristotle, a matter of public rather than private concern. The point is not primarily about who should *fund* education, though that too is part of it for Aristotle. The point is, much more fundamentally, about the *content* of education. Because the way citizens are educated determines what sorts of characters they will have, and what sorts of characters they have determines in turn the character of the overall social and political order, the state must be concerned with how citizens are educated. It must ensure that they are made "sound," as he puts it—that they have the right moral habits and correct views about the nature of things.

Aristotle's position is thus importantly different from those usually associated today with liberals and conservatives, though it also overlaps in part with each. Liberals firmly support public provision and funding of education, and want the state rather than individuals to determine its content. Conservatives, meanwhile, favor the free market in education no less than in other areas, and have—understandably, given the current orientation of governments—come to emphasize that parents rather than the state should determine its content. But liberals also emphasize lifestyle diversity, feminism and sexual liberation, multiculturalism, the inculcation of an attitude of suspicion of authority and of traditional institutions and moral convictions, a relaxation of discipline, contemporary academic fads over the classical curriculum, and so on. Aristotle would be horrified by all of that. He would agree with liberals that the state should fund education and enforce a certain kind of content. But he would agree with a more conservative view about what the content should be—that education should uphold the family and traditional sex roles; inculcate patriotism, respect for authority, and a common culture; enforce discipline; avoid faddish and pop culture topics and emphasize the classics; and so on.

But let's return to the thread of argument in Aristotle's *Politics* and look more carefully at how he addresses the content of education. What should be its overall aim? All ends or goals, he notes, are either instrumental in nature or good in themselves, and the former exist for the sake of the latter. For example, war is fought for the sake of securing peace, work exists for the sake of leisure, and things having mere utility exist for the sake of what is noble. Education must ultimately aim at what is of intrinsic worth or good in itself, even if it also involves learning things that are merely useful.

Leisure, in particular, plays a central role in Aristotle's account of the aim of education. But it is crucial to understand what he means by "leisure," and modern readers are bound to read into it things he does not mean, or even things positively contrary to what he has in mind. Aristotle emphasizes in Book VIII, Chapter III of *The Politics* that leisure is not the same thing as play or relaxation. Play or relaxation has only a utilitarian value, insofar as it is a means of resting mind and body—of recharging our batteries, as people say today—so that we can get back to work. Play has instrumental value, then, insofar as it exists for the sake of work. But leisure does *not* exist for the sake of work. Rather, and to repeat, work exists for the sake of leisure. And leisure, as Aristotle understands it, is not refraining from activity but rather activity devoted to what he calls "civilized pursuits" or what is "elevated," to what is of intrinsic worth.

What he has in mind are activities such as philosophy, music and poetry, and in general what today would fall under the label of "high culture." However, I hasten to add that this does not entail the sort of snobbishness that this expression is bound to call to mind today. As the philosopher Roger Scruton has noted, there is in modern times a tendency sharply to set off high culture from the rest of culture and to surround it with a wall of forbidding academic jargon and theory.[3] As a result, high culture has come to seem the preserve of a small elite possessing special expertise or credentials. There are interesting reasons why this occurred, some of them understandable if wrongheaded and some quite suspect, but the point is that it is not the way Aristotle understands that to which leisure is devoted. To be sure, that is not to say that Aristotle has egalitarian views about culture—he most definitely does not, and, as we'll see, he would be very critical of much contemporary pop culture. But neither does he think of leisure as devoted exclusively to abstractions which only the most powerful philosophical minds (like his own) are capable of understanding.

Hence, consider philosophy. It is devoted, most fundamentally, to questions about the general structure of reality and the ultimate causes of things. Its core is metaphysics, which studies notions such as substance, accident, essence, causation, time, space, and so on. For Aristotle, the capstone of metaphysical knowledge is philosophical theology, which, by way of rational argumentation and analysis, discovers the existence of, and something of the nature of, the divine prime Unmoved Mover of the world—that is to say, of God. And since God is the ultimate explanation of things and the most perfect object of desire that could exist, Aristotle judges in *The Eudemian Ethics* that:

> Whatever choice or possession of natural goods—bodily goods, wealth, friends and the like—will most conduce to the contemplation of God is the best; this is the finest criterion. But any choice of living that either through excess or through defect hinders the service and contemplation of God is bad.[4]

3. See Roger Scruton, *An Intelligent Person's Guide to Modern Culture* (St. Augustine's Press, 2000), especially chapters 7 and 8.

4. *Eudemian Ethics* VIII.3, 1249b20. Quoted from Aristotle, *The Eudemian Ethics*, trans. Anthony Kenny (Oxford University Press, 2011), 148.

Naturally, then, the leisure that education is meant to prepare us for will involve, among other things, the contemplation of God. Now, Aristotle's account of God's existence and nature—developed in Book VIII of his *Physics* and Book XII of his *Metaphysics*—is of a decidedly technical philosophical nature. It is part of his more general theorizing about the nature of motion as the actualization of potential, involves an analysis of the nature of causation, and so forth. Few people have the taste or aptitude for such abstractions. But as Richard Kraut notes in his book on Aristotle's political philosophy, Aristotle uses the term "philosophy" in different ways, sometimes in a narrower and more technical sense but sometimes in a looser sense, which includes the less rigorous contemplation of higher things that the average person might engage in no less than the academic.[5] As Kraut also notes, Aristotle regards popular religion with a certain measure of respect despite its lack of philosophical sophistication, and it can be seen as at least an approximate expression of the truths of philosophical theology.[6] Thus, though Aristotle himself did not and indeed could not have said so, it seems clear that religious worship of the kind with which we are familiar today would count as a kind of contemplation of the highest things that is the aim of leisure, and that which education should prepare us for.

When directly addressing the topics of leisure and education in *The Politics*, what Aristotle says the most about, as it happens, is music. I'll return to that presently. But whether it concerns philosophy, music, or some other aspect of high culture, Aristotle emphasizes that leisure, and the education that prepares us for it, should be directed primarily at what has worth in itself, rather than what is merely useful. "To be constantly asking 'What is the use of it?'" says Aristotle, "is unbecoming to those of broad vision and unworthy

5. Richard Kraut, *Aristotle* (Oxford University Press, 2002), 197–98.

6. Kraut, 204.

of free men."[7] To be sure, he acknowledges that acquisition of practical skills is also a component of education, and it goes without saying that instruction in reading, writing, and arithmetic is as useful in work and everyday life as it is preparatory for more advanced study in the humanities and sciences. But to make the acquisition of useful skills the primary rather than a secondary aim of education is, for Aristotle, to let the tail wag the dog.

Aristotle also emphasizes that education should avoid focusing excessively on one area of study, even an area of intrinsic worth. Excessive focus either on acquiring practical skills or on one area of study such as music or athletics, he says, makes one what he calls a "mechanic" rather than truly educated.[8] What he means is that it orients the mind too much in the direction of acquiring and exhibiting technical proficiency rather than toward leisure and contemplation. If the focus of your education is, say, preparing to run a business, or on doing what it takes to win as many athletic medals or compete in as many musical recitals as you can, then it is essentially utilitarian in nature rather than aimed toward what has worth in itself.

Aristotle makes a related point about moral instruction, which is a precondition of having the right sort of character to contemplate the highest things, and thus must also be a part of education. Such instruction must aim at the acquisition of all the virtues, and avoid overemphasizing some of them over the others. This, he says, is an error that was manifest in ancient Sparta, which put an exaggerated emphasis on the single virtue of courage. This not only entailed an atrophy of the other virtues, but corrupted even courage itself, brutalizing the Spartans and making them "like wild animals."[9]

---

7. *Politics* VIII.3, 1338a37, at p. 457.

8. *Politics* VIII.2, 1337b4; VIII.4, 1338b24; and VIII.6, 1341b8, at pp. 454, 459, and 471.

9. *Politics* VIII.4, 1338b9, at p. 458.

These points entail another significant difference between Aristotle's account of education and the views that tend to prevail today. Career preparation is now treated as the chief end of education, even where, and indeed perhaps especially where, education at the college and university level is concerned. The areas of study that Aristotle regarded as those having the greatest and intrinsic worth are often dismissed as impractical and thus a waste of time, sometimes even by otherwise conservative people. (Consider, for example, Senator Marco Rubio's mockery of philosophy majors during the 2016 election campaign.) Modern education, again especially at the highest level, also tends toward specialization.

Mētis: Habituation and Tacit Knowledge

There is yet another respect in which modern attitudes differ sharply from Aristotle's. It is common today to think of being educated as a matter of book-learning—of having read the right things, heard the right lectures, holding the right opinions, and having access to the right body of information. People take parenting classes, and Human Resources departments offer training sessions in how to get along with colleagues and customers—as if these interpersonal skills can be conveyed like recipes or driving directions.

This is likely at least in part an inheritance from Descartes's radical sundering of mind and body at the beginnings of modern philosophy. Famously, for Descartes, the material world in general and the human body in particular are mere unthinking, mechanical clockwork. Human thought and understanding float entirely free of it. Contemporary intellectuals generally reject Descartes's conclusion that the mind should be thought of as an entirely immaterial or non-physical substance. But they often nevertheless continue to conceive of the mind in a way that entirely abstracts it from the body, as when they characterize it as a kind of software or computer program that is implemented in the machine that is the brain. Now, if you model intelligence this way, it is easy to think of learning as essentially just a matter of adding further information to a database.

For Aristotle, though, we are, again, by nature rational *animals*. Our animality, and thus our being embodied beings, is no less essential to us than our rationality, and deeply influences the nature and exercise of that rationality. Now, one of the consequences of this is that human understanding is not merely a matter of having the right information but also a matter of having the right habits of acting and feeling, and these are bodily attributes no less than mental ones. They have to do with what the twentieth-century philosopher Michael Polanyi called the "tacit dimension" in human knowledge,[10] or what his contemporary Gilbert Ryle characterized as "knowing *how*" as opposed to "knowing *that*."[11]

To get an idea of what they mean, consider that you cannot learn to ride a bike, or paint a picture, or hold a conversation simply by reading a book about these things. Being able to ride a bike is, more than anything else, a matter of having certain skills which can be acquired only through actually trying to do it—until, through trial and error, one finally is able more or less unthinkingly to move one's arms and legs in just the right way. It simply cannot be captured in a step-by-step description that one might write down or memorize. Being able to paint a picture involves a bit more than that sort of thing, insofar as you have to conceptualize and understand what the picture is supposed to represent. All the same, actually getting that onto the canvas requires manual dexterity, and an intuitive sense of what simply "looks right" that cannot be easily expressed in words. As with learning to ride a bike, acquiring bodily habits and the ability to judge by sight what works and what does not comes about only by practice. Similarly, one acquires skill in

10. Michael Polanyi, *The Tacit Dimension* (Doubleday, 1966).

11. Gilbert Ryle, "Knowing How and Knowing That," *Proceedings of the Aristotelian Society* 46 (1945–46): 1–16.

holding a conversation only by actually having conversations and thereby coming to know by imitation of the example of others what sorts of topics are appropriate under what circumstances, how to read body language, and so on. Polanyi characterizes the knowledge we exhibit in cases like these as "tacit" rather than explicit because it is embodied in habits rather than explicitly formulated propositions, and is usually very difficult and in some cases even impossible to formulate that way. Ryle thus calls it "know *how*" in contrast to "knowing *that*" such-and-such a proposition is true.

Now, it is not just that tacit knowledge or know-how is different from explicit knowledge of propositions or book-learning. The deeper point is that the first kind of knowledge is, for embodied beings like us, more *fundamental* than knowledge of propositions or book-learning. You need to acquire the capacity to communicate with others before they can relay information to you verbally. You need a certain amount of experience to acquire an intuitive sense of what books are worth reading in the first place. You need to have a certain degree of patience with prolonged periods of listening and reading if you're ever going to sit still long enough for much information to get into your mind in those ways. All of this involves acquiring, by following the example and instructions of parents and peers, certain habits of acting and feeling. It is not *itself* a matter of picking up the right bits of information from a book or lecture.

Aristotle doesn't use the same jargon as Polanyi or Ryle, but he takes a very similar view, and it is central to his account of education. On the one hand, he says, "reason and intelligence are the end to which our nature tends" as its goal or final cause.[12] All the same, temporally speaking, "the unreasoning is prior to that which possesses reason . . . [as] is shown by the fact that, while passion and will as well as desire are to be found in children even right from birth, reasoning and intelligence come into their possession as they grow

12. *Politics* VII.15, 1334b12, at p. 439.

older."[13] Moreover, the specific way these sub-rational faculties are molded in the early part of a person's life has a dramatic impact on how his rational faculties develop later on. Accordingly, for Aristotle, the education of the passions, the appetites, and the will must precede the book-learning we associate with the education of the intellect. We must first learn the right habits of feeling and acting before we can think well.

Culture and Character Development

What this entails, Aristotle tells us, is that we need to be very careful about the company children are allowed to keep and the speech, images, stories, and the like to which they are exposed—what today we would think of as the popular culture they are surrounded by. What is spoken of by peers or presented in movies, books, music, social media, and the like as acceptable or unacceptable, admirable or contemptible, exciting or boring, well-informed or ignorant, etc. will affect what children themselves come to judge in those ways. And it will largely be picked up by imitation and by effects on children's passions and appetites, since the young lack experience, knowledge, and reasoning capacity and are largely driven by pleasure and avoidance of pain. As a result, Aristotle says, children should not be permitted to keep company with people prone to exhibit behavior and ways of speaking that are vulgar, coarse, insolent, or undignified.[14] Nor should they have access to stories, images, plays, poems, and the like that present debased actions or ways of living in a positive way. These sorts of influences will corrupt their character by habituating them into disordered ways of feeling and acting, making the vices attractive and the virtues unattractive, and making it more difficult for reason to govern the passions and appetites.

13. *Politics* VII.15, 1334b12, at p. 439.
14. *Politics* VII.17, at pp. 446–47.

Aristotle devotes particular attention to the importance of music, both as a potential source of moral corruption in the young and, when it is good, as a crucial component of the leisure that education is meant to prepare us for. Naturally, part of this has to do with what we would today call the lyrics that are put to music. As Ernest Barker notes in his book on Plato's and Aristotle's political thought: "Music, in the sense in which it was used by the Greeks, meant more than our music; and it may be defined as poetry wedded to the music, whether of voice or instrument, required for its proper presentation."[15] As with images and stories and other forms of speech or writing, the lyrical or poetic content of music can represent and encourage either what is noble or what is base, what is virtuous or what is vicious, and thereby promote a certain kind of character.

But Aristotle emphasizes that much of the influence of music for either good or ill has to do too with the emotional states that melody and rhythm can put us into, even apart from any lyrical content. He writes that "in rhythm and in tunes there is the closest resemblance to the real natures of anger and gentleness, also of courage and self-control, and of the opposites of these, indeed of all the other kinds of character."[16] Again, he says that "in music . . . character is present, imitated in the very tunes we hear," so that on hearing some melodies "men are inclined to be mournful and solemn," whereas with others "they are in a more relaxed frame of mind," and yet another sort "puts men into a frenzy of excitement."[17] He continues:

> The same is true also of the different types of rhythm: some have a steadying character, others an unsettling, and of these latter some give rise to vulgar movements, some to those more worthy of free men. It follows from all this that music has indeed the

15. Ernest Barker, *The Political Thought of Plato and Aristotle* (Dover, 1959), 432.
16. *Politics* VIII.5, 1340a18, at p. 465.
17. *Politics* VIII.5, 1340a18, at p. 466.

> power to induce a certain character of soul, and if it can do that, then clearly it must be applied to education.[18]

Aristotle says that the actual playing of music, and not just listening to and learning about it, should be part of education. The point of this, however, should in his view be to increase the student's understanding of and appreciation for music rather than acquiring the highest degree of technical proficiency. Interestingly, as with athletics, so too with music Aristotle warns against too great an emphasis on such proficiency, lest the student become too specialized.

It goes without saying that Aristotle would take a very dim view of much modern popular music, and that here we see once again a sharp contrast between his approach to education and attitudes that prevail today. In his 1987 bestseller *The Closing of the American Mind*, Allan Bloom devoted a famous chapter to criticizing modern pop music from the classical philosophical point of view represented by thinkers like Plato and Aristotle. It was probably the most controversial part of the book, even among conservatives otherwise sympathetic with Bloom. Aristotle would not have been surprised. Commenting on Aristotle's teaching on music, Barker notes that music derives much of its attraction from the way that, like sleep and socializing, it affords pleasure that dulls the pain of work. But just as sleeping and socializing can degenerate into chronic laying about or constant partying, so too immersion in music can become addictive. Of those who fall into this habit, Barker writes:

> They take a drug meant for the healing of pain, when they have no pain: they become, as it were, opium-eaters. A man who turns to music in this spirit is one who, as Plato says, surrenders his soul to be flooded through his ears with sound, until it loses its proper balance and adjustment.[19]

---

18. *Politics* VIII.5, 1340a18–1340b10, at p. 466.
19. Barker, *The Political Thought of Plato and Aristotle*, 437.

As with our use of alcohol, food, sex, and other things that are good in themselves but prone to excess, if we moderns are touchy when a thinker criticizes our attachment to music, that may be precisely a sign that we ought to listen. (I am not speaking from a high horse, by the way, since my own tastes in popular music run from Led Zeppelin to Steely Dan to the Beastie Boys!)

Conclusion: Aristotle Against Modern Education

That completes my survey of Aristotle's account of education. Let me end by reiterating the main objections Aristotle would raise against modern education. First, he would object to its failure to fulfill the basic function of education, which is to mold citizens who will uphold the social order and contribute to the common good. Hence he would object to those on the contemporary political right who see education as a purely private matter, and to those on the contemporary political left who seek to inculcate in the young an attitude of suspicion of the social order and the authorities who govern it, liberation from traditional moral restraints, divisive identity politics, and so on.

Second, Aristotle would be critical of the contemporary tendency to conceive of education primarily as a matter of preparation for a career. Naturally, he'd object also to the associated tendency to value subjects that are useful over those that have intrinsic worth but little or no utility. Third, Aristotle would object to the hyper-specialization of modern academic life. Fourth, he would criticize the tendency to think of education as essentially a matter of book-learning and to neglect the moral habituation and acquisition of tacit knowledge that must precede the sort of education one gets from books and in the classroom. Fifth and finally, he would object to modern education's blindness to the potentially morally corrupting effects of popular culture, and especially of what he would regard as the wrong kinds of music.

Modern educators like to think of themselves as promoting critical thinking. If they want to prove their sincerity, they might demonstrate it by taking to heart and grappling with Aristotle's critique.

5 Augustine

Michael P. Foley

It hardly needs saying that St. Augustine of Hippo (354–430) is a major source of Catholic education and its renewal. Augustine's conversion to Christianity after a dramatic and riotous youth is perhaps the second most famous and important conversion in Church history, second only to that of Saint Paul. A flower of classical Roman education, Augustine lived to see the barbarians literally at the gates. An intellectual who wanted a quiet monastic life, he was instead compelled to become a priest and bishop who would hammer the heretics of his day so effectively that St. Jerome, who was not known for his lavish praise, called him the second founder of Christianity.

We can analyze Augustine's legacy in the realm of education by thinking of his success as an author, as a preacher, and as a teacher.

As an author, there is no doubt that Augustine was a success. We have over 3,000,000 words from his writings, far more than from any other figure from antiquity, pagan or Christian. And we have those words in large part because they are so good. Even during the "Dark Ages" that followed late antiquity, scribes labored to save his every syllable. Reading Augustine in the twenty-first century, it is easy to see why: there is a timeless freshness, a relatability, a "relevance" in Augustine's work. In the words of Karl Jaspers, Augustine was one of the three great authors of the West "who thought with his blood."[1]

Augustine also scores high marks as a preacher. The well-trained *rhetor* with an outstanding memory could preach extemporaneously

1. As quoted in Ernest Fortin, "Reflections on the Proper Way to Read Augustine the Theologian," *Augustinian Studies* 2 (1971): 260. The other two, incidentally, are Kierkegaard and Nietzsche, although one is also reminded of Blaise Pascal.

for two hours to his rapt congregation, which was standing the entire time (there were no pews in the fourth and fifth century). Augustine's canons wrote down his homilies in shorthand, transcribed them, and then submitted them for his approval before publishing them. Augustine's Sunday homilies were so popular that the organizers of Hippo's games and circuses (chariot races) scheduled their performances around his Mass schedule for fear of a low attendance.

But curiously, Augustine's record as a personal teacher is mixed. His good friend Alypius was a student of his and credits Augustine for breaking his addiction, at least temporarily, to the bloodthirsty games. Alypius was auditing a course in the back of the class when Augustine randomly cracked a joke at the expense of people who enjoyed this kind of entertainment. Alypius thought that the remark was directed at him and mended his ways, even though it was not.[2] Augustine, in other words, was a good teacher at that moment, but only by accident.

Although Augustine's education of Alypius can ultimately be deemed successful, the same cannot be said for his tutoring of Licentius. Licentius was one of two pupils that Augustine brought with him to a villa in Cassiciacum in the autumn of AD 386 in order to prepare for his baptism. As the so-called Cassiciacum dialogues attest, Licentius, despite some signs of great promise, was a squirrely soul, erratically avowing and disavowing Academic skepticism, obsessing over tragic love poetry, and worst of all, caring more for his reputation than his pursuit of wisdom. Augustine's reactions were perhaps equally uneven, ranging from tender affection and high praise to ad hominem putdowns, angry admonitions, and breaking down into tears. In reading the Cassiciacum dialogues, one gets the distinct impression that Licentius had an unintentional knack for getting under Augustine's skin. Nine years after Cassiciacum, Licentius wrote an obsequious letter to Augustine in an effort to show

2. See Augustine, *Confessions*, 6.7.12.

how much he had grown, but the plan only reignited Augustine's irritability. "With a sad and pitiful heart,"[3] Augustine tells Licentius that he is still "most dangerously shackled" to worldly and mortal things and has an allergy to the liberating "shackles of wisdom."[4] As for any improvement in Licentius's poetic skills, Augustine is icily indifferent. "What is your golden tongue to me," he tells his former pupil, "when your heart is iron?"[5]

Most likely, Augustine's greatest success as a personal teacher was with his illegitimate son Adeodatus, who died at a tender age. Of him Augustine writes:

> You had made him well. He was barely fifteen, yet he was more intelligent than many a grave and learned man. In this I am but acknowledging to You Your own gifts, O Lord my God, Creator of all and powerful to reshape our shapelessness: for I had no part in that boy but the sin. That he had been brought up by us in Your way was because You had inspired us, no other. I do but acknowledge to You Your own gifts. There is a book of mine called *De Magistro*: it is a dialogue between him and me. You know, O God, that all the ideas which are put into the mouth of the other party to the dialogue were truly his, though he was but sixteen. I had experience of many other remarkable qualities in him. His great intelligence filled me with a kind of awe: and who but You could be the maker of things so wonderful? But You took him early from this earth, and I think of him utterly without anxiety, for there is nothing in his boyhood or youth or anywhere in him to cause me to fear.[6]

My essay has three main parts. First, I look at Augustine's anthropology of eros in *On Christian Doctrine*. Second, I examine

---

3. *Epistle* 26.6, translation mine.

4. *Ep.* 26.2.

5. *Ep.* 26.4.

6. *Confessions* 9.6.14, trans. Frank J. Sheed (Hackett, 2006).

the three kinds of self-knowledge that are found in Augustine's writings, especially the Cassiciacum dialogues and the *Confessions*. And third, I raise two questions about how Augustine's teachings intersect with our current situation.

An Unprejudiced Estimator of Things

Augustine's *On Christian Doctrine* has long been recognized as a groundbreaking and influential work. With its extended discussion of the distinction between signs and things, it is hailed as the first work on semiotics, and with its famous image of despoiling the Egyptians, it provides a Christian rationale for appropriating knowledge wherever it is found, even if it is found among the pagans. *On Christian Doctrine* was the most important blueprint for education in the Latin West for at least half a millennium.

But I would like to focus not on what Augustine foregrounds—namely, various signs and things—but on a fascinating anthropology of eros that lies in the background. *On Christian Doctrine* was not written to be a textbook on education but to help readers better understand Sacred Scripture. The only reason to want to understand Sacred Scripture better is to become a better knower of reality; and the only reason to want to become a better knower of reality is to become a better lover of reality (and its Creator). Aristotle famously defines man as a rational, political animal. Augustine would agree, but because he views the human person largely in terms of his/her desires, I would say that for Augustine, man is the ultimate love-animal, the creature of infinite desire. And this capacity for infinite desire can go well or badly. As Dante would note centuries later, it is our loves that are the seed of every virtue and every vice.[7] Every soul in Hell, Purgatory, and Heaven is there because of what they loved and how they loved it. Love is the key to everything, but not all loves are created equal.

7. See *Purgatorio*, XVII.91–105.

Book One of *On Christian Doctrine* is famous for its distinction between use and enjoyment. God is to be "enjoyed," that is, loved for His own sake, while everything else is to be "used," that is, loved for the sake of, or in light of God. The distinction can be particularly difficult in English, because "using someone" makes it sound like you are exploiting someone for selfish ends, but for Augustine, "use" is simply loving someone or something to the right degree and in the right way. He writes:

> Now he is a man of just and holy life who is an unprejudiced estimator of things and who keeps his affections also under strict control, so that he neither loves what he ought not to love, nor fails to love what he ought to love, nor loves that more which ought to be loved less, nor loves that equally which ought to be loved either less or more, nor loves that less or more which ought to be loved equally.[8]

Note the two conditions for justice and holiness, and ultimately, happiness: we need to become "an unprejudiced estimator of things," someone who sees the world and what is beyond it accurately. The word here for "unprejudiced" is *integer* or whole—not broken, dented, or warped, but intact and pristine. And second, we need to discipline our affections or loves so that there is a perfect alignment between our subjective loves and the objective order of lovable things.

This is the reason for despoiling the Egyptians; this is the reason for Christians to acquire a liberal arts education, or to study science or anything else for its own sake: it is to know reality better and to love it better.

An Unprejudiced Estimator of Self

But for Augustine, becoming an unprejudiced estimator of things requires becoming an unprejudiced estimator of self. Indeed, an

8. *On Christian Doctrine* 1.27.28, trans. J. F. Shaw (Dover Publications, 2009).

Augustinian view of education is more concerned about *self*-knowledge than the various branches of knowledge. In one of his first dialogues called the *Soliloquies*, which depicts Augustine and his own Reason as separate characters, Reason asks Augustine what he wants to know, to which Augustine replies: "God and the soul." "Nothing more?" Reason persists. "Nothing whatsoever!" Augustine exclaims. Later, when Reason asks Augustine to come up with the briefest and most perfect prayer that he can, Augustine prays: "O God, ever the Selfsame: may I know myself, may I know Thee. Amen."[9]

One can understand Augustine's preoccupation. The injunction to know thyself is at least as old as the Oracle of Delphi, and it essentially became the cornerstone of classical philosophy as evidenced in Socrates's famous aphorism, "The unexamined life is not worth living." Despite their differences, the one thing that all the myriad schools of Socratic and post-Socratic philosophy in antiquity had in common was a desire to acquire or at least approximate self-knowledge. But self-knowing was not just the purview of the philosopher; it was also a priority of the early and medieval Church. In the 1970s a French scholar by the name of Pierre Courcelle collected all the references he could find to knowing oneself, starting with Plato and ending with St. Bernard of Clairvaux in the twelfth century: He filled two massive volumes and even then could have kept going.[10]

And I trust that this quest for self-knowledge is still relevant to us as members of a university community, for it seems to me that one of the differences between training and education is that training helps you master a particular set of practical skills (such as mechanical repair or computer programming) while education, especially

9. Augustine, *Soliloquies*, trans. Michael P. Foley (Yale University Press, 2020), 1.2.7, 2.1.1. Translations of the Cassiciacum dialogues (*Against the Academics, On the Happy Life, On Order*, and *Soliloquies*) are taken from my four-volume translations and commentary, published by Yale University Press in 2019 and 2020.

10. Pierre Courcelle, *Connais-toi toi-même; de Socrate à saint Bernard [Know Thyself: From Socrates to St. Bernard]* (Études Augustiniennes, 1974–75).

higher education, helps you see and understand the world better, and that understanding (one would hope) includes a better understanding of oneself. I am tempted to say that if our students spend years under our tutelage and graduate without gaining any self-knowledge whatsoever, they might be entitled to a full refund, but I am also poignantly aware of the fact that it may be just a little bit their fault for not paying attention.

In any event, let us turn to St. Augustine and see how he can help us with the quest to know oneself.

The first thing to recognize is that Augustine does not think that there is only one kind of self-knowledge but at least *three*: intellectual self-knowledge, moral self-knowledge, and religious self-knowledge. As it turns out, these are the subjects of books seven, eight, and nine of the *Confessions*, respectively. Augustine describes the attainment of each kind of self-knowledge as involving a "conversion" or a "return to oneself," but what one discovers as a result of each return is different in each case.

Intellectual Self-Knowledge

The first kind of self-knowledge that Augustine acquired, thanks to a reading of the books of the Platonists, was intellectual.[11] I do not know if intellectual self-knowledge is the hardest to attain, but it is certainly the hardest to explain. For philosophers like Plato, the key breakthrough is to recognize that there are two kinds of reality: sensible reality, the world of space, time, and matter that is accessible to our bodily senses; and intelligible realities, the world of unchangeable realities or ideas that is accessible to the mind or intellect alone. In this room, for example, there are two chairs and

11. Augustine did, of course, experience an intellectual conversion of sorts when he read Cicero's *Hortensius* at the age of eighteen or nineteen (see *Confessions* 3.4.7), but as we will see, that turn to the love of wisdom is not what is strictly meant by the terms "intellectual conversion" and "intellectual self-knowledge."

two people but not the number two. "Twoness," so to speak, is not something I can touch, taste, or see, but it is real; in fact, it is in some ways more real than two chairs because unlike a chair it is an eternal and immutable reality that existed before the creation of the universe and will exist after its eventual destruction. In Plato's Allegory of the Cave, getting outside the cave means discovering intelligible reality.

For much of his life, Augustine's goal was to understand the Christian teaching that God is an intelligible reality and not a sensible reality, or to put it in more biblical language, that God is spirit and not body. But every time he tried, he kept thinking of God in terms of some material analogy. To give one example: Augustine pictured the universe as a sponge and God as water that filled every nook and cranny of the sponge but was still different from the sponge. The problem with this analogy is that it leads to absurdities, for if it is true, there is "more God" in an elephant than in a sparrow, "more God" in a fat man than in a thin man. But what alternative is there to understanding God materially?

For Augustine, the key is first to know something that we all have and are in fact using right now: our minds. For the very minds we are using right now are prime examples of a reality that is intelligible (and intelligent, of course) but not sensible. In other words, the mind is not the brain. Our brain is a sensible reality, a material organ, while our mind is an intelligible reality, pure spirit. Certainly, our mind makes great use of the brain, but that does not mean that the mind *is* the brain. Neuroscience can trace the activities of the brain when a person is thinking, but it is tracing correlation rather than causation. Does a mental insight happen because certain neurons in the brain fire, or do certain neurons in the brain fire because the mind is having an insight?

Here is how Augustine described his predicament:

> Thus I was so gross of mind—not seeing even myself clearly—that whatever was not extended in space, either diffused or

> massed together or swollen out or having some such qualities or at least capable of having them, I thought must be nothing whatsoever. My mind was in search of such images as the forms my eye was accustomed to see; and I did not realise that the mental act by which I formed these images was not itself a bodily image: yet it could not have formed them unless it were something and something great.[12]

Note the problem: Augustine kept thinking that for something to be real, it must be spatial, it must be locatable on a Cartesian grid. He did not realize that God is not in space; space is in God, but not spatially. And note the solution: the mental act that struggles with the difference between sensible and intelligible reality is itself an intelligible reality. It is obviously real, for if it was not, it would not be struggling: only things that are real struggle.

Here is how Augustine describes his breakthrough, precipitated by a reading of the books of the Platonists:

> Being admonished by all this to return to myself, I entered into my own depths, with You as guide; and I was able to do it because You were my helper. I entered, and with the eye of my soul, such as it was, I saw Your unchangeable Light shining over that same eye of my soul, over my mind. It was not the light of everyday that the eye of flesh can see, nor some greater light of the same order, such as might be if the brightness of our daily light should be seen shining with a more intense brightness and filling all things with its greatness. Your light was not that, but other, altogether other, than all such lights. Nor was it above my mind as oil above the water it floats on, nor as the sky is above the earth; it was above because it made me, and I was below because made by it. He who knows the truth knows that Light, and he that knows the Light knows eternity.[13]

---

12. *Confessions*, 7.1.2.

13. *Confessions*, 7.10.16.

By intellectual self-knowledge, then, we do not mean falling in love with the life of the mind or becoming a bibliophile of the best that has been thought and written, as excellent as those things are. We mean the discovery of one's mind as an intelligible reality that is participating in the Supreme Intelligibility we call God.

There are two obstacles to an intellectual conversion. The first is our daily habits, which privilege the sensible world.[14] There is nothing wrong with being a human person, an embodied soul that receives data from the senses before proceeding to intelligible universals. But because our intellects develop slowly over time, our fixation with the senses gets a head start. Moreover, even as students or teachers who would rather contemplate the Platonic Forms all day, we spend most of our mental energies during our waking hours thinking about things within the world of space, time, and matter, and this can give the impression that the only reality is the world of space, time, and matter.

The second obstacle is sin, which mires us even further in the passing world. In the *Confessions* Augustine writes that he was not able to savor his intellectual breakthrough for very long because he was "soon torn away" by his own weight and "fell again with torment to lower things."[15] Intellectual acumen and judgment are different from moral integrity but still connected: my sins *do* have a negative impact on my ability to think clearly, dispassionately, and maturely.

Moral Self-Knowledge

In addition to intellectual conversion, there needs to be a moral conversion. What is the point of being wise when you remain, as Augustine says of himself, "the vile slave of evil desires?"[16] Besides a conversion of one's intellect or understanding, there needs to occur a conversion of

14. *On Order*, 1.1.3.
15. *Confessions*, 7.16.22.
16. *Confessions*, 4.16.30.

one's behavior or *mores*. And as with intellectual breakthrough, a moral breakthrough can come through moral self-knowledge.

Moral self-knowledge consists of knowing oneself as a sinner, clearly and decisively, without any excuses or evasions, and it is important because it begins the process of repentance and healing, for the first step to any cure is a proper diagnosis. The obstacles to moral self-knowledge are fairly clear. First, we do not want to know ourselves as a sinner because the truth is too ugly. As Augustine writes: "[Men] love truth when it enlightens them, they hate truth when it accuses them. Because they do not wish to be deceived and do wish to deceive, they love truth when it reveals itself, and hate it when it reveals them."[17]

Aesop tells the story that when Jupiter made Man, he gave him two knapsacks, one for his neighbor's faults and one for his own. The Man kept the one for his neighbor's faults in front of him and the one for his own on his back. In the *Confessions*, when Augustine recounts finally seeing his moral failings for what they were, he uses a similar image of hiding behind himself:

> You [O God], turned me back towards myself, taking me from behind my own back where I had put myself all the time that I preferred not to see myself. And You set me there before my own face that I might see how vile I was, how twisted and unclean and spotted and ulcerous. I saw myself and was horrified.[18]

It takes a small miracle to see oneself as one truly is, in no small part because the miracle is so resisted.

A moral conversion can be prompted in different ways. In Augustine's life it was a combination of interpreting an everyday event as a sign from heaven, the sound of a neighborhood kid singing "Take and read," as well as hearing stories of people just like him

17. *Confessions*, 10.23.34.

18. *Confessions*, 8.7.16.

who were able to leave their sin behind. After hearing their testimonies, Augustine says:

> But there was no way to flee from myself. If I tried to turn my gaze from myself, there was Ponticianus telling what he was telling; and again You were setting me face to face with myself, forcing me upon my own sight, that I might see my iniquity and loathe it.[19]

In that crucial moment, he was able to overcome all the clever dodges, rationalizations, justifications, and excuses and to see himself as he truly was. And thanks to it, moments later he was healed.

The reluctance to see the truth about ourselves is a particularly difficult obstacle because it is fueled by a desire to be seen a certain way by the people around us, what Rousseau calls *amour propre*. In other words, we spend our lives hiding our own dark and disordered hearts from our neighbors, so much so that we start hiding it from ourselves. In the *Soliloquies*, Reason declares "there is no better way of seeking the truth than by questioning and answering," and *yet* "hardly anyone can be found who isn't ashamed of being refuted in a disputation." As a result, "it's almost always the case that the matter under discussion, one that's off to a good start, is booed off the stage by the rowdy hullabaloo of stubbornness and all the while souls are being ripped apart."[20]

A second obstacle is the power of sinful habit. As Augustine explains in the *Confessions*, we can abuse our free will in such a way that we effectively lose it. "Because my will was perverse it changed to lust, and lust yielded to become habit, and habit not resisted became necessity."[21] That is as tidy a summary of Aristotle's *Nichomachean Ethics* as one can find, even though Augustine never read

19. *Confessions*, 8.7.16.
20. *Soliloquies*, 2.7.14.
21. *Confessions*, 8.5.10.

the *Ethics*. Similarly, he writes that moments before his moral conversion, he "still shrank from dying unto death and living unto life. The lower condition which had grown habitual was more powerful the better condition which [he] had not tried."[22]

Religious Self-Knowledge

Moral conversion begins the life of ethical excellence and makes one fit to have the best kind of friendships. That said, neither intellectual nor moral conversion satisfies the deepest yearnings of the human mind and heart. Something more is needed, both as a completion and grounding of these conversions and in order to bring the human person to ultimate happiness. Hence the need for religious conversion, which in biblical terms is the replacement of one's heart of stone with a heart of flesh (see Ez 36:26) that enables one to love the Lord God with one's whole heart, whole soul, and whole strength (see Dt 6:4–5). Religious conversion is a surrender to divine love. It is "religious" in its modern meaning as ordered toward a formal and communal worship of God, but it is also "religious" in its ancient meaning as a binding (*religio*) of the soul to God. For Augustine, both senses are operative in the sacrament of baptism; and for Augustine, such a binding in the Christian religion does not involve a restriction but an expansion of one's freedom as well as a perfection or completion of the other two conversions, for in addition to knowing the good and doing the good, the individual is now capable of fully loving the good. "Without doubt," Saint Monica concludes in one of her son's dialogues, "this is the happy life, the life that is perfect. And we must presume that we who are hurrying to it can be brought to it by a firm faith, a lively hope, and an ardent charity."[23]

Religious *self-knowledge*, then, is the knowledge of oneself as a creature and as a beloved child of God. It makes moral self-knowl-

22. *Confessions*, 8.11.25.

23. *On the Happy Life*, 4.36.

edge bearable, for with religious self-knowledge comes trust in the help of the Lord and the possibility of forgiveness. It also completes intellectual self-knowledge, which tops out at the recognition that my knowing is somehow tied into God. If intellectual self-knowledge enables us to know the good and moral self-knowledge enables us to do the good, religious self-knowledge enables us to love the good. Finally, religious self-knowledge is crucial because self-knowledge and knowledge of God go hand in hand. Augustine's twin obsession to know "God and the soul" is inextricably intertwined. And, of course, the obstacles standing in the way to a religious conversion are any of the things that prevent or undermine religious faith. Augustine identifies two opposite vices that are particularly deadly: despair and presumption. Despair that you will ever find the truth effectively discourages you from embarking on a quest for truth, and so too does presumption, the "false opinion that [you] have already discovered the truth,"[24] for if you think that you already possess the truth, you will not feel the need to go looking for it. Similarly, despair over your sins being forgiven militates against religious conversion, as does the presumption that you have no sins that need forgiving.

Two Final Questions

Having surveyed the three kinds of self-knowledge in Augustine's thought and their obstacles, we conclude with two questions concerning their practical applications to contemporary Catholic higher education.

First, how responsible is the modern Catholic university for encouraging all three forms of education? In his *Idea of a University*, for example, John Henry Newman thinks of the university as the primary locus for intellectual formation, while moral formation is

24. *Against the Academics*, 1.1.1.

the responsibility of the college. Newman had in mind the University of Oxford, which is comprised of thirty-nine colleges (residence halls, and then some) and four permanent private halls of religious foundation. But what about universities not founded on this model?

Second, what is the relationship between these Augustinian kinds of self-knowledge and modern forms of self-knowledge? On one hand, since the 1960s an emphasis has been placed on "consciousness raising" or "raising awareness" about certain aspects of our existence, particularly our participation in a system or society that is unjust. The most recent iteration of this sensibility is the so-called Woke movement. My question, then is: are consciousness-raising and awareness-raising and being Woke extensions or updated versions of the quest for Augustinian self-knowledge, *or* are they substitutes for it, a sign that we have given up on the old quest for self-knowledge?

It is beyond the scope of this presentation to answer this question, but I conclude with one consideration. Much of Woke thought is predicated on a victimology that involves a strict binary of victim and victimizer, in which it is possible to be only one or the other. And if you are not a victim, the next best thing is to empathize radically with the victim to avoid the stigma of being an oppressor.

One problem with this binary is that it blocks self-knowledge by presupposing that victims cannot be oppressors. And yet this is not true. Several years ago the *Wall Street Journal* reported a growing problem in the Republic of Ireland, which only recently has had to deal with a significant minority population within its borders.[25] Middle Eastern and Nigerian immigrants are often the subject of ignorant microaggressions (statements like "You are beautiful—for a black woman") and sometimes outright violence. Felicia Olusanya, a poet and author who came to Ireland from Nigeria at the age of

25. Alistair MacDonald and Paul Hannon, "In Ireland, Push Intensifies for Hate-Crime Laws," *Wall Street Journal Eastern Edition* (July 23, 2020), A16.

eight and who "has experienced racism, including slurs, hostile looks and monkey noises," does not attribute this behavior to a racist or white supremacist ideology but to a fixation on their past mistreatment by the British. "There is a lot of, 'We can't be the oppressor because we have been oppressed,'" Olusanya reports. And thus, the Irish have blocked an insight into their own moral culpability by their own narrative of victimology.

At the very least, we can say that being an unprejudiced estimator of things or an unprejudiced estimator of self requires moral courage and a strong stomach. And how shall we help our students acquire such a heart and such a stomach when they are steeped in a cultural marinade of entitlement and brittle resentment?

6 Boethius

Jeffrey S. Lehman

Against wisdom evil does not prevail. She reaches mightily from one end of the earth to the other, and she orders all things well.

—Book of Wisdom 7:30–8:1 (RSVCE)[1]

In a general audience held on Wednesday, March 12, 2008, Pope Benedict XVI offered reflections on two important advocates of Catholic liberal education: Boethius and Cassiodorus, contemporaries[2] who, as the Holy Father notes, "lived in some of the most turbulent years in the Christian West and in the Italian peninsula in particular."[3] In the same address, Pope Benedict gives a brief yet illuminating summary of the man Boethius and his life's work:

> [B]orn in Rome in about [AD] 480 from the noble Anicius lineage, [Boethius] entered public life when he was still young and by age 25 was already a senator. Faithful to his family's tradition, he devoted himself to politics, convinced that it would be possible to temper the fundamental structure of Roman society with the values of the new peoples. And in this new time of cultural

1. See *Consolation of Philosophy*, III.12.

2. Anicius Manlius Severinus Boethius, commonly known as Boethius, lived ca. AD 480 to 524; Flavius Magnus Aurelius Cassiodorus Senator, commonly known at Cassiodorus, lived ca. AD 485 to 585. Cassiodorus was the immediate successor of Boethius as the *magister officiorum* under Theodoric "the Great," who, though initially well-disposed toward Boethius, sent him to prison in 523 and had him brutally tortured and executed the following year.

3. Benedict XVI, "Boethius and Cassiodorus," General Audience, Pope Paul VI Audience Hall, March 12, 2008, https://www.vatican.va/content/benedict-xvi/en/audiences/2008/documents/hf_ben-xvi_aud_20080312.html.

> encounter[4] he considered it his role to reconcile and bring together these two cultures, the classical Roman and the nascent Ostrogoth culture. Thus, he was also politically active under Theodoric, who at the outset held him in high esteem. In spite of this public activity, Boethius did not neglect his studies and dedicated himself in particular to acquiring a deep knowledge of philosophical and religious subjects. . . . [H]e also wrote manuals on arithmetic, geometry, music and astronomy, all with the intention of passing on the great Greco-Roman culture to the new generations, to the new times. In this context, in his commitment to fostering the encounter of cultures, he used the categories of Greek philosophy to present the Christian faith, here too seeking a synthesis between the Hellenistic-Roman heritage and the Gospel message. For this very reason Boethius was described as the last representative of ancient Roman culture and the first of the Medieval intellectuals.[5]

Pope Benedict's comments here help us to see the significance of Boethius and his life's work. On the one hand, Boethius "devoted himself to politics," seeking to bring into harmony the centuries-old political institutions and educational traditions of Roman society with the values and emerging culture of the reigning Ostrogoths and other Germanic tribes from the north who had descended upon Rome. Just four years prior to the birth of Boethius, the Western Roman Empire finally succumbed to the vast numbers of Goths and other non-Roman peoples who had fled their homelands (thanks in large part to the invading Huns) and entered Roman territory to stay. In 476 the last

4. In this collection of essays, see Michael Waldstein's insightful comments on "encounter" in Benedict's writings.

5. Benedict XVI, "Boethius and Cassiodorus." In the final sentence, Benedict alludes to the oft-quoted comment of Lorenzo Valla (c. 1407–1457), an Italian Renaissance humanist, educator, and Catholic priest, who referred to Boethius as the "last of the Romans, first of the scholastics." Howard Rollin Patch traces the origin of this description in *The Tradition of Boethius: A Study of His Importance in Medieval Culture* (Russell & Russell, 1935), 127.

Roman emperor, Romulus Augustulus, was deposed by the Germanic barbarian king, Odoacer, and the Roman Senate sent the imperial insignia to Zeno, who was then the Eastern Roman Emperor. The "cultural encounter" of which Benedict speaks and which Boethius fostered was an attempt to retain what was truly good in Roman civilization and to reconcile it with the budding culture of the new rulers of the territories that had until recently been the Western Roman Empire.

On the other hand, Boethius also "dedicated himself in particular to acquiring a deep knowledge of philosophical and religious subjects." Rather than neglecting his studies due to the demands of political service, Boethius instead threw himself into a painstaking examination of philosophy and theology. In addition, he also wrote handbooks on the four mathematical arts that we now know as the *quadrivium*, thanks to Boethius, who first used this term in the introduction to his work on arithmetic.[6] As Benedict points out, Boethius does all this "with the intention of passing on the great Greco-Roman culture to the new generations, to the new times." Finally, "in his commitment to fostering the encounter of cultures, [Boethius] used the categories of Greek philosophy to present the Christian faith, here too seeking a synthesis between the Hellenistic-Roman heritage and the Gospel message." In his person and in his work, then, Boethius sought a triple reconciliation—between Roman and barbarian culture broadly understood, between the active and the contemplative lives, and between the Greco-Roman heritage and the Christian Gospel. We could also add a fourth—the reconciliation of Plato and Aristotle. Boethius set himself the task of translating all of Plato and all of Aristotle in order to show, among other things, the deep unity of the teachings of these two great philosophers. All of this, we should recall, Boethius endeavored to do within "some of the most turbulent

---

6. For an English translation of this work on arithmetic, see Michael Masi, *Boethian Number Theory: A Translation of the De Institutione Arithmetica* (Editions Rodopi B. V., 1983).

years in the Christian West." Given the economic, political, and cultural turbulence within which we find ourselves today, we do well to consider the works and the legacy that Boethius has left for us as we seek to renew Catholic education in our own time. In what follows, I will offer both a taste of Boethius's *magnum opus*, the *Consolation of Philosophy*, and a general overview of his works and influence, placing particular emphasis on three closely related themes: wisdom, the liberal arts, and persons—*both* divine *and* human. Let's begin with a detailed consideration of a few passages from Book I of what one eminent scholar has called Boethius's "dazzling masterpiece,"[7] the *Consolation of Philosophy*.

Consolation of Philosophy, Book I

Consolation of Philosophy is undoubtedly one of the greatest philosophical dialogues in the Western tradition.[8] Within this philosophical dialogue, the image of Lady Philosophy as physician is fundamental to the drama that unfolds in the work.[9] In the first book

7. Henry Chadwick, *The Consolations of Music, Logic, Theology, and Philosophy* (Clarendon Press, 1981), v.

8. Anyone who has had the joy of reading and discussing the *Consolation* with students knows how remarkable their encounter with this philosophical dialogue can be. Whether they first come across it in a well-ordered classical high school curriculum or later on in college, students often identify the *Consolation* as among the most influential and important books that they've ever read. For an in-depth treatment of the *Consolation of Philosophy* as a philosophical dialogue, see Chapter VI of my *Socratic Conversation: Bringing the Dialogues of Plato and the Socratic Tradition into Today's Classroom* (Classical Academic Press, 2021), 151–81. My comments in this section of the essay draw from portions of that chapter. For a good source on the philosophical dialogue in general, see Vittorio Hösle's *The Philosophical Dialogue: A Poetics and a Hermeneutics*, trans. Steven Rendall (University of Notre Dame Press, 2012).

9. Among those who have reflected upon education in the Western tradition, there is a common tendency to draw out a parallel between medical doctors and teachers. For an excellent example of this outside Boethius, see St. Thomas Aquinas's "On the Teacher" (*Disputed Questions on Truth* 11).

of the *Consolation*, we are introduced to the characters, Boethius the patient and Philosophy the physician, and made aware of the patient's despondent condition. In the four books that follow, Philosophy undertakes a gradual curative regimen in an attempt to heal Boethius of his malady. Reflecting upon this therapeutic image and how the author employs it yields crucial insight into the nature, purpose, unity, and structure of this work. We can only make a modest beginning of this reflection here. To direct our study, let us start with a question: *How does Lady Philosophy exercise her therapeutic art in the Consolation of Philosophy?*[10] To make progress in answering this query, we must consider three elements of the work: the characters in the dialogue, the initial condition of Boethius, and the cure proposed and carried out by Lady Philosophy in the course of their conversation.

Let's commence with the characters. We first meet Boethius, who is composing elegiac verses of self-pity as the work opens (I.m.1). For the sake of clarity, we should distinguish between "two Boethiuses"—one, the author of the *Consolation of Philosophy*; and the other, the patient who comes under the care of the physician, Lady Philosophy, within the dramatic context of the written work.[11]

10. Such guiding questions are present in every great philosophical dialogue—either explicitly, implicitly, or a bit of both. Many thanks to my dear friend and fellow Senior Fellow of the Boethius Institute, Matthew Walz, who first suggested this question to me many years ago while we were each teaching Sophomore Seminar at Thomas Aquinas College.

11. A similar distinction is in order when considering St. Augustine's *Confessions* and Dante Alighieri's *Commedia*. Indeed, it is not difficult to see that these three works—*Confessions*, *Consolation of Philosophy*, and *Commedia*—are part of an ongoing literary, philosophical, and theological conversation. Undoubtedly, Boethius was inspired by and responding to Augustine's *Confessions* (as well as other works of Augustine, notably his early dialogue, *Soliloquies*); and Dante, in turn, was inspired by and responding to both Augustine and Boethius. Dante's indebtedness to Boethius is pervasive in the *Commedia*, even though is it usually implicit. Placing Boethius among the Doctors in the Paradiso, Dante identifies him as the "blessed soul who exposes the deceptive world to anyone who gives ear to him."

We should also keep in mind the time of the dialogue as it relates to these two Boethiuses. The dialogue recounts the conversation of the patient Boethius with Philosophy; as the dialogue unfolds, Philosophy teaches him and leads him gradually toward health. Boethius the author, in contrast, has already undergone the therapeutic regimen of Philosophy and recalls and reconstructs their conversation in written form.[12] Thus, the reader is placed within Boethius's own reflections on his condition both as he is experiencing it (i.e., as it is presented within the drama of the dialogue) and as he looks back upon the experience, having reconciled himself to himself (i.e., once he has attained a state of recollection) after these reflections are complete.

Significantly, Boethius the soon-to-be patient begins in a state of total passivity: "Wounded Muses tell me what to write, and elegiac verses bathe my face with real tears" (I.m.1.3–4).[13] In other words, he has completely abandoned himself to despair, passively receiving the communications of the Muses and composing self-absorbed verses of lamentation.[14] Indeed, he longs for "Death, . . . [who he says] turns a deaf ear to the wretched and cruelly refuses to close weeping eyes" (I.m.1.13–16). Boethius begins so engrossed in self-pity that he is unable to see anything else; he is wallowing in the depths of despair yet incapable of judging his own condition—blinded by his own tears, indeed, but blinded even more by his state of mind.

12. Robert McMahon, *Understanding the Medieval Meditative Ascent: Augustine, Anselm, Boethius, and Dante* (The Catholic University of America Press, 2006), 211.

13. Boethius, *The Consolation of Philosophy*, trans. and ed. Scott Goins and Barbara Wyman, Ignatius Critical Editions (Ignatius Press, 2011). All quotations of the *Consolation* are from this edition.

14. For a similar reading, see Krista Sue-Lo Twu, "This Is Comforting? Boethius's *Consolation of Philosophy*, Rhetoric, Dialectic, and 'Unicum Illud Inter Homines Deumque Commercium,'" in *New Directions in Boethian Studies*, ed. Noel Harold Kaylor, Jr. and Philip Edward Phillips, Studies in Medieval Culture Series 45 (Western Michigan University Press, 2007), 34.

Within the context of the dialogue, there is one element of Boethius's passivity that is particularly telling: namely, his silence.[15] Granted, silence *can* be a virtue.[16] The studious pupil who attends carefully to the teachings of a master is often silent. But this silence typically follows much active conversation, questioning the principles of the master to see that they are sound, raising reasonable objections to arguments along the way, and so forth. This is a silence that is born of prior, often vigorous dialectical exchange. By contrast, there is the silence of one who passively receives the opinions and sentiments of others, never attempting to weigh their relative merit or concordance with the truth.[17] Regrettably, the silence of Boethius in these opening lines is of the latter sort. He passively receives poetic "inspiration" from the Muses, allowing his passions to get the better of him.

Lady Philosophy comes on the scene in the first prose section of Book I. She appears standing above Boethius, a woman of "majestic countenance" with "flashing eyes" (*oculis ardentibus*) that penetrate beyond those of ordinary men (I.1.1). Unlike Boethius the patient, she can *see things clearly*.[18] Significantly, "her height

---

15. Seth Lerer makes much of this in his reading of the *Consolation*, contrasting the "listlessness of the prisoner's laments with the power of Philosophy's eloquence"; Lerer, *Boethius and Dialogue: Literary Method in The Consolation of Philosophy* (Princeton University Press, 1985), 102.

16. A notable example of silence as a virtue is the general movement of St. Augustine's *Confessions*, which moves from the dispersive loquacity of prideful human speech to reverent silence before the eternal Word.

17. This is a particularly alluring temptation to many today in our social-media-saturated world.

18. The entire pedagogy of the dialogue is in a sense focused on restoring Boethius's ability *to see things as they are*. Explicit references as well as subtle allusions to regaining one's sight permeate the *Consolation*. When we see things as they are, we are able to render sound judgments. Thus, Lady Philosophy seeks to restore Boethius's vision so that he can once again judge rightly both his own situation and the providential ordering of all things by God.

seemed to vary: sometimes she seemed of ordinary human stature, then again her head seemed to touch the top of the heavens" (I.1.2). Lady Philosophy's varying height is certainly symbolic, most likely to be interpreted in connection with the Greek letters on her robe: "At the lower edge of her robe was woven a Greek Π, and at the top the letter Θ, and between them were seen clearly marked stages, like stairs, ascending from the lowest level to the highest" (I.1.4). The Π and Θ stand for the two species of philosophy, the practical and theoretical, respectively. Lady Philosophy is able to lead men to action in this world through practical philosophy (e.g., ethics, politics, and economics); she is also able to lead them to contemplation through theoretical philosophy (e.g., natural science, mathematics, and metaphysics). And as the stairs would imply, she can guide them gradually from one to the other. More importantly, the varying height of Philosophy makes clear that she can direct her students in a philosophical ascent to the highest things, culminating in an approach to God. This ability is crucial to the healing of Boethius. Among other things, the cure conducted in Books II-V can be understood as a stepwise ascent whose ultimate goal is to bring Boethius back to God.[19,20]

19. Anna Crabbe argues in a similar manner: "This motif of ascent, which recurs frequently, is reflected in the general movement of the work as the vicissitudes of politics and the material world are left behind and the argument turns more positively to a pursuit of knowledge and enlightenment." "Literary Design in the *De consolatione philosophiae*," in *Boethius: His Life, Thought and Influence*, ed. Margaret T. Gibson (Basil Blackwell, 1981), 243–44. See also McMahon, *Understanding*, 214–26.

20. The concluding lines of Book V make this quite clear. In her final exhortation to Boethius, Lady Philosophy says: "[N]ot in vain are hopes and prayers placed before God, since when they are just, they cannot be without effect. So let us shun vices and cultivate virtues, lifting our minds to the proper hopes and offering humble prayers on high. For, if you wish to speak the truth, a great necessity has been placed upon you men to do good, since you live [in the presence of] a judge who sees all things" (Goins & Wyman, 173).

Let's return to the beginning of the dialogue. While the Muses of poetry make only a cameo appearance in the *Consolation*, we are surely meant to contrast them with Lady Philosophy, who no sooner comes on the scene than orders them to leave immediately, calling them "whores from the theater" (*scenicas meretriculas*) and "sirens" (I.1.8).[21] Tellingly, Philosophy reveals the Muses as *false physicians*: "They cannot offer medicine for [Boethius'] sorrows; they will nourish him only with their sweet poison. They kill the fruitful harvest of reason with the sterile thorns of the passions, they do not liberate the minds of men from disease, but merely accustom them to it" (I.1.8–9). Philosophy, on the other hand, offers true medicine for her patient's sorrow; she aims to reinvigorate his reason, thereby enabling him to subdue his passions; and she seeks to liberate his mind, restoring him to the dignity he once knew.[22]

All of the above sounds well and good, and we might naturally expect Philosophy to take such a stance toward poetry. In Boethius the author's time, there was already a longstanding tension, if not outright opposition, between poetry and philosophy. And Philosophy's peremptory dismissal of the Muses is undoubtedly a literary echo of Socrates's banishment of the poets from the ideal city in Plato's *Republic*. Even so, in both Plato and Boethius the relation between philosophy and poetry is far more nuanced than may appear at first. For while Plato's Socrates banishes the poets, he nevertheless engages in poetry himself, creating a host of poetic images as the dialogue unfolds. Socrates even speaks of making an "apology in images" (488a) and ends the conversation with the remarkable

---

21. On which, see Helen M. Barrett, *Boethius: Some Aspects of His Times and Work* (Russell and Russell, 1965), 77–78, and Crabbe, "Literary Design," 77–78 and 249.

22. By incorporating suffering and sorrow into his overall account of the happy life, Boethius goes well beyond most, if not all, of the Greek philosophies of ancient times. As a Christian author, he seeks to give an account of suffering that makes sense in light of the incarnation. This is a huge topic in Boethius, one which we cannot treat in sufficient detail here.

"myth of Er" in Book X (614b ff.). In like manner, Boethius the author's Lady Philosophy sends the Muses of poetry packing; but no sooner are they dismissed than she announces: "Leave him to be cured and made strong by *my Muses*" (I.1.11; emphasis added). From this point on, the literary form of the *Consolation* alternates between poetry and prose.

Furthermore, the poems of the *Consolation* are not mere window dressing for the philosophy of the prosaic sections. To begin with, many of the poems are quite excellent on their own terms.[23] And although they frequently revisit the themes of the immediately preceding prose sections, providing relief from the rigors of philosophic discourse, they often do so in ways that clarify or even carry forward the overall argument.[24] Thus, there is a "dialogue" of sorts between the prose and poetry of the *Consolation*, a dialogue that underscores certain points, refines others, and brings about a further level of dialectical exchange that transcends the scope of the prosaic argument. Moreover, we know from Boethius himself that he probably *did not* include the poems simply as an amusing diversion from the serious matter of the dialogue.[25] For Boethius, as for many ancient and medieval authors, "poetry was made to

23. The crowning achievement is no doubt the ninth poem in Book III (on which, see Chadwick, *The Consolations*, 234–35).

24. This view is defended in different ways by Barrett (*Boethius*, 77); Richard Green, introduction to *The Consolation of Philosophy*, by Boethius, trans. and ed. Richard Green (Macmillan Publishing Company, 1962), xxi; V. E. Watts, introduction to *The Consolation of Philosophy*, by Boethius, trans. V. E. Watts (Penguin Books, 1969), 20; and Elaine Scarry, "The Well-Rounded Sphere: The Metaphysical Structure of the *Consolation of Philosophy*," in *Essays in the Numerical Criticism of Medieval Literature*, ed. Caroline D. Eckhardt (Bucknell University Press, 1980), 99–103.

25. In the opening paragraph of his theological tractate *Quomodo Substantia*, Boethius remarks: "[I] would rather bury my speculations in my own memory than share them with any of those pert and frivolous persons who will not tolerate an argument unless it is made amusing" (as quoted in Scarry, 92–93).

please and to teach, or, more precisely, to please *in order* to teach."[26] A careful reading of the poetry of the *Consolation* reveals that it is integral to the overall argument. There is a delicate interplay between poetry and prose, creating a dialogical whole that is greater than either of its parts.

Even though the poetry is integral to Philosophy's therapeutic plan, it would be a mistake to infer from this that the prose and poetry are on a par. As one reader has put it, "It is not by accident that the *Consolation* begins with verse and ends with prose."[27] Lady Philosophy's purged poetry is consciously subordinated to her philosophic ends.[28] Its aim is to help restore the order that has been lost in the soul of her patient. Over the course of the remaining four books, Philosophy seeks to restore the powers of Boethius's soul to their rightful order and proper function. One of these powers is the imagination, a faculty that mediates between sensation, whose object is material and particular; and reason, whose object is immaterial (or formal) and universal.[29] The imagination shares the formality of its object[30] with reason; it shares the particularity of its object with sensation. At least one purpose of the poetry in the *Consolation* is

---

26. Green, introduction to *The Consolation of Philosophy*, xxi; emphasis in original. This account echoes that of Horace in the *Ars Poetica*, who says, "Poetry wants to instruct or else to delight; / Or, better still, to delight and instruct at once." *The Epistles of Horace*, Book II, bilingual edition, trans. David Ferry (Farrar, Straus, and Giroux, 2001).

27. Watts, introduction to *The Consolation of Philosophy*, 20.

28. We have already seen Philosophy's reference to "my Muses" in I.1. In the first prose section of Book II, she says she will "use the sweet persuasion of rhetoric, which is suitable enough *if it does not contradict the truths of philosophy*, and . . . the grace of Music, *a servant of mine* . . ." (emphasis added). In this context, rhetoric and music are part of the poetry of the *Consolation*.

29. For a similar line of reasoning based upon the imagination as a mediating faculty, see Scarry, "The Well-Rounded Sphere," 99 ff.

30. Referred to in the *Consolation* as an "image" (*imago*), "figure" (*figura*), or "form" (*forma*).

to restore the faculty of imagination to its rightful place in the hierarchy of the soul's faculties. *In a certain sense,* as the imagination mediates between sensation and reason, so too the poems with their images mediate between the prosaic sections.[31] Furthermore, the final poem of each book includes an admonition to look up (toward reason) rather than down (toward sensation). Philosophy is determined that the poetry point beyond itself to higher things.[32] Thus far we have focused on the character of Boethius, we turn now to his condition.

We have already made some headway toward determining Boethius the patient's condition in our treatment of him as a character. Let's resume our discussion where we left off with Lady Philosophy. After ejecting the Muses of elegiac poetry and installing her own Muses in their stead, the focus turns once again to Boethius, whose sight is still so "dimmed by tears" that he cannot recognize Philosophy: "I lay there astonished, my eyes staring at the earth [*in terram*], silently waiting to see what she would do" (I.1.13). In the "song" that follows, Philosophy reproves Boethius for his anxiety, reminding him that he was once a man "free beneath the open heaven" who "sought the causes of things"; now, however, he lies "bound down by heavy chains, the light of his mind gone out; his head is bowed down and he is forced to stare at the dull earth" (I.m.2.27).

At least three details from these passages shed light on Boethius the patient's condition at this point in the dialogue: his silent passivity, his earth-bound gaze, and his literal and figurative bondage. Earlier we drew attention to Boethius's initial silent passivity; here too he waits in silence for his unknown deliverer to take action. Boethius is truly a *patient* in the basic sense of the word—that is, one

---

31. This insight is Scarry's ("The Well-Rounded Sphere," 102). There are obvious limitations to this analogy.

32. This, of course, is also why the *Consolation* ends in prose, not poetry. For an excellent account of poetry in the *Consolation*, see Gerard O'Daly, *The Poetry of Boethius* (Duckworth, 1991).

who "suffers" or undergoes action rather than carrying it out himself. Second, there is his earth-bound gaze. Philosophy's reference to the "dull earth" (*stolidam terram*) reminds us of Boethius's own comment earlier about staring at the earth. He only looks downward; he cannot redirect his eyes upward to higher things. Third, and closely connected with the first two, is his bondage. He was once a free man; now he is bound by chains. The dramatic setting for the *Consolation* is during his imprisonment by Theodoric, as Boethius is awaiting execution. As deplorable and unjust as this literal, physical imprisonment is, it is only external. Even when his body is bound with physical chains, his mind can still be free. But as Philosophy tells us, "[T]he light of [Boethius'] mind has gone out." From her vantage point, Boethius's internal bondage is far worse than what physical chains or any other external constraints could do to him. In essence, Boethius the patient has relinquished his freedom; he has snuffed out the light of his mind by allowing his disordered passions to overcome his reason. Enlightened freedom and its recovery is one of the recurring themes throughout the *Consolation*. It becomes explicit in the discussion of providence and free will in Book V, a discussion that "hinges on the question of '*libertas*' [freedom]."[33] So in one sense, the movement of the *Consolation* is a movement from the darkness of bondage to the light of freedom.

What, however, are the nature and cause of this bondage? We get our first glimpse in the second prose section, where Philosophy rebukes Boethius: "I gave you weapons that would have protected you with invincible power, if you had not thrown them away" (I.2.3;

33. Crabbe, "Literary Design," 242. The connection with freedom and its recovery is crucial; she elaborates: "It is not just the material world in general, but actual imprisonment and exile, perhaps even physical chains and certainly physical death towards which [Boethius] must learn indifference in order to return to his former philosophical state. The paradox involved in the apparently identical nature of his physical and spiritual situation and the long struggle to establish the unreality of the physical prison and escape the reality of mental chains provides the work's impetus."

see also I.m.4). As for his silence, Philosophy says it is due to shock, not shame. The latter would be better, she contends, for it would imply a least some recognition of his disgraceful condition. After the rebuke, she offers him some words of comfort: "There is no danger. You are suffering merely from lethargy, the common illness of deceived minds. *You have forgotten yourself a little,* but you will quickly be yourself again when you recognize me. To bring you to your senses, I shall quickly wipe the dark cloud of mortal things from your eyes" (I.2.5–6; emphasis added). When she does just that, Boethius the patient is then able to recognize her: "I saw that she was Philosophy, my nurse, in whose house I had lived from my youth" (I.3.2). Philosophy's initial diagnosis—that Boethius has "forgotten himself a little"—appears to have some merit. After wiping "the dark cloud of mortal things" from his eyes, Boethius is able to recognize her. This is just a beginning, though.

Shortly thereafter, she encourages him to "uncover [his] wound," which he does at length in the fourth prose section.[34] Boethius the patient recounts how, inspired by the example of Plato's philosopher-king, he embarked upon a life of public service. In his determined efforts to safeguard justice, Boethius made many powerful enemies who eventually used their power (and rampant political corruption in the regime) to entrap him. The whole of the fourth prose section is a "long protestation of innocence"[35] that calls into question God's providential justice in governing human affairs. Similar themes are underscored in the embittered prayer that follows: "You govern all things, each according to its destined purpose. Human acts alone, O Ruler of All, You refuse to restrain within just bounds. Why should uncertain Fortune control our lives? . . . Ruler of all things, calm the roiling waves and, as You rule the immense heavens, rule also the earth in stable concord [*firma stabiles . . . terras*]" (I.m.5.48).

34. I.4 is by far the longest prose section in Book I.

35. Chadwick, *The Consolations*, 227.

This response makes clear to Philosophy that Boethius's condition is far worse than she had initially supposed: "When I first saw you downcast and crying, I knew you were in misery and exile. But without your story I would not have known how desperate your exile is. You have not been driven out of your homeland; you have willfully wandered away" (I.5.2–3). As with Boethius's imprisonment, so with his exile: the outward, physical exile is far less devastating then the inward, spiritual one.[36] He is dissociated from himself, estranged from himself, exiled from himself. Furthermore, his exile is self-imposed.[37] The severity of the problem is evident in his response to Philosophy's request to uncover his wound. She "asks what is wrong with *him*, but he responds by telling her what is wrong with *the world*."[38] He interprets his plight in an entirely earthbound, physical way; and as his prayer indicates, he asks for an external, physical solution—*firma stabiles terras*—"make the earth stable!"[39] Given the severity of the case, Philosophy decides upon a treatment plan that is carefully proportioned to his condition: "[B]ecause you are upset by sorrow and anger, and so blown about by the tumult of your feelings, you are not now in the right frame of mind to take strong medicine. For the time being, then, I shall use more gentle treatment, so that your hardened and excited condition may be softened by gentle handling and thus prepared for more potent remedies" (I.5.11–12).

---

36. Again, Green: "His exile from Rome represents his separation from the true country of the mind, a self-imposed wandering in an alien land of transitory satisfactions. . . ." (introduction to *The Consolation of Philosophy*, xxiii).

37. Compare St. Augustine's comment in his *Confessions*: "I sighed after such freedom, but was bound not by an iron imposed by anyone else but by the iron of my own choice" [VIII.v.10]. Saint Augustine, *Confessions*, trans., with an introduction and notes by Henry Chadwick (Oxford University Press, 1991), 140.

38. Twu, "This Is Comforting?," 35–36; emphasis in original. This amounts to a tragic inversion of G. K. Chesterton's comment when asked, "What is wrong with the world?"

39. Twu, 36.

In the next prose section, Philosophy asks Boethius a series of questions to test his state of mind (*statum mentis*; I.6.1). First, she asks him a few questions leading up to one about how the world is governed. He is perplexed by the question and doesn't know how to respond (I.6.3–8). She next asks what the end or goal (*finis*) of all things is. He says that he has heard it once, but grief has dulled his memory; he does know, however, that all things come from God (I.6.10–12). Finally, she comes to the question, "What is man?" (*Quid homo sit*). Boethius replies that he is "a rational animal, and mortal" (*rationale animal atque mortale*). Philosophy encourages him to say more, asking whether he knows anything else about what he is. He responds, "No, nothing" (*Nihil*; I.6.14–16). "Now," she says, "I know another cause of your sickness, and the most important [*maximam*]: you have forgotten what you are" (I.6.17).

This exchange between patient and physician is crucial to understanding Boethius's condition.[40] Recall Philosophy's initial, provisional diagnosis: "You have forgotten yourself a little." Since that initial diagnosis, she has been tirelessly laboring to help her patient remember himself. The more Boethius says, the more he reveals just how grave his condition is. When Philosophy finally asks him what man is, she is not looking for the common textbook answer; rather, she is trying to get him to remember *who he is in relation to God*—that is, he has an immortal soul with a destiny beyond the death of his mortal body.[41] Another way of putting this is to say that the account Boethius gives fails to consider that humans are persons created by God and for a personal relationship with him. We will return to the importance of personhood below. For now, we

40. In the analysis that follows, I am indebted to the insightful reading of this passage proposed by Twu (37).

41. "Merely to answer the question 'What is man?' with the Aristotelian definition 'a rational, mortal animal,' is to disclose a loss of awareness of one's higher self and of the guiding hand of providence in ordering the world" (Chadwick, *The Consolations*, 227).

should note that this is precisely what he is most deeply confused about in his own account of his current situation and the prayer that follows it. With head downcast and eyes focused on the "dull earth," he has no hope either of knowing himself or of understanding his place in the providential plan of God.[42]

With her patient's telling admissions of ignorance in mind, Philosophy gives her full and final diagnosis:

> You are confused because you have forgotten what you are, and, therefore, you are upset because you are in exile and stripped of all your possessions. Because you are ignorant of the purpose of things, you think that stupid and evil men are powerful and happy. And, because you have forgotten how the world is governed, you suppose that these changes of your fortune came about without purpose. Such notions are enough to cause not only sickness but death. (I.6.18–19)

Philosophy's diagnosis lays out the three fundamental causes of her patient's sickness. In the order of her dialectical examination, they go from least to most grave; in the diagnosis, the order is reversed. Beginning with the least grave, Boethius acknowledges *that* the world is governed by God, but he does not know *how*. Ignorance of how the world is governed leads Boethius to believe that his reversal of fortune occurred with no purpose. Second, while he believes God to be the source or origin (*principium*) of all things, he is ignorant of the end or purpose (*finis*) of all things. Lacking this knowledge, he has come to believe that wicked men are powerful and happy. Finally, the greatest (*maximam*) cause of his illness is that he has forgotten what he is. This lack of self-knowledge gave rise to his willingness to surrender himself to grief, self-pity, and even despair at the loss of his position and possessions. In typical Socratic fashion,

42. For Boethius, who follows Augustine on this point, genuine self-knowledge is grounded in a knowledge of God.

Philosophy begins by revealing to her patient the knowledge of his own ignorance—Boethius comes to know what he does not know. With this three-fold diagnosis in place, we are poised to see how Philosophy's plan of treatment unfolds. The first book has introduced us to the characters and informed us of the patient's condition. The remaining books take up the cure—that is, the "consolation" of Philosophy, strictly speaking.[43]

Wisdom, the Liberal Arts, and Persons

For present purposes, instead of exploring her consolation in detail, I want to draw attention to three fundamental concerns that Boethius the author keeps at the forefront of his mind from his earliest writings to this, his final work: wisdom, the liberal arts, and the human person. The three are closely connected in the passages from Book I that we have been considering. First and most obviously, Lady Philosophy is a personification of *philosophia,* that is, the love of wisdom. In Book I, Lady Philosophy encourages and exhorts Boethius to *return* to the love of wisdom. As the remainder of the *Consolation* makes clear, this wisdom is the fulfillment of the natural

43. One might be tempted to think that Philosophy's threefold diagnosis would serve as a principle of the order and structure of the remaining books. Although she does address each of the three issues in one form or another, they do not serve as a "key" to the order and structure of Books II-V. For details on where each of the three diagnoses is addressed, see Barrett, *Boethius*, 81; and McMahon, *Understanding*, 241–42. Among the many helpful accounts of the whole work, see Myra L. Uhlfelder†, *The Consolation of Philosophy as Cosmic Image*, Medieval and Renaissance Texts and Studies 474 (Arizona Center for Medieval and Renaissance Studies, 2018); John Marenbon, *Boethius* (Oxford University Press, 2003), 96–163; Paul A. Olson, *The Journey to Wisdom: Self-Education in Patristic and Medieval Literature* (University of Nebraska Press, 1995), 117–46; and Edmund Reiss, *Boethius* (Twayne Publishers, 1982), 80–153. P. G. Walsh offers a useful summary in the Oxford World's Classics edition: Boethius, *The Consolation of Philosophy*, trans., with an introduction and notes, by P. G. Walsh (Oxford University Press, 1999), li–lii.

human desire to know the truth; but it is also the *loving* pursuit of order. Recalling the opening quote from the Book of Wisdom, let's now consider it in light of the preceding verses as well:

> [22b] For in [Wisdom] there is
> a spirit that is intelligent, holy,
> unique, manifold, subtle,
> mobile, clear, unpolluted,
> distinct, invulnerable, loving the good,
> keen, irresistible,
> [23] beneficent, humane,
> steadfast, sure, free from anxiety,
> all-powerful, overseeing all,
> and penetrating through all spirits
> that are intelligent and pure and most subtle.
> [24] For wisdom is more mobile than any motion;
> because of her pureness she pervades and penetrates all things.
> [25] For she is a breath of the power of God,
> and a pure emanation of the glory of the Almighty;
> therefore nothing defiled gains entrance into her.
> [26] For she is a reflection of eternal light,
> a spotless mirror of the working of God,
> and an image of his goodness.
> [27] Though she is but one, she can do all things,
> and while remaining in herself, she renews all things;
> in every generation she passes into holy souls
> and makes them friends of God, and prophets;
> [28] for God loves nothing so much as the man who lives with wisdom.
> [29] For she is more beautiful than the sun,
> and excels every constellation of the stars.
> Compared with the light she is found to be superior,
> [30] for it is succeeded by the night,
> but against wisdom evil does not prevail.
> [8:1] She reaches mightily from one end
> of the earth to the other,
> and she orders all things well.

Clearly, this is a capacious vision of wisdom. In *Consolation* III.12, Lady Philosophy leads Boethius the patient to much the same conclusion, i.e., that wisdom (or the highest Good) rules all things mightily and orders all things well.[44] Thus, bound up in the truth and goodness of wisdom is also the beautiful ordering of all things. The one who seeks wisdom naturally seeks to discern this beautiful order in the cosmos; beyond this, though, such a seeker also makes every effort to see that this same beautiful order is present within himself.[45] Thus, the attainment of wisdom is inseparable from the perfection of our nature. Recall that in her assessment of Boethius, Lady Philosophy first notes that he has "forgotten himself a little" and ultimately concludes that he has "forgotten what he is." Once a student of wisdom, the natural pursuit of a well-ordered human being, Boethius must return to himself by returning to wisdom. Only then can he become "recollected" and return soul and body, reason, will, and passions, to their proper order.

For centuries in the Western tradition up to the time of Boethius, there were certain studies—studies we now call the "liberal arts"—that enabled the student to begin and to sustain this process of discerning order and of bringing about order within himself. On

44. Although some scholars doubt the connection between what Lady Philosophy says here and the passage from the Book of Wisdom, there are convincing reasons for concluding that this is exactly what Lady Philosophy intends to bring to mind. For an overview of this question, see the Goins & Wyman edition, notes 90 and 103.

45. Compare the following passage from Plato's *Timaeus*: "God devised and bestowed upon us vision to the end that we might behold the revolutions of Reason in the Heaven and use them for the revolvings of the reasoning that is within us, these being akin to those, the perturbable to the imperturbable; and that, through learning and sharing in calculations which are correct by their nature, by imitation of the absolutely unvarying revolutions of the God we might stabilize the variable revolutions within ourselves" (47 b/c). By observing the beautiful order in the heavens, one is able to imitate the order of the cosmos within one's own soul. Plato, *Plato in Twelve Volumes*, vol. 9, trans. W. R. M. Lamb (Harvard University Press, 1925).

the surface of the *Consolation*, we see one of these arts, namely, dialectic, dramatically portrayed in the philosophical dialogue itself. In their common pursuit of the truth through the give-and-take of philosophical inquiry, Lady Philosophy and Boethius model and enact the search for wisdom through logically stating, questioning, responding to, and reconciling truths in what has been said. At a deeper level, the *Consolation* also incorporates the arts of the quadrivium—arithmetic, geometry, music, and astronomy. For now, suffice it to say that the *Consolation of Philosophy* draws upon many, if not all, of what would later be called the seven liberal arts. Although these arts came to be considered the proper *beginning* of a liberal education, we must avoid two common confusions about them today. First, while a liberal education begins with the liberal arts, it is neither necessary nor even desirable to assume that other studies—for example, biology or business or whatever—must *also* be liberal arts. This is the misconception of many so-called "liberal arts colleges and universities" who either tacitly or explicitly assume that a "liberal arts education" is simply one that requires some significant number or variety of courses outside one's major field(s) of study. Another common error is to assume a "one-and-done" approach to the liberal arts. In other words, on this view the liberal arts are indeed distinct from other fields of study; but they are treated as subjects one should take at the beginning of an education and that can safely be dispensed with and forgotten thereafter. On the contrary, the liberal arts as traditionally construed are *essentially human arts*—arts that are perfective of our nature as human knowers, arts that one can and should continue to practice throughout one's life. While biology and business are not liberal arts, one who approaches these studies with a mind actively enlivened by the liberal arts will no doubt learn biology and business more quickly and more thoroughly than one who simply approaches these studies as "information" that must be assimilated and applied as needed to so-called "real-world" problems.

This brings us to our third consideration: the person. Anyone who reads the *Consolation of Philosophy* immediately sees that the work is nothing if not deeply personal. A conspicuous example of this is the fourth prose element in Book I (and the poem that follows) that was mentioned above, where Boethius pours out his heart to Lady Philosophy, protesting the intense and unjust pain and suffering that he is currently enduring. One key aspect of what it means to be a human person is the irreducible and non-transferable character of each person's interiority. While we share a common human nature, each of us is a distinct person, unique and irreplaceable. St. Augustine focuses the reader's attention on such interiority throughout his *Confessions*, especially in the first ten books (as well as in other writings of his). This aspect of human personhood is on display in Book II of the *Consolation*, where we find that "man can only experience authentic happiness within his own interiority."[46] As we will see shortly, Boethius's reflections on the human person had a significant influence on later thought on the topic—especially among the Catholic personalists of the twentieth and twenty-first centuries (e.g., St. John Paul II, Robert Spaemann, and Pope Benedict XVI).

With these three enduring concerns of Boethius in mind, let's turn to his writings to see how they have influenced the development of Catholic education through the centuries and to get a sense of how they could contribute to the renewal of Catholic education today.

The Works of Boethius

The earliest works we have of Boethius are his writings on the liberal arts. Most likely, he wrote *De arithmetica* around 500 and *De musica* around 510, both heavily influenced by works of Nicomachus of Gerasa (bearing similar titles) and the latter also by Ptolemy's *Harmonica*. There is some evidence that Boethius wrote an entire treatise on

46. Benedict XVI, "Boethius and Cassiodorus," 2.

geometry, but only fragments remain. He also translated many works on logic, including Porphyry's *Isagoge* and the entire *Organon* of Aristotle, composing commentaries on most of these works as well. Boethius wrote several original works on logic: *De divisione, De syllogism categorico, De topicis differentiis,* et alia. Since there were already good guides in Latin to the arts of grammar and rhetoric—the works of Donatus and Priscian for the former, and many works by Cicero as well as Quintilian and others for the latter—he did not compose independent guides to these liberal arts. Even so, Boethius makes ample use of the arts of grammar and rhetoric in the *Consolation* as well as in his *Opuscula Sacra,* theological works on a variety of topics.

To give a sense of the importance of the liberal arts as Boethius saw them, Henry Chadwick draws attention to a passage from his commentary on Aristotle's *Categories.* There Aristotle makes the unobjectionable assertion that if something is to be known, it must be knowable. Conversely, he points out that something can be knowable without anyone knowing it for two reasons: (1) either because it has yet to be discovered (the example given here is the method of squaring the circle) or (2) because it has been forgotten and must be rediscovered with much effort. "This last observation fascinated Boethius," Chadwick notes, "and his commentary on this passage treats it as a word for his own times." Chadwick continues:

> It is his [Boethius'] great fear that amid the general collapse of higher studies in his time, the knowledge acquired by the philosophers and scientists of classical Greece may simply be obliterated by a failure of transmission [*In Cat.* ii, 230C]. Books may lie in libraries but, if they are to survive for more than a generation, they need users who understand and value their contents or they will rapidly suffer from neglect, and the valuable space they occupy will be applied to other purposes. "It is one thing to have reason, another to use it," he writes [*In Porph. Isag.* II]. "To abandon the stretching of one's mind's power is to lose it" [*Perih.* ii, 79]. Or, with a sharper point, "Men who have long been idle in

> using their minds adopt positions from which they never move, and learn nothing until their old age" [*Intr. ad syll. cat.* 762C].

As Pope Benedict XVI pointed out in the general audience referred to above, Boethius wrote on the liberal arts "with the intention of passing on the Greco-Roman culture to . . . new generations [and] new times." Alongside the *Consolation*, Boethius's works on arithmetic and music were copied and used for centuries as key sources for education.[47] Arguably, today we stand as much in need of a renewal of *the actual practice of the liberal arts* as did those for whom Boethius originally wrote—if not more so.

Turning to his *Opuscula Sacra*, two are especially worthy of note in the present context. Above, we saw the connection in the mind of Boethius between wisdom and order. In chapter 2 of his *De Trinitate*, Boethius lays out three divisions of speculative science: natural science, which "deals with motion and is not abstract"; mathematics, which "does not deal with motion and . . . is not abstract"; and theology, which "does not deal with motion and . . . is abstract" (3). In a contemporary translation that bears the title *The Division and Methods of the Sciences*, and is part a larger commentary on Boethius's *De Trinitate*, St. Thomas Aquinas provides a literal commentary on this chapter and then offers a detailed exploration of Boethius's comments on the division and methods of the speculative sciences. Both the original work of Boethius and Thomas's commentary on it assume a much broader idea of what counts as a science, one that could help Catholic educators today in seeing both the order of the disciplines and the way that this order can serve them in teaching their students the unity and integrity of all knowledge.

47. As Scott Goins and Barbara H. Wyman point out in the introduction to their critical edition of the *Consolation*, "Studies in manuscripts have demonstrated the general availability of these works [*De arithmetica*, *De musica*, and *Consolation*], the surviving examples of which equal the works of Saint Augustine and the Bible in their extent, number, age, and completeness" (xiii).

Another important contribution from the theological works of Boethius is the definition of a person found in his treatise *Against Eutyches and Nestorius*. In the process of responding to Christological heresies defended by the two men named in the title, Boethius defines a person as an "individual substance of a rational nature" (*naturae rationabilis individua substantia; Contra Eutychen et Nestorium*, 3). This definition was to have a great influence on later reflections on persons divine and human. Much as Christian authors before him had done (e.g., Tertullian in Latin [*persona*] and Justin Martyr in Greek [*prosopon*]), Boethius here employs the term in speaking of God. All these authors were seeking to speak truly either of the Holy Trinity, as one Being in three persons, or of Christ as one person with two natures, or both. In time, the understanding of God as personal becomes the ground for understanding human beings as persons, who are made in the image and likeness of God. As Robert Spaemann points out, "Boethius's definition, though by no means unchallenged, lies behind all medieval discussion of the person. . . ."[48] What is more, it remains the starting point for the consideration of persons by influential Catholic personalists of the twentieth and twenty-first centuries, such as St. John Paul II, Pope Benedict XVI, and Spaemann himself.

Finally, we return to the *Consolation of Philosophy*, by far Boethius's best-known work today. In his book *The Discarded Image: An Introduction to Medieval and Renaissance Literature*, C. S. Lewis, speaking of the *Consolation*, says, "Until about two hundred years ago it would . . . have been hard to find an educated man in any European country who did not love it." As we noted above, the *Consolation of Philosophy* draws together the three perennial considerations of Boethius—wisdom, the liberal arts, and persons. If you haven't read (and re-read) the *Consolation* already, I encourage you to do so.

48. Robert Spaemann, *Persons: The Difference Between 'Someone' and 'Something,'* Oxford Studies in Theological Ethics (Oxford University Press, 2006), 29.

Boethius was brutally tortured and executed at the hands of Theodoric in 524 at forty-four years of age. He was canonized as Saint Severinus Boethius by Pope Leo XIII in 1883 and is buried in San Pietro in Ciel d'Oro in Pavia, Italy, in the same church where St. Augustine of Hippo is laid to rest. St. Augustine's large and ornate tomb is at the center of the sanctuary. The tomb of Boethius, much smaller and more modest, is in the crypt immediately beneath the tomb of Augustine. This is fitting, since Boethius, although a great teacher himself, was a remarkable student of the writings of St. Augustine. One could reasonably say that Boethius's writings on the liberal arts, philosophy, and theology support the magnificent work of this great Doctor of the Church. If you ever find yourself in Milan, make time for a day trip to Pavia to visit the tombs of Augustine and Boethius, two saints who have left a rich legacy for the renewal of Catholic liberal education today.

Saints Augustine and Severinus Boethius, pray for us!

7 Cassiodorus

Erik Z. D. Ellis

Historical Context: The Sixth-Century World

Magnus Aurelius Cassiodorus Senator was born into a distinguished Roman family around the year 485, within a decade of 476, when the last western emperor of the divided Roman empire, Romulus Augustulus, was forced to abdicate by Odovacer, an Ostrogothic military commander in Roman service. Odovacer informed Zeno, emperor in Constantinople, of the abdication and suggested that the West might do without a replacement. Although historians since the eighteenth century have dated the "Fall of the Roman Empire" to this event, no one at the time, or indeed for centuries afterwards, would have seen this most recent barbarian interference in Roman politics as remarkable. Odovacer was merely participating in a tradition that had been well and thoroughly established for centuries, following the examples of Stilicho, Alaric, Attila, and numerous other barbarian warlords who had been the power behind the throne and yet refused to take it. For the time being, the Roman Senate continued to serve its ancient functions, taxes went out from Italy eastward, and the *aureus*, the imperial golden coin, continued to bind Western Europe to the Eastern and the Southern Mediterranean in what modern economists might term an economic union.

As Henri Pirenne demonstrated more than a century ago, the watershed between antiquity and the Middle Ages is the seventh rather than the fifth century.[1] Asian spices and Egyptian papyrus

1. The "Pirenne Thesis" is given fullest expression in the 1937 *Mohammed and Charlemagne*, which ought to have displaced the "Gibbon Thesis" and *The Decline and Fall of the Roman Empire* as the starting points for thinking about the transition from antiquity to the middle ages.

continued to flow into Frankish Gaul until the Caliphs made the Mediterranean an Islamic lake. It was only as Arab armies crossed the Bosporus and the Pyrenees in the early eighth century that the seaborne empire of the Romans, which had ensured peace and prosperity since the days of Augustus, finally and truly came to an end. For most of the next millennium, the Romans in the east would use their diminished army and navy and still immense cultural and ceremonial prestige to keep the eternal flame burning, though not in Rome itself. Overland routes, always slow and expensive, had already become treacherous as a seemingly endless succession of steppe peoples streamed into Europe from the fourth century onwards. Now for its descendants in the West, the Roman Empire would be an idea and a challenge more than a political reality. Despite these shocks to the *status quo*, the industry, faith, and diligence of educators, scholars, clergy, religious, and jurists ensured the continuity of Roman culture and the catholicity and orthodoxy of the Church.

And yet, things were changing, however slowly, already in the sixth century. The population of Rome numbered perhaps 1 million in 410, the year the city's sack by Alaric put St. Augustine into a catatonic state and inspired him to write *City of God*. By the time of Pope St. Gregory the Great, a little less than two centuries later, the population had declined to 30,000. Historians have identified many reasons for this precipitous decline. During the sieges and sacks of late antiquity, the famed aqueducts of ancient Rome had been cut. Lack of fresh water and malnutrition encouraged the spread of disease, which meant that the weakened defenders had neither the corporate manpower nor the individual strength to repair their damaged infrastructure once the sieges were lifted. Over some three centuries, these problems compounded, and natural disasters in the sixth century roughly coincided to ensure one of history's greatest demographic cataclysms.

Along with nomadic incursions, epidemics have always been the chief enemy of interdependent, highly urbanized civilizations.

In the sixth century, the Roman and Persian empires suffered a particularly virulent outbreak of plague that has uncharitably been called "Justinianic" but that modern genetic studies have identified as *Yersinia pestis*, a precursor to the same Bubonic plague that through mass depopulation and the subsequent socio-economic revolution kickstarted the transition from medieval to modern culture in the fourteenth century. The first breakout occurred in 541, and cases recurred at intervals through about 750. Five years before, chroniclers throughout the world witnessed a mysterious event that historians now term the "volcanic winter of 536." An as yet unidentified volcano shot forth tons of matter into the atmosphere, causing a diffusion of the sun's rays. Justinian's court historian Procopius writes that "the sun gave forth its light without brightness." Temperatures dropped, crops failed, and famine ensued. This state of affairs continued for some years, perhaps prolonged by subsequent volcanic activity. Cassiodorus discusses the difficulties produced by the event in his official correspondence, speaking of a year without seasons in which the sky assumed a sickly pallor and the sun took on a blue tinge.[2] For observers in the sixth century, time itself seemed to have stopped. The climactic changes were so severe and prolonged that scholars now posit the existence of a "Late Antique Little Ice Age." When the plague arrived, it ran rampant through an already reduced, weakened, and demoralized population.

Religious and Political Tensions

As if sent to complete a disastrous triple, violent earthquakes struck the eastern Mediterranean from Alexandria to Antioch in 551. Due to high population density, the most destructive of these was the one that hit Beirut, home to the most famous school of Roman law

---

2. Cassiodorus, *Variae*, ed. S. J. B. Barnish (Liverpool University Press, 1992), 12.25.2.

in the East, which had long been an island of Latinity in a sea of Hellenism. A massive tsunami wiped out many of the great ancient coastal cities, Beirut itself suffered massive destruction, and damage extended as far inland as the Jordan Valley. This was the societal and natural setting into which Cassiodorus was born and in which he worked, first as a civil servant, then as a minister of God.

Cassiodorus's lifetime did not see the fall of the Roman Empire, but it did witness the end of antiquity, at least in the West. The urban and maritime civilization that made the Mediterranean went into long decline as trade became more limited and the general level of culture sank the further north one travelled. Though social and political bonds were weakening, it would be a grave mistake to assume, as once was common, that the ancient cultural and economic links were broken. Even after all of these shocks, the West remained surprisingly cosmopolitan. Theodore, a seventh-century Greek-speaking Syrian archbishop of Canterbury and John Scotus Eriugena, a ninth-century Irish scholar whose subtle and profound knowledge of Greek, learned in his Irish monastery, are merely the best-known examples of the continuing vitality of the classical and Christian tradition in the West. The number of surviving pilgrims' accounts to Rome and Jerusalem, surely representing only a small fraction of the actual number of pilgrimages made in the half-millennium between Cassiodorus and the First Crusade, are enough to dispel the old story of the Dark Ages. The light did indeed grow dim, sputtered, and even went out in a few places, but it was never fully extinguished, and Cassiodorus was one of the most important of those who worked to keep the fire burning.

Despite five hundred years of principate and dominate, the republican traditions of Rome remained strong among the old Italian families. "Old" here is a relative rather than an exact term. The Roman socio-political system was famous for a form of generational mobility that might see a family go from slavery to senatorial rank in 150 years. Horace, the greatest Latin lyric poet and a subtle philosopher, was the son of a freedman and the grandson of a slave. Since Republican times, the Roman elite had had a way of exhausting itself in civil wars, making space for *novi homines* or "new men" to enter public service, complete the *cursus honorum,* and eventually displace and replace the old patrician families. Among the great classical Latin authors, one finds very few other than Caesar who were proper Romans: Cicero, Livy, and Virgil were all from Cisalpine Gaul; Lucan and the two Senecas were Spanish; Augustine was, like Terence, who could be called the earliest classical Latin author, an African. Although these families represented the infusion of new blood in the *Res Publica,* they sought to enrich rather than to destroy the systems they inherited. Change was of course constant, but it was conservative and organic rather than sudden and revolutionary.

The fourth and fifth centuries were periods of intense theological discussion and therefore, conflict. In what many observers considered a miraculous turn of events, the Roman emperor Constantine embraced Christianity just a few decades after his predecessor, Diocletian, inaugurated the most severe and widespread persecution of Christians in the history of Church. Constantine found that his Church was deeply divided on Christological issues and sought to establish a basis of conformity. At issue was the reconciliation of Christ's humanity with his divinity. Followers of the priest Arius, whom history calls the Arians, emphasized Christ's humanity to the extent that he could appear to be completely subordinated to the Father, even a creature. When their doctrine was excluded by the formula now termed the Nicene Creed, their preachers left the empire and found receptive audiences among the Germanic tribesmen.

Arian Christianity spread quickly among these groups and became closely tied to their ethnic identity. The Vandals, who took Africa and the Mediterranean islands; the Visigoths, who settled Spain; the Ostrogoths, who settled Italy; and the Lombards, who would follow after them, were all Arian Christians rather than the pagans many imagine them to be. Their unorthodox faith gave them a certain participation in wider Mediterranean culture but allowed them to remain apart from their Roman subjects and preserve a distinct identity. The Goths, at least, had the Bible in their own language and had developed something like a classical liturgical register for it, which they preserved for many centuries. Many of the archaic Christian terms in English, like "church," "blessing," and "housel" have their origins in this early and largely forgotten form of Germanic Christianity.

As Newman tells us, allegiance to the Nicene, Catholic faith or to Arian Christianity implied ethnic identity, such that already in the fifth century, the terms "Roman" and "Catholic" were synonymous.[3] These tensions had profound reflexes for Cassiodorus's political and religious careers. This ethnic tension tied to religious doctrine also endangered the cultural unity and communion of the Western and Eastern Romans. Theological dispute had not of course ceased with the Council of Nicaea. The fifth century witnessed the articulation of models of Christ's nature that sought to redress the problems with Arianism and were in danger of moving to the other extreme, allowing Christ's divinity to blot out his humanity. This spectrum of doctrine, called "Monophytism" or "Miaphytism," was condemned at the Council of Chalcedon in 451. While this met with general approval in both Old and New Rome, large numbers of Christians in the patriarchates of Alexandria and Antioch rejected the Chalcedonian definition. As with Arianism, allegiance to one doctrine or another tended to track with ethnic differentiation as Coptic and Syriac identities and literatures emerged after almost a millennium of Greek cultural hegemony. In Italy, heterodoxy was a marker of Germanic otherness, as intentionally cultivated by the occupiers as it was resented and abhorred

3. See Newman's discussion in John Henry Newman, *An Essay on the Development of Christian Doctrine* (London: James Toovey, 1845), 6.3.5.

by the occupied. In the East, competition with orthodoxy, articulated in Greek and enforced by the Roman state, gave expression to native resentment of centuries of cultural and political subordination by their own groups of northern occupiers.

The Life and Public Career of Cassiodorus

Given the great economic importance of Egypt and Syria, the emperors in Constantinople were of course eager to heal divisions and return all members of the Church to Roman unity. In 482, the emperor Zeno issued the *Henotikon*, which we might translate into English as the "instrument of unity." Acacius, the patriarch of Constantinople responsible for drafting the document, intended to provide definitions in language loose enough to allow a certain plasticity of interpretation. In the end, the *Henotikon* pleased no one and only made things worse as the two sides lined up to point out the document's failures rather than to appreciate its irenic intent. Over the next two years, Pope Felix III sought clarification from Acacius, and when the latter continuously delayed, excommunicated him in 484. The "Acacian Schism" between Rome and Constantinople would last until 519, very nearly an entire biblical generation.

Rome itself was hardly better off. Even within the Catholic community, there was bitter division, stemming from a disputed papal election and resulting in a local schism that lasted more than a decade. Simony and politicking, which had been infecting the Roman Church for some time already, became normalized in the period known as the "Ostrogothic Papacy." While orthodoxy and catholicity remained intact, scandal ran rampant as senatorial families competed with one another to win their non-Catholic king's approval for their candidacy with more or less open payouts, factionalism, and the promise of control and division of the Church's temporalities after election. Accommodating the unfortunately well-established practice of subjecting clerical tenure to imperial approval to the new realities of Germanic kingship, this state of affairs sowed the seeds of the investiture controversies that would be harvested at the beginning of the second millennium.

It was into this late Roman world, riven by social, political, economic, and religious conflict and threatened by changing weather and natural disasters, that Cassiodorus was born and came of age. Cassiodorus's family had come to Italy from Syria a few generations back, settling in the South, which had for centuries been called Magna Graecia and which still sustains pockets of Greek speakers throughout Calabria and Sicily. Urban life in Syria had been conducted in Greek since the days of Alexander, and the family name, Kassiodoros, is evidence that the clan had Greek roots. The Cassiodori had almost certainly been involved in public service for many centuries in the east when our Cassiodorus's ancestors decided to establish an Italian branch; "Senator" was his surname, inherited from his forbears, rather than his title, an indication of the family's successful entry into the establishment. These Cassiodori at some point became allied to the ancient Gens Anicia, making our Cassiodorus a cousin of Anicius Manlius Severinus Boethius, the subject of another chapter in this handbook, and a relation of the Symmachi, another powerful and influential family that produced consuls and popes. The Anicii were reputedly the first of the old families to embrace Christianity, but their change of faith in no way diminished their historical commitment to the cultivation of *Romanitas*. Already in the fourth century, members of this circle, including the grammarian Donatus, the commentator Servius, and the philosopher Macrobius, worked to reconcile the pagan tradition and the Christian faith. Among their activities was the editing of Vergil and the production of large manuscript codices containing his work, examples of which, incredibly, have survived to the present day. Without their work, it is unlikely that the Virgilian tradition, including both the Poet's works and the mass of commentaries that had grown up around them, would have been transmitted to posterity. As we will see, Cassiodorus followed this example in both theory and practice in the last phase of his life.

We know very little of Cassiodorus's early life. One of the first secure dates is his consulship in 514, nearly forty years into the Gothic dominion of Italy and a sign of the still relatively intact functioning of Roman institutions. He held in addition to this highest republican office a number of other titles, offices, and positions in both imperial and Gothic service. In 525, he succeeded Boethius as Theodoric's "prime minister." The king died the following year, ushering in a decade of internecine intrigue and warfare among the Goths that further destabilized Italy and practically invited Justinian to attempt reconquest of the Latin homeland. Once hostilities commenced, civil government broke down, and Cassiodorus decided to observe the progress of the war from Ravenna, where his attentions turned away from secular matters to philosophy and theology. It is also likely that at this time he took up some of the ascetic practices that would anchor his second life as a monastic, first in Constantinople and then at Vivarium, the monastery he founded in southern Italy.

As Roman quaestor and praetorian prefect for a Gothic king, Cassiodorus had to navigate delicate political and social realities. Roman and Goth were not equal before the law; rather, each was governed according to his own law. The Roman civil and canon law (in the sixth century, the border between the two was indistinct) competed and mixed with the legal traditions that the invaders had brought with them. This situation gave rise to the so-called "Leges Barbarorum," which cast the oral law of the Germanic tribes into the Latin language and something like Roman form. This double legal system worked well in theory, but it was not practical for the two communities to stay isolated, and soon, individuals with mixed Gothic and Roman parentage upset the precarious balance this state of affairs had produced. So long as Goths murdered Goths, and Romans swindled Romans, it was trivial to reckon *wergild* or indemnify injury. But if an individual with a Gothic mother and a Roman father cheated a Goth with a Roman grandparent, under which system of laws was the judgment to be made? Decades spent finding equitable answers to these questions gave Cassiodorus a subtle intellect.

The major source for Cassiodorus's public career is the collection of the *Variae*; Cassiodorus's modern biographer has derided his subject's Latin style as "wooden and artificial,"[4] but others have admired his baroque purple prose. In ages different from our own, when "His serene highness" was, rather than "Mr. President," the standard form of address for the head of state, Cassiodorus's brand of rhetoric met with greater approval. As Isocrates and Thomas More knew and demonstrated, rhetoric becomes most necessary precisely when politics becomes most dangerous. Anyone can give an elected official a piece of his mind; it takes a highly trained and cultivated orator to admonish a tyrant while outwardly appearing to offer a panegyric. The delicate political realities of the sixth century demanded a finely articulated rhetoric, and Cassiodorus was a master of the niceties of language that helped ensure that the sword did not completely replace the pen as the principal instrument of governance in Italy.

The Written Word: Rhetoric and Orthography

Beyond this, the *Variae* served later generations as a massive collection of formularies, an early version of the *artes dictaminis* that would be the backbone of medieval training in the art of writing. Although Cassiodorus's time and the period immediately following have traditionally been called the "Dark Ages," it is important to spend some effort on this word "writing," for it is precisely in this period that classical rhetoric ceases to be a primarily oral phenomenon. As the occasions for persuasive public speaking grew fewer and fewer in the midst of near-constant warfare and the decline of urban life, the importance of the written word became, somewhat paradoxically, ever larger.

4. J. J. O'Donnell, *Cassiodorus* (University of California Press, 1979), ix.

Despite the trouble that our continued use of fourteenth-century orthographic conventions poses to even native English speakers, this oddity of our language ensures that even with a wide divergence in oral performance, Australians, Minnesotans, and Scottish Highlanders can all write the same language and be reasonably sure that the message will come across. A teacherly concern for spelling and good style is characteristic of all of Cassiodorus's works, and it is surely a sign of an abiding interest in the niceties of language that his final work, written when he was perhaps 93 years old, is *De Orthographia*. Cassiodorus compiled this textbook from the old Roman grammarians to ensure that the younger brothers in the monastery would not write a Latin that their peers in Gaul or Spain could not understand. This ultimate expression of Cassiodorus's concern for posterity surpassed previous guides to spelling, which had merely catalogued common mistakes, and built a foundation for literate culture in a world moving rapidly away from it. This effort ensured that Latinity would be participatory and productive, the object not merely of language study but of language acquisition. The long-lived and beautiful tradition of medieval Latin, although by no means an unchanged continuation of its classical pagan and patristic ancestors, is nonetheless a sign of Cassiodorus's success.

One final remark on the *Variae* that sheds light on the working methods and self-understanding of its author: to the twelve books of formulas and official correspondence, many manuscripts append a shorter work of Cassiodorus, *De Anima*. While the congruence of the two works may not have been Cassiodorus's original intent, it did have authorial sanction, and later readers have sought to find meaning in the arrangement.[5] This book adds one, the monad, to the sequence of twelve, a significant number, and both stands apart from them and completes them. In this numerological

5. Cassiodorus, *Explanation of the Psalms* [*Expositio Psalmorum*], ed. W. J. Burghardt, T. C. Lawler, and P. G. Walsh (Paulist Press, 1990), 145.2.

scheme, Cassiodorus echoes what Boethius wrote in the *De Arithmetica* and the literary architecture of St. Augustine's *Confessions*, a work also in thirteen books. Having published a carefully curated collection of the working materials of his public career, Cassiodorus turned to the contemplation of his own soul and of the nature of all souls. Over sixteen chapters, he poses and answers twelve questions about the origin, meaning, and destiny of human life and the discernment of human character. In two final chapters, he provides a summary of his work and charts a path forward both for himself and his readers:

> And so we have closed our little work with the number twelve, which adorns the heavens with a variety of constellations, which fills the year with the charm of the months, which has yielded in a providential arrangement the principal winds for the needs of the earth, which divides the hours of day and night into equal parts, so that rightly even this calculation, which is consecrated in such great arrangements of natural things, might be joined to the interpretation of the soul. It remains, wisest men who flourish in your intelligence, once we have passed over the mass of this world safely, to offer ourselves swiftly to that divine mercy through which the vision of the thinker is most fully illuminated. Let us understand Him, let us love Him, and then we truly know our souls, if we are wise through His beneficence. For He is the powerful and perfect master who speaks truth to our soul and enables us to perceive what He has said with enlightened mind. In the school of Christ indeed no heart can be found unteachable that has committed itself to him with wholeness of mind, nor can the heart be ignorant of what it seeks nor lose what it has gained by pious payment.[6]

Having achieved the highest estate of merely human honor, as did his predecessors St. Augustine and Boethius, Cassiodorus calls

6. Cassiodorus, *Institutes of Divine and Secular Learning [Institutes] and On the Soul [De Anima]*, ed. James W. Halporn (Liverpool University Press, 2004), 17.

his readers to conversion and marks his own. His mature understanding of his public service was not, as might be imagined in one who watched the political institutions that he worked so hard to preserve crumble around him, as something done in vain. Cassiodorus's was not a *contemptus mundi* but rather a deep *caritas* that saw his secular work as a preparation for the divine office he undertook in the changed circumstances of the second half of his life.

From Public Service to Divine Contemplation

Between the *Variae* and *De Orthographia*, Cassiodorus wrote the two works on which his modern reputation principally rests: the *Expositio Psalmorum* and the *Institutiones Divinarum et Saecularium Litterarum*. There is no unambiguous evidence for this period of Cassiodorus's life, but a likely conjecture is that he had a long period of "enforced leisure" following the fall of Gothic Italy that may have been something like house arrest. Though a Roman, Cassiodorus had dutifully served Gothic masters for decades and was likely suspected by the Eastern Romans when they retook the Italian peninsula. Perhaps retirement from public life and transfer to Constantinople, where he could be watched, was the cost of his freedom. Instead of fighting this state of affairs, Cassiodorus embraced his new environment and changed status, turning to the Psalms, the biblical text that was the flesh and bones of monastic life. Over the next two decades, he directed his labors towards the production of a commentary that would serve many as their first port of entry to the mighty flow of Psalm interpretation.

Two keys to the work's success are its form and limitation. Although Cassiodorus expressed his intention to expound the text of the Psalter according to the several senses of Scripture,[7] he gave disproportionate space to the allegorical sense. While much denigrated over the last two centuries, appreciation for the allegorical

7. *Expositio Psalmorum*, Praef.14.3.

sense is once again growing as Christians recognize it as the key to understanding the ties that bind the Old and New Testaments as well as the network of typological resonances that define the relationship between the liturgy and scripture. The Psalms, as individual poetic works, and the Psalter, as the earliest and even pre-Christian liturgical book of the Church, have always served individual Christians in finding their own lives reflected in the life of Christ, and the life of Christ as the exegetical key that fulfills the Old Testament and makes it comprehensible. In a sense, Cassiodorus's *Expositio* is his record of his own encounter with the "honey of souls"[8] that awakened his religious vocation and sustained it until the end of his earthly life.

For medieval and especially monastic Christians, reflection on the Psalms in this manner became, along with the Mass, a primary means of mimetic ascent. Cassiodorus's chief contribution was to formalize the mystagogical mode of the early Christians into something that could be packaged, taught, and repeated. It was an accommodation of divine inspiration to the methods of classical education. Where the early Christians had lived in tight-knit communities in urban centers ringing the Mediterranean basin, Cassiodorus's contemporaries were quite literally fleeing for the hills and contemplating the disappearance of literate culture. The sixth century demanded forms of culture that were portable and easily transferable. It needed handbooks. So, the *breviarium* became a useful and necessary literary form. Just as Boethius's *Consolatio* summarized Plato and Aristotle, St. Benedict took the centuries-old tradition of desert monasticism and packaged it in a "little rule for beginners," and Justinian reduced and reconciled a millennium of Roman law in his *Institutes* and *Code*, so Cassiodorus made the Psalter available to Christians who, in the changed circumstances of the sixth century, had not the leisure, learning, space, or wealth to develop or maintain libraries of homilies and commentaries.

8. *Exp. Ps.*, Praef.1.2.

Something like a law code, Cassiodorus's handbook follows a repeated formula in his treatment of each Psalm: *titulus, divisio, expositio,* and *conclusio*. The *titulus* explains the traditional headings of each Psalm, the *divisio* demonstrates how meaning and performance work in tandem in each Psalm's structure, and the *expositio* provides a verse-by-verse reading, usually running two to five pages. The *conclusiones* offer a summary of the preceding three sections, often taking the form of prayer. For this reason, later generations used these, isolated from the main text, to nourish their own devotional life. It is important to remember that Cassiodorus was the first to attempt such a project, and he brought it to completion in such a way that it long remained the work of first recourse for those seeking a better understanding of the Psalms they prayed and chanted day in and day out. Taken on this basis, it is hard to imagine a biblical commentary that has had more influence, however quiet and unacknowledged, in the history of the Church. In our regime of novelty, chaotic pace of life, surrounded by mass-produced goods, we make the mistake of taking order and regularity for granted. Cassiodorus had no such luxury and had to make order out of the chaos he was given. So, his monks and the monks that followed them would be the primary agents of ordered simplicity in a world grown disordered and complex. The forms of intellectual and spiritual life were sustained by ideas from antiquity but transmitted in the form Cassiodorus gave them.

The *Expositio* was not only a summary of the tradition of Christian interpretation of the Psalter; it was also a general guide to the craft of reading and something like a beginner's manual of literacy and the three arts of language and the newly canonized quadrivium, the four arts of number named by Boethius in Cassiodorus's lifetime. Cassiodorus filled his book with marginal signs that modern editions unfortunately omit:[9]

---

9. O'Donnell, *Cassiodorus*, 160.

Figure 7.1.

P̂P	*idiomata*, i.e., *propriae locutiones* of scripture		
☧	necessary dogmas	$\overline{\text{TOP}}$	*topoi*
Ᵽ	definitions	$\overline{\text{SYL}}$	syllogisms
$\overline{\text{SCHE}}$	schemata	$\overline{\text{AR}}$	arithmetic
$\overline{\text{ET}}$	etyologies	$\overline{\text{GEO}}$	geometry
$\overline{\text{RⱣ}}$	interpretations of names	$\acute{\text{M}}$	music
$\overline{\text{RT}}$	rhetoric	*	astronomy

In continuity with the practice of Alexandrine scholiasts, these signs served to concentrate reader's focus and act as reference points that functioned as both page numbers and subject index. The ☧, made famous by the emperor Constantine, pointed to passages of the Psalms that had some bearing on the pressing theological issues of the day, while the * asterisk, literally a "little star," drew the gaze and minds of students upwards to contemplate the perennial order of the heavens. This system of signs made it possible for students and teachers to use the Psalter as a guide to both secular and divine letters. Cassiodorus was confident that the arts were not "invented" by pagan antiquity but rather discovered. They were merely and profoundly an adequate account of reality. The pagans had not created them; they had rather done an excellent job of documenting, articulating, and teaching them, and this teaching was not only useful but also necessary for a proper understanding of all literature, which included scripture. What Cassiodorus accomplished was the reconciliation of secular and Christian learning, showing the indispensability of the classical liberal arts for the interpretation of scripture.

For much of the last two centuries, Cassiodorus has suffered condemnation as a writer and intellect of the second or third rank. The nineteenth century decisively rejected the Baroque and lost the aesthetic capacity to appreciate the highly mannered style of the

Variae. In the same period, scholars' command of the classical languages declined just as, paradoxically, their interest in sources increased. This strange state of affairs was powered by the production and wide availability of translations of the Greek and Latin classics into the vernacular languages. Where before, students had been expected to approach Greek through Latin, and therefore Hellenism through *Romanitas*, students now read Homer and Plato in English, French, or German, leaving Vergil and Cicero, whose works had been the foundation of literate culture for almost two millennia, to gather dust and seem quaint in comparison to their more original Greek prototypes. Why bother with Platonism when one could have Plato? Why bother with Christianity when one could have the Synoptic Problem and the Historical Jesus?

In a similar way, Cassiodorus's *Expositio Psalmorum* lost its standing as the intermediary through which one approached St. Augustine's *Enarrationes in Psalmos* and the whole patristic tradition of Psalm interpretation. Now, we take a shortcut, walking past the tidy garden of Cassiodoran exegesis to wander in the woods of Augustinian homiletics. Such an approach is fine for those who have a merely historical interest in texts, but those who are interested in cultivating philosophy as a way of life, in learning and inculcating a discipline of reading, who wish not only to study a tradition but also to participate in it, would do well to recover the old understanding of "the apt" along with "the true, the good, and the beautiful." The "apt," an intermediate excellence identified by Isocrates and developed by Cicero, is the means by which human beings learn the disciplines that adduce to knowledge of the transcendent. It is what Werner Jaeger called *paideia* or simply, culture. Knowledge of its proper use is "teaching" or "education," and Cassiodorus was a master of the craft. In comparison to St. Augustine, Cassiodorus was not an original thinker. But, like his father in the faith, Cassiodorus was keenly interested in cultivating intellects and forming characters. Perhaps because his rhetorical training had been employed in legal and state matters, he saw less vanity in it than did the bishop of Hippo. From this same experience, he likely derived ways of thinking and writing that, though less free, were more disciplined. St. Augustine will always be the common theologian of Latin Christianity, but the bulk, profundity, and diffusion of his works will always perplex all but the most brilliant and diligent of his readers. Cassiodorus constructed a system of levies and dikes that tamed the exegetical flow but still lead the courageous and persistent upriver and out to the sea of Augustinian interpretation.

Reconciling Classical and Christian Learning

Cassiodorus was a master teacher and an author of textbooks so successful that they can be said not only to have charted but to have actualized the path by which Latin Christians would become orators, philosophers, and theologians for the next millennium and more. It is curious that so much of the common inheritance of literate culture should have been lost so recently, and unchecked historicism is the culprit. Only quite recently have educators begun recovering tools, like the *Disticha Catonis*, that enabled literacy in the past, and it is still rare to find scholars who appreciate the moral aspects of education as much as the intellective. The ancients, medievals, and early moderns understood that establishing habits of mind were decisive in preparing the intellect for the complex objects of contemplation it would encounter near the end of the process of formal education. Cassiodorus's *Expositio* is just such a tool, and the fact that it is "the only formal commentary on the entire Psalter surviving from the patristic era"[10] demands that it be given more consideration and fame than it has hitherto received.

Cassiodorus's work on the Psalms consumed perhaps the majority of the nearly two decades he spent in Constantinople. Once

10. O'Donnell, 136.

Roman rule had been restored, or at least Gothic rule had become impossible, Cassiodorus returned to Italy and spent the rest of his life in his native Squillace, where he had converted his family estate into Vivarium. Scholars today call Vivarium a monastery, and that is what it was, but it was not and could not have been a Benedictine monastery. Benedictine monasticism, which was of course only just being established in Cassiodorus's lifetime, for many centuries coexisted and mingled with older forms. Few would today consider St. Augustine a monk, although his post-conversion retirement to Cassiciacum was something like a monastic retreat, and he, as bishop, presided over communities of Christians who lived in common following a set of his precepts that later centuries would call the *Rule of St. Augustine*. Cassiodorus's Vivarium was neither a patrician's country estate nor a medieval monastery, but rather something in between. Unlike St. Benedict's Monte Cassino, it was not a fortified mountain redoubt but rather a charming seaside plantation whose name might best be translated as "park," in the same sense that Jane Austen used to describe the balance achieved between nature and artifice in the grounds surrounding England's great houses. It was a complex consisting of vegetable and botanical gardens, an oratory, a library, dormitories, and most famously, manmade pools stocked with fish to nourish the brothers, pilgrims, and the infirm with both beauty and food. Since Vivarium was planned to maximize beauty rather than defense, it was thoroughly destroyed by the disturbances that continued to rage throughout Italy in the seventh century, not rebuilt, and has left few traces of its existence. In fact, identification of the site is uncertain, and no substantial archaeological or manuscript evidence has been positively identified with the place.

The primary legacy of Vivarium is spiritual rather than material, although, as we shall see, the spirit of Vivarium continues to animate the way most Christians physically interact with the Bible today. The spiritual legacy is twofold, as the title of Cassiodorus's most famous work, *Institutiones Divinarum et Saecularium Littera-*

rum, demonstrates. This work, like the *Expositio*, can be understood as a working out and concretization of Augustinian thought. In this case, Cassiodorus gave definite shape to the theory of St. Augustine's *De Doctrina Christiana*, which is often called the charter of Christian education. St. Augustine envisioned but did not establish a Christian form of education. The Roman school system was still intact in his day, and Christians could influence and direct it, but radical reform was neither possible nor widely desired. In Cassiodorus's time, all civil society had collapsed or was mortally wounded. As St. Gregory the Great tells us of St. Benedict's school days, even in the capital, the proud legacy of Roman education was a shadow of a shadow, poorly carried on and directed at vanity.[11] Cassiodorus, brought up under the old system but unable to keep it going, had to reinvent education.

A New Model of Education

In times of great crisis, there cannot be a question of going back or of transmitting the current state of things to future generations. The questions "what can be preserved," and "how much," must be brought to the forefront. If one hears that the enemy army will arrive in three days, and one has a well-stocked library containing the wealth of five centuries of literary production but only one oxcart to move it to a safe location, what does one take? In such circumstances, it becomes all the more impressive that a full 35 of the 147 books of Livy's *Ab Urbe Condita* made their way through the maelstrom of late antique destruction. Great masses of material were lost, but enough survived to sustain culture, and in the majority of cases, the survivals were the product of conscious selection rather than happenstance.

11. St. Gregory gives us this detail in the prologue to Book II of his *Dialogues*, which is often excerpted as the *Life of St. Benedict*.

Cassiodorus was one of the primary agents of this process of selection, preservation, and transmission. Some have described the *Institutes* as a card catalogue, a mere user's guide to the books that happened to be in Vivarium's library, but this underestimates the great care Cassiodorus took in selecting the contents of that library. A better comparison would be to call it a curriculum guide or course catalogue, a rationalized system of education and the prototype of the *ordo disciplinarum* that would define medieval education. Cassiodorus gave his monks a set of books and told them how to read them and in what order. He gave them a comprehensive vision of how the arts served philosophy and theology and how each was a part of an integral whole. Just as importantly, he gave them not only a vision of the great ideas but also the tools and textbooks that cultivated the disciplines needed to access them. For the first time, the liberal arts had a definite and real consummation in theology, rather than the useful or coincidental relationship they had had in St. Augustine's time. We can best see Cassiodorus's plan by reading his own words:

> When I realized that there was such a zealous and eager pursuit of secular learning, by which the majority of mankind hopes to obtain knowledge of this world, I was deeply grieved, I admit, that Holy Scripture should so lack public teachers, whereas secular authors certainly flourish in widespread teaching. Together with blessed Pope Agapetus of Rome, I made efforts to collect money so that it should rather be the Christian schools in the city of Rome that could employ learned teachers—the money having been collected—from whom the faithful might gain eternal salvation for their souls and the adornment of sober and pure eloquence for their speech. They say that such a system existed for a long time at Alexandria and that the Hebrews are now using it enthusiastically in Nisibis, a city of Syria. But since I could not accomplish this task because of raging wars and violent struggles in the Kingdom of Italy—for a peaceful endeavour has no place in a time of unrest—I was moved by divine love to devise for you,

> with God's help, these introductory books to take the place of a teacher. Through them I believe that both the textual sequence of Holy Scripture and also a compact account of secular letters may, with God's grace, be revealed.[12]

This brief account is something like an autobiography that also serves as a summary of the sixth century. Cassiodorus could have become desperate when his plans to found an urban, papal academy were frustrated by the rapid social and political changes of his day, but instead, he chose to improvise and make the best contribution he could to his contemporary culture and to posterity given his particular circumstances. Some of the most significant changes that he had to confront were the closure of schools, the breakdown of society, and the scarcity of teachers. Where teaching had always been a primarily oral activity, Cassiodorus laid the basis of the textual culture we have inherited from the Middle Ages, an educational and cultural regime where learning takes place "not so much by their speech as through your eyes."[13] In a world where metropolitan life was becoming impossible, Cassiodorus found a way to condense the rich texture of antique orality into a set of written precepts that enabled students to "learn what is to be read in proper order."[14]

Further, he impressed on his students that "[w]hatever has been found in Divine Scripture on [the liberal arts] will be better understood if one has prior acquaintance with them."[15] Just as the Angels used Jacob's ladder to make possible the journey from Earth to Heaven, so those who read Cassiodorus's *Institutes* and implemented its system of education would enable their own ascent to "Holy Scripture through the excellent commentaries of the Fathers."[16] In the same

12. *Institutes*, Praef.1.
13. *Institutes*, Praef.5.
14. *Institutes*, Praef.5.
15. *Institutes*, Praef.6.
16. *Institutes*, Praef.2.

passage, Cassiodorus explains the necessity of cultivating proper scribal habits to ensure the faithful transmission of scripture, and in the absence of printing, digital typesetting, and automated grammar and spell checkers, the monks had to become proficient in all of the disciplines of written culture and become guardians of language.

Taken together, the first book of the *Institutes* was Cassiodorus's formalization of St. Augustine's *De Doctrina Christiana*, and the second book was a concrete plan for experiencing Boethius's *Consolatio Philosophiae*. In Cassiodorus's regime of education, the Psalms became the primary means of cultivating Latinity, literacy, and a fundamental knowledge of the liberal arts. Students followed this with a definite sequence of the seven liberal arts, culminating in eloquence, philosophy, and theology. Cassiodorus gave us this model, and his spiritual descendants took it to every corner of the globe. What they established was textual culture, knowing that the Latin *textus* has the same etymon as *textile*. Both things are woven from many strands, and when used together, secular and divine letters make a garment more elegant and durable than would be possible for either in isolation. St. Benedict had assumed that the monastery would have a library, but he did not mention a scriptorium. For the association of book production with monasticism, we must look to Cassiodorus. To Benedictine *Ora et Labora*, Cassiodorus added an emphatic *Et Scribe!*

This textual culture, depending on the classical tradition and fulfilled in the reading of scripture, was a radical reconciliation of an ancient tension in Latin Christendom. The Greek Fathers, starting with St. Paul at the Areopagus,[17] had always held a more positive view of classical learning than did their Latin brethren. In the Greek tradition, Clement of Alexandria had paved the way for later Christian use of the classical tradition,[18] and St. Basil the Great

17. Acts 17:22–23.

18. *Stromata*, 1.20.

gave lasting form to the marriage of Christian theology and Greek Paideia when he described the classics as a great sea that, being lesser than the sun of divine truth and nearer to humanity, could therefore reflect it and make it easier for human beings to approach.[19] The early Latin tradition, from Tertullian through Ss. Jerome and Augustine, was much more cautious, and even came close to denying that the secular arts were of any use at all to the Christian.[20] There is no easy way to account for this, but one might trace it back to a vocational difference. The majority of the Greek Fathers were educators and philosophers. The majority of Latin Fathers were lawyers and orators. It seems likely that the Latin Fathers were embarrassed by the practical and lucrative ends to which they had put their training in the liberal arts, and they needed a century and more to exorcise their collective guilt for the late Roman (mis)use of classical culture.

When contemporary Christians leave off their reading of the Latin Fathers in the early fifth century, they accordingly take with them an overly negative view of Latin Christendom's evaluation of pagan antiquity. As has been remarked, the Roman senatorial families, the ancestors of Boethius and Cassiodorus, had participated in the baptism of *Romanitas* over the span of the fourth and fifth centuries, and by the sixth century, a more positive attitude was possible. Their work was to copy, edit, and codify the Vergilian tradition and reduce libraries of papyrus scrolls to a few magnificent codices. In doing so, they baptized Vergil, expunging St. Augustine's guilt and ensuring that the *Aeneid*, *Georgics*, and *Eclogues* would guide Dante as far as poetry and wisdom could take him and prepare him to respond to grace and revelation.

19. *Address to Young Men on Greek Literature*, 2.

20. See St. Jerome's *Ep*. 22 for his famous "Dream of Cicero" and St. Augustine's *Confessions* 1.12 for his account of his early education and the tears he shed for Dido.

The Legacy of Cassiodorus: Textual Culture

Like his ancestors, Cassiodorus's importance is best encapsulated in his concern for codification, as both abstract intellective process and as concrete craft producing large and comprehensive yet portable codices. Of these codices, none was more important than the *Codex Grandior*. This is the conventional name given to a now lost manuscript, the first complete Latin Bible to have been bound in a single volume. It was compiled and produced at Vivarium on Cassiodorus's orders. In the next century, the codex made its way to Rome, perhaps to the library of St. Gregory the Great, where an Anglo-Saxon pilgrim acquired it. He took it to Monkwearmouth-Jarrow, the twin monasteries in the extreme north of England, dedicated to Ss. Peter and Paul and home of the Venerable Bede. There, three copies were made: one for St. Peter, one for St. Paul, and one for Pope Gregory II, whose namesake had been the agent of the Anglo-Saxon conversion to Christianity. The *Codex Grandior* and the two copies that stayed in England perished during the Reformation and the Dissolution of the Monasteries, but the third copy found a home at a monastery on Monte Amiata near Florence. This copy, called *Codex Amiatinus*, is the oldest Latin Bible in existence. Due to its antiquity and the purity of its text, it was used at the Council of Trent to help define the text and canon of scripture and again in the twentieth century to bring the text of the Latin Bible promulgated at Vatican II into closer conformity with St. Jerome's prototype.

At each stage of history, the survival of culture depends on groups of individuals banding together to ensure the vitality of tradition. That vitality is enabled by careful discernment of what is most important and valuable in the tradition coupled with a dynamic approach that can make the best use of the opportunities offered by a particular time and place. Even in a time of great crisis, Cassiodorus and his community searched for and perfected new forms, like the single-volume Bible and the marriage of the life of prayer with textual scholarship, to accommodate their tradition to the needs of their day. In our own time, we should not spurn the honest work of conservation as we pass on the fundamental disciplines that sustain literate culture. We must recognize that the humble work of authoring textbooks and designing curricula is the means by which culture is sustained and the next Renaissance made possible.[21]

21. For further reading, see: S. J. B. Barnish, "The Work of Cassiodorus After His Conversion," *Latomus* 48, no. 1 (1989): 157–87; Jacob Hammer, "Cassiodorus, the Saviour of Western Civilization," *Bulletin of the Polish Institute of Arts and Sciences in America* 3, no. 2 (1945): 369–84; Paul Meyvaert, "Bede, Cassiodorus, and the Codex Amiatinus," *Speculum* 71, no. 4 (1996): 827–83; D. A. Olsen, *The Honey of Souls: Cassiodorus and the Interpretation of the Psalms* (The Liturgical Press, 2017).

8 Benedict of Nursia

David P. Deavel

Introduction: Benedict's World, Our World

A joke told in some Catholic circles circa 2020 had it that things were pretty much like the dark ages. After all, it went, we have two popes, a plague, and civilization seems to be collapsing. Another joke had it that the year was just like the fall of the Roman Empire, but with better wi-fi.

As an optimist, I have to tell you that, apart from certain precincts in blue states, nobody's afraid of the Covid plague anymore and those "Benevacantists" who believed Pope Benedict XVI was the true pope who would spring back into the office at some point have now either joined the Sedevacantists who simply think the see of Peter is empty or have reconciled themselves to saying they think Pope Francis was just a bad pope. Some might call this progress.

As a realist, however, I have to tell you that civilization is probably still collapsing. But the wi-fi works well even in places that are disordered.

I begin this way because these jokes have more than a bit of truth in them. Society and the Church are in decay. And that is what many people thought in that golden time we call the patristic era, the age of the Fathers of the Church. In his 1859 essay, "The Benedictine Schools," St. John Henry Newman quotes a homily from St. Gregory the Great from about the year 600 AD.

> Behold, my brethren, we already see with our eyes what we are used to hear in prophecy. Day by day is the world assaulted by fresh and thickening blows. Out of that innumerable Roman *plebs* what a mere remnant are ye at this day! Yet incessant scourges are still in action; sudden adversities thwart you; new

> and unforeseen slaughters wear you away. For, as in youth, the body is in vigour, the chest is strong, the neck muscular, and the arms plump, but in old age the stature is bent, the neck is withered and stooping, the chest pants, the energies are feeble, and breath is wanting for the words; so the world too once was vigorous, robust for the increase of its kind, green in its health, and opulent in its resources, but now on the contrary it is laden with the weight of years, and is fast sinking into the grave by its ever-multiplying maladies. Beware, then, of giving your heart to that which, as even your senses tell you, cannot last for ever.[1]

As Newman observes, at almost all times there is some popular notion that evil is coming. The world, we might say, is always going to hell, whether traveling in a handbasket or not. But the distinction of those early years of the Church was that it wasn't just the unlearned man crying out; it was the saint and the scholar, too: "As St. Gregory looked out for Antichrist in the sixth century," Newman observes, "so had the Martyrs of Lyons in the second, St. Cyprian in the third, St. Hilary and St. Chrysostom in the fourth, and St. Jerome in the fifth. It was the sober judgment of the wisest and the most charitable, that the world was too bad to mend, and that destruction was close upon it."[2]

Now, neither St. John Henry nor I recount these views with the purpose of encouraging skepticism about the world's end or the Lord's return. Destruction of everything will indeed happen and judgment will come. We know neither the day nor the hour, but we know the events will happen. No, we recount these dismal views of the world to remind ourselves of the fact that as bleak as many things seem today, they have seemed just as bleak in past ages that

1. John Henry Newman, "The Benedictine Schools," reprinted in *A Benedictine Education: The Mission of Saint Benedict & The Benedictine Schools*, ed. Christopher Fisher (Cluny Press, 2020): 60. Newman is quoting Gregory's Homily I.1.
2. Newman, "The Benedictine Schools," 61.

we now look upon as golden. Whether or not this is the final end of history or just the end of an age of the Church, it is an age in which Jesus is still the Lord and in which we can become saints conformed to his will.

And we have much better wi-fi, no?

St. Benedict was born around 480 into a world in which the Roman Empire was indeed collapsing and the Church was not looking so hot either. In an essay on his life, Dom Aelred Sillem notes that "alike in the Church and in civil society, the background of [Benedict's] life was one of conflict."[3] Around 498 there was a schism in the Roman Church on the election of Pope Symmachus that lasted for sixteen years. By 537 Pope Vigilius had taken over from Pope Silverius, the latter having been accused of betraying Rome and deposed by the Roman General Bellisarius.

So too in the political sphere, where there was some good government from King Odoacer, and then Theodoric, but then a Gothic War to reconquer Italy started in 535, a war that would lead to a great deal of famine and suffering for the monks and those around them.

And yet, Dom Aelred notes that St. Gregory, whom we have just quoted as to the darkness of the age, relates, in his famous *Dialogues*, book two of which is a life of Benedict, almost nothing of the ecclesial strife and only a few hints of the famine and suffering.[4] So, too, the only thing we have of Benedict's own writing, the famous Rule, gives precious little of that strife or suffering. Though the suffering is indeed real, the deeper truths in Benedict's life have to do with the eternal. But they certainly were understood amid the strife.

---

3. Dom Aelred Sillem, "St. Benedict," in *Benedict's Disciples*, ed. D. H. Farmer (Fowler Wright Books Ltd., 1980), 27.
4. Sillem, 27.

His Life

He was born, as noted, around 480, in Nursia, which is near Spoleto. His father was a Roman who was likely a member of the "provincial gentry rather than . . . the patrician background which later tradition claims for him."[5] We know from Gregory's life that Benedict had a sister named Scholastica who had been dedicated to God as a baby, which indicates that his family were seriously Christian. We know nothing of his childhood from Gregory other than that he "had the heart of an old man."[6] He attended school in Rome where he became increasingly frustrated with the bad morals of his fellow students. "So, hardly had he entered the world," Gregory tells us, "than he recoiled from it, fearing that the worldly knowledge he had just begun to acquire would suck him entirely down into its bottomless whirlpool." Dropping his studies, the young man, "learnedly ignorant and wisely unskilled,"[7] left Rome with his nurse and went about forty miles away to a town called Enfide where they lived with a community of pious people. Traditionally, he was said to have been around fourteen when this happened, but most scholars think he was likely about nineteen or twenty.

He may initially have just wanted to get away from the wickedness of Rome, but his goal was very soon to live the religious life. After some time in this town, he snuck away from the nurse and went a couple miles away to the valley of Subiaco where he lived in a cave over which hung a monastery. He made friends with a monk named Romanus, who, without letting the abbot know, gave Benedict the habit and also regularly let food down to this young hermit.

---

5. Sillem, 23.

6. From the Prologue to Gregory the Great, *Life of Benedict*, trans. Hilary Costello and Eoin de Bhaldraithe, with commentary by Adalbert de Vogüé (St. Bede's Publications, 1993), 3.

7. Prologue to Gregory the Great, *Life of Benedict*, 3.

For a man later to be famous for his Rule (*regula* in Latin), all of this seems a bit irregular. Benedict himself would later say that hermits should be taken from among those who have already lived the monastic life in community. But the young man in the cave soon gained a reputation for holiness. After three years, a nearby monastery asked him to become their abbot. Benedict reluctantly accepted this invitation since he knew that his way of life was very different from theirs, but they begged. As expected, he found the monastery far too lax. For their part, the monks found that their hermit-abbot was far too strict and tried to poison him, so he returned to his cave where his holiness and indeed his miracles became more widely known.

Eventually, other young men in search of the monastic life came to him and asked for guidance. Given that these were not established monks set in their own ways, he accepted this call to spiritual fatherhood and set up twelve monasteries in the valley. In each there was an abbot. In a thirteenth monastery he lived with some specially chosen disciples. His life from this point on was engrossed in the running of these monasteries and the seeking of God that is involved in them. At a certain point he wrote his famous Rule for these monasteries, a monastic rule that eventually dominated western monasticism and proved flexible enough to be adopted and adapted by a great many groups.

A Plan to Save Civilization? Or to Seek God?

Many who have a surface acquaintance with the man might ask, "So what was his plan to save civilization? Can I find it in any of his writings?" And the answer to this is a (perhaps to some) astounding, "No." For St. Benedict—Father of the West, Patron of Europe, Patron of Students, Father of Western Monasticism—had no particular plan to save civilization. Though Benedictine monasteries would later be renowned for their role as intellectual centers, sites of economic life, and even wielders of political power, that was all in the future, byproducts that were sometimes judged as legitimate developments, sometimes as corruptions that needed reform and return to an earlier vision by both onlookers and Benedictines themselves.

What was that earlier vision? As Newman puts it in an essay titled "The Mission of St. Benedict," Benedict's own plan was that of all monastics at the time, and it can be described without embarrassment as a negation of worldly life:

> Their one idea then, their one purpose, was to be quit of [the secular world]; too long had it enthralled them. It was not a question of this or that vocation, of the better deed, of the higher state, but of life and death. In later times a variety of holy objects might present themselves for devotion to choose from, such as the care of the poor, or of the sick, or of the young, the redemption of captives, or the conversion of the barbarians; but early monachism was flight from the world, and nothing else. The troubled, jaded, weary heart, the stricken, laden conscience, sought a life free from corruption in its daily work, free from distraction in its daily worship; and it sought employments as contrary as possible to the world's employments,—employments, the end of which would be in themselves, in which each day, each hour, would have its own completeness;—no elaborate undertakings, no difficult aims, no anxious ventures, no uncertainties to make the heart beat, or the temples throb, no painful combination of efforts, no extended plan of operations, no multiplicity of details, no deep calculations, no sustained machinations, no suspense, no vicissitudes, no moments of crisis or catastrophe;—nor again any subtle investigations, nor perplexities of proof, nor conflicts of rival intellects, to agitate, harass, depress, stimulate, weary, or intoxicate the soul.[8]

If you wanted to put it in a more positive way, however, you might do well to use Newman's description of a three-fold positive

8. Newman, "The Mission of St. Benedict," in Fisher, *A Benedictine Education*, 10–11.

plan of Benedict and the monastic movement as a whole at that time: "Their object was rest and peace; their state was retirement; their occupation was some work that was simple, as opposed to intellectual, viz., prayer, fasting, meditation, study, transcription, manual labour, and other unexciting, soothing employments."[9]

If you want an even more basic definition than that, Benedict's own notion of what he was about was this: *quaerere Deum*, to seek God. Pope Benedict XVI made this point in an address in 2008: "First and foremost, it must be frankly admitted straight away that it was not their intention to create a culture nor even to preserve a culture from the past. Their motivation was much more basic. Their goal was: *quaerere Deum*. Amid the confusion of the times, in which nothing seemed permanent, they wanted to do the essential—to make an effort to find what was perennially valid and lasting, life itself. They were searching for God."[10]

Thus we come at last to the first and most important lesson for Catholic educators that we take from Benedict. We are here for renewal of Catholic education, but renewal always comes from seeking God first. It is always and everywhere the truth that we must seek first the kingdom of God and his righteousness and remember that all these things will be given to us only in God's good time. As Catholic educators, we have to remember that the most important things are not our plans, our funding, our curricula, or any of the other things that are, of course, important in the practical order. The most important thing is for us to seek God so that we can pass on what is perennially valid and lasting—life itself. It is a simple lesson, but it is not easy at all. As Professor Waldstein observed in an earlier chapter, "disciple" means "learner." What we want to pass on first and

9. Newman, "The Mission of St. Benedict," 12.

10. Benedict XVI, "Meeting with Representatives from the World of Culture," Address, The Holy See, September 12, 2008, https://www.vatican.va/content/benedict-xvi/en/speeches/2008/september/documents/hf_ben-xvi_spe_20080912_parigi-cultura.html.

foremost is not merely our learning but our state as learners, disciples. That is passed on only from person to person.

Poetic Learning

But is there something that distinguishes the kind of intellectual discipleship that might be characterized as Benedictine? Newman thought there was. He described the history of Christian education as characterized by three "discriminating badges" that correspond to three founders and their religious orders. St. Ignatius and the Jesuits have characterized the modern age with their badge of the practical; St. Dominic and the Order of Preachers marked the middle of the Church's life with the scientific; and to Benedict he ascribes the poetic badge. This poetic element is central:

> It demands, as its primary condition, that we should not put ourselves above the objects in which it resides, but at their feet; that we should feel them to be above and beyond us, that we should look up to them, and that, instead of fancying that we can comprehend them, we should take for granted that we are surrounded and comprehended by them ourselves. It implies that we understand them to be vast, immeasurable, impenetrable, inscrutable, mysterious; so that at best we are only forming conjectures about them, not conclusions, for the phenomena which they present admit of many explanations, and we cannot know the true one. Poetry does not address the reason, but the imagination and affections; it leads to admiration, enthusiasm, devotion, love. The vague, the uncertain, the irregular, the sudden, are among its attributes or sources.[11]

For those of you who have read Josef Pieper's *Leisure the Basis of Culture*, this should seem familiar to you. The Benedictine age is characterized not by *ratio*, the form of reason that works on finely

---

11. Newman, "The Mission of St. Benedict," 20.

honed premises and conclusions but instead on *intellectus*, that form of reasoning that takes in the vision of the world as an item of mystery created by a God who is an even greater mystery. It is a vision that is underpinned ultimately by the virtue to which Benedict dedicates an entire chapter in his Rule: humility.

Pray, Work, Read, and Be Happy

How is this poetic vision gained? The Benedictine way has often been characterized by the phrases *opus dei*, the work of God, and *ora et labora*, prayer and labor. While later figures thought of *opus dei* as the work of praying the Divine Office, it seems that Benedict took the term in the more holistic fashion that the modern group called Opus Dei thinks of it—as the entire life offered to God. In Benedict's case, the entire monastic life.

While later forms of monasticism, filled almost entirely with priest-monks, ended up with a day crammed to the gills with liturgical prayer, Benedict's original form of life balanced the *ora* and the *labora*. In fact, it was a life of three parts: prayer, work, and reading.

Clearly, the communal prayer of the Divine Office was important, but so, too, was the work that the Benedictines engaged in. Many people have mistakenly thought that *ora et labora* means work is prayer. It does not—that would be *ora est labora* or, more likely, *ora labora est*—but it is one of those happy misreadings that bears a truth. For the work they did was indeed a form of prayer, a form of the *Opus Dei*. And as such, it was just as poetic as the chants in the monastic Churches. Newman says of them: "They were not dreamy sentimentalists, to fall in love with melancholy winds and purling rills, and waterfalls and nodding groves; but their poetry was the poetry of hard work and hard fare, unselfish hearts and charitable hands. They could plough and reap, they could hedge and ditch, they could drain; they could lop, they could carpenter; they could thatch, they could make hurdles for their huts; they could make a road, they could divert or secure the streamlet's bed, they could bridge a torrent."[12]

In the age of the digital, I think Benedict and his disciples speak to us of what we need to do: though our students are not all destined to be monks, they actually need to be helped away from their screens and pushed back into the world that God created, to have access to manual labor of some sort or another.

Several of my children are attending a classical school in Houston called the St. Constantine School. Though it is not Benedictine or even Catholic officially (the "Saint" before Constantine should have tipped you off), part of what attracts us to the school is that they promise us that our younger children will have lots of time outside during the day. Not only that, but, in the midst of Houston, it is a school that has gardens and animals such as sheep to be taken care of by the students. And one of my sons can sign up for an elective on theater that includes building sets.

This matches up quite well with the Benedictine vision. As scholars have noted, the Benedictine schools were from the beginning geared toward younger boys, most of whom would be assumed to be working out in the world at some point—often with their hands. If in a different age there was less need to educate children to work with their hands, I think today Catholic educators need to think much more about including such training at lower levels.

But there is that other part of monastic life—the reading, which is prescribed for about four hours a day for the monks. Dom Jean LeClercq, in his classic *The Love of Learning and the Desire for God: A Study in Monastic Culture*, reminds us that while reading in the past might well have been silent reading, it was usually different: "in the Middle Ages, as in antiquity, they read usually, not as today, principally with the eyes, but with the lips, pronouncing what they saw, and with the ears, listening to the words pronounced, hearing what

12. Newman, "The Mission of St. Benedict," 28.

is called 'the voices of the pages.'"[13] Of course, those who know about ancient texts know that they did not all have the same systems of spacing and punctuation that we do now. Words and sentences were printed together, making it necessary for the reader to read aloud in order to ascertain the meaning.

But even with our modern systems of spaces between words and punctuation, the same necessity exists. I don't know about you, but, having been teaching at the college level for twenty years, my impression has been a gradual downward trend in the ability to read texts on the part of many students—with a precipitous drop since Covid. I don't mean merely that students are not able to give sophisticated readings of texts; I mean that the ability to read at all is very low. Vocabularies and the ability to read at a basic level have shrunken precipitously. Recent articles on drops in reading ability match what I have seen in the classroom for eighteen- and nineteen-year-olds.

What many of my colleagues and I at the college level have found is that one cannot assume that students have read the assigned texts, and even when they have, that they have read with any degree of understanding. Many of us have gone back to old-fashioned methods of having students not only learn grammar at a basic level but also read aloud during class and listen to each other. They often cannot hear the voices of the pages. Those in classical education already will know that this learning to read is very important. They will resonate with Dom LeClercq's understanding of the three necessary phases of the activity of reading: "to speak, to think, to remember."[14] And of course, in the case of reading the Bible and the Church Fathers, we might add that this was a work that had a moral component to it. LeClercq observes that the monastic school was a

13. Jean LeClercq, *Love of Learning and the Desire for God*, trans. Catherine Misrahi (Fordham University Press, 1961), 15.
14. LeClercq, 16.

combination of the classical school and the rabbinical school since its main focus was not on the study of grammar or literature for its own sake but on the texts of Christian faith.[15]

Now, if you are looking for a course of study from St. Benedict, however, there is none. Unlike the Jesuits with their *ratio studiorum*, or course of studies, the Benedictines never actually had one. While Benedict's Rule seems to assume some understanding of grammar and literature, his was not a scientific but a spiritual curriculum. If it was Benedictine monks who eventually saved the documents of antiquity by copying them out and produced works of literary art, that was not part of his plan. It was simply another bit of useful work like building bridges and digging ditches.

But here, too, I think, we have something that is helpful to our own age. We do not require any copying out of important documents by hand at this particular moment. But that act of transcription by the monks, the copying out of texts, is something that seems to me well worth thinking about at all levels of education. For it is a form of manual labor—labor of the *manus*, or hand—that has something profoundly important about it. Too many studies have shown that those who write out their notes by pen or pencil retain much more of what they are learning than do those who are tap-tap-tapping away on their laptops. Copying out important texts and writing down one's thoughts on paper seem to me important elements of Benedict's world and his monasteries that have immediate applications.

If work and reading are important to the monastic life and to the education of the young, so too is that first element of monastic life: prayer. And this is an element that goes back to the earlier point about what the teacher is transmitting, as well as to the discussion of reading.

While kids in Catholic schools are not likely to pray the entirety of the Divine Office, it seems incumbent on schools and teachers to

15. LeClercq, 18.

include prayer—Mass, certainly, but also other times of prayer—as part of the learning. The success of this prayer will be in part dependent upon students seeing that this is not a thing that teachers are just getting over mechanically but a real and important part of the day's learning, a thing that the teachers are in fact engaging in. But it will also be dependent on that very teaching of children to read in such a way that they can speak, think, and remember the words of God—that they can hear the voices on the page and perceive the Divine Voice.

That's what grammar, logic, and rhetoric are all about. Those very skills of reading are indeed practical arts and liberal arts. We want students to be able to read, write, and think with power. We even want them to be humanists who love those classical authors as did later Benedictines. But we want them to be a particular kind of humanist. LeClercq gives us a good distinction: "If humanism consists in studying the classics for their own sakes, in focusing interest on the type of ancient humanity whose message they transmit, then the medieval monks are not humanists. But if humanism is the study of the classics for the reader's personal good, to enable him to enrich his personality, the monks are in the fullest sense humanists."[16] We might even call them divine humanists.

The Catholic educational tradition did indeed build on Benedict and that poetic tradition. The medieval systematic and scientific ways and the modern practical ways are not betrayals of Benedict or the past. Nor are they simply substitutes for the poetic vision of Benedict and his monks. By talking about Benedict's badge as that of the youngest phase of the Church, Newman does not mean that the age of poetry is gone; nor does he think that the age of the scientific—in the old sense of the word as a systematic approach to knowledge, not merely dealing with natural science—has gone either. No, the Church carries with her all the characteristics of her

16. LeClercq, 133.

entire life. Catholic, after all, does not merely mean geographically universal, but universal with regard to time as well. The scientists and the practical types today desperately need that poetic, receptive vision of the world and of God that Benedict gives us.

Fatherhood

But there is one final aspect of Benedict's monasteries that we can latch onto. And that is his idea of what an abbot should be, given in the second chapter of his Rule.[17] It is an idea that I have been appealing to throughout this chapter, because I think it is applicable not just to abbots or abbesses, but also to teachers who are ultimately vicars of Christ the Teacher. So here are five aspects from the chapter.

First, Benedict thinks of the abbot as a shepherd who cares for the sheep in place of the father. He observes that the shepherd will be held to account "when the sheep have yielded no profit" (2, 7), but, if the shepherd has been faithful, "always striving to cure their unhealthy ways, it will be otherwise: the shepherd will be acquitted at the last judgment" (2, 8–9). He repeats this warning at the end of the chapter. We who are called teachers ought to remember the Lord's words about not many of us being called teacher.

Second, the abbot teaches in two ways: by word and example. The example is more important than the words. Those of us with our own children know that they do as we do and not as we say. So, too, do our students.

Third, the abbot cannot show favoritism. Discipline should be fairly and equally given. There shall be no teacher's pets if one is teaching in a Benedictine vein, though this clearly does not mean that there will not be some students who may not receive special attention either because they are behind or further ahead.

17. I will be quoting Benedict's Rule from *RB 1980: The Rule of Benedict in English*, ed. Timothy Fry (Liturgical Press, 1981).

Remember that Benedict himself put hand-picked men in his own, thirteenth monastery.

Fourth, the abbot must follow St. Paul's instruction to Timothy in 2 Timothy 4:2 and use argument, appeal, and reproof. "This means," Benedict says, "that he must vary with circumstances, threatening and coaxing by turns, stern as a taskmaster, devoted and tender as only a father can be. With the undisciplined and restless, he will use firm argument; with the obedient and docile and patient, he will appeal for greater virtue; but as for the negligent and disdainful, we charge him to use reproof and rebuke" (2, 24–25). Is there better advice for teachers, headmasters, and headmistresses who are dealing with very different students?

Finally, this necessity of firm, fair, but flexible treatment must be applied on an individual basis. "He must so accommodate and adapt himself to each one's character and intelligence that he will not only keep the flock entrusted to his care from dwindling, but will rejoice in the increase of a good flock" (2,32). The old question, "So what do you teach?" always has one final answer: students. Those who love the Lord will love those entrusted to their care and instruction.

Benedict's Task, Our Task

In the time since the beginning of this essay, civilization has not stopped collapsing. Nor have books on the apocalypse been relocated from their present place in the "current events" section. Nor have we gained from this essay any kind of plan to save civilization, western or otherwise. But what I hope what you have gained from this little tour through Benedict's life and legacy is the sense that he is indeed our older brother in the faith, who can tell us what to do when things fall apart: *quaerere Deum*! Seek God! He can give us a plan for life: pray, work, and read—and see the poetry that runs through the world. And he can tell us a bit about what it means to be a teacher and shepherd in the manner of Christ, who is the great shepherd and the image and right hand of the Father.

Renewal starts with us, each one of us, seeking the kingdom of God and its righteousness in the face of a world of great evils and in the sight of the students God has given us. Let us teach them to read, to speak, to think, and to remember so that they might have the ability to discern what is perennially valid—life itself and seeking God.

9 Alcuin

Richard Meloche

To state the obvious: our modern education system is in crisis, unable or unwilling to equip young souls with the necessary tools to achieve authentic human happiness. The principal cause of this crisis is the ever-increasing gap between the revealed truths of the Catholic faith and beliefs about how these truths ought to inform—in very concrete ways—how we go about the important business of educating the young.[1] Undoubtedly, the task of restoring modern culture pivots upon how we respond to this educational drama. The following is a modest proposal on how to mend the gap by turning to the wisdom of the past, in particular to the educational reforms implemented by one of the West's greatest educators, viz. Bl. Alcuin of York.

Alcuin stood at the crossroads of the transmission of ancient learning in the Middle Ages, serving as a key conduit, being "the most learned man of his time" (as Charlemagne's biographer, Einhard, put it).[2] He received the fruit of monastic learning in his native Northumbria, which in turn had been transmitted by missionaries from the storehouse of Ireland, and passed it on to the continent through his work in the Carolingian Empire. Alcuin's cooperation with Charlemagne bore immediate fruit in the rise of cathedral and monastery schools and also laid the foundation through them for

1. Alcuin of York's treatise on the liberal arts puts it this way: "It will be easy to show you the way of wisdom, provided you seek it purely for God's sake to preserve the purity of your own soul, and for the love of virtue; if you love it for its own sake, and do not seek in it any worldly honour and glory or, still less, riches or pleasure. . . ." Quoted in Augusta Theodosia Drane, *Christian Schools and Scholars* (G. E. Stechert and Co., 1910), 139.

2. Einhard, *The Life of Charlemagne*, trans. Lewis Thorpe (Penguin Books, 1969), 85.

the rise of the university. Another of Charlemagne's biographers, a monk of St. Gall, praised Alcuin's achievement: "And his teaching bore such fruit among his pupils that the modern Gauls or Franks came to equal the ancient Romans or Athenians."[3] Though we might fault the monk for exaggeration, it is true that the scholastics depended upon the work of Alcuin for their later achievement, which might be said justly to rival Rome and Athens. For this reason, we can call Alcuin a father of Western education.

The King

It is impossible to grasp the cultural and educational impact of Alcuin of York without first mentioning his patron and friend, and one of history's most central figures, viz. Charles the Great. Alcuin and Charles are so intimately intertwined that one cannot fully understand the impact of Alcuin's educational reforms without first sketching the cultural impact of the reign of Charles.

Charles the Great, or simply Charlemagne, enjoys a unique and commanding position in the history of the Christian era. The roughly eight hundred years which precede him (marked by the decadent rise and subsequent destruction of the Roman imperium) pivots upon his rule with the eight hundred years that followed, ending abruptly with the rise of the modern era. Providentially, Charlemagne squarely sits at the fulcrum of ancient history. As such, he is a crucial figure bridging the gap between the old ancient order and new modern era and is thus central to understanding that vast period of time known as Christendom.[4]

Charlemagne was born in 748 AD, the son of Pippin, the grandson of Charles Martel and the great-grandson of Pepin of Herstal.

---

3. Monk of St. Gall, *The Life of Charlemagne*, trans. Lewis Thorpe (Penguin Books, 1969), 62.

4. The modern era beginning in the sixteenth century is demarcated as specifically post-Christian.

Before his birth, his forefathers had been able to seize greater and greater authority from the long-reigning Merovingian dynasty. The Merovingians had grown increasingly corrupt and inept, and in 751, Charlemagne's father, through political and ecclesial alliances and eventual military conquest, was finally able to formally depose the Merovingian king, Childeric III. The transfer of royal authority from the Merovingian kingship to the house of Pippin—by official papal coronation in 754 at the Basilica of St. Denis—marks the formal establishment of the Carolingian dynasty and the first historical papal crowning of a civic ruler[5] Pippin and his wife Bertrada ruled the Franks until Pippin's death in 768. His short reign was preoccupied with waging various military campaigns to curb Lombardian incursions into papal territories and suppressing revolts within his own borders. Subsequently, the dynasty that Charlemagne inherited when he assumed the crown in 768 was still very much languishing from the neglect and cultural impoverishment of the previous Merovingian rule.[6]

Much of what we know of Charlemagne and his reign comes from three contemporary sources, viz. *Vita Karoli Magni* (his earliest biography), the *Annales Mettenses Priores* (a sort of Carolingian house-history), and the letters of Alcuin.[7] Modern scholars tend to question the historical accuracy of all three and argue that they provide more insight into the motives of the authors than the actual life and governance of Charlemagne.[8] The authors themselves, however,

---

5. *Liber Pontificalis,* "Life of Stephen II," c. 27, trans. Raymond Davis (Liverpool University Press, 2009), p. 64, where the consecrations are dated to January 754.

6. Pippin was succeeded by his two sons, Charlemagne and Carloman. Carloman died in 771, leaving Charlemagne to govern the entire Frankish kingdom.

7. See Einhard, *The Life of Charlemagne,* trans. David Ganz (Penguin Books, 2008); Bernhard von Simson, ed., *Annales Mettenses Priores* (https://archive.org/details/annalesmettenses00sims/page/n7/mode/2up); Alcuin, Letters 27–174, in Alcuin, *Opera Omnia* (*PL* 100).

8. See, for example, Janet L. Nelson's article "Charlemagne the Man," in *Charlemagne: Empire and Society,* ed. Joanna Story (Manchester University Press, 2005), 22–37.

inform the readers of their motives. Einhard, the author of *Vita Karoli*, for example, states that he intends to detail "the manner of life" (*vitae modus*) of Charlemagne in order to commemorate a man whose deeds "can scarcely be imitated."[9] To do so, he argues, requires the novel use of "Ciceronian eloquence" and not the straightforward prose common in similar early medieval hagiographies. The implication is that Charlemagne's life and office were perceived—rightfully so—as wholly unique and beyond imitation.

These early sketches of Charlemagne's life can be divided into three principal areas: his victorious and triumphant military campaigns, the inner sanctity or "mores" of the king, and the administrative governance of his kingdom. In all three areas, Charlemagne is convincingly depicted as a singular "great man" ("*excellentissimus*").[10] In his own lifetime he was already hailed as '*Carolus Magnus*' and styled as the "reborn Constantine" who was destined to usher in the idealized '*civitate Dei*' as described by St. Augustine in his theo-historical masterpiece *The City of God*.[11] Like his father, he was an exceptional military tactician and was convinced of his vocation to be a "warrior-king."[12] Charlemagne desired to "re-establish the ancient authority of the city of Rome" and for forty-five years tirelessly waged wars with his legendry sword *Joyeuse* in defense of the Church or the furthering of his kingdom.[13] He conducted a series

---

9. Einhard, *Vita Karoli* [Life of Charlemagne] in *Charlemagne's Courtier: The Complete Einhard*, trans. Paul Edward Dutton (Broadview Press, 1998), preface.

10. Adjectives used to describe Charlemagne frequently use the superlative; for example: *benignissimus* (most benign), *gloriosimmimus* (most glorious), *mitissimus* (most gentle), *celmentissimus* (most merciful), *prudentissimus* (most prudent), *pissimus* (most pious), and the standard epistolary formula for addressing Charlemagne: *excellentissimus* (most excellent). See David Ganz, "Einhard's Charlemagne: The Characterization of Greatness," in *Charlemagne: Empire and Society*, ed. Joanna Story (Manchester University Press, 2005), 42.

11. See St. Augustine, *City of God*, trans. Marcus Dods (Modern Library, 2000).

12. See William J. Slattery, *Heroism and Genius* (Ignatius Press, 2017), 99.

13. Einhard, *Vita Karoli*, c. XXVII.

of campaigns against the Saxons in the North, successfully conquered the Lombards and expanded power and control over Avars in the East, won over the fiercely independent Bretons in the west, and famously seized the Iberian Peninsula from the Basques as recorded in the medieval epic poem, *The Song of Roland*. His efforts resulted in the almost doubling of the size of the kingdom which he had inherited and establishing an empire that was distinctively animated by Christian principles and ideals.

Importantly, Charlemagne's greatness extends beyond his capacity to wage war. Utilizing principles of medieval physiognomics, Einhard explains how Charlemagne's inner sanctity was suitably reflected in both his outward appearance and in his charitable relationships with others and God. Charlemagne is described as "large and strong" with a "cheerful and attractive face." His appearance, the reader is told, "was always stately and dignified, whether he was standing or sitting" and his "gait was firm, [and] his whole carriage manly."[14] Although a man of great wealth, Einhard emphasizes that he hated pomp and shunned extravagant displays of money. Rather, he preferred the dress of the "common man," liked the simple fare of the huntsman (i.e., roasted meats), had no tolerance for drunkenness, and often assisted the poor.[15] Similarly, his virtuous disposition was manifest in his manifold relationships. Einhard repeatedly informs the reader that Charlemagne greatly "loved," "honored," and "reverenced" his family and friends. He had a particularly intense devotion to his children, whom he never dined or traveled without. And he cherished his daughters so deeply that "he never wanted to give any one of them in marriage . . . but kept them all with him until his death."[16] Although normally in complete control of his emotions, Einhard recounts how he cried

14. Einhard, *Vita Karoli*, c. XXII.
15. *Vita Karoli*, c. XXIII.
16. *Vita Karoli*, c. XX.

bitterly at the death of his closest friend, Pope Hadrian.[17] His moral integrity and rightly ordered loves were ultimately animated by his deep conviction of the truths of the Christian religion. Einhard explains how Charlemagne "cherished with the greatest fervor and devotion the principles of the Christian religion."[18] His religious piety was largely due to the influence of three key paternal figures: his father, Pippin; Fulrad, the abbot of St. Denis; and his confessor, the Irish priest Cathulf. From all three, Charlemagne learned to staunchly defend the Church, to dutifully adhere to her norms, and to piously perform his private prayers and devotions.[19]

Lastly, his administrative greatness is seen in his capacity to govern as a Christian stateman. Charlemagne greatly admired the grandeur of the old Roman Empire, but was interested in creating a new social order—an *imperium Christianum*—that would integrate the Catholic faith, with Roman order, and Germanic culture. The attempt to forge a unified Christian empire from desperate barbarian and fiercely independent kingdoms was a grand feat that required both diplomacy and a powerful hand. His model of rule was informed almost entirely by St. Augustine's portrayal of the Christian emperor found in his bedside book *De Civitate Dei*. Augustine explains that the Christian ruler is to "make [his] power the handmaid of His majesty by using it for the greatest possible extension of His worship;" he is to "fear, love, worship God;" he is to be "slow to punish, ready to pardon;" and "grant pardon, not that iniquity may go unpunished, but with the hope that the transgressor may amend his ways." The emperor is to "do all these things, not through ardent desire of empty glory, but through love of eternal felicity."[20] This ideal required the harmonious merging of the socio-

17. *Vita Karoli*, c. XIX.
18. *Vita Karoli*, c. XXVI.
19. *Vita Karoli*, c. XXVI.
20. St. Augustine, *City of God*, trans. Marcus Dods (Modern Library, 2000), bk. V, ch. 24.

political order with Church governance. Only with such an alliance, with pope and emperor working together for the flourishing of the citizenry, would the earthy polis be transformed into the City of God. Thus, Charlemagne envisioned himself, not as another Caesar, but as a Christian leader charged by God with ushering in a new socio-political order, demarcated by unprecedented peace and prosperity.

His capacity to excel in these three areas (warcraft, moral integrity, and governance) was greatly augmented and made possible by the cadre of scholars that Charlemagne invited to his court to provide him with instruction and counsel. The members of this court shared Charlemagne's nation-building enthusiasm and they thus formed a tightly knit group who aided the king in every policy, decision, and decree aimed at forming and shaping the new society. Among his counselors was the master grammarian Paulinus of Aquileia, the Latinist Peter of Pisa, the renowned poet Angilbert, and the mystic of Saint-Mihiel, Smaragdus, who famously penned the *Royal Road*, a manual of mystical theology. Of these distinguished scholars, there was one man, however, who Charlemagne uniquely favored. In his quest to establish a truly Christian empire, Charlemagne befriended and leaned most heavily upon a scholar from Northumbria, Alcuin of York.

The Teacher

Before coming to the aid of Charlemagne, Alcuin of York lived a relatively quiet life in the Anglo-Saxon kingdom of Northumbria. The date and place of his birth are not recorded, but most scholars place his birth in or near the *civitas Euborica* (the city of York) in the year 735.[21] As a small child "of noble English stock," he entered the local

21. Frobenius, Mabillon, and Lorentz, whom most of the later biographers follow, state that Alcuin's birth could not have occurred earlier that 735. See Lorentz, *Alkuin*, 9.

cathedral school with other children of the aristocracy.[22] The school introduced the young Alcuin to the rudiments of both sacred and secular studies. In his poem *De Sanctis Eboracensis Ecclesiae*, he details the kind of education that he had received at York:

> To some he made the grammar understood
> And poured on others rhetoric's copious flood.
> The rules of jurisprudence these rehearse,
> While those recite in high Aonian verse,
> Or play Castalia's flutes in cadence sweet
> And mount Parnassus on swift lyric feet.
>
> Anon the master turns their gaze on high
> To view the travailing sun and moon, the sky
> In order turning with its planets seven,
> And starry hosts that keep the law of heaven.
>
> The storms at sea, the earthquake's shock, the race
> Of men and beasts and flying fowl they trace;
> Or to the laws of numbers bend their mind
> And search till Easter's annual day they find.
>
> Then, last and best, he opened up to view
> The depths of Holy Scripture, Old and New.
>
> Was any youth in studies well approved,
> Then him the master cherished, taught and loved;
> And thus the double knowledge he conferred
> Of liberal studies and the Holy Word.[23]

---

22. Rolph Barlow Page, *The Letters of Alcuin* (The Forest Press, 1909), 9; Epp. 20, 19, 43, 47.

23. *Versus de Sanctis Eboracensis Ecclesiae*, vv.1535–1557. A digital copy of the manuscript can be found at the James Catalogue of Western Manuscripts, Trinity College, https://mss-cat.trin.cam.ac.uk/Manuscript/O.2.26.

As revealed in this poetic description, the liberal arts (*artes liberales*) were very much a part of his formal education.[24] Unlike much of the rest of the continent, which had seen a contracting of liberal education after the fall of Rome, the liberal arts were flourishing at the cathedral school of York. This was due, in part, to the early Celtic missionaries who had brought over from Gaul not only the faith, but also the study of the trivium and quadrivium. Many of those early missionaries would have been formed at the Abbey of Lérins, which was one of the few places in continental Europe where the study of Aristotle, Cicero, Virgil, Varro, and Isidore—the ardent champions of liberal education—remained. Having thus been formed and with great evangelical zeal, these Irish missionaries quickly established communities of learning throughout Ireland, and by the seventh century the learning eventually passed to the kingdoms of Britain. In 669, Theodore of Tarsus, a man well acquainted with the Hellenic-Roman educational tradition, became archbishop of Canterbury. He brought with him not only a keen knowledge of the liberal arts but also Roman order and discipline. To the north, the twin monasteries of Wearmouth and Jarrow were founded by the erudite Benedict Biscop in 674 and 684, respectively. As abbot, Benedict sought to establish Wearmouth-Jarrow as *the* center of learning in all of Britain. The monasteries themselves were built by masons and glassmakers from Francia and the libraries were populated and enriched by texts from both Lérins and Rome. Under his direction, many fine scholars and clerics were formed, the preeminent being none other than the Venerable Bede (ca. 673–735). One of Benedict's closest friends was Egbert, who in 732 became the

24. In his poetic description a number of the liberal arts are discernable. He explicitly lists grammar, rhetoric, astronomy, and "laws of numbers," i.e., arithmetic. "Jurisprudence" is a reference to canonical law. The "storms" and "earthquakes," as well the reference to "men," "beasts and flying fowl" belong to Isidore's geometric study of things occupying space. Poetry is included under "Aonian verse" and "Parnassus," and music may possibly be included in the reference to "Castalia's flutes."

Bishop of York and shortly thereafter founded there the cathedral school. He appointed as master of the school the Anglo-Saxon scholar Æthelbert. According to modern historian Peter Blair, the cathedral school at York, under the leadership of Æthelbert and the support of Egbert, quickly became the preeminent school in Briton and eventually surpassed the educational prowess of Wearmouth-Jarrow.[25] Of prime importance at the school was the library, which was the largest collection of books to be found in Europe outside of Rome. According to Alcuin, Æthelbert was able to amass "all the Latin writers" in addition to "those that glorious Greece transferred to Rome."[26] Although this is likely poetic embellishment, the library did include the works of the great champions of liberal education, viz. Boethius, Cassiodorus, and Bede. In addition, the catalogue of books at York also included works by Cicero, Virgil, and the grammarians Donatus and Priscian, as well as many of the Latin fathers such as Lactantius, Augustine, Jerome, Ambrose, Hilary, and Gregory the Great. Importantly, "Aristotle" is also numbered as one of the many authors present in Æthelbert's renowned library.[27]

It is here, under the guidance of master Æthelbert, and nourished by one of the grandest libraries, that Alcuin received his education in the "freeing arts," crowned by a thorough formation in the mysteries of the Catholic faith. In 766, Æthelbert advanced to the archbishopric of York on the death of Egbert, leaving the headship of the cathedral school vacant. In his place, his most renowned student, Alcuin, was appointed master. Under Alcuin's vigilant care and prudent guidance, the school greatly enlarged and advanced in regional status. Many students sought out his instruction and he

---

25. Peter Hunter Blair, *The World of Bede* (Cambridge University Press, 1990), 225.

26. *Versus de Sanctis Eboracensis Ecclesiae*, vv.1535–1561.

27. Most likely only Aristotle's logical works were at the cathedral school at this time and although Alcuin may have been able to read Greek (on account of the regional influence of Theodore of Tarsus), the texts categorized were most likely all latinized versions.

was soon regarded as the most astute master in all of Britain. We know of only a handful of his students, mostly from his many letters of correspondence. Distinguished among them are Eanbald, Witzo, Fridugis, and Sigulf. Eanbald would become archbishop of York and the other three, so attached to their master, would follow him to Francia. For fourteen years, Alcuin faithfully fulfilled his office, passing on all that he had received.

His tenure at the cathedral school was interpreted by two successive journeys to the Continent, the last of which led to his permanent withdrawal. On his first trip (sometime before 766) he joined Æthelbert on his pilgrimage to Rome to find something new in the way of books and studies.[28] This initial sojourn was consequential, for on their return they stopped at Pavia to listen to a public debate between Peter of Pisa and a certain Jewish scholar named Lullus. Peter of Pisa was the king's instructor of grammar and thus they had the good fortune of meeting Charlemagne, who was in attendance. His second trip occurred in March of 781. This trip was motivated by the death of his beloved friend and mentor Æthelbert.[29] Eanbald, who had succeeded Æthelbert as archbishop of York, sent Alcuin to Rome to obtain his pallium from the pope. On this second trip he happened to meet Charlemagne once again, this time in Parma, and was invited by the Frankish king to leave his native Britain and take up residence in Aachen to teach in his palace school. Alcuin was hesitant to give up his place as master of the school at York, but promised Charlemagne to come if he could receive blessings from both his new archbishop Eanbald and the Northumbrian king Ælfwald. Upon his return to York, Alcuin secured both secular and sacred approval and soon thereafter departed for the Francia capital in 782 to take up his charge as Master of the Palace School.

28. *Versus de Sanctis Eboracensis Ecclesiae*, vv.1457, 1458. See "Quos (libellos) habui in patria per bonam et dovtissimam magistri mei industriam vel etiam mei ipsius qualemcumque sudorem," *Ep* 121.

29. *Ep* 148, p. 239. Cf. *Versus de Sanctis Eboracensis Ecclesiae*, vv.1589–1595.

The motives that persuaded Alcuin to leave York were threefold. Firstly, the death of Æthelbert deeply affected Alcuin. Alcuin loved Æthelbert as a father and mourned his passing with great sorrow.[30] This death may have emotionally swayed Alcuin to seek work in a place not saturated with the painful memories of his old master. Secondly, Northumbria's political and cultural climate was destabilizing, and this made the conditions for learning less than ideal. The golden age of Northumbrian learning was waning, and there arouse a suspicion of the liberal arts. Reflecting upon his time as master at York, he wrote, "there are few who care to know such things, and what is worse, those who seek to study them are considered blameworthy."[31] Subsequently, Alcuin was keen on finding an environment truly conducive to living a life ordered to the acquisition of truth. And lastly, and perhaps most significantly, Alcuin was an enthusiastic admirer of Charlemagne. His letters attest to his approval of Charlemagne's campaigns to enlarge the domain of civilization and spread the truths of the Gospel. To Alcuin's mind, the Merovingian kings had left Francia in a state of utter disrepair. The monasteries had long been destroyed or repurposed for purely secular purposes; centers of learning had almost been completely abandoned; language had devolved and fragmented; and the copying of manuscripts had all but ceased. Thusly, Alcuin understood his departure for Francia as an apostolic partnership with Charlemagne to advance the cause of Christ and in turn restore Christian culture to all of Europe. "I have not come to Frankland," proclaims Alcuin, "nor remained there for love of money, but for the sake of religion and the strengthening of the Catholic faith."[32]

Alcuin was forty-seven years of age when he arrived at Charlemagne's court in Aachen. He was a seasoned administrator and a

30. *Ep* 148, p. 239. See *Versus de Sanctis Eboracensis Ecclesiae*, vv. 1589–1595.

31. See Andrew West, *Alcuin and the Rise of the Christian Schools* (Charles Scribner's Sons, 1912), 37–38, quoting a letter to Charlemagne.

32. *Epp.* 178, 198, 171, 41, 217, 43. Cf. Alcuin's *Adversus Elipandum*, bk. 1 chap. 16, Migne CCI, 251.

skilled master teacher, and quickly set to work restoring the culture through education. His task upon arrival was not a continuation of the learning that he had begun at York, but more primitively, to establish the foundations of learning and to diffuse those foundations as far and as wide as possible. For such a task he was exceptionally well equipped. By all accounts Alcuin was a truly integrated teacher. In addition to the years of cultivating the habits of the mind, Alcuin was also exceedingly practical. He understood that wisdom, that "chief adornment of the soul," cannot be "lightly won." Rather, he rightly understood that to have a society properly ordered required the crossing and ascending of certain "intervening plains and slopes."[33] It is to these educational "plains and slopes" that we now turn.

The Plan

Alcuin's first act as the newly appointed "Deputy of Education and Culture" was, quite surprisingly, to stock the forests of Europe with boar and deer.[34] He realized that in order to have a revitalization of education one has need of the prerequisites of learning, viz. books and writing instruments. The deer would provide the velum to write upon, while the boar hair was utilized for the brushes. In addition to this very necessary practical good, the stocking and subsequent hunting of animals compelled the good people of Europe to be exposed to nature—to the real—which has a unique pedagogical purpose. Drawing upon the principles of classical education, Alcuin understood that the formation of the mind first requires the formation of the imagination. What has been later defined as the "poetic mode," a primitive or initial encounter with reality via the senses and the emotions are the necessary foundation for the higher modes of

---

33. Alcuin, *Grammatica* (PL 101), quoted in R. B. Page, *The Letters of Alcuin* (Bibliolife, 2009), 78–79.

34. See Pierre de Cointet, Barbara Morgan, and Petroc Willey, "*The Catechism of the Catholic Church*" *and the Craft of Catechesis* (Ignatius Press, 2008), 8–14.

learning contained in the trivium. Alcuin deeply understood this pedagogical structure and thus began his educational and cultural reforms by having his people first experience the depth, beauty, and goodness of God's salvific love communicated to man through nature. This wonderous encounter with unadulterated reality stirs up in them some deep-down longing that cannot be satiated until it acquires—in its fullness—the object of its yearning. This "wondering" then became the ground, the foundation, of a well-formed Catholic people and culture, which developed into Christendom—this prolonged period of Catholic culture, a synthesis between gospel and culture—that saw the unprecedented flourishing of humanity: universities, hospitals, art, religion (the mendicant and military orders), architecture, science, trades, and guilds.

Having acquired the necessary tools of learning and having thickened the imaginations of the people with robust contact with reality, Alcuin then initiated his next phase of educational renewal. Working intimately with certain monastic communities, he ordered the establishment of scriptoriums and had the monks begin the tedious task of copying the remnant texts that had survived the centuries of neglect. To do so both quickly and accurately, he and his student Fredegrise developed a uniformed minuscule, with clear and distinct spacing, paragraphs, and rules governing the use of lower- and upper-case letters and punctuation. The "Carolingian" minuscule thus greatly hastened the time it took to copy and recopy texts, dramatically reduced textual errors, made both reading and writing much easier, and facilitated the rapid dissemination of literature throughout the kingdom. Alcuin's second phase thus resulted in a twofold good: first, it reorganized and prioritized the work of many of the monastic communities and made them dynamic centers of learning, and second, the distribution of readable books throughout the realm established a culture of learning that hitherto had not been possible.

In the same practical manner, his last and most essential reform was to ensure that the spirit of friendship animated all his efforts and informed all his educational relationships. Alcuin labored to form deep and lasting friendships with gifted teachers throughout the empire and, having formed them according to his own profound comprehension of the truth, he sent them out to establish their own schools throughout the newly established regime.

He began his educational project by first forming an inner circle of students. At the palace school, he gathered to himself Charlemagne and his family (queen Liutgard and their children: Charles, Pepin, Lewis—who would succeed his father as emperor—and his daughters Rotrud and Gisela, along with his son-in-law Angilbert); his three prized students who followed him from York—Witzo, Fridugis, and Sigulf; and the future bishops and archbishops of important ecclesial Francia sees, viz. Theodulf, Riculf, and Arno. Additionally, Charlemagne's dear friend and eventual biographer, Einhard, also joined them.[35] The diverse makeup of this initial class—old and young; male and female; lettered and unlettered—often made instruction difficult; however, Alcuin's warmth, wit, and general jocularity made him a most likable figure. He famously gave all his students fanciful and playful pseudonyms (and himself was known as Master Albinus, with the nickname Flaccus), and his love for his students is most evident in the many letters penned to this initial group of students.

One particular fruit of his work can be found in his influence on the Emperor himself. Charlemagne could read Latin, though he could not write it well,[36] and gladly partook of the bestowal of the liberal arts in his court. We have received a written dialogue between Charlemagne and Alcuin on the nature of rhetoric, which opens with the Emperor praising the *magister* for the gifts he had bestowed and seeking more:

35. See Andrew West, *Alcuin and the Rise of the Christian Schools* (New York: Charles Scribner's Sons, 1892), 42–43.

36. We shouldn't think of the Emperor as an intellectual slouch, for he began composing a German grammar, partially in hopes that law could be written in the German language in the future. See Drane, *Christian Schools and Scholars*, 126.

> Since God has led you and brought you back, O revered Master Alcuin, I pray that a short time be allowed me in which to question you about the precepts of the art of rhetoric; for I remember you once said that the strength of this art lay wholly in dealing with public questions. As you very well know, in the course of the duties of government and the cares of State, we are constantly wont to be busy with questions of this kind; and it seems absurd not to know the rules of an art when the necessity of using it confronts us daily. To the extent that you have partly opened for me by your few previous remarks the portals of the rhetorical art and the gates of dialectical subtlety, you have made me very eager for these disciplines, and more especially so because the other day you wisely conducted me into the storehouse of the arithmetical science, and revealed also to me the splendor of astronomy.[37]

More importantly, however, Alcuin exercised a moral influence on the Emperor, resisting his compulsion of tithes from newly converted tribes and the use of force to induce their baptism. He writes to Charlemagne in a letter, "If the same pains had been taken to preach to them the easy yoke and light burden of Christ as has been done to collect tithes, and to punish the slightest infringement of the laws on their part, then they would no longer abhor and repel baptism."[38] Charlemagne took the rebuke to heart, leveled primarily at his treatment of the Saxons, and he changed course after the conquest of Hungary. A similar influence can be found toward Charlemagne's sons: "In his letters to the young princes Alcuin freely points out their faults, and gives them excellent advice. 'Seek,' he writes, 'to adorn your noble rank with noble deeds; let humility be in your heart, and truth on your lips; and

---

37. *The Rhetoric of Alcuin & Charlemagne*, trans. Wilbur Samuel Howell (Russell & Russell, 1965), 67.

38. Alcuin, Letter 111, quoted in Rolph Barlow Page, "The Letters of Alcuin" (PhD diss., Columbia University, 1909), 53.

let your life be a pattern of integrity, that so God may be pleased to prosper your days.'"[39]

Having thus educated this inner circle of educators, he then charged them with establishing their own schools—animated with same spirit of friendship—with an eye towards universal primary education. Through a series of successive decrees, Charles and Alcuin established an educational system rooted in cathedrals and monasteries forming not only clerks but the laity as well. The formation was certainly rudimentary, but each child—whether rich or poor—received a sound formation in reading, writing, and arithmetic, along with the basics in Latin and chant.

Sr. Augusta Theodosia Drane provides a sound overview of the nature of Charlemagne's schools:

> In the Capitular of Aix-la-Chapelle, published in 789, Charlemagne required that minor schools should be attached to all monasteries and cathedral churches without exception, and that children of all ranks, both noble and servile, should be received into them. At the same time the larger and more important monasteries were to open major schools, in which mathematics, astronomy, arithmetic, geography, music, rhetoric, and dialectics were taught; and these again were of two descriptions. Some were interior, or claustral, intended only for the junior monks, while others were exterior, or public, and intended for pupils as well secular as ecclesiastic. Some monk, qualified by his learning, was appointed scholasticus, and if none such were to be found in the community, it was not an uncommon practice to invite a monk from some other religious house to take charge of the school. A claustral and an exterior school often existed attached to the same monastery or cathedral, governed by separate masters, the scholars of the claustral school forming part of the community, while those of the exterior school, though subject to a certain claustral discipline, did not follow the same religious exercises.

39. Quoted in Drane, *Christian Schools and Scholars*, 127.

> Lay students were received in these exterior schools, and that far more extensively than is commonly supposed, most popular writers having represented the monastic schools as exclusively intended for those in training for the religious life, thus confusing together the interior and exterior schools. Public schools of this kind were erected at Fulda, St. Gall's, Tours, Hirsauge, Hirsfield, Gorze, Fleury, L'Isle Barbe, Fontanelles, and Ferrières, as well as at many other monasteries and cathedrals, a list of which is given by Mabillon.[40]

Out of these schools sprang a culture well acquainted with the true, good, and beautiful. The fruit of Alcuin's educational reforms are clearly seen in the synthesis between culture and Gospel.

With their establishment, Alcuin could retire from court. He returned to England for two years, but Charlemagne continued to employ his service, combatting numerous heresies, especially a new form of adoptionism that had arisen in Toledo. Alcuin resigned himself to retirement within the Frankish Empire, exiled from his homeland, and he was appointed to the chief abbey of France, Marmoutier in Tours, the monastery of St. Martin himself, where he developed a model school.

The Takeaway

So what do Alcuin and his reforms have to do with us? In many ways we are now living in a time that resembles the Dark Ages of the fifth through eighth centuries. The gap between Gospel and culture is as wide today as it was then. Barbarians may not be seen riding around on shaggy ponies with crossbows in hand; however, the presence of a neo-barbarism is overtly evident everywhere.

Barbarism is nothing other than the appetites and emotions of man prevailing over the intellect. We can detect their kind in politics,

40. Drane, 131.

in the academy, on the streets, and in our families. Unfortunately, instead of being draped in bearskins, the neo-barbarians come wearing suits, and instead of crossbows they wield an even deadlier weapon, namely PhDs and corrupting ideologies. They take us unaware, because there is no sign of sword or fire, and everything seems to work as it should—often even better. In fact, one of the tactics of the neo-barbarian is to hide cultural upheaval in technological triumphs. But the statistics do not lie: our culture is sliding into barbarism.

The family, the basic unit of culture, is crumbling: nearly half of American children live without a father in the home and 40% to 50% of marriages end in divorce, with Catholic marriage only faring slightly better. Our respect for the fundamental reality of human life is almost nonexistent: the majority of women between fifteen and forty-four use contraception; in an increasing number of states, there are more deaths than births. Our children are being raised in unhealthy, immoral environments: eight- to twelve-year-olds spend large portions of the day on screens, and by the age of eleven, the average child has already been exposed to explicit pornography. Our understanding of social organization and relations has become skewed: half of US millennials have favorable views of socialism, and many social media platforms have begun limiting speech.

Even in our Catholic communities, we are decreasing in our awareness of and respect for the sacramental realities of the Church. Only one baptized child out of five receives First Holy Communion. Over half of children raised Catholic fall away by age seventeen, and over three-quarters by twenty-one. The number of Catholic schools has decreased by half, and students who attend them are *less* likely to identify as "Catholic."

So if we are living in a new Dark Age, we need a new Alcuin, someone to enliven learning not only within a small group, but within the Church and culture more broadly. He models how to unite the Gospel and culture through fostering authentic friendships grounded in Christ. We find an educational extension of this principle in the employment of Socratic dialogue. We can also follow his example in employing a robust, yet whimsical return to the primary sources of our Christian heritage. This will include the Great Books, but Alcuin emphasized the teaching of Sacred Scripture and the Church Fathers primarily, pointing us to the true source of the wisdom we so desperately lack. He oversaw the dissemination of manuscripts to make these precious authors much more widely available. Alcuin also demonstrates the need for an authentic and robust engagement with reality, employing the daily work of the monastery and the home, and contemplating God's created works. He models this for us not only in his teaching of the liberal arts, but also as a poet.

Conclusion

And it is as a poet that we will give Alcuin the last word, as he teaches us to attend to the realities of earthly life, but also to look beyond them. We begin with his poetic description of the glory of Charlemagne:

> O face, face more shining than gold thrice refined,
> Happy he who always is with thee.
> The head illustrious, the chin, the neck so beautiful,
> The hands of gold, that banish poverty.
> The breast, the legs, the feet, all laudable,
> All shining forth in beauty and in strength.[41]

Even the glory of emperors fades, and so too their servants. He composed the following poem as an epitaph for his tomb in Tours:

> Here halt, I pray you; make a little stay,
> O wayfarer, to read what I have writ,
> And know by my fate what thy fate shall be.

41. Quoted in G. F. Brown, *Alcuin of York* (E. S. Gorham, 1908), 245.

What thou art now, wayfarer, world-renowned,
I was; what I am now, so shall thou be.
The world's delight I followed with a heart
Unsatisfied: ashes am I, and dust.

Wherefore bethink thee rather of thy soul
Than of thy flesh; — this dieth, that abides.
Dost thou make wide thy fields? In this small house
Peace holds me now; no greater house for thee.
Wouldst have thy body clothed in royal red?
The worm is hungry for that body's meat.
Even as the flowers die in a cruel wind,
Even so, of flesh, shall perish all thy pride.

Now in thy turn, wayfarer, for this song
That I have made for thee, I pray you, say:
"Lord Christ, have mercy on thy servant here,"
And may no hand disturb this sepulchre,
Until the trumpet rings from heaven's height,
"O thou that liest in the dust, arise,
The Judge of the unnumbered hosts is here!"

Alcuin was my name; learning I loved.
O thou that readest this, pray for my soul.

Before his death, writing to his emperor-friend, he expressed hope that his work would endure: "In the morning I sowed in Britain studies which have flourished for a generation. Now as it were towards even I do not cease with blood grown cold to sow in Francia. And in both places I hope that by the Grace of God the seed may spring."[42] His work certainly brought forth enduring fruit in medieval learning, but, as a holy man, considered Blessed in his memory, he recognized and expressed the most importance inheritance in perpetual light:

42. Quoted in Charles W. Colby, *Selections from the Sources of English History* (New York: Longmans, Green & Co., 1899), 18.

Eternal Light, shine into our hearts;
Eternal Goodness, deliver us from evil;
Eternal Power, be our support;
Eternal Wisdom, scatter the darkness of our ignorance:
That we may seek Your face
With all our heart and mind and soul and strength.[42]

42. Alcuin of York: Eternal One," Harvard Square Library, accessed October 29, 2024, https://www.harvardsquarelibrary.org/poetry-prayers-visual-arts/alcuin-eternal-one/.

10 Hugh of St. Victor

Andrew Salzmann

While Hugh of St. Victor is often called the *alter Augustinus*—"another Augustine"—he has not left us a detailed account of his life along the lines of Augustine's *Confessions*. What he did leave, a rather short *Soliloquium de arrha animae*, has been likened to a spiritual autobiography.[1] We have a clearer picture of Hugh's inner life than his worldly one. From the vantage point of the end of his life—the *Soliloquium* appears to be his final work—Hugh confesses his thanks to the Lord:

> You have given me to know you more truly, to love you more purely, to believe in you more sincerely, and to follow you more ardently. You have given me a keen awareness, an agile mind, a tenacious memory, a ready tongue, pleasing speech, convincing teaching, effectiveness in work, graceful demeanor, progress in studies, results in undertakings, consolation in adversities, caution when things go well. Wherever I have turned, there your grace and mercy preceded me.[2]

His fellow canons appear to have agreed. His entry in the necrology of St. Victor notes, "He received so excellently the gift of heavenly wisdom given him from on high that in the whole Latin Church no one could be found comparable to him in wisdom."[3] St. Bonaventure,

---

1. Paul Rorem, *Hugh of Saint Victor* (Oxford, 2009), 11.
2. *Arrha* 63; Hugh Feiss, OSB, "Hugh of St. Victor, *Soliloquy on the Betrothal-Gift of the Soul*," in *On Love*, ed. Hugh Feiss, Victorine Texts in Translation 2 (New City Press, 2012), 225.
3. Jerome Taylor, *Origin and Early Life of Hugh of St. Victor: An Evaluation of the Tradition*, Texts and Studies in the History of Mediaeval Education 5 (University

perhaps the best-known of his intellectual descendants, offers similar praise, writing that in his age Anselm had excelled in teaching doctrine, Bernard of Clairvaux in teaching morals, Richard of Saint-Victor in teaching contemplation, but "Hugh excels in all three."[4]

About the events of his life, Hugh himself offers little more than this passage, which obfuscates as much as it enlightens:

> From boyhood I have dwelt on foreign soil, and I know with what grief sometimes the mind takes leave of the narrow hearth of a peasant's hut, and I know, too, how frankly it afterwards disdains marble firesides and paneled halls.[5]

Hugh was born around 1096, but where and to whom has been hotly contested until only recently. Later Victorines asserted that Hugh had grown up in German-speaking Saxony, and while a case was made that he had been born in French-speaking Flanders, Dominic Poirel has argued convincingly in favor of the traditional account, in part due to a detail from the *Soliliquium* itself. A twelfth-century Victorine calendar commemorates one Reinhard of Halberstadt, a cleric who had studied in Paris before founding of the Augustinian community of St. Pancras in Hamersleben; Hugh dedicated the *Soliliquium* to these canons.[6] With this connection established, other details fall into place. Hugh becomes the son of

---

of Notre Dame Press, 1957), 59–60. Translation in Feiss, *Soliloquy on the Betrothal-Gift of the Soul,*" in *On Love*, VTT 2, 186n4.

4. Bonaventure, *De Reductione Artium et Theologian*, trans. Sister Emma T. Healey, in *Works of Saint Bonaventure I* (Saint Bonaventure University, 1955), 27–29.

5. *Didasc.* 3.19; Hugh of St. Victor, *The Didascalicon of Hugh of Saint Victor: A Medieval Guide to the Arts*, trans. Jerome Taylor (Columbia University Press, 1991), 101. All subsequent references to Taylor refer to this translation.

6. Dominique Poirel, "*Hugo Saxo*. Les origins germaniques de la pensée d'Hugues de Saint-Victor," *Francia. Forschungen zur westeuropäischen Geschichte* 33, no. 1 (2006): 163–69. See also Patrice Sicard, *Hugues de Saint-Victor et son école* (Brepols, 1991), 13–17.

Conrad, Count of Blankenburg, and his departure from Saxony with another uncle, also Hugh, may perhaps be explained by political tensions with the emperor. It is well documented that these two Hughs, uncle and nephew, arrived at the Abbey of St. Victor in Paris after having first gone to obtain a relic of the martyr St. Victor from his principal shrine in the city of Marseilles.[7] The elder Hugh, previously archdeacon of the church of Halberstadt, is honored in the necrology of St. Victor for endowing the abbey "magnificently with gold, silver, precious vestments, tapestries, carpets, and various other coverings"; indeed, it concludes, "our church was constructed at his expense."[8] Poirel speculates that Hugh arrived at St. Victor already well-educated and began teaching in 1115, at about nineteen years old. Hugh, then, is the bright and well-educated son of wealthy Saxon nobles, well-connected with his local church and familiar from childhood with Augustinian life.

The most indisputable fact about Hugh's biography is that he was a teacher. Certainly by 1120 Hugh was engaged in instruction at the abbey's school, teaching both members of the community and students who lived outside the monastery. He is called "master" by 1127 and became head of the school by 1133.[9] Nothing else definitive can be said except that he died February 11, 1141, apparently at the age of 44.[10] Demand for his students, shaped by an education which sought to restore the intellect and reform the will, meant that many abbeys sought Victorines to serve as their abbot. By the end of the twelfth century, the Abbey of St. Victor had become the mother house to a significant federation stretching from England to Rome.[11]

---

7. Taylor (1957), 59–60; translation in Feiss (2012), 186n4.

8. Taylor (1957), 59–60; translation in Feiss (2012), 186n4.

9. Rorem, *Hugh of Saint Victor*, 11.

10. Cf. PL 175:CLXIII; cited by Rorem, 11.

11. Robert Porwoll, "Introduction," *Victorine Restoration: Essays on Hugh of St Victor, Richard of St Victor, and Thomas Gallus*, ed. Robert J. Porwoll and David Allison Orsbon, Cursor Mundi 39 (Brepols, 2021), 32–33.

The Aims of Education: Perfection, Healing, Joy

For Hugh, human beings are, by nature, learners. Our need for education is not an effect of original sin; "to be born without knowledge," he writes, "is nature, not guilt." When Hugh speaks of the ignorance which is a punishment of original sin, he describes it not as the need to learn but rather as a slowness or even inability to learn what would have been naturally easy for unfallen human beings to see and understand: "to be born in that vice by which afterwards they are hindered from a knowledge of truth is guilt, not nature."[12] Without this vice, our senses "would take on without labour the judgment of truth instructed by those things which were seen externally."[13] Although Hugh believes the first man "immediately from the beginning of his creation" received both "a perfect knowledge [*scientiam*] and understanding [*cognitionem*] of . . . that [truth] which was appropriate to first perfection," and that he received it "not by study or any teaching" but rather "by a single and simple illumination of divine aspiration," there was still a greater perfection about which humanity needed to learn.[14] Unfallen humanity would still have pursued its completion in the Wisdom of God through learning and would have learned readily.

Hugh thus speaks of God providing three "books" from which humanity would learn Wisdom: "Wisdom was a book written within; the work of [W]isdom a book written without," so that, read properly, Wisdom would lead the human soul to the Love of God.[15] Created as they were in a unfinished condition, not yet confirmed in grace, Adam and Eve needed to read the Book of Wisdom to

12. *Sacr.* 1.7.32. All translations of *De Sacramentis* are taken from *Hugh of Saint-Victor on the Sacraments of the Christian Faith*, trans. Roy Deferrari (Wipf & Stock, 2007). Here, Deferrari, 137.

13. *Sacr.* 1.7.32; Deferrari, 137.

14. *Sacr.* 1.6.12; Deferrari, 102.

15. *Sacr.* 1.6.5; Deferrari, 97.

achieve beatitude; for that purpose, the Book of Wisdom was written within their souls. But the same Wisdom was also written "without," outside their souls. First, it was written in the works of creation, and this was done "for joy" (*ad iocunditatem*); second, it was written in the works of redemption, and this was done "for healing" (*ad sanitatem*). The aims of education, then, are the completion of the human person in beatitude, the experience of contemplative joy, and healing of the effects of sin.

The First Aim: Reading the Book of Wisdom to Complete the Human Person

In order to understand how reading the Wisdom of God would complete the human person, we have to understand that, for Hugh, there is a deep correspondence between the human soul and the created world. Properly seen, this correspondence means that the created world can reveal to the student of creation truths about human nature and its relationship to God. The created world can do this because both it and the human soul are fashioned after the Trinity.

In the first place, Hugh understands the Trinitarian character of the human person through Augustine's psychological analogy. He explains it as follows:

> Consider these three: the mind, understanding, and love. From the mind is born understanding; from the mind and understanding together, love arises. Understanding arises from the mind alone, because the mind generates understanding from itself. But love arises neither from the mind alone nor from understanding alone, for it proceeds from both. First there is mind, then mind and understanding, and afterwards mind, understanding and love.[16]

---

16. *De tribus diebus*, 21.3. Translation by Hugh Feiss, OSB, "Hugh of St. Victor: *On the Three Days*," in *Trinity and Creation*, ed. Boyd Taylor Coolman and Dale M. Coulter (New City Press, 2011), 85. Cf. also *Sacr.* 1.3.21 and 1.3.27.

The integrity of the human person is constituted by a human mind (*mens* or *memoria*) which bears the image (*imago*) of Christological Wisdom "according to reason" in the intellect and likeness (*similitudo*) of pneumatological love "according to love of virtue" in the will.[17] Thus, Hugh can conclude, "God inhabits the human heart in two ways, namely, through learning and love [*per cognitionem . . . et amorem*]."[18] Or, again, "The integrity of human nature . . . is attained in two things—in knowledge and in virtue."[19]

In the second place, Hugh understands the Trinitarian character of the created world through the triad of "power, wisdom, goodness." Creation and each thing within it testifies to the creating Trinity in that each thing is brought into existence through a power which Hugh associates with the Father, then brought to proper form through a wisdom which Hugh associates with the Son, only to find its purpose or end in a *utilitas* (usefulness) which speaks to the goodness or kindness of the Holy Spirit, the Love-of-the-Father-and-the-Son.[20] Hugh believes that the reason that Genesis relates the account of God forming the world gradually is precisely to reveal these progressive perfections of being (*esse*), beautiful being (*pulchrum esse*), and blessed or happy being (*beatum esse*).[21] Human beings

17. *Sacr.* 1.6.2; Deferrari, 95; cf. *Didasc.* 1.1.

18. *De archa Noe*, I.3. Quoted and translated by Harkins, 96.

19. *Didasc.* 1.5; Taylor, 52

20. *De tribus diebus*, 1.2–1.4.

21. "For even the rational creature itself was first made unformed in a certain mode of its own, afterwards to be formed through conversion to its Creator; and therefore matter unformed but afterwards formed was shown to it, that it might discern how great was the difference between being (*esse*) and beautiful being (*pulchrum esse*). And by this it was warned not to be content with having received being from the Creator through creation, until it should obtain both beautiful being and happy being (*beatum esse*), which it was destined to receive from the Creator" (*Sacr.* 1.1.3; Deferrari, 9). For more on the distinctions between *esse*, cf. Boyd Taylor Coolman, "*Pulchrum esse*: The Beauty of Scripture, the Beauty of the Soul, and the Art of Exegesis in Hugh of St. Victor," *Traditio* 58 (2003): 175–200.

would learn that the world itself had been created progressively, "first made unformed and then formed," moving from being (*esse*) to beautiful being (*pulchrum esse*), only to be consummated at the end of time with being happy (*beatum esse*). If creation itself was a "work in progress," humanity would then readily understand that it, too, remains to be completed. Reflecting that nothing could be impossible for a God who somehow quickened slimy matter and then joined it to the radically different nature of a rational spirit, "man might know that . . . by no means would it be impossible for [God] to elevate the lowness of the rational creature . . . to participation in His own glory."[22] Humanity itself could trace the path from *esse*, to *pulcrum esse*, to *beatum esse*—that is, beatitude with God.[23] All this would be learned through "reading" the Book of Wisdom written in the soul and in Creation. It is profoundly striking that the need to learn through observation and introspection is by no means an effect of original sin but rather one of the most naturally human activities.

The Second Aim: Reading the Book of Nature to Bring Joy

A second aim of education is to discover the special joy which comes from contemplating the forms of Wisdom read simultaneously within (that is, in the soul) and without (that is, in creation). The Victorines were inspired by Paul's claim that "the invisible things of him, from the creation of the world, are clearly seen, being understood by the things that are made." Inspired by Augustine's inner ascent, the Victorines sought to move *per visibilia ad invisibilia*, proceeding "from visible things to the invisible, turning inward in the process."[24] Hugh explains our ability to "see" God in visible things

22. *Sacr.* 1.6.1; Deferrari, 94.

23. *Sacr.* 1.1.3; Deferrari, 9.

24. Ineke van't Spijker, "*Non quaerat extra se, qui haec propter se facta credit:* Hugh of Saint-Victor's Pedagogy," in *Omnium expetendorum prima est sapientia: Studies on Victorine Thought and Influence*, ed. Wanda Bajor, Michal Buraczewski, and

and in invisible things with his famous doctrine of the "three eyes." Drawing his inspiration from Augustine, he distinguishes between the "eye of the flesh" (*oculus carnis*) by which the soul sees the visible things of the world, the "eye of reason" (*oculus rationis*) by which the soul sees and understands itself and those things within itself, and the "eye of contemplation" (*oculus contemplationis*) by which the soul sees and rejoices in God.[25] Human beings share the eye of the flesh with animals and the eye of reason and contemplation with the angels, but only human beings have both. Thus, humanity

> was placed in a middle position, that he might have sense within and without; within for invisible things, without for visible; within through the sense of reason, without through the sense of the flesh, that he might go in and contemplate and might go out and contemplate . . . the sense of man was permitted to go to both, and find refreshment in both, to go by cognition, to be refreshed by love.[26]

The ability to see God interiorly with the eye of reason and exteriorly with the eye of the flesh allows the soul to contemplate God at all times, regardless of its attention span. Thus the soul can be refreshed with the love of the Holy Spirit wherever it turns.

More than merely reinforcing each other, however, the discovery that the same Wisdom is written both within the soul and without it in the world is the occasion of a kind of joy which is uniquely proper to the human race, what we can call "the joy of sacramental-

---

Marcin Jan Janecki, and Dominique Poirel, Bibliotheca Victorina 29 (Turnhout, 2021), 119. See Dale M. Coulter, *Per visibilia ad invisibilia: Theological Method in Richard of St. Victor*, Bibliotheca Victorina 19 (Brepols, 2006).

25. *Sacr.* 1.10.2; Deferrari, 167. See also *In Hierarchiam coelestem* (PL 175:976A-B). For more on the *oculus* or *acies mentis* in Augustine, see Frederick van Fleteren, "*Acies mentis*," in *Augustine Through the Ages: An Encyclopedia*, ed. Allan Fitzgerald and John Cavadini (Eerdmans, 1999), 5–6; cf. Augustine, *trin.* 15.21–23).

26. *Sacr.* 1.6.5; Deferrari, 97; cf. *Didasc.* 3.10.

ity." What Hugh means by "joy" is not merely a passion, the body's unreflexive reaction to external *stimuli*.[27] On the contrary, it is, like love, a rational movement of will; in fact, while Hugh when describing the psychological analogy of the Trinity says in some places that the mind and understanding give rise to love, in others he explains that they give rise specifically to joy (*gaudium*).[28] For Hugh, this joy could be called "sacramental." Like sacramental grace emerging from the juxtaposition of word and form, the joy of sacramentality has the particular character that it is the fruit of the juxtaposition of seeing the same Wisdom written in the soul and the world. Hugh understands that experiencing a truth which one has first seen expressed in the mind's eye then expressed in the physical world yields a particular kind of delight (*iocunditas*), the delight of the artist whose painting turns out just the way she pictured it in her mind. The perfect expression of the spiritual in the physical gives a deep joy, one which is not merely provisional, but eschatological; it will constitute one of the joys of heaven. Thus Hugh explains that God sends us "light and sweetness":

> One [light] is for illumination, the other [sweetness] for refreshment. . . . Refreshment makes what is within delightful [*iucundum*]; illumination reveals the joy which is without; both are required for full joy [*gaudium plenum*]. For if you are refreshed in one and lacking in the other, it is not perfect joy [*laeitita perfecta*], but is mixed with sadness. Seek therefore refreshment, so that what is within you may be delightful [*iucundum*] to you; seek

27. Augustine "saved" the experience of joy from the Stoic suspicion that joy, as an unreflexive passion erupting into the soul from the irrational parts of the body, was dangerous to a well-reasoned life. By understanding joy as a rational movement of the will, joy is no longer a threat to a well-reasoned life. Hugh follows Augustine in this understanding of joy. Cf. William S. Babcock, "The Human and the Angelic Fall: Will and Moral Agency in Augustine's *City of God*," in *Augustine: From Rhetor to Theologian*, ed. Joanne McWilliam (Wilfrid Laurier University Press, 1992), 137.

28. *Sacr.* 1.3.31; Deferrari 59.

> also enlightenment, so that what is without may be delightful [*iucundum*] to you."[29]

Then, Hugh invites us, "Look at this world, which offers so many spectacles of delight [*iucunditatis*]!"[30] The student who discovers Wisdom while reading the "books" of Creation and of the soul discovers that "a divine pedagogy is woven into the very texture of the world and its history."[31] To learn in such a symbolic, sacramental world is itself a source of delight.

The Third Aim: Reading the Book of the Incarnation to Heal the Sinner

By nature, then, human beings were called to be educated by reading creation to make a final turning (*conversio*) to God in love, and to take everlasting joy in the continued reading of the same Wisdom expressed interiorly in the soul and sacramentally in creation. However, after the fall into sin, the reading of the Book of Wisdom written within and without is no longer possible:

> As long, therefore, as [the soul] kept these eyes [of the flesh, of reason, of contemplation] open and uncovered, it saw clearly and discerned rightly, but, after the shades of sin had entered upon it, the eye of contemplation indeed was extinguished so that it saw nothing, but the eye of reason was made bleared so that it saw doubtfully. That eye alone which was not extinguished remained in its clarity and as long as this [bodily eye] has clear light it has undoubting judgment. . . . [Fallen humanity] has not the eye of contemplation, [and so it] is not able to see God and the things that are in God.[32]

29. *Commentariorum in hierarchiam caelestem* 7 (PL 175, 1063C-D); my translation.

30. *De tribus diebus*, 12.

31. Spijker, "*Non quaerat extra se*," 117.

32. *Sacr.* 1.10.2; Deferrari, 167.

It is important to note that this fall is not a fall into "total depravity": The eye of reason is only bleared and doubtful, not completely blinded. Some truth remains within its grasp. To lack the illumination of reason completely would mean entering into a state of bestiality.[33] Nonetheless, as noted above, humanity now bears within it the vice of being "impeded from recognizing the truth when they ought," and of failing to respond to the truth with virtue and love.[34] Sin has deformed the human soul, and this sin "is understood to be the corruption . . . which we take by birth through ignorance in the mind, through concupiscence of the flesh."[35] Sin is "the violation of proper measure," the disintegration of self, the loss of form. The deformed soul—as a triad of memory, intellect, and will—must now be restored, be reconstructed, through the imposition of form and order.[36] Healing is necessary.

That medicine is nothing other than Wisdom, the "highest curative [*solamen*] in life."[37] Wisdom will come again, not as the source of the soul's intellect nor as the form impressed upon creation, but rather as the incarnation of Christ.

> Wisdom was a book written within; the work of wisdom a book written without. But He willed afterwards that it still be written otherwise without, that wisdom might be seen more manifestly

---

33. Fallen humanity continues to participate in that "threefold power of the soul"—sustaining the vegetative body, animating sensible perception, and "grasping things present" or "understanding of things absent," the specific motion which "belongs to humans alone" (*Didasc.* 1.3; Taylor, 49–50).

34. *Sacr.* 1.7.32; Deferrari, 137.

35. *Sacr.* 1.7.28; Deferrari, 134.

36. Boyd Taylor Coolman, *The Theology of Hugh of St. Victor: An Interpretation* (Cambridge University Press, 2010), 65–69. Cf. *Sacr.* 1.7.16.

37. *Didasc.* 1.1; Taylor, 47. Or again, "As God, He created you with me; He alone came to you as a human being. . . . He is the form; He is the medicine; He is the example [*exemplum*]; He is the remedy" (*Tribus Diebus* 24.3; Feiss, 89). Or, finally, "This is our entire task—the restoration of our nature and the removal of our deficiency" (*Didasc.* 1.5; Taylor, 52).

> and be recognized more perfectly, that the eye of man might be illumined to the second [exterior] writing, since it had been darkened to the first [exterior writing]. Therefore, He made a second work after the first, and that was more evident, since it not only pointed out but illumined. He [Wisdom] assumed flesh not losing divinity. . . . Therefore, there was one book written once within, and twice without; [written without] first through the foundation of visible things, secondly without through the assumption of flesh."[38]

Note that this third writing of the book of Wisdom, the second outside of the soul, makes it easier for the bleared eye of reason to read, in the Scriptures, a message which otherwise might be lost, and it restores the possibility of contemplating God's Wisdom in the world.

Concretely, this restoration means the restoration of memory and "the contemplation of truth and the practice of virtue."[39] As Hugh describes the process of this restoration in his "guide for readers," the *Didascalicon*, "There are four things in which the life of the just man is now practiced and raised . . . to its future perfection—namely, study or instruction, meditation, prayer, and performance. Then follows a fifth, contemplation, in which, as if by a sort of fruit of the preceding steps, one has a foretaste, even in this life, of what the future reward of good work is."[40] We can preface these four (or five) steps with two preparatory steps. First, the formation of life; for Hugh, learning occurs within the broader context of the (re)-formation of the student's daily habits. Second, the restoration of memory, which Hugh describes in the preface to his *Chronicon*. We

38. *Sacr.* 1.6.5; Deferrari, 97–98.

39. *Didasc.* 1.8; Taylor, 55. Note that the restoration of memory is not included in this citation. However, in *Didasc.* 1.1, Hugh notes that the woundedness of memory is indeed part of the problem of the human condition and seems to include its restoration when he says that "we are restored through instruction" (Taylor, 47).

40. *Didasc.* 5.9; Taylor, 132.

can therefore summarize Hugh's spiritual program with seven stages, though again he himself names four or five.[41]

Table 10-1.

Activity	Principal Work(s) by Hugh
Formation of Life	*De institutione novitiorum*
Exercise of Memory	The *Chronicon, vel del tribus maximis circumstantiis gestorum.*
Reading	Scriptural Reading: *De scripturis*[a] General Reading: The *Didascalicon*
Meditation [including psychegram]	*Libellus de formatione arche* (or *De arca Noe mystica*); *De meditatione*
Prayer	*Virtuti orandi*
Performance	*Archa Noe*
Contemplation	Various Mystical Treatises, such as the *De arrha animae*

a. For Grover Zinn's argument that the *De scripturis* (*On Sacred Scripture*) was intended to be Hugh's introduction to the sacred page, see Grover Zinn, "Hugh of St. Victor's *De scripturis et scriptoribus sacris* as an Accessus Treatise for the Study of the Bible," *Traditio* 52 (1997): 116–21; and Franklin Harkins, *Reading and the Work of Restoration: History and Scripture in the Theology of Hugh of St Victor* (Pontifical Institute of Mediaeval Studies, 2009), 142–43.

---

41. The justification for prefacing the acts of reading (read through the *De scripturis* and *Didascalicon*), meditation, prayer, performance, and contemplation with the formation of life (and the *De institutione novitiorum*) with the *Chronicon* (and the formation of memory) can be found in the *Indiculum* of Gilduin. This index was written by Hugh's abbot after Hugh's death, and lists Hugh's works in "a specific order" which Paul Rorem considers an intentional introduction to Hugh's works (14). Indeed, Rorem structures his whole introduction to Hugh based on the order in which his works are listed in the *Indiculum*. I have departed from Rorem's order only in splitting up the two Ark treatises (*Libellus de formation arche* and *Archa Noe*) given that the *Libellus de formation arche* fits more clearly into Hugh's idea of meditation. For an edition of the *Indiculum*, see Joseph De Ghellinck, "La table des matières de la première edition des oeuvres de Hugues de Saint-Victor," *Recherches de sciences religieuses* I (1910): 270–89, 385–96.

Importantly, the general shape and progression of Hugh's thought as presented by Abbot Gilduin move from the mastery of creation and history (through the formation of life and of memory) through to the mastery of doctrine and thought (through the intellectual acts of reading and meditation) to the mastery of prayer, action, and contemplation (all volitional acts). Creation, history, and memory are all appropriated to the Father; doctrine, thought, and intellect are all appropriated to the Son; prayer, action, contemplation, and will are all appropriated to the Spirit.

Much could be said about the Trinitarian shape of the many triads in Hugh's thought.[42] A few of these triads, however, can be listed right here:

Table 10-2.

Father	Son	Holy Spirit
Power	Wisdom	Goodness
Memory	Intellect	Will
History	Doctrine	Performance
Creation	Recreation	Eschaton

Note, then, that Hugh's wholistic educational program "rounds the bases" of the faculties of body and soul. The formation of good habits of behavior within the novice is a kind of bodily prolegomena to learning. Beginning with the formation of the memory, the intellect proceeds to seek truth by learning through reading and retaining what is learned, before the will seeks virtue by petitioning through prayer and growing through performance. The soul, now perfected in memory, intellect, and will, returns to creation newly able to con-

42. For a longer explanation of the Trinitarian structure of Hugh's thought based on his *De tribus diebus*, see A. B. Salzmann, "The Holy Spirit and the Life of the Christian According to Hugh of St. Victor: Dator et Donum, Cordis Omne Bonum" (PhD diss., Boston College, 2015), 60–75.

template God through it, saving the sweetness of God's presence in all it knows.

The *Chronicon*: History and Memory

The healing of the soul thus begins with the healing of memory. When Hugh speaks about the restoration of memory, he is not simply concerned with the disinterested recall of information: he is speaking about the restoration of the heart of human identity as made in the image of God; he is speaking about the restoration or reform of the human soul. Hugh lays out his most fundamental advice for improving memory in the preface of the *Chronicon*, a book which offers a list of biblical names, dates, and places which his students were intended to memorize in preparation for reading the Bible. Hugh considered the facts of history to be "the foundation of all knowledge, the first to be laid out together in memory." Invoking the image of a money changer who can quickly make change because his purse is divided into many different compartments, preventing a burdensome, disastrous, and ineffective confusion, Hugh informs his students that the most basic key to memory is to recognize that memory is like this money changer's bag:

> Consider how you ought to gather together in [your heart] the precious treasures of wisdom and set them in order, so that you will know the individual receptacles for each one. And then, set what you have placed in those receptacles for storage in such an order that, when reason requests it, you will be able easily to find it by means of memory, to know it by means of understanding, and to set it forth by means of eloquence.[43]

43. *Chronicon*, translated by Grover A. Zinn as "On the Three Most Important Circumstances of Deeds, that is, Persons, Places, and Times," in *Interpretation of Scripture: Practice*, Victorine Texts in Translation 6, ed. Frans van Liere and Franklin T. Harkins (New City Press, 2016), 138.

Hugh draws deeply from the history of Western memory techniques to help his students in the task of remembering, having apparently read Cicero and the *Ad Herennium* on memory.[44] Students are advised to remember based on "number, place, and occasion." As Franklin Harkins describes, the ultimate aim of *memoria* was "to make a particular text a part of oneself, to allow it to be inscribed in one's heart in order to build character, promote citizenship, instill prudence, engender piety, and ultimately attain perfect happiness."[45] As the Father begets the Son, so those facts locked in the treasure chest of memory will conceive worthy thoughts.

The *Didascalicon*: Reading for Transformation

Hugh gives his prescription for the healing of the sin-wounded soul in his famous *Didascalicon*, a reader's guide written to give structure and purpose to education. It is difficult to overstate the importance of this work in the history of Western education. We have eighty-two extant manuscripts, full or partial, with a remarkable spread across Europe: France, Germany, Austria, Italy, England, the Low Countries, Spain, and Slovenia. Interest in the work stayed high through the centuries; twenty-three to twenty-six of the manuscripts have been dated to the twelfth century, eighteen to twenty-three of them from the thirteenth, nine to eleven from the fourteenth, twenty-one or twenty-two from the fifteenth, and even two or three from the final decades of manuscript writing in the sixteenth century. They were owned by major abbeys and centers of learning, as well as a diverse group of religious orders: Augustinians of course; not just the Victorines, but also the Norbertines and Crosiers; Bene-

44. For an explanation of Hugh's use of the Western memory tradition, see Harkins, 14–41. See also Mary Carruthers, *The Book of Memory: A Study of Memory in Medieval Culture*, 2nd ed. (Cambridge University Press, 2008).

45. Harkins, *Reading and the Work of Restoration*, 35.

dictines and Cistercians; even the Franciscans.[46] As a project, it stands among Augustine's *De doctrina Christiana*, the *Institutions* of Cassiodorus, Isidore of Seville's *Etymologiae*, John of Salisbury's *Metalogicon*, or the Jesuit *Ratio studiorum* for the clarity and scope of its Christian educational vision. As Jerome Taylor notes, at the same time that the schools at Bologna, Salerno, Tours, and Orleans were beginning to specialize in law, medicine, or the arts, when the School of Chartres was focusing on the *quadrivium* and Abelard on the Trivium, when the Cistercians were shying away from scholastic education itself, Hugh, and afterwards the Abbey of St. Victor with him, resisted such specialization, setting forth a program "insisting on the indispensability of a whole complex of the traditional arts and on the need for their scientific pursuit in a particular order by all."[47] For both its sensitivity to the needs of students and its actual influence across history, the *Didascalicon* places Hugh in the company of the Church's great educators.

Confronted with a work that bills itself as a guide for readers, one may ask whether "reading" and "teaching" are truly the same. At first glance, reading appears to be a profoundly individualistic activity, teaching a fundamentally communal one. In Hugh's time, however, reading was a collective activity, and the collective activity of reading was—along with the sermon, the *collatio*, and other forms of speeches—the primary mode of instruction.

46. Patrice Sicard, *Iter Victorinum: La tradition manuscrite des œuvres de Hugues et de Richard de Saint-Victor; Répertoire complémentaire et études, avec un index cumulatif des manuscrits des œuvres de Hugues et de Richard de Saint-Victor*, Bibliotheca Victorina 24 (Brepols, 2015), 208–15.

47. Taylor, 4.

Figure 10.1. Image: Hugh of St. Victor. Unknown Miniaturist, French (active 1190s Paris). Illumination on parchment. Bodleian Library, MS Laud Misc. 409 (Oxford Manuscript). Photo: © Bodleian Libraries, University of Oxford

Book One of the Didascalicon*: A Broad Curriculum; or, What One Ought to Read*

Hugh begins his guide for readers by discussing what one ought to read. While one might expect that he would give a list of things to read, he instead discusses Wisdom itself. One is to read Wisdom, the Logos which gives form to all things. Because Wisdom gives form to all human activities, however, one should read "the theoretical consideration of *all* human acts and pursuits," which can each be said to belong "with equal fitness" to philosophy, the pursuit of

Wisdom.[48] Hugh explains that the Wisdom pursued by philosophy has two parts. The first part of Wisdom is understanding (*intelligentia*), which investigates the truth of changeless, spiritual things (the theoretical arts of the mathematical quadrivium, or of physics, or of metaphysical theology) and which assists us in the delineation of moral action (the practical arts of ethics, economics, and politics). The second part of Wisdom is knowledge (*scientia*), which investigates earthly things and which therefore engages in all the arts proper to supporting the human body.[49] These practical arts are especially necessary to alleviate the weakness of the body brought on by sin, for our temporal part must be "cherished and conserved" in proportion to its weakness. The discussion of "what to read" and the extent of Wisdom concludes with the language arts of the Trivium. These, says Hugh, existed in an instinctive form from the beginning, but they were the last of the arts to be properly distinguished; they were developed and refined out of the need to eliminate errors which had arisen in the study of the other arts.[50]

Book Two of the Didascalicon: *An Integrated Curriculum, or the Order in which to Read*

The second book sets out to give the order in which the four families of arts (theoretical, practical, mechanical, and logical) should be read, and to explain how all the twenty-one arts fit within these four families. It is tempting to think that the order in which Hugh discusses the arts is, in fact, the sequential order in which they ought to be read. The order Hugh gives, however, contrasts with the order in which his works are listed by Gilduin's *Indiculum*, and it is that sequence which seems more intuitive. It could be argued that the order presented here is more logical than experiential. One may wonder why

48. *Didasc.* 1.4; Taylor, 51.

49. *Didasc.* 1.7-8; Taylor, 54–55.

50. *Didasc.* 1.11.

Hugh goes through the work to give a logical ordering to all branches of human knowledge; it is intricate. Dominique Poirel has suggested that this classification of knowledge is "the most important attempt since Aristotle to order the whole of knowledge."[51] But the book begins by emphasizing the importance of Wisdom as form, and it recalls Hugh's belief that the proper organization of ideas is necessary for them to be memorized and understood. Thus, while the arts are not listed in the sequence of study, they are listed in terms of their logical priority and relationships to each other. By understanding which arts depend upon other arts, one can form an integrated view of the curriculum, which helps students to see the relationships and causal dependencies between subjects of study; this, in turn, helps students to form a cohesive worldview.

Book Three of the Didascalicon: *Meditation and the Manner in which to Read*

The third book is a treasure-trove of advice for a life of study. Hugh gives his readers a kind of "accessus" to the arts, listing the primary authors and titles to be studied. He then encourages the reader to prepare for this reading list by mastery of the seven liberal arts, offering a well-loved definition: They are the arts considered by the ancients "to excel all the rest in usefulness that anyone who had been thoroughly schooled in them might afterward come to a knowledge of the others by his own inquiry and effort rather than by listening to a teacher," the best tools by which to "prepare for the mind's complete knowledge of philosophic truth."[52]

Study of the liberal arts is not the only preparation, however; the scholar must have a certain way of life. Hugh writes that there

51. Franklin T. Harkins, "Introduction to the *Didascalicon*," in *Interpretation of Scripture: Theory*, Victorine Texts in Translation 3, ed. Franklin T. Harkins and Frans van Liere (New City Press, 2013), 68–69.

52. *Didasc.* 3.3; Taylor, 86–87; cf. also *Didasc.* 2.20 and 3.4.

Figure 10-2. The Branches of Learning According to Hugh of St. Victor

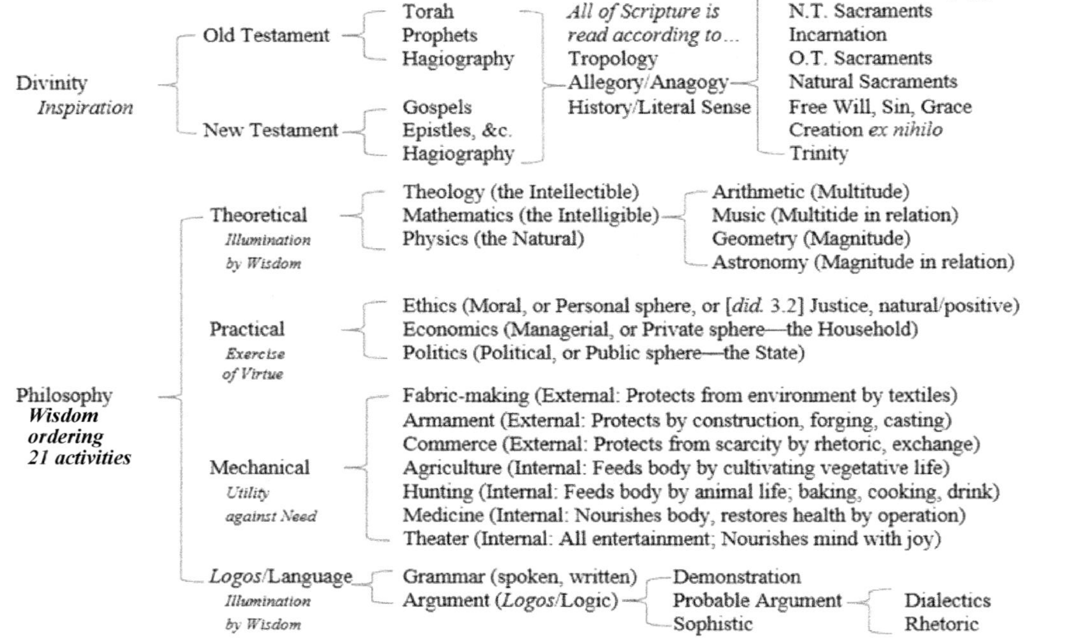

are three things necessary for study: endowment, practices, and disciplines. One cannot do much to increase the natural endowment for learning which God gives to each soul, but one can adopt practices and disciplines which are conducive to a scholarly life. Hugh explains these by offering a significant exegesis on a passage he draws from a contemporary, Bernard of Chartres:

> "A humble mind, eagerness to inquire, a quiet life,
> Silent scrutiny, poverty, a foreign soil.
> These, for many, unlock the hidden places of learning."[53]

Eagerness to inquire, scrutiny, and a foreign soil are the practices, or rules for living; a scholar must be more dedicated to truth than to earthly things or love of one's native home, and must practice the scrutiny of meditation. Humility, interior quiet, and parsimony or frugality are rules for study: a scholar must look down on no person, no book, and no field of study, but must be humble before "the special gift which natural endowment has given to every man," convinced that one can learn at least something from everything and everyone.[54] A scholar must discipline the will against desire while living without concern for luxury.

Hugh then discusses the method by which one ought to read a text. He establishes that a text has a *literam* or "letter" (the grammatical construction and arrangement of the words on the page), a *sensum* or "sense" (the ready and obvious meaning of the text), and a *sententiam* or "inner meaning" (the deeper understanding of a text which can only be achieved by interpretation and analysis).[55] One must progress from the letter, to the sense, to the inner meaning. In analyzing the material, the teacher "begins with those things which are better known and, by acquainting us with these, works . . . to matters which lie hidden."[56]

---

53. *Didasc.* 3.12; Taylor, 94.
54. *Didasc.* 3.13; Taylor 96.
55. *Didasc.* 3.8; Taylor, 92.

Thus, teaching begins "from things which are finite, or defined, and proceeds in the direction of things which are infinite, or undefined." The teacher is also to move from universals to particulars by means of an analysis (*dividendo*) or reasoning which proceeds primarily by divisions and distinctions. Starting with the more general idea, one descends to an understanding of the various particulars which instantiate the universal principles under discussion.

Hugh observes that the whole usefulness of education depends upon one's ability to remember it.[57] Thus he insists that one must read in such a manner that one can remember what one has read. The way to do this he calls *meditation,* the next step—after reading—in the soul's restoration. As one reads, one must "gather" by "reducing to a brief and compendious outline things which have been written or discussed at some length."[58] The most important task in creating this outline is to identify the organizing principle of the work one is reading "upon which the entire truth of the matter and the force of its thought rest."[59] Once an adequate outline is developed, one must somehow remember the outline. Again, Hugh warns "not to rejoice a great deal because you have read many things, but because you have been able to retain them."[60] One way to retain them is to project this outline upon some image, such as a harp, or a house, or the form of a church; then, one easily meditates upon the outline by recalling the image. Hugh famously developed a single image, the Ark of Noah, upon which to project an outline of the whole world of knowledge.[61] The Victorine student who had mas-

---

56. *Didasc.* 3.9; Taylor, 92.

57. *Chronicon*; Liere and Harkins, 141.

58. *Didasc.* 3.10; Taylor, 93.

59. *Didasc.* 3.10; Taylor, 93.

60. *Didasc.* 3.11; Taylor, 94.

61. *De Arca Noe Mystica.* See Conrad Rudolph, "'First I Find the Center Point': Reading the Text of Hugh of Saint Victor's *The Mystic Ark*," *Transactions of the American Philosophical Society* 94, no. 4 (2004).

tered this image had a summary of all sacred and secular knowledge upon which to meditate at leisure.

Books Four, Five, and Six: Reading Scripture

The last three books of the *Didascalicon* shift from secular to the sacred page.[62] It is not possible here to go into a deep discussion of Hugh's exegesis.[63] Hugh begins his treatment of reading the Scriptures with an explanation that Scripture has three senses.[64] While his distinction between the literal and spiritual senses of Scripture follows in the long tradition of Christian exegesis, it is rooted in his general approach to exposition, by which any reading—sacred or secular—is understood to have a text (the words themselves), a sense or obvious meaning, and an inner meaning "which can be found only through interpretation and commentary."[65] The literal/historical sense is always the starting place: "First you learn history and diligently commit to memory the truth of the deeds that have been performed, reviewing from beginning to end what has been done, when it has been done, where it has been done, and by whom it has been done"; one can only proceed to the logical, doctrinal sense of the text (allegory) once "you have first been grounded in history."[66]

62. For a discussion of the literature on the relation of faith and reason in Hugh's *Didascalicon*, see Andrew Benjamin Salzmann, "Hugh of St. Victor," in *A Companion to Medieval Christian Humanism*, ed. John P. Bequette (Brill, 2016), 142–67.
63. For a full overview of Hugh's exegetical practice and writings, see Andrew Benjamin Salzmann, "A Trinitarian Introduction to Hugh of St. Victor's Exegesis," in *Victorine Restoration: Essays on Hugh of St Victor, Richard of St Victor, and Thomas Gallus*, ed. Robert J. Porwoll and David Allison Orsbon, Cursor Mundi 39 (Brepols, 2021), 45–97.
64. *Didasc.* 5.2.
65. *Didasc.* 3.9; Cf. *Didasc.* 6.8-11, in which Hugh aligns "the letter" with the literal sense, "the sense" and "deeper meanings" with the spiritual senses.
66. *Didasc.* 6.3; Taylor, 138. See Grover Zinn, "*Historia fundamentum est*: The Role of History in the Contemplative Life According to Hugh of St. Victor," in *Contemporary Reflections on the Medieval Christian Tradition: Essays in Honor of Ray C. Petry*, ed. G. H. Shriver (Duke University Press, 1974), 135–58.

The truth learned through the allegorical sense then shapes our understanding of how we are to act. The literal/historical, allegorical/doctrinal, and tropological/moral senses map well onto the three faculties of the human person listed in Hugh's account of the psychological analogy (mind, intellect, and love) as well as the three qualities of the cosmological triad (power, wisdom, and loving-kindness). Furthermore, the order in which the three exegetical arts are to be studied reflects the logical priority of the Trinitarian relations. The literal sense is the memory of God's powerful works, which then generates the allegorical sense, which is the proper mode of understanding the wisdom behind these works. Finally, the tropological sense, which instructs the will to live according to God's loving-kindness, proceeds from the literal and allegorical senses. Thus, Hugh's scriptural curriculum involves memorizing the narrative of Scripture, understanding its doctrinal meaning, and finally exercising its virtues in the moral life.

Beyond the *Didascalicon*

In a short overview of Hugh's understanding of education, it is not possible to give the next steps of Hugh's spiritual program—prayer, performance, and contemplation—the attention they deserve. However, they have more to do with the perfection of the will (and its affect) than of the intellect. Thus, meditation on what one has learned should change how one feels. In *De virtute orandi*, he explores how words of prayer arouse devotion, which is the heart of prayer.[67] He explores nine types of prayer and nine types of feelings.[68] The petitioning of prayer naturally advances to the performance of good works.[69] The Ark has already been imprinted upon the

67. *Virtute orandi* 4-6; Hugh Feiss, *Writings on the Spiritual Life*, Victorine Texts in Translation 4, ed. Christopher P. Evans (New City Press, 2013), 325.

68. *Virtute orandi* 6–9.3 and 14.2–3.

69. *Didasc.* 5.9.

memory by the exercise of the intellect; now it must be built with the will through the exercise of virtue: "Whosoever makes it his endeavor to cut himself off from the enjoyment of this world and cultivate virtues, must with the assistance of God's grace"—called down through petitionary prayer—"erect within himself a building of virtues" which shares the proportions of the ark.[70] Ultimately, these virtues will receive the heaven-sent fire of charity which will lead the soul to the sweetness of contemplation.[71]

The Influence of Hugh of St. Victor on the Renewal of Catholic Education

As the author of one of the major, if not the primary, educational text of the Middle Ages, Hugh is one of the most obvious resources for those interested in the renewal of education. Perhaps one of the most prominent reforming voices in Christian education to draw on Hugh is Dorothy Sayers. While Sayers is often credited with inspiring some of the founders of the Classical Education movement, she describes her project as "neo-Medievalist"; she frequently refers back to what was done in the Middle Ages, though without naming which medieval authors she is invoking.[72] Nonetheless, a compelling case can be made that Sayers is drawing from Hugh's *Didascalicon*. The very title of her famous 1947 Oxford address, "The Lost Tools of Learning," evokes Hugh's description of the liberal arts as the *instrumenta* (tools) of learning.[73] Sayers has been critiqued for articulating a vision of Trivium in which it consists

---

70. *Archa Noe* 1.18; A Religious of CSMV, trans., *Ark of Noah*, in *Hugh of Saint-Victor: Selected Spiritual Writings* (Harper and Row, 1962), 72.
71. Cf. *Archa Noe* 3.1. For an overview of Hugh's idea of exercising the will to build virtues, see Salzmann, "The Holy Spirit and the Life of the Christian," 292–312.
72. Unfortunately, no working draft of the speech exists in her papers (held at Wheaton College, in Illinois) which could shed light on this question.
73. *Didasc.* 3.3. See Dorothy Sayers, *The Lost Tools of Learning* (GLH Publishing, 2017).

not of three arts (grammar, logic, rhetoric) but of three stages of study which can be applied to any subject (the study of fact, of thought, of action).[74] Her proposed curriculum for theology, however, tacks closely with Hugh's: first, the memorization of an outline of Scripture as "grammar" or the literal sense; second, the rational structure of Christian doctrine as "logic" or the allegorical sense; finally, the renewed appreciation of the beauty, but also the actionability, of the content studied as "rhetoric" or the tropological sense. The Trinitarian, triadic structure of Sayers's proposal is similarly Hugonian. Thus, Hugh appears to be an indirect influence at the origin of the Association of Classical Christian Schools, whose founder was inspired by Sayers.[75] More recently, major figures in the ACCS engaged Hugh directly.[76]

Hugh's thought was also influential on a major voice in the renewal of specifically Catholic, liberal education: Stratford Caldecott. While Caldecott's *Beauty and the Word* cites Hugh and Sayers on only a few pages, Hugh's influence in it is tectonic. The work is structured around remembering (associated with other Paternal moments like grammar, history or *mythos*, and imagining the real), thinking (associated with other Christological moments like dialectic, Logos, and knowing the real), and speaking (associated with other pneumatological moments like rhetoric, ethos, and com-

74. E.g., "Dorothy Sayers is NOT talking about the true medieval Trivium. She is proposing a modernized program of study that borrows the 'progression' idea from the Trivium, but is re-oriented around 'stages of learning' and not specific knowledge and skills. Whereas the Trivium consisted of three specific arts, she is now referring to three different stages that resemble the Trivium by way of analogy. This is *not* classical education, but something she is inventing on the spot." William C. Michael, OP, "Against Dorothy Sayers," Classical Liberal Arts Academy, updated Dec. 24, 2024, https://classicalliberalarts.com/blog/against-dorothy-sayers-2009/.

75. Douglas Wilson, *The Case for Classical Christian Education* (Crossway, 2003), 87.

76. Kevin Clark and Ravi Scott Jain, *The Liberal Arts Tradition: A Philosophy of Christian Classical Education*, 3rd ed. (Classical Academic Press, 2021), e.g., 110.

munity in the real).[77] While one might have expected the triad remembering-thinking-speaking to terminate in a different, more volitional term than "speaking" such as love or morals, Caldecott makes clear that "speaking" is indeed as pneumatological as those would have been: "you cannot communicate a truth that has not changed you."[78]

Other thinkers have drawn on Hugh's theory of reading sacred literature and its intentional movement from the formation of memory to formation of intellect to formation of will through reading, meditation, prayer, and performance to suggest more effective ways of reading secular literature. Brett Bertucio suggests that educators could adopt the *Didascalicon's* methods into a "pedagogy of *metanoia*," in which the text is allowed to give "ontological substance to the reader in the pattern of her essential nature."[79] Hugh's '*lectio divina*' need not be limited to scripture, but in fact can help us to recover a properly Christian literary theory, rather than one grounded in critical hermeneutics or "autonomous models" of student learning. Such a proposal makes concrete the manner in which a Great Books education strives to go beyond mere plot-analysis of a text while remaining firmly grounded in the text itself.

This list is not exhaustive. One could also mention, for example, Hugh's influence on Ivan Ilych, a noted advocate of "unschooling." Still other compelling aspects of Hugh's educational program remain to be mined, like his emphasis on the connection between learning and the form of life which is suggested by his instruction

77. Stratford Caldecott, *Beauty in the World: Rethinking the Foundations of Education* (Angelico Press, 2012). He specifically cites Hugh on the importance of history/mythos and the dynamic motion from the literal sense of Scripture to the spiritual senses (110–11).

78. Caldecott, 86.

79. Brett Bertucio, "*Paideia* as *Metanoia*: Transformative Insights from the Monastic Tradition," *Philosophy of Education* 71 (2015): 514.

to novices, or a modern retrieval of his emphasis on memorization as the restoration of the "treasure chest of the heart."[80] Hugh's rich pedagogical thought will continue to reward careful study and to inspire Catholic educators as new readers call new attention to different aspects of his *oeuvre*.

80. Brett Bertucio, "The Monastic Turn: 400–1150," in *A History of Western Philosophy of Education in the Middle Ages and Renaissance*, ed. Kevin H. Gary (Bloomsbury Academic, 2021), 47.

11 Dominic and Thomas Aquinas

Josef Froula

The purpose of this chapter is to supply an account of the nature and purpose of Catholic education according to the writings of St. Thomas and in the context of the Dominican charism. To this end, I hope to accomplish three things. First, I will touch briefly on the essentials of Dominican life that gave rise to the unique contribution of St. Thomas to the Church. Second, as the principal focus of my presentation, I will explain what is most fundamental to Catholic education in the mind of St. Thomas. Third, I will conclude with some examples of how St. Thomas's understanding manifests itself in the practical pursuit of Catholic education.

The Dominican Charism

Because the particular life and writings of St. Thomas Aquinas were able to flourish only in the context of the charism given by the Holy Spirit to St. Dominic, I will begin by supplying an account of how the Dominican way of life contributed to the realization of Catholic education.

St. Dominic frequently repeated in his exhortations and letters the injunction "Always study!"[1] His insistence on study as the foundation of preaching was not without controversy in the twelfth and thirteenth centuries. In fact, Peter of the Cells (1115–1183), a Benedictine bishop of Chartres, wrote, "Blessed school in which Christ himself teaches our hearts by his Word, where, without studies and courses, we assimilate the secrets of eternal bliss. No need to buy

1. Guy Bedouelle, OP, *St. Dominic: The Grace of the Word* (Ignatius Press, 1987), 156.

books, no professors to be paid, no gatherings for debates, no sophisms to unravel."[2] In contrast, St. Dominic approved of the subordination of common life, at certain times, to study and preaching. Visitators sent by the provincial chapter to Dominican Houses were instructed to ask three questions: "Do the brothers live in harmony, are they assiduous in their studies, and are they fervent in preaching?"[3] A new essential bond was thus formed between study and preaching for the sake of the salvation of souls. St. Dominic's sons were not merely to cultivate a fervent prayer and intellectual life, but to pass on the fruits of their charism to the faithful by combatting error and cultivating rectified minds among the faithful. Every convent or priory had a doctor assigned to it and was a school of theology in its own right. Centers for Dominican studies became faculties of theology who were thence introduced into medieval universities. We owe to St. Dominic, then, the very archetype of what Catholic institutions of higher learning are today. Without his inspiration to transform the culture of those surrounding him with the unsurpassed wisdom of sacred theology, St. Thomas would have been unable to teach and preach in the manner that he did. Our Holy Patron of all Catholic schools and Universal Doctor of natural and revealed truth could not have been our guide and model of Catholic liberal education without the charism of St. Dominic that he embraced. We therefore owe our understanding of intellectual perfection to St. Thomas, but first to St. Dominic who made the work of the Angelic Doctor possible. Using the writings of St. Thomas as a guide, I hope to manifest what is most essential to Catholic education.

What "Catholic Liberal Education" Means

I should first note, however, that when I refer to Catholic education, I have in mind Catholic *liberal* education. This is the education

2. Bedouelle, 157.

3. Bedouelle, 158.

which is for its own sake and specifically ordered to the perfection of the mind. In the *Summa Contra Gentiles*, St. Thomas defines "free" as "that . . . which is for its own sake" (Book I Ch. 72). Here, "for its own sake" means simply "for the sake of the perfection of man himself" as opposed to being ordered to some other practical or useful end. So, one who is free is able to devote himself to those pursuits specifically ordered to the perfection of the faculties of the soul. In contrast, a slave is treated as a mere possession that is ordered to the good of his master. This is why slavery is dehumanizing and wrong: slaves are not treated as human beings who realize within themselves their own ends, but as objects that exist for the sake of someone else.

Following this understanding of freedom, then, an education that is liberal or free is an education which is for its own sake. In other words, it is ordered to the kind of knowledge which is an end in itself because it forms and perfects the human person. St. John Henry Cardinal Newman puts it this way in *The Idea of a University*: "I am asked what is the **end** of University Education, and of the **Liberal** or Philosophical Knowledge which I conceive it to impart: I answer, that . . . it has a very tangible, real, and sufficient end, though the end cannot be divided from that knowledge itself. Knowledge is capable of being its own end . . . sufficient to rest in and to pursue for its own sake."[4] Saint John Paul II makes the same point in *Ex Corde Ecclesiae*. He says, "The basic mission of a University is a continuous quest for *truth* through its research, and the preservation and communication of *knowledge* for the good of society."[5]

My treatment of Catholic education here, then, is limited to Catholic liberal education. This, however, is not to say that Catholic schools that exist for practical purposes do not deserve the name.

---

4. John Henry Newman, *The Idea of a University* (Longmans, Green & Co., 1907), Discourse V, 103. Emphasis added in bold.

5. John Paul II, *Ex Corde Ecclesiae* [Apostolic Constitution], The Holy See, August 15, 1990, §30, https://www.vatican.va/content/john-paul-ii/en/apost_constitutions/documents/hf_jp-ii_apc_15081990_ex-corde-ecclesiae.html.

We need Catholic nurses, doctors, lawyers, and real estate investors who work in accord with Catholic principles every bit as much as we need Catholic thinkers and educators.

Given that a liberal education, according to the traditional meaning of the term, has as its purpose the attainment of that knowledge which is ordered to human perfection, it remains to determine how this perfection is accomplished.

The Order in Catholic Liberal Education

St. Thomas teaches us at the beginning of the *Summa Contra Gentiles* that it belongs to the wise man to establish order: "Sapientis est ordinare."[6] The wise man not only orders his mind by knowing the order in creation, but causes order in man-made things, such as the order in a course of studies. Just as the order in creation is God's greatest work, the most distinctive characteristic and most essential element of any school is the order in the curriculum. I will now argue that this is the case and offer further support and defense for the fundamental principles and practices of the Catholic College.

In his commentary of the *Ethics*, St. Thomas distinguishes between two kinds of order that should be observed in every endeavor. The first of these is the order among the parts of a whole, such as the order found in artifacts that are made up of different material parts. For example, the parts of a house have an order among them regarding their position with respect to each other: the foundation is at the bottom, upon which stand the walls, upon which is mounted a roof. Also, there is a sequential order among the parts. The foundation must be built first, and then the walls, because the foundation can exist without the walls, but the walls cannot exist

6. "It is the task of the wise man to order." St. Thomas Aquinas, *Summa Contra Gentiles* (Marietti, 1934), Book I, Ch.1; and *In Ethicorum*, Lectio 1, Paragraph 1 *Opera Omnia Sancti Thomae Aquinatis* (Musurgia, 1948), 17. See Aristotle, *Metaphysics*, 982a 15–19.

without the foundation. The second kind of order is that of things to an end: a house is ordered to the end of providing shelter. The second kind is superior to the first because the order of things to an end determines the order among the parts, and is that for the sake of which the order among the parts exists. It is *because* a house is ordered to providing shelter that its parts are arranged in a certain way.[7]

Accordingly, "the end is everywhere the chief thing,"[8] uniting and governing everything else, dictating which parts are to be used and how they are to be ordered. For this reason, the good of any whole is determined by how fittingly its parts are ordered to its proper end. Nothing is more important when establishing or governing an institution than rightly determining the end or purpose of the whole and properly ordering the parts of the whole to the end.

Because all liberal education has as its aim intellectual perfection, the curriculum should be directed to this purpose. The intellect, however, is perfected most of all by knowing the highest truths. And because God is the highest object of our knowledge, the greatest possible intellectual perfection consists in knowing the truth about him. But the highest truths about God are those truths of revelation that transcend the power of reason to discover or judge.[9] Because these truths are known most profoundly by the science of sacred theology, this science is the end of liberal education in its fullness. Since sacred

7. See St. Thomas, *In Ethicorum*, Lectio 1: "Invenitur autem duplex ordo in rebus. Unus quidem partium alicuius totius seu multitudinis adinvicem, sicut partes domus ad invicem ordinantur: alius est ordo rerum in finem. Et hic ordo est principalior quam prius." ["A twofold order is found in things. One kind is of the parts of a certain whole or multitude to each other, such as the parts of a house being ordered among themselves. The other is the order of things to an end. And this kind of order is superior to the first."] (All translations are mine.) We also find this distinction in Book XII, Chapter 10 of Aristotle's *Metaphysics*, 1075a11–25.

8. Aristotle, *Poetics*, 1450a23.

9. The two greatest truths of our faith are the Trinity and the incarnation. Of these two, the Trinity is superior because it is true independently of, and is the cause of, the incarnation: the Trinity can exist without the incarnation, but not the reverse.

theology is the end, it necessarily determines the order among the other parts of Catholic liberal education that exist for its sake.

From this it follows that what is most essential to a Catholic college is that all the arts and sciences be *ordered by* and *ordered to* the wisdom of sacred theology. This twofold order in the curriculum, that of the parts among themselves and that of things to an end, therefore, is what most of all distinguishes the Catholic College. St. Thomas confirms this when he says, "All sciences and arts are ordered to one thing, namely, to man's perfection, which is his happiness."[10]

A Curriculum Ordered to Sacred Theology

In order for a college to be truly Catholic, it is necessary that the curriculum be directed to understanding the Catholic faith, the truths of which are the most perfective of the intellect. Because the highest possible perfection of the mind consists in understanding the Catholic faith, all other kinds of knowledge that bear on this understanding are undertaken principally for its sake. So the philosophical sciences are *ordered to* theology[11] in the sense that they are studied chiefly for the sake of contemplating the highest truths about God. The inferior sciences prepare the learner for the superior, while the superior sciences strengthen and illuminate the inferior. Yet the value of the inferior sciences is not exclusively (even though chiefly) in contributing to the learning of the superior. The reason for this is that whenever something is done for two purposes, one of which is higher than the other, it is done for the higher purpose more than the lower one. The lower disciplines, therefore, are learned primarily for the purpose of understanding God.

---

10. "Omnes autem scientiae et artes ordinantur in unum, scilicet ad hominis perfectionem, quae est eius beatitudo." *In Metaphysicorum* Proemium, *Opera Omnia Sancti Thomae Aquinatis* (Musurgia, 1948).

11. It is the task of sacred theology to explicate the articles of faith and to reason from these articles as principles of the science.

At first, it may seem that saying that the lower disciplines are studied first and foremost for the sake of theology is at odds with saying that these disciplines are studied for their own sake. What sense does it make to say that the knowledge of natural philosophy, for example, is its own end if it is primarily a means of knowing something else?

Saying that the knowledge of natural philosophy is its own end means that this knowledge is perfective of the mind *even if* it is not applied to any other science beyond it. Yet this does not prevent it from being so applied. Further, because the sciences of natural and sacred theology perfect the mind in an immeasurably higher way, natural philosophy is more worth knowing for their sake than it is for its own sake. This point deserves some elaboration, since it is a key element in understanding not only the relationship between faith and reason but also the essential character of truly Catholic liberal education according to St Thomas.

Though philosophy is studied chiefly for the sake of theology, there is a way in which it is studied for its own sake that is important to emphasize: there is a proper and immediate end of every science that we must embrace as our own habit of knowledge in order for it to be useful for a higher science. Unless we see the truths of philosophy independently of their application to theology, they lose their power of being so applied. For the truths of philosophy are not true because they are useful for theology. Rather, they are useful for theology because they are true. As St. Thomas observes, "faith presupposes natural knowledge, just as grace presupposes nature and perfection something that can be perfected."[12] Grace builds on but never supplants nature. We cannot have faith in what has been revealed without first having knowledge of natural things because the belief in a truth divinely revealed always includes or presupposes

---

12. *Summa Theologiae* I Q2 A1 ad 1: "fides praesupponit cognitionem naturalem, sicut gratia naturam et ut perfectio perfectibile."

something that we know by reason alone. For instance, we cannot have faith in the teaching of the First Vatican Council that the existence of God can be known with certainty by reason alone unless we first know the more universal truth that the mind can come to know with certainty the existence of things outside itself. If we deny the possibility of having natural knowledge of things in reality, or of proving the existence of anything at all, as many modern philosophers do,[13] we must also deny that we can know the existence of God by natural knowledge.

In the same vein, growing in our knowledge of theology demands that we grow in natural knowledge first: the more firm a grasp we have of philosophy, the more able we will be to arrive at the truths of natural theology and to understand the meaning of truths divinely revealed. For example, the more clearly we perceive the definition of motion, the sharper will be our understanding of St. Thomas's first way of arguing to God's existence. Also, understanding the analogous use of the name "relation" as applied to the Trinity directly depends on an understanding of relation in the first sense of the word: the better we understand relation in the natural world, the better our understanding of relation in God can be. Pope St. John Paul II makes this point in *Fides et ratio*: "Without philosophy's contribution, it would in fact be impossible to discuss theological issues such as, for example, the use of language to speak about God, the personal relations within the Trinity, God's creative activity in the world, the relationship between God and man, or Christ's identity as true God and true man."[14]

---

13. See David Hume's *Dialogues Concerning Natural Religion*, Part IX, where Cleanthes propounds this view: "There is no being, therefore, whose non-existence implies a contradiction. Consequently there is no being, whose existence is demonstrable." Quoted from *The Empiricists: Locke, Berkeley, Hume* (Doubleday, 1974), 483.

14. John Paul II, *Fides et ratio* [Encyclical Letter], The Holy See, September 14, 1998, §66, https://www.vatican.va/content/john-paul-ii/en/encyclicals/documents/hf_jp-ii_enc_14091998_fides-et-ratio.html.

Even for those who admit the necessity of philosophy for theology, though, there is a dangerous pitfall to be avoided. There is a tendency to see philosophy as a necessary evil, something to get out of the way because it is necessary only for some further end. The reason that this tendency is so perilous is that if students desire philosophy only for the sake of theology, and not at all for its own sake, failing to see the truths of philosophy for themselves, then philosophy loses entirely its usefulness for theology. It is of the utmost importance to cultivate an abiding wonder about the truths of philosophy. This is among the many things that St. Thomas does so well. Paradoxically, for philosophy to attain its greatest usefulness for theology, we must hold that usefulness in abeyance and attend to the lower disciplines by themselves, and, at least for a time, for themselves. Each art and science plays its proper role in the cultivation of the intellectual virtues that perfect the soul. The more we attend directly to these, the better these habits will be formed. In order for this to happen, however, students must be driven by a powerful desire for knowledge for its own sake. They must engage in the pursuit of wisdom with spontaneous zeal. Any learning, real and true, is a pleasure to the learner. But this pleasure comes only from satisfying a desire to know something purely for the sake of knowing it, which desire is a necessary component of wonder.[15] If students lack a passion for a discipline, they will have but a tenuous hold on the truth. What we enjoy acquiring, we long retain; what we assume begrudgingly, we shed with haste.

15. In "Wonder and Skepticism," Marcus R. Berquist says, "Now when we say that the man of wonder has a passion for knowledge, we imply that he desires the knowledge for its own sake, and not because of some usefulness that it might have" (unpublished lecture, September 13, 1985). See also Marcus R. Berquist, "Learning and Discipleship": "The second characteristic [of the man who wonders] is that he *desires to know*, not just in some momentary way, but wants to know so badly that *he is willing to devote his life to the quest of what he does not know.*" *The Aquinas Review* 6, no. 1 (1999): 41.

Even worse than thinking that philosophy is only for the sake of theology is the failure to see the need for all the parts of an authentic liberal education for theology in the first place. There is a widespread view that other disciplines are not necessary for perfecting our understanding of divinely revealed truth. Mark Brumley says in his article, "What Makes Catholic Education Catholic?" that "the *principal purpose* of Catholic education is to *form disciples*—people who *know* Christ, *follow* Christ and make him *known*. Not excellence in education, as important as that is. . . ."[16] At least in the way he words it here, the author speaks of knowing Christ as one end and excellence in education as another, as if each could exist without the other. In reality, however, Catholic education is a unified whole in which "excellence in education" consists chiefly in "knowing Christ" and the Trinity through knowing the lower disciplines, without which a more profound understanding of these central mysteries of our faith cannot exist.

Sadly, the absence of theology's sapiential function and its isolation from the rest of the curriculum also persists in many Catholic colleges. Recently, a prominent Catholic university inaugurated a new department that they describe as follows: "The Department of Catholic Studies, which is the University's only department that intentionally and directly reflects the University's Mission and Catholic Identity, provides students with a solid, interdisciplinary foundation in the Catholic Intellectual tradition. . . ."[17] Aside from the difficulty of having only one department that reflects the mission of the university (in which case it would not even be a university, let alone a Catholic one), it is trou-

16. Mark Brumley, "What Makes Catholic Education Catholic?" *National Catholic Register*, September 3, 2013, https://www.ncregister.com/news/what-makes-catholic-education-catholic.

17. "The Department of Catholic Studies," Sacred Heart Catholic College, accessed November 12, 2024, https://www.sacredheart.edu/academics/colleges—schools/college-of-arts—sciences/departments—schools/catholic-studies/.

bling that any reflection of Catholic identity outside of one department should be regarded as unintentional. If this is true, then their statement is inconsistent with itself: the university would have no Catholic identity at all. Courses that undermine the Catholic faith would be consistent with this description of the school. The examination of this aberration is helpful by its contrast: for a college to have a truly Catholic identity, courses outside of theology should not only never contradict the faith, but they should also be subject to it and, in accord with its sapiential function, ordered by it.

A Curriculum Ordered by Sacred Theology

The sciences have no existence independent of a mind. At the very beginning of the mind's journey along the natural road to wisdom are common conceptions to which all later conclusions can be traced. As one advances from a lower science to a higher one, as from natural philosophy to first philosophy, the higher knowledge necessarily depends upon the lower: the knowledge of being as such cannot be attained without the knowledge of mobile being. Also, knowledge of the first cause depends upon the knowledge of subsequent causes because the first cause can be known only through knowing those causes first. Yet the knowledge of subsequent causes does not depend upon the knowledge of the first cause. Thus, knowledge of the higher sciences requires knowledge of the lower ones, but not the reverse. It is therefore within the scope of the metaphysician to say how his science differs from natural philosophy, but the natural philosopher is not in a position to speak about metaphysics.

Thus, distinguishing the lower sciences of philosophy and determining their proper methods belongs to metaphysics. And if there is a science that surpasses metaphysics, it must belong to this science to judge the others and to distinguish between itself and the others. Therefore, because the knowledge of theology surpasses all the other sciences, it belongs to this science to order and guide the disciplines beneath it.[18]

The Faith guides and guards the human mind even in its progress through the lower sciences known by reason alone. Therefore, these lower disciplines are also *ordered by*[19] sacred theology. This is what distinguishes a Catholic school from a secular one. Not only is the understanding of divinely revealed truth the primary purpose of the secular disciplines, but it also serves as a governing principle, giving order to those disciplines.

One of the most prominent ways that the order among the parts of the curriculum manifests itself is the sequence in which the sciences are studied. This is the first kind of order mentioned earlier by St. Thomas: the order among the parts of a whole. St. Thomas speaks of the order in which the disciplines of philosophy should be studied in his commentary on Aristotle's *Ethics:*

> Therefore this will be the proper order of learning: first, boys should be instructed in logical matters, because logic teaches the way of the whole of philosophy. Second, they are to be instructed in mathematics, which neither requires experience nor transcends the imagination. Third, they should be taught the natural sciences which, although they do not exceed sense and imagination, do nevertheless require experience. Fourth, they are to be instructed in the moral sciences, which require both experience and a soul free from the passions, as is maintained in the first

---

18. It is for this reason that theology is called the queen of the sciences and philosophy her handmaid. Philosophy is subject to and in the service of theology. For this reason, there is no such thing as the "philosophy of religion" as it is commonly understood: it belongs to theology to judge philosophy, not to philosophy to judge theology.

19. St. Thomas says, "sacra doctrina non supponit sua principia ab aliqua scientia humana, sed a scientia divina, a qua, sicut a summa sapientia, omnis nostra cognitio ordinatur." ["sacred doctrine does not take its principles from another human science, but from divine science, by which, as from the highest wisdom, all our knowledge is ordered."] *Summa Theologiae,* I Q1 A6 ad 1.

> book. Fifth, they should be taught matters concerning wisdom and divine science, which transcend imagination and require a vigorous mind.[20]

Is following St. Thomas's order really an example of divinely revealed truth giving order to the secular disciplines? Isn't the order among the secular disciplines knowable by reason alone? Because the order among the lower disciplines does not depend on revelation, it is certainly knowable by reason alone. Yet, because we cannot know this order without already being wise, it is nearly impossible to attain this knowledge on our own: we must know the disciplines in order to follow them in the right order, yet we must follow them in the right order in order to know them. To escape this quandary, students must trust in the authority of a teacher if they are to make genuine progress toward wisdom. When placing our trust in a teacher, Catholics have the benefit of not having to rely on purely human authority: the Magisterium guides us even in matters of philosophy. This is because, as explained earlier, understanding revelation to the degree that we are able is not possible without the natural knowledge that philosophy supplies. Pope St. John Paul II says in *Fides et ratio*, "... philosophy, like theology, comes more directly under the authority of the Magisterium and its discernment, because of the implications it has for the understanding of revelation, as I have already explained. The truths of the faith make certain demands which philosophy must respect

20. "Erit ergo hic congruus ordo addiscendi, ut primo quidem pueri logicalibus instruantur, quia logica docet modum totius philosophiae. Secundo autem instruendi sunt in mathematicis quae nec experientia indigent, nec imaginationem transcendunt. Tertio autem in naturalibus, quae, etsi non excedant sensum et imaginationem, requirunt tamen experientiam; quarto autem in moralibus, quae requirunt et experientiam et animum a passionibus liberum, ut in primo habitum est. Quinto autem in sapientialibus et divinis quae transcendunt imaginationem et requirunt validum intellectum." St. Thomas Aquinas, *In Ethicorum*, Book VI, Lectio 7, *Opera Omnia Sancti Thomae Aquinatis* (Musurgia, 1948).

whenever it engages theology."[21] Therefore, because philosophy comes under the authority of the Magisterium, the teaching office of the Church whereby divine revelation is clarified, there is a way in which the order among the sciences falls under the purview of divinely revealed truth.

St. Thomas holds a unique place as the Universal Doctor of the Catholic Church. He is the only theologian mentioned by name in the Code of Canon Law, the documents of the Second Vatican Council, and the Program of Priestly Formation as a required guide for teaching theology and philosophy. In addition to the many magisterial statements commending St. Thomas's teaching, at least two popes have made sure to use the word "magisterium" when enjoining us that we take St. Thomas as our guide, model, and teacher in the study of both philosophy and theology.

First, in *Lumen Ecclesiae,* Pope Paul VI says, "A little time later, we called our attention to the 'return to St. Thomas,' an unexpected return certainly, but marvelous, which confirms what the supreme magisterium had said about him, that he is the authorized and irreplaceable guide of philosophical and theological studies."[22] Second, Pope St. John Paul II says in *Fides et ratio,*

> The philosophical disciplines should be . . . based upon the philosophical heritage which is enduringly valid [the *philosophia perennis*]. . . . These directives have been reiterated and developed in a number of *magisterial documents* in order to guarantee a solid philosophical formation, especially for those preparing for theological studies. (§60)
>
> If it has been necessary from time to time to intervene on this question, to reiterate the value of the Angelic Doctor's insights

---

21. John Paul II, *Fides et ratio,* §77.

22. Paul VI, Apostolic Letter *Lumen Ecclesiae* [Apostolic Letter], The Holy See, November 20, 1974, §2, https://www.vatican.va/content/paul-vi/la/apost_letters/documents/hf_p-vi_apl_19741205_lumen-ecclesiae.html.

> and insist on the study of his thought (*doctrina*), this has been because *the Magisterium's directives* have not always been followed with the readiness one would wish. (§61)
> It should be clear in light of these reflections why the **Magisterium** has repeatedly acclaimed the merits of St. Thomas's thought (*doctrina*) and made him the guide and model of theological studies. (§78, bold emphasis added)

The teaching of the Church, therefore, directs us to St. Thomas as an essential guide and model, pointing us toward his "method, doctrine, and principles" (Pius XI, *Studiorum Ducem*, §30) in both philosophy and theology.

It is important to make one qualification here. Though the Magisterium has consistently enjoined upon us the obligation to take St. Thomas as our teacher, this does not mean, of course, that he is inerrant or that no further development is possible in philosophy and theology.

The Church's teaching on St. Thomas does mean, however, that we cannot go wrong in adhering to his fundamental principles and method. The fundamental principle that learning begins with the senses that we can trust and progresses to reason cannot be mistaken. This doctrine of teaching and learning forms the basis for the order of the disciplines, which proceed from those things that can be sensed and imagined to those that cannot.

Another such example of a fundamental doctrine that cannot be mistaken is the distinction between a substance, which cannot exist in another subject, and its accidents, which cannot naturally exist by themselves, but only in a subject. If St. Thomas is wrong about this fundamental principle, then it would also follow that the Church has erred in her approbation of him. This philosophical principle is part of the Church's teaching on the Eucharist, which is that bread is changed into the substance of Christ, while only the accidents of bread remain. If one denies altogether the existence of substance, and thinks that substances are really just conglomerations of their accidents, it is not possible to have faith in the Eucharist. For there would be no difference between the accidents of bread and bread itself. Yet we must believe that the accidents of bread in the Eucharist are not bread. One must adhere, therefore, to Aristotle's distinction between substance and accident in order to accept the Church's teaching on the Eucharist.[23] So, we need not adhere to every assertion of St. Thomas, but we must adhere to his fundamental principles, method, and doctrine in order to be his disciples and disciples of the teaching Church.

This discipleship of St. Thomas, though borne of a steadfast adherence to the teaching of Christ and his Church, is confirmed in our ability to grasp the truth that we learn from St. Thomas. Though we begin our studies by trusting the Church to choose our teacher for us, as we progress along the path to wisdom, we can see more clearly the necessity of following this path. After proceeding from logic to mathematics to natural philosophy to ethics to metaphysics, one is able to see the necessity of studying logic first because it is continually needed in all the other disciplines. One also sees the necessity of following the natural order of learning from sensible things to purely intelligible ones, progressing from the study of the natural world to the knowledge of the First Cause.

These principles of St. Thomas that guide and govern education offer many practical applications for educators. Here are some examples.

1) Begin with what is more known or easier to know and proceed to what is less known or more difficult to know.

For example, in biology, one ought to begin with animals and progress to plants. Because animals are more like us than plants, their

23. The *Catechism of the Council of Trent* says, "In order that the body of our Lord be present in the Sacrament, it remains, therefore, that it be rendered present by the change of the bread into it. Wherefore it is necessary that none of the substance of the bread remain." *Catechism of the Council of Trent*, trans. John McHugh, OP, and Charles Callan, OP (Marian Publications, 1976), 236.

life and operations are more known to us. As we study animals, one ought to begin with the study of the behavior of the whole animal and then proceed to the study of its anatomical parts. Again, this is because the actions of the whole are first known to us and easier to know than the function of its parts. Because knowledge begins with the senses, what is more easily sensed is more easily known.

This order is reversed in modern biology, which almost invariably begins with the cell, which is considered the fundamental unit of life. Rudolf Virchow (1821–1902), the father of modern pathology and biological studies, states, "According to my ideas, this [the cell] is the only possible starting-point for all biological doctrines." He continues, "Every animal presents itself as the sum of all vital unities, every one of which manifests all the characteristics of life. The characteristics and unity of life are to be found only in the definite, constantly recurring structure, which every individual element displays. Hence it follows that the structural composition of a body of considerable size, a so-called individual, always represents ... an arrangement of a social kind, in which a number of individual existences are mutually dependent. ..."[24] According to modern biology, then, we begin with the cell because life is found only in the cell. Yet this is contrary to what is self-evident to us—that human beings and other animals are unified substances and individual, undivided lives. Charles DeKoninck puts it this way, "the man who hopes to arrive at some definition of life ... should never begin with the study of what is alive very obscurely, if alive at all. Why not begin with horses? He can see them without a microscope. Or why not start with the kind of thing that asks what horses are? which eventually constructs microscopes and finds itself faced with the obscure forms of life?"[25]

24. Rudolf Virchow, *Cellular Pathology as Based upon Physiological and Pathological Histology*, trans. Frank Chance (London: John Churchill, 1860), 68.

25. Charles De Koninck, *The Lifeless World of Biology*, in *The Hollow Universe* (University of Notre Dame Press, 1960), 45.

2) Because what is universal is better known, we should begin with what is universal or common, and proceed to what is particular or distinct.

St. Thomas makes this point in his commentary on Book I, Chapter 1 of Aristotle's *Physics*. He says that "those things which are better known to us are confused, and such are the universals; therefore it is necessary that we proceed from universals to singulars."[26] In the study of plant life, for example, the distinction between trees and grasses is more evident than the distinctions among the families of trees. And the distinction among families is more certain than the distinction among genera, which is more certain than the distinction among species. I am more sure that the plant in front of me is a tree than I am that it is an oak; and I am more sure that it is an oak than a red oak; and I am more sure that it is a red oak than it is *quercus palustris* (a pin oak).

In his *Parts of Animals,* Aristotle supplies a practical example of why proceeding from universal to particular makes sense in natural science. He says, "ought we rather to deal first with the attributes which they have in common in virtue of some common element of their nature, and proceed from this as a basis for the consideration of them separately? Now it is plain that if we deal with each species independently of the rest, we shall frequently be obliged to repeat the same statements over and over again."[27] Beginning with the universal, then, makes sense because it is in accord with the natural order of learning.

3) Because we proceed from the senses to reason, making observations for oneself is better than relying on the authority of others.

In his *Anatomical Exercises on the Generation of Animals,* William Harvey says, "Nor is any long refutation necessary where the

26. *Commentary on the Physics,* Lectio I, #6.
27. *Parts of Animals,* 639a 18 and 23.

truth can be seen *with one's proper eyes*; where the inquirer by simple inspection finds everything in conformity with reason; and where at the same time he is made to understand how unsafe, how base a thing it is to receive instruction form others' comments without examination of the objects themselves. . . ."[28] William Harvey manifested this principle in his own writings by doing dissections and vivisections to discover the circulation of the blood and overturn the errors of two millennia of biology. These experiments of his can be repeated in the lab so that students arrive at the same level of certainty that he had.

To supply another example, students of astronomy should rely not only on books but on their own observations of the motion of the heavenly bodies to learn for themselves with certainty the truths of physics. Then, by a careful study of Ptolemy, Copernicus, Kepler, and Newton, they can come to know with certainty that the planets travel in elliptical paths around the sun, rather than merely believing the experts who tell us that this is so.

In the science of chemistry, also, one should rely on the senses and proceed to an understanding of material and agent causes through this sense knowledge. For example, rather than believing that water is composed of hydrogen and oxygen, a simple electrolysis experiment can show that water can be broken down into these two elements.

Summing up this point, William Harvey, who relies heavily on the Aristotelian principles that he enunciates, says, "Diligent observation is, therefore, requisite in every science, and the senses are frequently appealed to. We are, I say, to strive after personal experience, not to rely on the experience of others"[29] "for indeed, there is nothing in the understanding which was not first in the sense."[30]

28. William Harvey, *Anatomical Exercises* (London, 1651), 1.

29. Harvey, 4.

30. Harvey, 2.

To sum up, in order for a program of Catholic liberal education to be true to its name, it must be ordered to understanding divinely revealed truth and the science of sacred theology that adopts this truth as its principles. Further, this truth must serve as a guide[31] and ordering principle of the other disciplines that are necessary for understanding it. Thus, in Catholic liberal education, the entire curriculum must be ordered to and ordered by sacred theology in a way that respects the natural order of learning. Our Faith is both the beginning of our path to wisdom because it orders and guides our progress, and the end because all of our efforts are directed to understanding it. The importance of rightly determining the necessary steps to the knowledge of God can hardly be overemphasized; for it is in this knowledge that our perfection, which is our happiness, principally consists.

31. There are many other ways that divinely revealed truth guides the other disciplines, such as the following. 1) It precludes the possibility of making deleterious errors—such as those about the moral life and the soul—that are contrary to doctrine. 2) It ensures the truth of those philosophical doctrines that are necessarily presupposed in divinely revealed truths. 3) It supplies assurance that arduous efforts to arrive at the knowledge of such things as the existence and attributes of God bear the promise of success.

12 Bonaventure

Randall B. Smith

We begin with an image. One of the most profound visual statements of the medieval Catholic educational ideal—namely, the integration of the disciplines of human wisdom in the light of the divine Wisdom incarnate—is portrayed in the tympanum over the right door to the main entrance of the Cathedral of Our Lady in the city of Chartres, France.

Chartres was the sight of a tremendous intellectual renaissance in the twelfth century, which witnessed not only the construction of this magnificent cathedral, but also the founding of a remarkable academic institution, the Cathedral school. This was an institution that brought together in one place for research and teaching many of the best and wisest scholars of the day, an institution which would serve as a model for the creation and development of that amazing medieval invention, the *university*.

For the great scholars and visionaries at Chartres, their challenge was to create an educational framework in which the disciplines of human wisdom might be married to the revelation of divine Wisdom in the person of Jesus Christ. This portal sculpture is an artistic expression of precisely that intellectual vision.

If you do an online search for an image of "the seven liberal arts and the western portal at Chartres," you will find several good photographs of the tympanum, some of which have the characters labeled. In the middle, you will see the famous *Sedes Sapientae*, or holy "Seat of Wisdom." Surrounding it in the archivolts are personifications of the seven liberal arts: on the bottom right, *grammar*, who is teaching two boys to write; moving then to the bottom left, we find *dialectic*, in whose right hand is a flower and in whose left hand is the head of a barking dog; proceeding around clockwise, we find *rhetoric*,

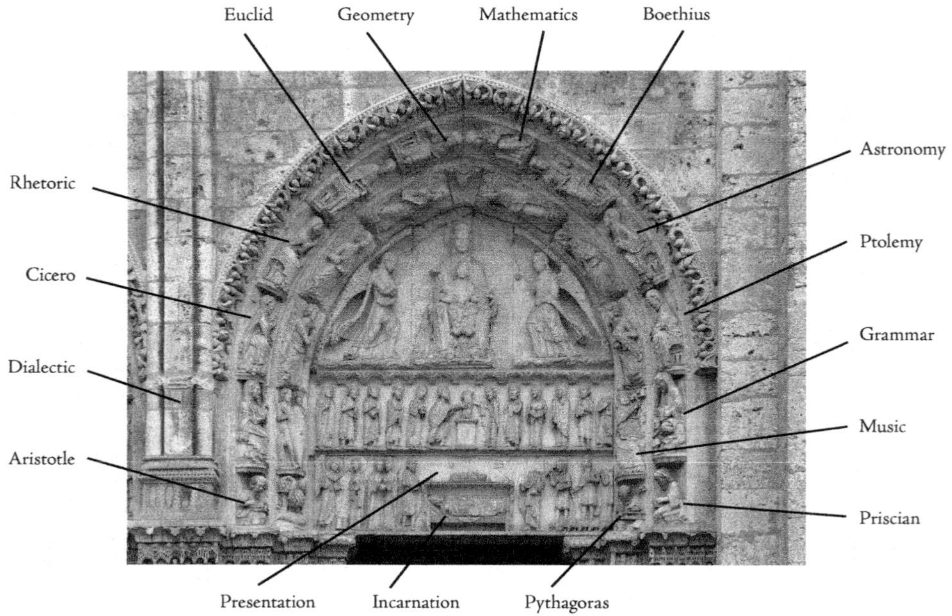

Image 12-1. Chartres-West, Right Tympanum: incarnation of Christ; the seven Liberal Arts. Source: Wikimedia Commons. Photo by Edelseider on Flickr.

who is pictured proclaiming a speech; *geometry*, who is shown writing figures on a tablet; *arithmetic*, whose attributes have been effaced over the centuries, so no one is sure what she is doing; *astronomy*, who is gazing up at the sky; and finally, moving to the inner archivolt, *music*, who is playing two instruments: the twelve-stringed harp and some bells. Underneath each of the Arts is a representation of the thinker classically associated with that discipline: Priscian for grammar, Aristotle for dialectic, Cicero for rhetoric, Euclid for geometry, Boethius for arithmetic, Ptolemy for astronomy, and most likely Pythagoras for music, about whom Cassiodorus had related the story that he had "invented the principles of this discipline from the sound of bells and the percussive extension of chords."

Here at Chartres, we see in concrete, visible form the artistic record of an attempt to integrate human wisdom, as exemplified by its instruments—namely, the seven liberal arts—with Wisdom incarnate in the person of Jesus Christ. The visual movement of the image goes in both directions. The arts and disciplines of human wisdom are seen as a preparation for an increased understanding of faith: they surround and support the image of Wisdom Incarnate in the center. By the same token, the Seat of Wisdom is pictured at the center as both the source and summit of all human wisdom. Mary sits at the center of the arts as a paradigm—as the "Seat of Wisdom"—because she is a model of one who obediently responded to God's word, thus giving birth (in her case, literally) to God's Wisdom Incarnate.

This point is emphasized in the two friezes below, both of which illustrate the events of the Christ's birth. In the bottom frieze (reading from left to right), we see the Annunciation, the Visitation, and in the middle, the birth of Christ, with the angel leading the shepherds in from the right, sheep in tow. In the top frieze, we see Mary and Joseph presenting Jesus at the altar in the Temple. If you look closely, you'll see that, unfortunately, likely due to violence done to the cathedral during the French Revolution, Christ is missing his head.

Image 12-2. Chartres-West, Right Tympanum, detail. Source: Wikimedia Commons. Photo by Edelseider on Flickr.

I am sometimes asked: "Doesn't Jesus look sort of a like a loaf of bread?" The answer is, yes, and it's not just because he's missing his head. Scholars tell us that these images were carved in response to a Eucharistic controversy raging at the time, in which certain groups were emphasizing the presence of the Risen Christ of heaven in the Eucharist, perhaps to the detriment of an understanding of the Eucharist which might include the living Christ who lived and walked the earth. Here at Chartres, we see an attempt to correct that potential misunderstanding by including within the Eucharistic imagery scenes from Christ's birth. This theological and historical context helps to explain why the artist pictures the child Jesus on top of an altar rather than in Mary's arms or in a manger.

Let me stress that such details are not merely artistic trivia. Lying behind this entire set of images is a conscious theology of incarnation and sacramentality. If God has created the world and reveals himself to us through his creation, then we have the possibility (as St. Paul tells us) of coming to know the invisible attributes of God through the visible things of creation. As in the visible, earthly elements of the Eucharist, we are meant to see the real presence of Christ, the Word made flesh, so also, in the visible, earthly elements of creation, we are meant to see the presence of God's creative word and wisdom. It would be a similar theology of incarnation that would allow the word and wisdom of God to become incarnate in actual, human language and thus, by extension, present and embodied on a written page such as the Scriptures.

Thus, we must learn to read *both* the Book of Nature and the Book of Scripture, for they are not mutually exclusive. Rather, they will ultimately illumine each other because they both have the one God as their author. Indeed, on the classical Christian understanding of the seven liberal arts, the trivium (or "threefold way"), which includes grammar, rhetoric, and logic, are precisely the disciplines that teach us how to read and understand the Book of Scripture; while the quadrivium (the "fourfold way"), the arts of geometry, mathematics, astronomy, and music, are those that guide us in our understanding of the Book of Nature. The portal image proclaims that this reading—whether of one book or the other—must be done in the light of the divine Wisdom incarnate.

We begin here, at Chartres, because it provides for us the general perspective from which we ought to view the vision of Catholic education we will find in Bonaventure. As we will see, there were important developments between the twelfth century and the thirteenth. But the underlying vision of the source and goal of an education is the same. So too, approaching Bonaventure's text from the perspective of this example of medieval sculptural imagery will, I hope, help us appreciate Bonaventure's creative use of imagery. That use of imagery can seem odd to first-time readers unused to the creative way medieval authors employed imagery. It's not the way modern theologians write books. But once we think of those odd features as "artistic" rather than merely "theological," the creativity and the beauty of Bonaventure's writing will become more apparent. But first, we need a little background to Bonaventure and the age in which he lived.

Francis, the Franciscans, and Bonaventure

It is unlikely that Bonaventure ever met St. Francis in person, but he attributed his recovery from a near-fatal illness when he was five to Francis's intervention, shortly after the saint's death on October 3, 1226. Francis was canonized a saint two years later, when Bonaventure was seven—though he was still, at this point, Giovanni di Fidanza, a young boy living in the small town of Bagnoregio in the Tuscany region of central Italy.[1]

Despite his long veneration for Francis, Bonaventure did not join the Franciscans right away when he came of age. Instead, he enrolled in 1235 as a layman in the Arts faculty at the University of Paris when he was fourteen years old. At Paris, he encountered the Franciscans, who had themselves arrived in the city only fifteen years before.

In 1219, Brother Pacificus, with a small group of friars, had journeyed to Paris and settled originally in a modest house near the church of Saint-Denis outside the city. As late as 1224, they had to go to a neighboring parish to celebrate their Offices, having no church of their own. Sometime later, they began the construction of a larger friary in Vauvert (*Vallis Viridis*), but it fell to the ground in 1229.

But then, in 1234, the year before young Giovanni de Fidanza arrived in Paris, King Louis IX bought some land and gave it as a gift to the friars. Pope Gregory IX confirmed this donation in 1236, and on December 8, 1239, the friars were granted permission for building. Here, over the next twenty-three years, the famous Fran-

1. In what follows, I am following the carefully worked out chronology found in Jay Hammond, "Dating Bonaventure's Inception as Regent Master," *Franciscan Studies* 67 (2009): 179–226. Hammond dates Bonaventure's birth at 1221. This section is a revised version of material that can be found at greater length and in greater detail in chapter 1 of *Bonaventure's Journey of the Soul into God: Context and Commentary*, forthcoming from Cambridge University Press.

ciscan "Convent of the Cordeliers" was built—"Cordeliers" being the name given to the friars because of the knotted cord (in Old French, *cordelle*) they wore around their waist.

And it was here, in 1236 or 1237, even before the construction of the larger convent had begun, that Alexander of Hales, the man who had introduced the *Sentences* of Peter Lombard as the basic textbook for the study of theology and who had, since his inception in 1220, been one of the most preeminent and influential regent masters at Paris, gave up all his worldly possessions and entered the Franciscan Order. When Alexander entered the order, he brought with him to the Franciscans his chair as regent master of Theology.

By 1221, the year of Giovanni's birth, Francis's early group of eleven brothers had grown to some 3000. That number would double again in the next twenty years. Clearly something dynamic was happening among the Franciscans, and men and women were being drawn to the order. By the time young Giovanni was completing his Master of Arts degree in 1243, Alexander of Hales had been a recognized Franciscan Master of Theology for seven or eight years, the bulk of the time Giovanni had been studying at Paris. And the construction of the new Convent of the Cordeliers would have been well under way. The Franciscans may have had poor beginnings in Paris, but they were clearly on their way up.

And so it was that, when Giovanni finished his Arts degree in 1243 or 1244, now roughly 23 years of age, he decided to join the Franciscans, taking "Bonaventure" as his religious name to celebrate his "good fortune" to be under the tutelage of both St. Francis and Alexander of Hales. Alexander is reported to have held the young Giovanni in the highest regard, having reportedly said of him that "in him Adam seemed not to have sinned."[2]

2. See "Catalogus generalium ministrorum ordinis fratrum Minorum" in *Monumenta Germaniae Historica* 32, ed. Oswold Holder-Egger (Hannoverae: Impensis Bibliopolii Hahniani, 1905–1913), 664.

The point of recounting this brief history is to show how much Bonaventure's entry into the order and subsequent development was bound up with those heady early days of the Franciscans in Paris as they grew from their simple beginnings in a small borrowed house outside the city and their faltering early projects to greater prominence, gaining the notice of even the great King Louis IX, culminating in the entry of Alexander of Hales to their ranks that secured for them a master's chair at the University and the beginning of construction on the Parisian convent that would become the home of so many great Franciscan students and masters in the coming years. Something dynamic was happening among the Franciscans, and Bonaventure wanted to be part of it. Not only would he become a valued part of it, in relatively short order, he would become a leading intellectual and spiritual light among the Franciscans, and shortly thereafter, its master general.

Bonaventure continued to write important theological texts throughout his life, even as master general of the order. The question of how the intellectual life ought to lead to the knowledge and love of God was one to which he returned several times during his life; the first time was in a lecture given as part of his inception ceremonies as Master of the Sacred Page (*magister sacra pagina*) at the University of Paris, a text we know in the modern world as *On the Reduction of the Arts to Theology*. He discussed the subject again, taking a different approach, in his *Journey of the Mind Into God*. And a third time, near the end of his life, he took it up again in his unfinished *Collations on the Six Days of Creation*. Each text is complex, and it would be impossible to cover adequately even one of them in a short chapter. But for our purposes, I propose to give the reader what I hope will be an interesting and informative introduction to a work now called *On the Reduction of the Arts to Theology*.

The Hierarchy of the Sciences and the Order of Leaning

Bonaventure was not alone in his concern to diagram the proper hierarchy and order of learning. There is abundant evidence that the question of hierarchy of the sciences and the order of learning was much on the minds of medieval masters during the thirteenth century.[3] Fr. James Weisheipl reports the three sources with the greatest influence on the development of the classification of the sciences in the thirteenth century were (1) "the Greco-Roman heritage of a liberal arts education"; (2) "the profound influence of Manlius Boethius"; and (3) the twelfth- and thirteenth-century translations from the Greek and Arabic, which helped make this schema intelligible to the Latins."[4]

The earliest Latin classification and exposition of the liberal arts seems to have been Terence Varro's *Disciplinarum libri IX* (116–27 BC). Varro's list of the arts included these nine: grammar, dialectics, rhetoric, geometry, arithmetic, astrology, music, medicine, and architecture. As a pragmatic Roman, Varro envisioned the liberal arts as preparations for the study of the more practical arts of medicine and architecture. These more pragmatic arts were dropped from later lists, leaving the classic seven liberal arts of the *trivium* (grammar, rhetoric, and logic) and *quadrivium* (geometry, arithmetic, astronomy, and music).

By the time Bonaventure composed the *De reductione*, the twelfth-century theologian Hugh of St. Victor (1096–1141) had added the more pragmatic, "mechanical" arts back into the mix in his *Didascalicon*. But instead of being the goal to which the other

3. This section contains a revised version of material that can be found at greater length and in greater detail in *Aquinas, Bonaventure and the Scholastic Culture of Medieval Paris: Preaching, Prologues, and Biblical Commentary* (Cambridge University Press, 2020), 251–88.

4. See James A. Weisheipl, OP, "Classification of the Sciences in Medieval Thought," *Mediaeval Studies* 27 (1965): 54–90, esp. 54. My discussion throughout this section is indebted to Fr. Weisheipl's article.

studies were to lead, the mechanical and pragmatic arts were now considered "lower" disciplines leading to the "higher studies" in the liberal arts: philosophy and theology.

This revaluation of values which resulted in the elevation of philosophy and theology had largely been accomplished during the Patristic period, when the classic tradition of the liberal arts was mediated through early Christian sources. The third-century Eastern Father of the Church Clement of Alexandria (c. 150–c. 215) insisted, for example, that young people should study all the liberal disciplines as a foundation for the higher study of philosophy, which was itself to be a preparation for the reception of Christian wisdom.[5] So too in the Latin West, Augustine was a proponent of students studying the seven liberal arts, but he viewed them, as had Clement before him, as preparatory for the reception of Christian doctrine and as an aid to its interpretation.[6] In the Early Middle Ages in the West, the knowledge of the seven liberal arts was kept alive in works such as Donatus's *Ars grammatica* (mid-fourth century AD), Martianus Capella's *De nuptiis Philologiae et Mercurii* (*On the Marriage of Philology and Mercury*, mid-fifth century AD), and Priscian's *Institutiones grammaticae* (late fifth or early sixth century AD).

The work of Boethius, the sixth-century Roman Christian, however, was to be of special significance for Christian authors, especially Christian theologians, in the twelfth and thirteenth centuries. Boethius, like many before him, divided philosophy into two kinds: theoretical and practical. But he was distinctive in maintaining there were three subdivisions of each. In his treatise *On the Trinity*—a work on which Thomas Aquinas was later to make a famous commentary[7]—Boethius conceived of a new threefold division of

5. See, e.g., Clement of Alexandria, *Stromata* I.5–7.

6. See, e.g., Augustine, *De doctrina christiana*, II.27–39.

7. Indeed, the English translation of the first part of Thomas's commentary on Boethius *De trinitate* by Armand Maurer was titled *The Divisions and Methods of the Sciences* (Pontifical Institute of Mediaeval Studies, 1986).

speculative philosophy elegant in its clarity and simplicity. The first division of speculative philosophy he called *naturalis*, or physics; the second, *mathematica*; and the third, *theologica*. The first, said Boethius, deals with forms that cannot exist or be considered apart from matter and motion. The second, *mathematica*, deals with forms that, although they can never actually exist separate from matter, can be considered apart from matter. The third, *theologica*, finally, deals with forms that exist apart from matter and motion.

According to Boethius, each branch of speculative philosophy had its own proper method. The method proper to physics and the other natural sciences (*naturalia*) he called *rationalibiliter*, by which Boethius had in mind the demonstrative process of reasoning that Aristotle had used in his works of natural science. The method proper to *mathematica* he called *disciplinaliter*, "disciplinary," a word derived from the Latin *disco, discere*, "to learn." It had long been held that mathematics was especially "teachable" because of the precision that its abstraction from matter and motion afforded it. The method needed in *theologica*, finally, Boethius described as *intellectualiter*, by which he meant that "theology" involves a contemplation and intellectual grasp not merely of "forms" but of that form that is pure *esse*.

This tradition of reflection on the liberal arts was further mediated to the Middle Ages through the *Institutiones* of Cassiodorus (562 AD) and the *Etymologiae* of Isidore of Seville (c. 600–625 AD) who, along with Boethius and Augustine, "served as the principal sources for all later discussions of the seven liberal arts and the tripartite division of philosophy."[8] Isidore divided philosophy into physics, ethics, and logic; he then subdivided each of these further, with physics subdivided according to the four arts of the quadrivium: arithmetic, geometry, music, and astronomy; ethics subdivided according to the four cardinal virtues: prudence, justice, fortitude, and temperance; and logic subdivided into rhetoric and dialectic.

8. Weisheipl, "Classification," 64.

A host of important medieval thinkers took up the question of the order and hierarchy of the sciences in the late twelfth and early thirteenth centuries, among them Clarenbaud of Arras (c. 1110–c. 1187), Gilbert de la Porrée (1085–1154), Thierry of Chartres (c. 1100–1150), Robert Grosseteste (c. 1175–1253), Robert Kilwardby (c. 1215–1275), Roger Bacon (c. 1220–1292), Albert the Great (1193–1280), and Thomas Aquinas (1225–1274).[9] The fact that all these highly regarded thinkers wrote important and widely circulated treatises on the divisions, methods, and hierarchy of the sciences indicates that the topic was of great interest and likely had generated no small amount of controversy in academic circles such as those at the University of Paris by the time Bonaventure incepted there in 1254.

The Influence of Hugh of St. Victor and the *Didascalicon*

The man with the most profound and direct influence on Bonaventure's account of the hierarchy of the sciences, however, was Hugh of St. Victor. In the *Didascalicon,* Hugh had reintroduced the mechanical arts back into the schema of the liberal arts. In place of medicine and architecture, the two arts Varro had listed, Hugh listed *seven* mechanical arts, likely to provide a nice sense of symmetry and balance with the seven liberal arts. These seven make for an interesting list: fabric making, armament, commerce, agriculture, hunting, medicine, and theatrics. Bonaventure simply reproduced Hugh's list in the *De reductione* and provided a broad enough description of each of the seven to show why the list was all-inclusive. "Hunting," for example, on Bonaventure's account, was not merely about hunting for animals, but included "every conceivable way of preparing foods, drinks, and delicacies." "Armour-making" included not merely the making of armor, but also "the production

9. For more on the thought of these men, I refer the reader again to Fr. Weisheipl's excellent article, esp. 66–94.

of every instrument made of iron or of any other metal, or of stone or wood."[10]

Hugh divided philosophy into theoretical, practical, mechanical, and logical. The *theoretical* branch of philosophy he subdivided according to Boethius's threefold schema: physics or natural philosophy, mathematics, and theology. Although Hugh was a Christian author, "theology" in this context should not be mistaken for the discipline of "sacred doctrine." "Theology" here meant, as it did for Boethius and Aristotle before him, the study of forms separated from matter and motion. It is more akin to what we today would call "metaphysics." Hugh divided *practical* philosophy in a Boethian manner, distinguishing ethics, economics (or domestics), and politics. Hugh divided the *mechanical* arts into the seven we discussed above: fabric making, armament, commerce, agriculture, hunting, medicine, and theatrics. And *logical* philosophy, finally, he distinguished into the classic three arts of the trivium: grammar, rhetoric, and dialectic. (See figure 1, next page.)

As we will see, Bonaventure reproduced nearly all the elements of Hugh's complex schema in the *De reductione*.

The Four Lights

As noted above, it appears that Bonaventure delivered an earlier version of *On the Reduction of the Arts to Theology* as the second of the two addresses he was required to give during his inception as a Master of the Sacred Page at the University of Paris. Shortly after he was elected master general of the Franciscan Order, he modified it by giving it a new opening paragraph.[11] When Bonaventure orig-

---

10. See Hugh of St. Victor, *Didascalicon of Hugh of St. Victor: A Medieval Guide to the Arts*, trans. Jerome Taylor (Columbia University Press, 1991).

11. The text that Bonaventure used at his *resumptio* was, as Joshua C. Benson has shown, an early version of a work scholars used to think came from late in Bonaventure's career: the *De Reductione Artium ad Theologiam* (*On the Reduction of the*

Figure 12-1. Hugh's Fourfold Division of Knowledge

1. Theoretical (*naturalis*)
    a. Theology: deals with forms separated from matter
    b. Mathematics: deals with forms of bodies considered apart from matter
        i. Arithmetic
        ii. Music
        iii. Geometry
        iv. Astronomy
    c. Physics: deals with forms in matter
2. Practical (*moralis*)
    a. Ethics
    b. Economics
    c. Politics
3. Mechanical: fabric making, armament, commerce, agriculture, hunting, medicine, theatrics
4. Logical (*sermocinales*)
    a. Grammar
    b. Dialectics
    c. Rhetoric

Arts to Theology). A quick comparison of the Latin version of the *De Reductione* in the Quaracchi edition with the critical edition of Bonaventure's *resumptio* published by Benson reveals that the sole difference is the first paragraph. See Joshua C. Benson, "Identifying the Literary Genre of the *De reductione artium ad theologiam*: Bonaventure's Inaugural Lecture at Paris," *Franciscan Studies* 67 (2009): 149–78; and "Bonaventure's *De reductione artium ad theologiam* and Its Early Reception as an Inaugural Sermon," *American Catholic Philosophical Quarterly* 85, no. 1 (2011): 7–24. The Quaracchi editors seem to have known of the manuscript containing this early version, but because the first paragraph was different from nearly all the other manuscripts of the *De reductione* they had identified, they assumed it was an aberrant copy. It was Prof. Benson's genius to realize that the manuscript contained Bonaventure's two inception addresses.

inally delivered the address, he introduced it with a quotation from Augustine's *Soliloquies*.

> Because all truth is sought in the light of the First Cause, according to what Augustine says in the first book of the *Soliloquies*: "Therefore," he says, "as in this visible sun we may observe three things: that it is, etc." [that it shines, that it illuminates: so in that God most far withdrawn whom you would wish to apprehend, there are these three things: that He is, that He is apprehended, and that He makes other things to be apprehended].[12]

When he later revised the text, he added a new first paragraph based on a passage from James 1:17: "Every good gift and every perfect gift is from above, coming down from the God of Lights." This verse had been a favorite of Hugh of St. Victor's, and since the basic conception of the hierarchy of the sciences in the *De reductione* owes much to Hugh's influence, it may have seemed fitting.

But in either case, we should not miss Bonaventure's message. All truth is made possible by the "light of the First Cause." Or to put this another way, all truth is made possible by a light "coming down from the God of Lights." As we are able to see because of the light of the sun, so we are able to know the truth because of the illumination we receive from God our Creator. This is the light "from above," the *superior* light.

But notice, in the text from Augustine's *Soliloquies*, "the light of the First Cause" is "most far withdrawn" from us. The God we wish to apprehend enlightens us, but he is too far above for us to see him directly. So how do we apprehend him? That light from above is medi-

---

12. I have included the whole passage from Augustine's *Soliloquies*, even though in the original manuscript, Bonaventure provides only the first several words followed by "et cetera," suggesting he could quote the text from memory and needed only those first words to help bring to mind the text he intended to use. "Although Bonaventure may have known the entire verse by memory, most of us do not, so I have taken the liberty of supplying the missing text in brackets.

ated to us, first, through the "light" of the sacred Scriptures. But as the light of the sun not only is and shines, but also illumines visible things so they can be seen, so too, the light coming down from God not only exists, it also shines in and through the Scriptures. But it also shines in and through three lower lights. There is, first, the exterior light of the mechanical arts; next, the inferior light of the sensitive cognition, and finally, the interior light of philosophical cognition. Above these three, as we have seen, is the superior light of sacred Scripture.

This fourfold division of "light" allowed Bonaventure to creatively retrofit Hugh's fourfold hierarchy into a new schema with the sacred Scriptures more clearly at the top. In Bonaventure's new schema, the *inferior* light is the light of sense knowledge—called "inferior" because it begins with an inferior object and requires the aid of corporeal light. The *exterior* light is the knowledge of the mechanical arts, which produce things "external" to us. The *interior* light is the light of philosophical knowledge by which we inquire into inner and hidden causes through principles in the recesses of the human mind. And the *superior* light is the light of the sacred Scriptures, the light that, by revealing truths transcending human reason, leads to higher things, the light sent down from on high by "the God of lights" (cf. James 1:17).[13]

The Interior Light and Hugh's Hierarchy of the Sciences

Bonaventure places Hugh's entire hierarchy of the sciences (minus the mechanical arts) under the heading of the "interior" light. His

13. A reader interested in a modern example of this sort of "dilation" should consult Avery Cardinal Dulles's book *The Catholicity of the Church* (Clarendon Press, 1987), in which the author structures his discussion around this fourfold distinction: "Catholicity from Above," "Catholicity from Below," "Catholicity in Breadth," and "Catholicity in Length." Throughout the remainder of this chapter, the English translation and the Latin text quoted have been taken from: Bonaventure, *On the Reduction of the Arts to Theology*, The Works of Saint Bonaventure, vol. 1, trans. with an intro. by Zachary Hayes, OFM (The Franciscan Institute, 1996).

schema reduces Hugh's hierarchy to these three divisions: (1) "natural" philosophy (theoretical), which includes both the mathematical disciplines (arithmetic, geometry, music, and astronomy) and physics; (2) "moral" philosophy (practical), which includes ethics, economics, and politics; and (3) "rational" philosophy (logical), which includes grammar, dialectic, and rhetoric. Compare the outline of Hugh's division of the sciences in Figure 1 with the outline of Bonaventure's divisions under "interior" light in Figure 2 below.[14]

Figure 12-2. Bonaventure's Division of Knowledge

1. Theoretical Knowledge (Natural Philosophy)
   a. Mathematics: deals with forms of bodies considered apart from matter
      i. Arithmetic
      ii. Music
      v. Geometry
      vi. Astronomy
   b. Physics: deals with forms in matter
2. Practical Knowledge (Moral Philosophy)
   a. Ethics
   b. Economics
   c. Politics
3. Logic (Rational Philosophy)
   a. Grammar
   b. Dialectic
   c. Rhetoric

In the first half of section 4 of the *De reductione,* Bonaventure sets forth this basic threefold division between rational, natural, and moral by describing it in three ways. The problem with his discussion is that he does not always keep the same order: in his first account, he lists "rational" philosophy first; in his second, "natural"

14. See esp. *De reductione,* 4.

philosophy comes first; and in his third, "moral." If one fails to notice this, the lists can be confusing.[15]

In his first account, he distinguishes the truth of *speech*, the truth of *things*, and the truth of *morals*. *Rational* philosophy considers the truth of *speech*; *natural* philosophy, the truth of *things*; and moral philosophy, the truth of *conduct*.

In his second account, he states that "since 'God is the cause of being, the principle of intelligibility, and the order of human life,' so we may find these in the illumination of philosophy." When the illumination of philosophy enlightens the mind to discern the causes of being, it is *physics*. When we are enlightened to know the principles of understanding, it is *logic*. And when the illumination involves the order of living, this is *moral philosophy*. Notice in this second list that the first and second categories have been reversed: he lists physics first, which would correspond to "natural" philosophy in the first list, and logic second, which would correspond to "rational" of "discursive" philosophy, the first item in the first list.

In his third account of this same threefold division, Bonaventure takes a different approach, stating that "the light of philosophical knowledge illumines the intellect itself and this enlightenment may be threefold." If it directs the *motive power*, it is *moral* philosophy, which enlightens us regarding the truth of life; if it *directs itself*, it is *natural* philosophy, which enlightens us regarding the truth of knowledge; and if it directs *the interpretive power*, it is *discursive* philosophy, which enlightens us regarding the truth of doctrine.

Since the terms can be confusing, I have attempted to diagram the lists together in one chart in Figure 12-3 below.

15. All three can be found in *De reduction*, 4.

Figure 12-3.

Category of Philosophy	Deals with:	Which explores:	Intellect directs:	Category of Truth:
Natural Philosophy a. Mathematics b. Physics	Truth of things	Causes of being	Intellect directs itself (to understand the truth of things)	Truth of knowledge
Moral Philosophy a. Ethics b. Economics c. Politics	Truth of conduct	Principles of understanding	Intellect directs the interpretive power (to interpret the truth of speech)	Truth of doctrine
Rational Philosophy a. Grammar b. Dialectic c. Rhetoric	Truth of speech	Order of living	Intellect directs the motive power (to move one to act in accord with the truth)	Truth of Life

From the Four Lights to the Light of the Six Days

The "superior" light, the light that is the "highest," is the light that illuminates respect to saving truth: this is the "light" of Sacred Scripture. This light is called "superior," says Bonaventure, for two reasons: first, because it leads to higher things by revealing truths that transcend reason, and second, because it is not acquired by human investigation but is sent down to us from "the God of Lights."

But note, these gifts *come down* from the God of Lights. What about the return? As we have seen, the "God of Lights" *illumines* us in various ways—through sense perception, the mechanical arts, the liberal arts, and sacred Scripture—but this illumination is not merely an end unto itself. We are illumined so we can achieve our ultimate end, which is union with him. So, after he has described in the first part of his text the ways in which God illumines us, it remained for Bonaventure in the second part to describe how they *lead us back to* God. This change of focus required a change of

Bonaventure's governing image: from the "four lights" in the first part to the "six days" in the second.

Rather than trying to describe this rather startling transition, it will be best simply to quote Bonaventure's text in full. After finishing his discussion of the last of the four "lights," the *superior* light of the sacred Scriptures, Bonaventure says this.

> From what has been said up to now it can be concluded that, according to our primary division, the light coming down from above is *fourfold;* nonetheless there are six differentiations of this light namely, the light of *sacred Scripture,* the light of *sense perception,* the light of the *mechanical arts,* the light of *rational philosophy,* the light of *natural philosophy,* and the light of *moral philosophy.* Therefore, in the present life there are six illuminations; and they have their evening, for all *knowledge will be destroyed.* And therefore they will be followed by a seventh day of rest, a day which knows no evening, namely, *the illumination of glory.*
>
> Therefore these six illuminations may very fittingly be traced back to the six days of formation or illumination in which the world was made, so that the knowledge of sacred Scripture would correspond to the creation of the first day, that is, to the formation of light, and so on with the rest, one after the other in proper order. And as all those lights had their origin in a single light, so too all these branches of knowledge are ordered to the knowledge of sacred Scripture; they are contained in it; they are perfected by it; and they are ordered to the eternal illumination by means of it. Therefore all our knowledge should come to rest in the knowledge of sacred Scripture, and particular in the *anagogical* understanding of Scripture, through which any illumination is traced back to God from whom it took its origin. And there the circle is completed; the pattern of six is complete, and consequently there is rest.[16]

16. *De reductione,* 6–7.

Why make this switch from the image of the four lights to the six days? First, it is not without scriptural warrant, since "light" is the first thing created on the first day—"And God said, 'Let there be light'"—and since in the Gospel of John's recapitulation of the creation story in Genesis—"In the beginning was the Word"—he declares that the Word is "the true light, which gives light to everyone" (Jn 1:9). In this way, there is light at the beginning of the Scriptures and light at the culmination in Christ.

So too, it seems likely that, having in the first section settled on an image that would let him make a suitable "division" of the sciences—one corresponding, as we have seen, with the schema set forth by Hugh of St. Victor in his *Didascalicon*—Bonaventure needed another image to communicate more clearly the idea that the sciences should culminate in a goal beyond themselves. His goal, after all, wasn't merely to *classify* the sciences, as a scientist or metaphysician might. Bonaventure set out to show how all human knowing was a reflection of the divine image meant to lead back to (*reducit*) union with God.

Using the image of the "six days" of creation let Bonaventure continue to use the image of light. But it also let him picture the movement of the days *toward* the Sabbath and to Christ—a movement of the disciplines leading mankind back to God, the source and summit of all things. The six "days" imagery let Bonaventure picture more adequately the "lights" of the sciences as *flowing forth from* God (since "light" is created on the first day) and *flowing toward* God (who is our "rest" on the seventh day). Getting the order of the arts and sciences right is the way the university sets up the proper "ladder" of ascent up the Platonic "divided line" so the students can raise their minds from the knowledge they gain in the disciplines to achieve an ever greater knowledge of, and relation to, God. Bonaventure's message to his confreres at the University of Paris was that what they were studying in their academic classrooms was meant to bear fruit in greater union with God.

The material from the four lights section gets reapportioned into the six days in the following way:

Superior Light: Light of Sacred Scripture: First Day
Inferior Light: Light of Sense Perception: Second Day
Exterior Light: Light of Mechanical Arts: Third Day
Interior Light: Light of Philosophical Science (threefold division):
Light of Rational Philosophy: Fourth Day
Light of Natural Philosophy: Fifth Day
Light of Moral Philosophy: Sixth Day
Illumination of Glory (New Culmination): Seventh Day

In the four "lights" schema, sacred Scripture was the "superior" light at the top. Here the Scriptures are the primary light which illumine all the rest. Note how the disciplines merely listed and divided in the earlier "four lights" schema are here set within a dynamic hierarchy, with sense perception at the bottom (since we come to know through sense perception) and moral philosophy, the knowledge of how to live one's life well, near the top, and with the "lights" of the various "days" leading ultimately to the seventh "day," union with God.

On this account, sacred Scripture is the first light that illumines all the rest, and it does so by keeping them directed to their primordial Source, which is also their ultimate End: the Triune God. Bonaventure's account of the three mystical senses of Scripture helps him make this transition from the "four lights" part of the treatise to the second part structured around the six days. The allegorical sense, he says, is concerned with *faith*; the moral sense with *morals*; and the anagogical sense with the ultimate goal of both, namely union with God. Therefore, claims Bonaventure, the whole of sacred Scripture teaches these three truths: the eternal generation of the Son and his incarnation in the person of Jesus Christ (the subject of the allegorical sense), the pattern of human life (the subject of the moral sense), and the union of the soul with God (the subject of the anagogical sense). Moreover, these three truths can be found "reflected in" or "illumined by" the lights of each of the following five "days" leading to the light of eternal glory on the seventh day.

Just as all the lights of creation "had their origin in a single light"—that is, the light created on the first day—so too all the "lights" of the various branches of knowledge "are ordered to the knowledge of sacred Scripture."

> [T]hey are contained in it; they are perfected by it; and they are ordered to the eternal illumination by means of it. Therefore all our knowledge should come to rest in the knowledge of Sacred Scripture, and particularly in the *anagogical* understanding of Scripture through which any illumination is traced back to God [*refertur in Deum*] from whom it took its origin. And there the circle is completed; the pattern of six is complete, and consequently there is rest.[17]

In Figure 12-4 below, I have diagrammed how, according to Bonaventure, the three basic truths of Sacred Scripture illuminate the other sciences, which in turn "lead back to" God.

This threefold schema is consistent across all the "days." Bonaventure's challenge is to see whether he can identify "vestiges" or "echoes" of (1) the generation and incarnation of the Word, (2) the moral pattern of human life, and (3) the union of the soul with God in *all* the arts and branches of knowledge. To see how he carries out this monumental task, we would need to get into the details of the "light" of each "day." I have provided a description of these details elsewhere, but there is not space for a complete commentary of that length and depth here.[18] So let's summarize based on what we have seen thus far.

---

17. *De reductione*, 7.

18. For a more complete description of Bonaventure's account of the "six days," see *Aquinas, Bonaventure*, ch. 11.

Figure 12-4.

First Day: Light of Sacred Scripture	Second Day: Light of Sense Perception	Third Day: Light of the Mechanical Arts	Fourth Day: Light of Rational Philosophy	Fifth Day: Light of Natural Philosophy	Sixth Day: Light of Moral Philosophy	Seventh Day: Illumination of Glory
Allegorical Sense: Generation and incarnation of the Word	Medium of knowledge	Production (skill of the artist)	Person speaking (mental concept)	Relation of Proportion	"Right": middle between extremes	
Moral Sense: Pattern of human life	Exercise of knowledge	Effect (quality of the effect produced)	Delivery (fittingness, truth, style)	Effect of Causality	"Right": guided by regulations of divine law	
Anagogical Sense: Union of the soul with God	Delight	Fruit of the work (usefulness of the product)	Purpose (express, instruct, persuade)	Medium of Union	"Right": when one's summit is raised upward (e.g., upright posture)	

The Summit of Human Learning

In the first book of the *Metaphysics*, Aristotle famously declared that "all men by nature desire to know" and to know the "highest" things. The "highest" knowledge, thought Aristotle, would be the knowledge of first principles and the causes of things, "for by reason of these, and from these, all other things come to be known."[19] Aristotle called this "highest science" by various names— "first philosophy," "first science," "wisdom," "theology"—and said that it provides knowledge of the first principles, causes, and good of all things. To pursue this knowledge, thought Aristotle, was to pursue the highest wisdom of which human beings are capable.

In the *De reductione*, Bonaventure shifted the summit of human learning upward—to God Himself. And although God is in his essence unknowable, Bonaventure accepted that he had made himself known through the revelation of Sacred Scripture. And so, he argued that all the disciplines in the Arts curriculum at the University of Paris, including the study of Aristotle's *Metaphysics*, needed to be illumined by the knowledge gained by reading sacred Scripture to be "seen" fully. To read and study these texts apart from divine revelation would be like trying to see the woman you intend to marry only in the dark.[20] Without seeing her in the light, you will fail to see and appreciate her true beauty, and failing to appreciate her beauty, your heart may fail to be drawn to her as it ought and as she deserves. So too, when the objects of the other sciences are "illumined" by the light and wisdom shining forth from the sacred Scriptures, it is only then that we finally see them in their full truth and beauty, and our hearts should be drawn to the Source of all Truth, Beauty, and Goodness—the First Cause, Highest Principle, and Complete Good of all things. When studied properly, all the sciences

19. Aristotle, *Metaphysics* I.2 (981a 1–25).

20. This image is mine, not Bonaventure's.

should lead us back to the Creator who has revealed himself in and through the sacred Scriptures.

For in those Scriptures, we find to our amazement that the First Cause, Highest Principle, and Complete Good of all things reveals himself to be a loving Father who has sent his eternally begotten Son into the world to redeem it from sin. He further extends this loving gift of himself and his eternal Son to us by sending us his own Spirit, whose loving gifts of grace help perfect our rational powers and even our baser, "earthier" powers: our irascible and concupiscible appetites. Our *irascible nature* is perfected, claims Bonaventure, "when it strives after the highest generosity," and our *concupiscible nature* is perfected "when it clings to the good." When we are angry, when we are motivated by wrath or fear, it is a wise counsel that advises: "Turn your mind to generosity." And when we are motivated by lust or greed or the desire for power and prestige, should we not consider whether the things we desire are truly for our good?[21]

And yet, if we are tempted to think of Bonaventure's "reduction" of the arts to theology as merely a medieval version of Plato's Allegory of the Cave in book 7 of *The Republic*, we should note an important difference.[22] Instead of the visible things of creation being mere shadows and illusions at the bottom of the cave, for Bonaventure, the created realities are truly *real*. They are meant to lead us upward to their Source and ours. Instead of Plato's false lights illuminating shadows in the cave, Bonaventure thinks of created reality as if it were a series of mirrors reflecting the light that comes down from above.[23]

21. See Plato's *Gorgias*, in which one of Socrates's primary goals is to show each of his interlocutors that many of the things men desire as good are merely apparent or illusory goods and are not in fact truly good.

22. Plato, *Republic* 7 (514a-520a).

23. This image of "mirrors" reflecting the light from above is one Bonaventure also uses in the *Itinerarium mentis in deum* (*The Journey of the Mind into God*). See, for example, *Itinerarium* 1.5: "in as far as we consider God in each of the above-mentioned ways as through a mirror or as in a mirror" (*ut per speculum et ut in speculo*).

That light gets dimmer as it is reflected, and we would be misled if we mistook what we can see in the dim light for what we would be able to see in the light of the sun. But there is a definite drive upward supplied in Bonaventure's vision by Christ and the Scriptures that is missing in Plato's vision of the cave.

Zachary Hayes has suggested that Bonaventure's accomplishment in the *De reductione* consists in this, the fact that:

> he incorporates all the familiar and new forms of knowledge in the arts and sciences into an all-embracing, theological framework and integrates them into the journey of the human spirit into God. All must be situated in the context of the going-forth from and the return of creation to God. . . . He argues, in effect, that spirituality and theology do not have to by-pass or bracket the so-called secular disciplines in order to find God elsewhere; for the entire world is drenched with the presence of the divine mystery. It is a world that bears at least the vestiges (=foot-prints) of God, and at some levels even the image and similitude of God. It is the task of the human person situated in such a world to learn how to detect the symptoms of that mysterious, divine presence.[24]

To this, I would add only that, for Bonaventure, learning how to detect "the symptoms of that mysterious divine presence" in the world in its various manifestations involved mastering the methods appropriate to each discipline. This was not a mysticism of the mountaintops; it was, rather, a very Franciscan reaffirmation of the truth and holiness to be sought and achieved in everyday life, study, and work.[25]

---

24. Hayes intro, *Reduction*, 11.

25. Étienne Gilson has written: "Saint Bonaventure's doctrine can be characterized as an 'itinerary of the soul toward God.' . . . It teaches 'how man goes to God through other things.' Accordingly, his outlook on man and things will be dominated by a twofold tendency: first, to conceive the sensible world as the road that leads to God; next, to conceive man as a creature naturally open to the divine light and God as revealing himself to man through the whole gamut of his illuminations." See *History of Christian Philosophy in the Middle Ages* (Random House, 1955), 332.

At the heart of this *reductio* of the other arts to theology is not only a clarity of the mind and a perfection of the rational powers, although these are important, but also a perfection of the will through the gift of charity. For Bonaventure, what should animate all one's studies in the disciplines is the conviction that we can find God in them—a conviction borne of the faith that God, out of his love, has revealed himself to us, and that we are creatures he made capable of both knowing and loving him. So we realize the highest potential and perfection of each discipline when we see in them a revelation of the God who loved us so much he became flesh for us, sacrificed himself for us on the cross, and rose to the right hand of the Father to send his Holy Spirit that we might be brought into a fuller union, a deeper communion with him.[26]

For Bonaventure, the truths of the Scriptures help to illumine the other disciplines, while the lesser lights of the other disciplines can, in turn, help us understand the truths of sacred Scriptures more fully. "It is for this reason," says Bonaventure, "that theology makes use of illustrations and terms pertaining to every branch of knowledge" because every branch of knowledge can build up faith, hope, and love, if we see them as containing self-revelations of the God of love in whom is our ultimate faith and hope.

Bonaventure's message was that one should engage in one's studies much as a lover studies his beloved; the more love he has,

---

26. Gilson, *History*, 333: "It is possible to find God by considering his creature, because the truth of things consists in their representing the primary and supreme truth. In this sense, all creatures are so many ways to God.... To describe it by a technical term, let us say that it is a resemblance of "expression," as a spoken word expresses its meaning. Considered from this point of view, therefore, what we call creatures, or things, constitute a sort of language, and the whole universe is only a book in which the Trinity is read on every page. And if one were to ask why God created the world on this plan, the answer would be very simply: the world has no other reason for being that to give utterance to God; it is a book which was written only that it might be read by man and be the unceasing reminder of its Author's love."

the more he notices, and the more he notices, the more it inspires the increase of his love. When one's studies are illumined by the light of the Holy Spirit and the sacred Scriptures, each discipline, each science, becomes a potential means of building up charity. Hence "the fruit of all the sciences," says Bonaventure, is:

> that in all, faith may be strengthened, God may be honored, character may be formed, and consolation may be derived from the union of the Spouse with the beloved, a union which takes place through charity: a charity in which the whole purpose of Sacred Scripture, and thus of every illumination descending from above, comes to rest—a charity without which all knowledge is vain because no one come to the Son except through the Holy Spirit who teaches us *all the truth, who is blessed forever*. Amen.[27]

---

27. *De reductione*, 26.

13 Ignatius of Loyola and the Ratio Studiorum

Fr. Robert J. Spitzer, SJ

In his article, "Old Wine in New Wine Skins," Michael Williams, SJ, articulates seven characteristics of Jesuit education inspired by the *Ratio Studiorum*:[1]

1. The primary spiritual objective: deep love of God and neighbor
2. Integration of the intellectual, moral, and spiritual dimensions of education
3. Stress on formation beyond information
4. Stress order: moving from simpler foundations to more complex concepts
5. Stress on active, rather than passive, education
6. Emphasis on the humanities and liberal arts
7. *Eloquentia perfecta*

I believe that Williams has revealed the Ignatian heart of the *Ratio Studiorum* that can continue to inspire Jesuit and Catholic education today. After teaching in a Jesuit high school and three Jesuit universities, and having been president of Gonzaga University for 11 years, I will attempt to summarize my viewpoint on what truly worked to inspire students in the Ignatian vision of Catholic education. I believe that it can help Catholic educators to successfully implement the heart of the *Ratio Studiorum* in both high school and university settings to develop strong Christian leaders for the good of the world and the kingdom of God. I will begin with a

1. See Michael Williams, SJ, "Old Wine in New Wine Skins," EDUignaciana.Tripod.com, 1997, 7–8. https://eduignaciana.tripod.com/docum/oldwine.pdf.

brief historical background and then examine a contemporary implementation of some of Williams's characteristics of the *Ratio Studiorum*.

I. Brief Historical Background of the Ratio Studiorum

When we look at the four parts of the *Ratio Studiorum* (hereafter "*RS*"),[2] Williams's seven characteristics may not be immediately evident. Nevertheless, they become quite apparent when we see the *RS* in light of St. Ignatius's vision for education articulated in the *Spiritual Exercises*[3] and *The Constitutions of the Society of Jesus*.[4]

The rules of the *RS* are the product of the collective reflections of dozens of educators inspired by St. Ignatius who had many years of experience learning by the school of "hard knocks." Frs. Jerome Nadal and Juan Polanco were desirous of standardizing Jesuit education because it literally grew exponentially from the time that Ignatius and his first companions started the Society of Jesus at the Church of Montmartre (Paris) in 1534. One hundred years after the Order's founding (1634), the Society had already started 444 schools! Well before that time, Nadal and Polanco recognized that with such rapid initiation of schools, they had to put together a "Jesuit brand" that synthesized the spiritual intention of St. Ignatius and the "best practices" and the collective wisdom of the leaders in the fast-growing area of primary and secondary education.

---

2. For a free online pdf, see *Ratio Studiorum*, trans. and intro Allan P. Farrell, SJ (Conference of Major Superiors, 1970), https://www.educatemagis.org/wp-content/uploads/documents/2019/09/ratio-studiorum-1599.pdf. The four parts of the *RS* are (1) rules for superiors and prefects, (2) rules for theology professors, (3) rules for philosophy professors, and (4) rules for foundational subjects—logic, grammar, rhetoric, and history.

3. See St. Ignatius of Loyola, "The Contemplation on the Love of God," Internet Sacred Text Archive, https://sacred-texts.com/chr/seil/seil35.htm.

4. See *The Constitutions* Part IV.

This occurred in several phases,[5] beginning with the collective writings of Nadal, Polanco, and several other influential educational leaders. The first attempt to standardize those writings occurred in 1581, undertaken by a committee of twelve during the generalate of Fr. Claudio Aquaviva. It then went through several drafts, followed by feedback and subsequent reflection in 1586, then in 1591, and finally in 1599, which produced the promulgated version. The *RS* became the standard for the Jesuit teaching method for about two centuries, until 1773, when the Society of Jesus was suppressed. An attempt was made to revitalize the *RS* after the restoration of the Society in 1814, but it did not have much effect beyond some of the seven characteristics articulated by Williams—particularly, the attention to retreats and the *Spiritual Exercises*, the three kinds of conversion, the attention to strong foundations and active learning, and above all, *eloquentia perfecta*.

II. The Primary Objective of Jesuit Education: A Lived Relationship with God in Jesus Christ

The primary intention of Jesuit education for St. Ignatius and his followers (to this day) is to help students develop a relationship with God in Jesus Christ, which they will hopefully foster throughout their lives. Though this is the primary objective of Jesuit education, it presupposes both apologetical and catechetical preparation to make that relationship intelligible and fruitful. Thus, reaching the primary objective entails significant work and study in the three kinds of conversion—intellectual, religious/spiritual, and moral (section III below). If these apologetical and catechetical objectives (toward the three kinds of conversion) are taking place in the classroom and extracurricular activities, the three major "Jesuit techniques" for helping students develop a relationship with Christ can

5. Allan P. Farrell, SJ, *The Jesuit Code of Liberal Education: Development and Scope of the Ratio Studiorum* (Bruce, 1938), 85–90, https://archive.org/details/jesuitcodeofliteooooounse.

reach their anticipated end: a living relationship with the Lord. So, what are these three "Jesuit techniques"?

1. Retreats (Section II.A)
2. Frequent Mass/Communion and Confession (Section II.B)
3. Communities of prayer and moral integrity (Section II.C)

II.A. Retreats

It will come as no surprise to anyone familiar with Jesuit education that retreats are central to our schools' mission. In secondary schools, *Kairos* retreats (sometimes called "Search" retreats) are part of students' experience in junior or senior year. These are often preceded by freshman and sophomore retreats, and in some schools, a short weekend Ignatian silent retreat is offered in the senior year. The *Kairos* (or "Search") retreat is part of what the Jesuits call the "*Schola Affectus*" (the School of the Heart). There is a component of Mass and prayer, some presentations to help students open their hearts to Christ, a time to receive notes of love and affirmation from parents and friends (called "polancos"—named after Fr. Juan Polanco), and a time to enjoy deepening Christian fellowship with one another. In my experience, these retreats are very effective for creating what the Jesuits call "hearts on fire."

Though these retreats can create an intense feeling of relationship with God, they need to be complemented by spiritual practices at school and by apologetical instruction, otherwise the intense feelings of the retreat will begin dissipating almost immediately until they are pushed into the recesses of the mind after a few weeks.

Most Jesuit universities have an extensive Search retreat program, but the most effective ones balance genuine religious/spiritual practice and content with the social/community content. Though many students might want more social content at first, they will have a much more beneficial religious and personal experience if Search retreats give at least equal emphasis to religious/spiritual content and practice.

There are three-day, four-day, and five-day adaptations of the *Spiritual Exercises* given to students at Jesuit universities. These can be remarkably effective for "jumpstarting" a deeper relationship with Jesus if students maintain silence and are serious about working with a spiritual director during the retreat. Fr. William Watson, SJ, has started several of these retreats at Georgetown University, Seattle University, and Gonzaga University.[6]

II.B. Frequent Communion and Confession

St. Ignatius of Loyola, following St. Thomas Aquinas, believed that frequent Communion was exceedingly efficacious in bringing about spiritual conversion, a deep love of Christ, and an appreciation for Scripture during the Holy Mass.[7] Allan Farrell states the following:

> The *Ratio Studiorum* stipulates that in accordance with Common Rules 2 to 4 for the Professor of the Lower Classes the teacher should begin each class with a prayer and the sign of the cross. He should monitor his students to ensure that they attend Mass during the week and on feast days and urge them to receive Holy Communion and to go to Confession frequently.[8]

Serious spiritual directors are aware of the multiple graces coming from worthy reception of the Holy Eucharist: the forgiveness of venial sins, healing from past sins, protection from the evil spirit,

---

6. William Watson, SJ, current president of Sacred Story Institute at the University of St. Thomas, Houston, may be available to answer questions on how to start a program for university students. Email bill.watson@sacredstory.net, and visit https://sacredstory.net/about/.

7. See Andrew Hofer, OP, "Frequent Communion for the Greater Glory of God: Thomas Aquinas and Ignatius of Loyola," in *Ignatius of Loyola and Thomas Aquinas: A Jesuit Ressourcement,* ed. Justin M. Anderson, Matthew Levering, and Aaron Pidel, SJ (The Catholic University of America Press, 2024), 135–66.

8. Allan Farrell, *The Jesuit Ratio Studiorum of 1599* (Conference of Major Superiors of Jesuits, 1970), 62–63.

the grace of conversion, a sense of deep peace and connection with the sacred, and above all, interior transformation in the heart of Christ.[9] This last gift, coming from "*cor ad cor loquitur*"—Jesus's heart speaking to our heart—was particularly important for the development of my vocation to the Jesuits.

When I was a freshman at Gonzaga University, I started going to daily Mass during Lent and became hooked. I continue that practice to this day. Throughout my college years, I noticed that my rather harsh, utilitarian outlook was being modified ever so slowly but surely. By the time I was a senior, I was convinced that my religion was the most important dimension of my life and that I wanted to commit myself to bringing Christ to as many as possible. Though some of this was attributable to my studies and retreats, I am convinced that the work of interior transformation was principally accomplished by the Lord in my daily reception of him in the Holy Eucharist. Frankly, I think the decline in vocations could be completely resolved if most Catholic schools strongly encouraged frequent reception of Communion at daily Mass.

Though frequent confession is harder to actualize today than at the time of St. Ignatius, encouraging students to build confession into their schedule once per month—or at least four times per year—is very important for progress in the spiritual life. Sometimes we really don't know the burden we carry around with us until we go to confession and feel that burden lifted by the extraordinary grace of that sacrament. I attend the Fellowship of Catholic University Students (FOCUS) annual conferences quite frequently and hear confessions, along with dozens of other priests, for about 7,000 students during a penitential vigil. The next day, the ambience of the conference and demeanor of the students (individually and collectively) is

9. See Robert J. Spitzer, SJ, "Father Spitzer's Resource Book," Magis Center, https://discover.magiscenter.com/hubfs/CC%20-%20Big%20Book%20Pdfs/BB-Vol-9-Eucharistic-Liturgy.pdf?hsLang=en.

palpably transformed. It feels like a huge burden has been lifted from them, allowing a confidence and joy of the Spirit to break through in a myriad of ways. I think we could lift the burden of sin from our students in all of our schools with some seasonal penitential services or penitential services during Search retreats, silent Ignatian retreats, and other retreats. If the FOCUS conference is any indication, it will make a remarkable difference to the atmosphere of your campus.

II.C. Communities of Prayer and Moral Integrity

According to the *RS*, ". . . no student at a Jesuit college or university is to be admitted to any extra-curricular activity unless he has been received into the Sodality of the Blessed Virgin."[10] Though the vast majority of our universities today do not have Sodalities of the Blessed Virgin, we do have spiritual communities that are dedicated to prayer, high moral integrity, and service to others. The power of these smaller spiritual communities in helping students to maintain a life of sacraments, prayer, and moral integrity cannot be overestimated, especially in our secularized society that seems to have as its objective a call to moral relativism, anti-transcendence, and over-indulgence. Though we do not see Sodalities in our universities and high schools, we see dozens of new smaller spiritual communities popping up in the form of Bible studies, Rosary groups, Wednesday adoration groups, fellowship societies, and the like. Organizations, such as FOCUS, Knights of Columbus student chapters, Cursillo prayer groups, and Charismatic Renewal prayer groups, are also bringing small group prayer and fellowship back to campuses. The reason seems obvious—with peer support and encouragement, it is almost effortless to integrate the sacraments and daily prayer into student life. This provides a foundation for peer support to live

10. Part II section 2/4/2a on Sodalities. See also C. E. Gavin, "The Sodality: Spiritual Honours Seminar," *The Heights* [Boston College] xl, no. 6 (1958): 6, https://newspapers.bc.edu/?a=d&d=bcheights19581121.2.32

according to the moral standards of Jesus and the Catholic Church as well as group service to those in need. Trying to do this by oneself in today's secular environment is very difficult, which may explain why so many of these organizations and their small groups have become so popular on hundreds of college campuses.

Though university professors and staff have their lives full of responsibilities, helping students to form these small groups or advocating for students to bring in one of the organizations sponsoring small groups (e.g., FOCUS and Knights of Columbus) can be of immeasurable help to generations of students on our campuses.

III. The Integration of Intellectual, Spiritual, and Moral Conversion

In his foundational work, *Method in Theology*, Bernard Lonergan distinguishes three interrelated kinds of conversion: intellectual, religious/spiritual, and moral.[11] I will briefly describe each below.

III.A. Intellectual Conversion

"Intellectual conversion" refers to a state of strong rational conviction about the existence and nature of God, Jesus, the transcendent soul, and other doctrines of the faith. This conviction is not based on one hundred percent certainty, but on reasonable and responsible belief from the preponderance of evidence brought together in what John Henry Newman called an "informal inference"[12]—mutual corroboration among multiple sources of antecedently probable evidence.

Since there is such a large preponderance of scientific and philosophical evidence which points to a higher transcendent intelligent

---

11. See Bernard Lonergan, *Method in Theology*, vol. 14 of *The Collected Works of Bernard Lonergan*, ed. Frederick Crowe and Robert Doran (University of Toronto Press, 1990), 144–55, 204–5, and 220–39.

12. See John Henry Newman, *An Essay in Aid of Grammar of Assent*, ch. 8, available at The National Institute of Newman Studies, www.newmanreader.org.

power standing at the origin of everything, we do not need to bet the bank on a single source of evidence. So, for example, we can take the mutual complementarity and corroboration of several antecedently probable sources of evidence—such as a metaphysical proof of God, the peer-reviewed medical studies of near-death experiences and terminal lucidity (showing the strong likelihood of consciousness surviving bodily death), the scientific evidence for a beginning of our universe and even a multiverse, the scientific evidence for transcendent intelligence as the source of the fine-tuning for life in our universe, and the philosophical arguments for a transphysical cause of self-consciousness and abstract conceptual intelligence—to ground the conclusion that there exists a transcendent intelligent cause of not only our universe or a multiverse, but also our transphysical soul, life after death, and even the whole of reality.[13]

Helping our students to be aware of this evidence, to discuss it, and affirm it is essential to our mission because without it most of our students will not move toward religious/spiritual conversion or moral conversion, and as a consequence, will benefit little from the religious/spiritual activities within our schools.

As the Pew[14] and CARA[15] surveys show, students need rational and scientific evidence for God, Jesus, and life after death if they

---

13. See, for example, Robert J. Spitzer, SJ, *Science at the Doorstep to God* (Ignatius, 2023); and *New Proofs for the Existence of God* (Eerdmans, 2010). See also Robert J. Spitzer and James Sinclair, "Fine-Tuning and Indications of Transcendent Intelligence," in *Theism and Atheism: Opposing Arguments in Philosophy*, ed. Joseph Koterski, SJ, and Graham Oppy (Macmillan Reference, 2019), 331–58.

14. See Michael Lipka, "Millennials Increasingly Are Driving Growth of 'Nones,'" Pew Research Foundation, May 12, 2015, www.pewresearch.org/fact-tank/2015/05/12/millennials-increasingly-are-driving-growth-of-nones/. See also Michael Lipka, "Why America's 'Nones' Left Religion Behind," Pew Research Foundation, August 24, 2016, www.pewresearch.org/fact-tank/2016/08/24/why-americas-nones-left-religion-behind/.

15. Courtney Mares, "Why Do Some Young People Leave the Church? A New Study Investigates," Catholic News Agency, January 17, 2018, https://www.

are not to become unbelievers by their junior year of college. Apparently, our contemporary culture so values rational, scientific, and empirical evidence that we must assume that for most of our students, intellectual conversion is necessary for religious/spiritual conversion; and if religious/spiritual conversion is needed for moral conversion in the Christian tradition, then failure to give the best possible contemporary rational and scientific evidence for God, Jesus, life after death, the soul, and the Church will lead to almost total failure in our mission to help students develop a lifelong relationship with the Lord. The reality is that intellectual conversion (supported by apologetical instruction) is the linchpin of practically everything else in our mission. Without it, we build the bronze statue with clay feet.

My institute, the Magis Center of Reason and Faith, in conjunction with the Sophia Institute for Teachers, has developed courses for middle school and high school to help students achieve intellectual conversion. The Assessment of Religious Knowledge (ARK) survey of Catholic schools in the U.S. measures both the knowledge and belief level of students from second grade to senior year (see arktest.org).[16] Though the knowledge of students goes up considerably from second grade to senior year, the **belief** score falls precipitously over the same period. The average belief score for seniors in Catholic high schools is a 67 (**D+**), which is so low that student perseverance in the faith is unlikely to make it past the freshman or sophomore year of college. If students take our senior year one-semester elective course called, "The Catholic Faith and Science," their belief score goes from a **67** (**D+**) to an **83** (**B**) in the

catholicnewsagency.com/news/why-do-some-young-people-leave-the-church-a-new-study-investigates-35699.

16. Assessment of Religious Knowledge (ARK) tests second through twelfth graders in Catholic schools with customizable tests, growth tracking, and individualized recommendations for both knowledge and belief. https://arktest.org/.

senior year, which has sufficient "sticking power" to last them into their collegiate experience.[17]

As important as apologetical studies are today, many Catholic schools (including Jesuit schools) have abandoned them—and most schools have no science-based apologetics at all. This is unfortunate, because science-based apologetics is the most effective kind for turning faith around and sustaining it. Thus, if we are to make our theology classes, retreat programs, and spiritual practices efficacious for the future faith lives of our students, we must reintegrate apologetics, especially science-based apologetics, into our classrooms. Though a one-semester course can be quite effective, the most effective, long-lasting way to do this is to have science-based apologetical material presented in middle school, which can bring students' belief scores up to an "A" by the senior year.[18]

III.B. Religious/Spiritual Conversion

Religious/spiritual conversion goes beyond intellectual conviction/conversion into the domain of the heart. It requires revelation from God because its objective is to establish a relationship with him. If we are to do this, philosophical and scientific evidence of God and life after death is not enough. We need to know what lies in the heart of that God and about the life he promises. Since science and philosophy cannot give us this information, we must turn to a source of revelation, and for the Jesuits, that source of revelation is Jesus Christ.

We need not take a blind "super-leap" to faith because God has left us with an immense amount of historical, exegetical, theological, and even scientific evidence of Jesus as his Son, who became incar-

---

17. Our Magis-Sophia high school course, "The Catholic Faith and Science" can be found at https://www.magiscenter.com/faith-science-courses.

18. Our Magis-Sophia middle school program called "Speak the Faith" can be found at https://www.magiscenter.com/blog/speak-the-faith and https://sophiateachers.org/product/speak-the-faith-teachers-guide.

nate to reveal the heart of God to us and initiate his Church.[19] So, reasonable and responsible intellectual conviction can help to ground our belief in Christ, but we will also need an act of the will to assent to Jesus's moral and doctrinal teaching as true and good—indeed, as the epitome of truth and goodness. When we do this, we open ourselves to an interpersonal relationship with Jesus through the Church which he initiated—the Church of the Holy Spirit, the sacraments, the Word, and the Magisterium (teaching authority) that will guide and empower us in the discovery and surrender to his unrestricted love. For the Jesuits in the *RS*, this religious/spiritual conversion is the nexus of the classroom and religious practice (see above section II).

The pluralism in our high schools, and especially in our universities, has caused most Jesuit institutions to deemphasize Christian religious/spiritual conversion as St. Ignatius understood it so that we won't leave non-Catholics and non-Christians out. Though I understand this motive, I think that Jesuit schools should get back to the business of Christian religious/spiritual conversion for all students who come from this faith tradition and that special accommodations be made for those who do not. If we weaken our mission to religious/spiritual conversion in both the classroom and our schools' religious practice, we barely achieve the mission for which they were originally intended since the earliest centuries of the Church—a mission which leaves our students with only a superficial connection to the heart of God in Jesus Christ.

There are two dimensions of religious/spiritual conversion that our schools should be developing—(1) the teaching of Christian

19. See, for example, Robert J. Spitzer, SJ, *Christ, Science, and Reason: What We Can Know About Jesus, Mary, and Miracles* (Ignatius Press, 2024), which examines not only the historical and exegetical evidence of Jesus's Sonship, but also the scientific evidence on the Shroud of Turin, Eucharistic hosts, and Marian miracles. See also Robert J. Spitzer, SJ, *Science, Reason, and Faith: Discovering the Bible* (OSV Press, 2023).

theology, and (2) the practical fostering of a relationship with Christ through retreats, frequent Mass/confession, and communities of faith and moral integrity (e.g., prayer groups, Bible studies, etc.)—see above section II.

III.C. Moral Conversion

There is an underlying assumption in the *Spiritual Exercises* and the *RS* that may not be as apparent today as in previous centuries—that we are involved in a cosmic struggle between good and evil. Though 68% of Americans indicate that they do believe there are angels and demons active in the world,[20] this belief does not seem to be taken seriously enough to incite deeper moral conversion.

Some teachers believe that speaking about an evil spirit would be too frightening for students; others believe that it is a throwback to a superstitious pre-scientific era, and still others do not make the connection to Jesus and the Church as our greatest protection against this evil spirit. This makes it difficult for our students to take Jesus's and the Church's moral teaching seriously. If students perceive no danger from cooperation with evil, they are likely to walk right into it, failing to recognize the danger into which they are putting themselves in this life and the next.

A good starting point for the discussion of the good spirit and evil spirit (and how they work) can be found in the "Rules for the Discernment of Spirits" in the *Spiritual Exercises.*[21] This can give stu-

20. Pew Research Center, "U.S. Religious Landscape Survey: Religious Beliefs and Practices," June 1, 2008, https://www.pewresearch.org/religion/2008/06/01/u-s-religious-landscape-survey-religious-beliefs-and-practices/.

21. St. Ignatius of Loyola, "Fourteen Rules for Discernment of Spirits," in *Spiritual Exercises*, https://www.documentacatholicaomnia.eu/03d/1491-1556,_Ignatius_Loyola,_Spiritual_Exercises,_EN.pdf#page=74. See also St. Ignatius of Loyola, "Eight Additional Rules for People of the Second Week," in *Spiritual Exercises*, https://www.documentacatholicaomnia.eu/03d/1491-1556,_Ignatius_Loyola,_Spiritual_Exercises,_EN.pdf#page=76.

dents a sense of the dangers presented by the evil spirit, inciting them to take moral teaching seriously. If students are skeptical about the existence of an evil spirit, you may want to refer them to some well-documented exorcism cases from reputable sources.[22] We cannot afford to leave students with the impression that conversion *ends* with a relationship with Christ (though it pervades everything in religious life); it must also be complemented with the need for and steps to moral conversion. If we do not take seriously the moral teaching of Christ and conversion towards it, we could weaken our relationship with him and fall into darkness.

The *RS* treats moral conversion in three interrelated dimensions:

1. Moral theological teaching, which not only explains the "what" of Jesus's teaching, but also the "why."
2. Relating moral conversion to spiritual conversion through the sacraments and prayer.
3. Good role models from the Jesuits, faculty, coaches, etc.

The first dimension of moral conversion (moral teaching) in the Jesuit tradition is quite rich and requires some explanation. First, as teachers are aware, many if not most of our students need to know *why* Jesus and the Church teach against so many current practices that popular culture believes are "just fine"—transgenderism, pre-marital sex, cohabitation, homosexual lifestyle, invitro fertilization, and much more. Our students truly want to understand why Jesus and the Church are not "in line" with the culture, particularly when popular culture criticizes and even cancels them for adhering to the Church's teaching. Hence, it is incumbent upon us as moral/ethical teachers to explain why being against transgen-

22. Richard Gallagher, MD, *Demonic Foes* (HarperOne, 2020)—The case of Julia. See also Thomas Allen, *Possessed* (iUniverse, 2000)—Full diary of the case of Robbie Mannheim. See also Robert J. Spitzer, SJ, *Christ Versus Satan in our Daily Lives* (Ignatius, 2020), ch. 3.

derism, etc., is not callousness, insensitivity, and ignorance on the part of the Church. We need to defend Jesus's and the Church's teachings by using *secular* university and professional studies (e.g., the *Archives of General Psychiatry*) to make the case that obeying Jesus's and the Church's moral teaching leads to significantly increased emotional health, spiritual health, relational health, and marital health. Conversely, disobeying Church teaching does the opposite, leading to increased rates of depression, anxiety, major psychiatric disorders, suicidality, and suicides.[23] I have developed a senior year elective course called *Challenges of the Modern World,* which makes this case at the level of seniors in high school.[24] This course shows how Jesus's view of covenant love is the interpretive key not only to his moral teachings, but also to spiritual, emotional, and relational health—precisely what we would expect from the revelation of the Son of God.

The second dimension of moral conversion is connecting it to spiritual conversion through the sacraments and prayer. Considerable attention is paid to the connection between moral and spiritual conversion in parts 1–3 of the *RS* because reception of the Holy Eucharist, the sacrament of reconciliation, and prayer are essential to resisting temptation, appropriating virtue, and becoming "the new self" in Christ (Col 3:10 and Eph 4:24). Much of St. Ignatius's *Spiritual Exercises* are focused on developing a deeper relationship with the Lord so that we will want to follow his moral teachings out of love for him (beyond fear). Though St. Ignatius warns us of the evil spirit and his attempts to seduce us into his darkness (a strong motivation for moral conversion), he wants us to experience the same

23. See Robert J. Spitzer, SJ, *The Moral Wisdom of the Catholic Church* (Ignatius Press, 2022), chs. 1–5.

24. Robert J. Spitzer, SJ, *Challenges of the Modern World* (Sophia Institute for Teachers, 2022). There is a faculty manual, student workbook, and videos—for a sample see: https://www.yumpu.com/en/document/read/67797049/magis-apologetics-ii-sample-lesson.

transformation that he did at Manresa[25]—revulsion at sin which breaks down our loving relationship with the Lord.[26]

The Jesuits consider this so important that they place major emphasis on developing spiritual practices, particularly through retreats, Mass, and frequent confession (see section II), which provide a solid foundation for deeper moral conversion. Two practices are emphasized:

1. Frequent confession, which helps students form their consciences and connect their love of Christ to resisting sin and obtaining forgiveness.
2. The Examen Prayer is a daily practice recommended in the *Spiritual Exercises* to integrate our relationship with Christ into our moral conversion.[27] When practiced faithfully, it helps us resist temptation and develop virtue out of love for Christ—who loved us first.

The third dimension of moral conversion, good role modeling from Jesuits, teachers, and coaches, is exceedingly important because students look up to teachers not only as academic authorities, but also as moral models. Disedification of young people can undermine their faith and moral resolve for decades, if not a lifetime.

IV. Strong Foundations, Active Learning, and *Eloquentia Perfecta*

Parts 2–4 of the *RS* give multiple examples of these three fundamental principles of Jesuit pedagogy—strong foundations, active

25. St. Ignatius of Loyola, *The Autobiography*, ed. J. F. X. O'Conor, SJ (Benzinger Brothers, 1900), 30–55 (chapters 2 and 3), https://www.gutenberg.org/cache/epub/24534/pg24534-images.html.

26. For an explanation of this, see Robert J. Spitzer, SJ, *Escape from Evil's Darkness* (Ignatius Press, 2021), chs. 4–6.

27. This is a simplified method of the Examen Prayer provided by Loyola Press. https://www.loyolapress.com/catholic-resources/ignatian-spirituality/examen-and-ignatian-prayer/how-can-i-pray-try-the-daily-examen/.

learning, and *eloquentia perfecta*. With respect to *strong foundations*, the Jesuits emphasized the Trivium and the Quadrivium in the lower grades (part 4 of the *RS*). The Trivium is the most basic foundation, stressing the essential building blocks for thinking, writing, and speaking—logic, grammar, and rhetoric. The classical approach has much value even today because it focuses on *mastery of method* by repeated exercises in the application of logic for thinking, grammar for writing, and rhetoric for public speaking. Many of today's students, through no fault of their own, are lacking these active skills so necessary for accurate thought, communication, and good judgment. Aside from diagraming sentences, freshman and sophomore students should become acquainted with informal fallacies, some basic rules for proper syllogisms, and some of the elements of style.[28]

The Quadrivium in middle school and high school emphasizes mathematics (arithmetic and geometry, and today, trigonometry, statistics, and if possible, calculus), science (astronomy and today, biology/life sciences, chemistry, and physics), and musical theory. Today, strong emphasis on history and social sciences must be added. Most Jesuit high schools do excellent work in these areas, while reinforcing and developing the skills of logic/argument, writing, and rhetoric/public speaking.

With respect to *active learning*, the *RS* (and many Jesuit schools today) emphasize three techniques:

1. Constant drilling on fundamentals and methods ("*repetitio est mater studiorum*"—repetition is the mother of learning). Without drilling, fundamental methods will not become habitual (second nature), which will inhibit critical thought, speaking, and writing throughout academic studies and life.

---

28. High school teachers could introduce students to some of the basic rules in William Strunk's and E. B. White's brief foundational work, *The Elements of Style* (Pearson, 1999). See also William Strunk, Jr.'s *Elements of Style Workbook* (Tip-Top Education, 2018).

2. Constant revisions of research and written work to achieve an excellent product. This technique is quite labor intensive for teachers, but makes an invaluable difference for the thinking and writing proficiency of students. Just filling a paper with red corrections and "leaving it there" is not enough. The student needs to go through the corrections with the teacher, not only to improve the organization and development of thought in the paper, but also to learn how to write a proper sentence and paragraph. The Jesuits also expected written work for history and science classes as well as literature and humanities. The students who master these skills become successful because of their capacity to think, write, and speak creatively and clearly.
3. *Oral arguments, public speeches, and debates*—both informally in class and formally in public competitions—is essential not only for clear communication, but also to put one's point across firmly in public and professional forums. The *RS* did not want Jesuit leaders to be obstreperous, but rational (*logos*), aware of their audience (*ethos*), and passionate to a precisely appropriate degree for that audience (*pathos*). The old Jesuit adages, "do not let your enthusiasm outstretch your content" and "do not be the most boring intellectual in the room," are reflections of how to build the balance between *logos*, *ethos*, and *pathos*. The only way of making this rhetorical capability second nature is to practice continually while receiving constructive criticism on how to improve.

As students progress into philosophical studies (part 3 of the *RS*) both in high schools and universities, another Jesuit discipline becomes essential—the mastery of higher viewpoints and the capability of making subtle distinctions on the basis of those viewpoints.[29] Higher viewpoints give us the freedom to test our and others' fundamental assumptions, which in turn, helps clarify our

29. Robert J. Spitzer, SJ, "Educating in the Jesuit Tradition," Catholic Education Resource Center, 2000. https://catholiceducation.org/en/education/educating-in-the-jesuit-tradition.html.

thinking. Many Jesuit students are aware of differences in the assessment of truth (e.g. rationalism, empiricism, and realism), ethics (e.g. utilitarianism, teleology, deontology, and natural law), freedom (e.g. determinism, absolute freedom, and partial freedom), economics (e.g. capitalism, socialism, and communism), and much more. The fundamental assumptions we choose will determine our principles, ideals, sense of truth, justice, personhood, happiness, suffering, love, purpose in life, and quality of life.[30] Our assumptions will also determine how we will interact with the culture, political community, and economic community, which will affect how we interact with almost every area of society. So, our fundamental assumptions will affect both our personal objectives and our social-cultural objectives, which in turn, will affect not only how we lead, but more importantly, what we are leading people to.

There is another reason for mastering higher viewpoints—to facilitate clear and helpful distinctions. Yet another Jesuit adage is, "Never deny, seldom affirm, always distinguish." When we are arguing, we will make little progress in finding common ground or persuading a person to change by simply denying an opponent's position out of hand. Similarly, it is not very helpful to affirm opponents' positions solely to appease them. True persuasion and progress are made when we can appeal to a higher viewpoint—a higher idea or set of ideas—that will enable us to make distinctions between positions on the basis of objective criteria. If, for example, I can say your assumptions are ethically utilitarian and epistemologically phenomenalist, whereas mine are natural law ethics and epistemological realism, we can now move the argument from mere positions on issues to the higher viewpoints standing behind those positions. If we can convince a person to clarify their assumptions

30. I have written two books articulating the various options for these fundamental categories: *Ten Universal Principles* (Ignatius Press, 2011) and *Healing the Culture* (Ignatius Press, 2000), 123–280 (chs. 4–8).

or even to change their previously unrecognized assumptions, we can progress toward agreement based on sound reasoning—and that makes us better influencers and leaders.

The expression "*eloquentia perfecta*" was coined in the *RS* as a way of referring to the end result of Jesuit education—the ability to express the ideals of faith and morals, knowledge and wisdom, and higher viewpoints and foundations in a coherent way for the purpose of education and leadership in organizations and the public forum.[31] Thus, *eloquentia perfecta* is the culmination of the spiritual and moral formation, the drilling on fundamentals, the constant revisions of papers and speeches, the mastery of higher viewpoints and distinctions, and the balance of *logos*, *ethos*, and *pathos*. Graduates who have cultivated this capability have painstakingly appropriated the background needed not only for independence of thought, but also a method for pursuing objective truth, the ultimate grounds of nature and reality (science and metaphysics), objective moral principles, the physical and spiritual grounds of personhood and freedom, and the ability to express the synthesis of these ideas in concrete situations for the common good and the kingdom of God. Yes—*eloquentia perfecta* includes not only subtle articulation and felicitous phrasing, but also the heights and depths of the categories of cultural discourse. Those possessing this ability are almost destined to be leaders because they possess both charisma and depth of knowledge and wisdom that can lead culture and society to higher levels of purpose, ethics, and the common good.

31. Patricia Bizzell, "Historical Notes on Rhetoric in Jesuit Education," in *Traditions of Eloquence: The Jesuits and Modern Rhetoric Studies*, ed. C. Gannett and J. C. Brereton (Fordham University Press, 2016), 42–43.

V. Developing Leaders for the Common Good and the Kingdom of God

Developing the intellectual and rhetorical skills in the *RS* (discussed in section IV above) is not enough to become leaders for the common good and the kingdom of God. Leaders must *care* about others and the common good—not only for this world, but also the eternal world revealed by our transcendental desires, conscience, metaphysical and scientific discoveries, and Christian revelation. St. Augustine's penetrating insight into human happiness, ethics, and reasoning cannot be overlooked when developing and expressing our ideals for self and culture:

> For thou hast made us for Thyself, and our hearts are restless until they rest in Thee (*Confessions* bk 1, ch 1).

This means that we cannot content ourselves with being leaders of a this-worldly common good. We must understand that the common good includes our transcendental, spiritual, and transphysical nature. We have desires for ultimate and perfect truth, love, goodness, beauty, and being that reveal our spiritual nature; and so we must include these highest dimensions of ourselves not only in our understanding of individual human beings, but also of the common good. If we underestimate and undervalue our dignity, destiny, and fulfillment by assuming a materialistic and this-worldly reductionism, our view of the common good will call everyone *downward*—to a mere shadow of our real transcendent and eternal selves. This leads to profound unhappiness, moral relativism, and a reduction of human beings from mystery to problem. This is evidenced by the American Psychiatric Association study (and several other complementary studies) showing that non-religiously affiliated people have significantly higher (double and triple) rates of depression, anxiety, anti-social aggressivity, substance abuse, familial tensions, suicidal ideation, and suicides than religiously affiliated people.[32] It is also evidenced by the correlation between the decline in religious affiliation and the decline in both objective moral values and willingness to listen to conscience.[33]

The *RS* calls educators to develop leaders for the common good in the highest and broadest meaning of that term—the common good of people who are spiritual and transcendent and who will only be satisfied by absolute, eternal, and perfect truth, love, goodness, beauty, and being. In order to do this, the *RS* sets out a plan to encourage students toward intellectual, religious/spiritual, and moral conversion. Of course, students are not expected to complete the conversion process, which continues throughout life. Rather, they are given a jumpstart into all three kinds of conversion (described in section III) in the hope that they will deepen their conversion through their religious practice, intellectual development, and moral practice and reflection. Thus, the leadership ideal of Jesuit graduates is fourfold:

1. To have a recognition of the spiritual and transcendent nature of every human being, and if Christian, to follow the revelation of Christ for their spiritual and eternal fulfillment. In that way they will treat each person as a transcendent mystery, rather than a "thingified" problem.
2. To be virtuous by embracing objective moral values, developing the four cardinal virtues—prudence/wisdom, temperance/self-control,

32. Kanita Dervic, M. A. Oquendo, and M. F. Grunebaum et al., "Religious Affiliation and Suicide Attempts," *The American Journal of Psychiatry* 161, no. 12 (December 2004): 2303–8, https://ajp.psychiatryonline.org/doi/full/10.1176/appi.ajp.161.12.2303. See also Harold Koenig, "Research on Religion, Spirituality and Mental Health: A Review," *Canadian Journal of Psychiatry* 54, no. 5 (2009): 283–91, https://journals.sagepub. com/doi/pdf/10.1177/070674370905400502; Raphael Bonelli, R. E. Dew, and H. G. Koenig et al., "Religious and Spiritual Factors in Depression: Review and Integration of the Research," *Depression and Research Treatment* (2012), https://www.hindawi.com/journals/drt/2012/962860/.

33. See the multiple studies in Spitzer, *The Moral Wisdom of the Catholic Church*, chs. 1–4.

fortitude/courage, and justice—and to embrace the theological virtues of faith, hope, and love (*caritas* and *agapē*) as the true objective of their interior transformation.

3. To be capable of *eloquentia perfecta* to the degree that their thinking, speaking, and writing capabilities will allow. This includes a strong foundation in fundamentals and developing the habits of logic, excellent writing, and rhetoric, to be effective communicators and leaders for the common good, and to have a vision of the common good capable of calling people to higher levels of purpose in life, ethics, freedom, love, personhood, society, and political economy. In other words, to have the capability to call people upward, rather than downward into the depths of materialism, utilitarianism, and ego-comparative narcissism.[34]
4. To have basic leadership skills (prudence) for formulating organizational goals and objectives, and developing consensus among internal and external stakeholders toward those objectives (communicating a vision clearly and charismatically), in a manner that is hardworking, self-sacrificial, and a good ethical model for the mission, goals, and stakeholders of the organization.[35]

The objectives of the *Ratio Studiorum* are not only relevant today, but needed more than ever. Though many Jesuit schools and universities still embrace spiritual practice (section II), intellectual, religious/spiritual, and moral conversion (section III), active learning, *eloquentia perfecta,* and leadership for the common good (sections IV-V), some schools and universities have declined in this noble mission, deemphasizing spiritual practice, intellectual conversion

---

34. I have developed a method to help students and adults move their purpose in life/identity from Level 1 (pursuit of pleasure and materialism) to Level 2 (pursuit of ego-comparative advantage) to Level 3 (pursuit of optimal contribution and relationship) to Level 4 (pursuit of transcendence and spiritual/faith-based purpose). See Robert J. Spitzer, SJ, *The Four Levels of Happiness* (Sophia Institute Press, 2024).

35. See Robert J. Spitzer, SJ, *The Spirit of Leadership* (Executive Excellence, 2000), chs. 6–18.

(apologetics), and moral conversion. As a result, their view of the common good has become focused on the present world, frequently substituting social justice for development of faith and morals. Though social justice is important, we must remember the emphasis in the *RS* toward what many Jesuits call "The faith that does justice." My hope in writing this chapter is to reinspire the leadership of our schools to reinvest in the vision of St. Ignatius of Loyola, who in his *Spiritual Exercises* and *Constitutions* provided the noble mission for Jesuit education.

14 Jean-Baptiste de La Salle and Don Bosco

Joe Heschmeyer

The State of Things

I will start with bad news: modern education is in a state of crisis. This is inclusive of, but not limited to, Catholic education. In 2008, in a letter to the faithful of Rome, Pope Benedict XVI spoke of what he called "the crisis of education." To see that things are problematic, you do not have to be someone working in education or of a certain theological persuasion, and Benedict points this out. He notes that his assessment is shared "by parents who worry about their children's future, teachers who are living the school crisis from within, priests and catechists who know from experience how difficult it is to teach the faith, and the children, adolescents and young people themselves who do not want to be left on their own to face life's challenges."[1]

Benedict makes two points, in particular, that I want to highlight. First, that things are going very badly, and second, that things seem to be getting progressively worse. This is true whether you share a Catholic vision of the *telos*—the goal—of education or not. If we ask what the purpose of a school is, we could broadly highlight four groups of answers. The first is that given by Plato and Aristotle, who say the point of education is to teach the young how to love the lovable and hate the odious in proper proportion. If a child hears about a person and a dog being hit by a car, and their heart goes out

---

1. Benedict XVI, "Presentation to the Diocese of Rome of the 'Letter on the Urgent Task of Education,'" February 23, 2008, https://www.vatican.va/content/benedict-xvi/en/speeches/2008/february/documents/hf_ben-xvi_spe_20080223_diocesi-roma.html.

for the dog more than the person, there's a failure of education. By the end of the educational process, they should be well adjusted to loving what is worthy of love, loving the greater things more than the lesser things, and hating the worst things more than the less-bad things. By that standard, how are we doing with the next generation? It does not seem like it's going well.

Another approach we can take on the purpose of schools is the explicitly Catholic one, Pope Pius XI being the exemplar of this. Pius says that "education consists essentially in preparing man for what he must be and for what he must do here below, in order to attain the sublime end for which he was created." And so, based on this, he continues, "it is clear that there can be no true education which is not wholly directed to man's last end."[2] In other words, any education that is not focused on how we get these kids closer to the beatific vision is not education in the fullest sense of the term. I do not have to tell you schools are not succeeding in that task.

You could also take a completely secular vision of education. John Dewey, the most famous advocate of this position, rejected the whole vision of education we saw in Pius, and tried to argue that education does not *need* an end or a purpose. Now, from an Aristotelian standpoint, that is nonsensical. Nevertheless, in his writings, he talks about the unifying aim of education being "the growth of the child in the direction of social capacity and service, [and] his larger and more vital union with life."[3] As long as we are producing well-adjusted functional members of society, we are succeeding in education. Yet, how are we doing on that front?

---

2. Pius XI, *Divini Illius Magistri* [Encyclical Letter on Christian Education], December 31, 1929, Papal Encyclicals Online, 7, https://www.papalencyclicals.net/pius11/p11rappr.htm.

3. John Dewey, *The School and Society* (Southern Illinois University Press, 1980), 55.

On the other hand, there is the common, ordinary, "man on the street" theory that education is simply the imparting of information. The teacher has a block of knowledge, and they just dump it into the heads of their kids. We can ask, once again, if you take that model of education, how are we doing? The answer seems to be—by any model of education, by any criterion used to judge the state of modern education—that we are failing. Whatever the goal we ought to be pursuing, we're not hitting *any* of them very well.

Benedict talked about the crisis of education in 2008. That year is as far from us as 2042 is in the other direction. And since then, as you would predict from reading Benedict's letter, things have gotten progressively worse. Now, of course, there have been compounding factors. I will give you just two headlines from June 21, 2023, the first from the *Washington Post*, which said that "National test scores plunge, with still no sign of pandemic recovery."[4] *U.S. News & World Report*, covering the same bad set of test scores, has an even more ominous headline: "U.S. Teens' Reading and Math Scores Feature Largest Declines Ever."[5]

As bad as the test scores are, there's something that I find more foreboding. Of the thirteen-year-old students they tested, a third of them said they never or hardly ever read for fun.[6] That is up from 22% a decade ago. In the last decade, we have gone from about 22% of kids with no love of reading to 33%. The signs are all in the wrong direction. Moreover, the number who took Algebra a decade ago was about 34%. That's down to 24%. Even if you said that we'll sac-

---

4. Donna St. George, "National Test Scores Plunge, with Still No Sign of Pandemic Recovery," *Washington Post*, June 21, 2023, https://www.washingtonpost.com/education/2023/06/21/national-student-test-scores-drop-naep/.

5. Lauren Camera, "U.S. Teens' Reading and Math Scores Feature Largest Declines Ever," *U.S. News*, June 21, 2023, https://www.usnews.com/news/education-news/articles/2023–06–21/u-s-teens-reading-and-math-scores-feature-largest-declines-ever.

6. Camera, "U.S. Teens' Reading and Math Scores Feature Largest Declines Ever."

rifice the Beatific Vision and we'll sacrifice love of literature as long as they know STEM, well, guess what? We're also spiraling out of control with STEM by every standard imaginable.

Education is in a state of ever-worsening crisis. Pope Benedict, therefore, warns that we are becoming like the pagans St. Paul describes in Ephesians 2:12, where he talks about the pagans as "having no hope and without God in the world." This is his description of the climate in schools today, producing a generation of people who have neither hope nor God.

This leads to a follow-up question: who do we blame? It is easy to blame the kids, the students, whether we are talking about college, high school, or grade school. But Benedict points out that it is not as though children today are born differently than those in the past. There are not new genetic defects, like a TikTok gene, that make one incapable of learning. If there's a generational gap where the young don't share the knowledge, beliefs, and values of the older generation, it's a *symptom* of the problem. It's not the *cause* of the problem, and all you've done is describe it.

What about the parents or the teachers? And Benedict responds that "yes," they are to blame—but not only them: "There is certainly a strong temptation among both parents and teachers as well as educators in general to give up, since they run the risk of not even understanding what their role or rather the mission entrusted to them is."[7] One of the problems is that there are many different visions of what education is supposed to be floating around parents and educators. One of the reasons we're failing is that we do not know what we are supposed to be doing. If we don't know the final cause, it is first in order of intent and last in order of execution. If we do not know where we are heading, we are not going to get there.

Behind this and beneath this, Benedict says, there is a cultural problem. A sick culture is giving rise to the confusion parents and

7. Benedict XVI, "Presentation to Diocese of Rome."

educators are experiencing. He says, "In fact, it is not only the personal responsibilities of adults or young people, which nonetheless exist and must not be concealed, that are called into question but also a widespread atmosphere, a mindset and form of culture which induce one to have doubt about the value of the human person, about the very meaning of truth and good, and ultimately about the goodness of life."[8] All of this is, in some way, "downstream" from culture—which we stand in a complicated relationship with.

Culture is, in a certain sense, the sum of human action, but it's also larger than any individual actor. As a parent, as an educator, we operate within a particular cultural space. I think every educator can tell you there's only so much you can do if the home life is in disarray, if the *cultural* life is in disarray, if your kids are consuming vicious (in the moral sense of the term) media constantly from TV, from internet, from apps on their phone—which they shouldn't have in the first place. There's only so much you, as an educator, can do. Everyone feels powerless, helpless, and overwhelmed.

I'm reminded here of the poem *The Second Coming* by William Butler Yeats, written shortly after the First World War. In the opening lines, he says,

> Turning and turning in the widening gyre
> The falcon cannot hear the falconer;
> Things fall apart; the centre cannot hold;
> Mere anarchy is loosed upon the world,
> The blood-dimmed tide is loosed, and everywhere
> The ceremony of innocence is drowned;
> The best lack all conviction, while the worst
> Are full of passionate intensity.[9]

---

8. Benedict XVI, "Presentation to Diocese of Rome."

9. W. B. Yeats, "The Second Coming," *Poetry Foundation*, https://www.poetryfoundation.org/poems/43290/the-second-coming.

A gyre is a circle, a rotation, a revolution—an image from falconry. The falcon circles and is meant to return. The problem, however, is that the revolution has gone off course. In the case of Catholic education, we wanted to follow the vision of Pius XI, until we threw it off in the sixties. Then, we wanted to compete with Harvard, to be prominent, prestigious, and well-accredited in the state-level systems. But the revolution went off-course, and the falcon can no longer hear the falconer. We have lost communication; we have lost touch, and our kids are like the falcons that have simply drifted away unintentionally.

Looking to the Saints for Help

That was the bad news, but now we can ask: "What can we do?" And as I said before, there are two saints I hope to employ in helping to solve this question and giving us a few practical tips for restoring some sanity to the world of education. The first is St. Jean-Baptiste de La Salle (1651–1719), and the second is St. Giovanni Bosco (1815–1888, "Don Bosco"); both are heavily associated with education.

Jean-Baptiste de La Salle is praised by St. John Paul II for what he calls "his pedagogical genius,"[10] and Pope Pius XII, in 1950, named him "the special patron of all teachers of children and youth."[11] That's a good set of recommendations. For Don Bosco, John Paul II called him the "father and teacher of young people"[12] and described him as "the perennial force of the educa-

10. John Paul II, "Message to Brother John Johnston," May 2, 2000, https://www.vatican.va/content/john-paul-ii/en/speeches/2000/apr-jun/documents/hf_jp-ii_spe_20000515_scuole-cristiane.html.
11. Quoted in "Jean-Baptiste de La Salle," *Nominis*, accessed November 9, 2024, https://nominis.cef.fr/contenus/saint/931/Saint-Jean-Baptiste-de-La-Salle.html.
12. Quoted in "St John Bosco (Canonized: 1934)," *Salesian Missions*, accessed November 9, 2024, https://salesianmissions.org/about-us/who-we-are/about-st-john-bosco/our-history/history-of-the-salesians/st-john-bosco-canonized-1934/.

tional apostolate,"[13] and more recently, Pope Francis encouraged young people to "look to him as the exemplary educator."[14] In short, we have Don Bosco, a teacher par excellence, and Jean-Baptiste de La Salle, a teacher *of teachers* par excellence. Wherever you find yourself, whether in the classroom directly or in administration helping to ensure the teachers are doing what they should, there is a saint for you.[15]

Jean-Baptiste de La Salle and the Need for Teacher Conversion

Let's turn first to Jean Baptiste de La Salle. To tie this back to the state of education, it is easy to feel overwhelmed and discouraged. It may help—or it may be just more discouraging—to know that we have been here before. I mentioned that John Paul II praises the pedagogical genius of de La Salle, but what he praises him for *specifically* is that he was "a distinguished pioneer in the popular education of children and youth. A true apostle, he knew how to serve the children who came to his schools, striving first of all to form their teachers."[16] If we have a problem in the schools, the first place to look is the teachers.

---

13. John Paul II, "General Address on May 23, 2001," https://www.vatican.va/content/john-paul-ii/en/audiences/2001/documents/hf_jp-ii_aud_20010523.html#:~:text=The%20perennial%20force%20of%20the%20educational%20apostolate%20of,places%20that%20are%20on%20the%20frontiers%20of%20civilization.
14. Anne Kurian-Montabone, "Saint John Bosco, 'Exemplary Educator,'" *Zenit*, January 31, 2018, https://zenit.org/2018/01/31/saint-john-bosco-exemplary-educator/.
15. There are roughly four different audiences in this field: college, high school, grade school, and homeschool. Those are four different needs. I'll try to extrapolate, at the broadest level, the principles that are of chief applicability. It's worth remembering that both men dealt with young all-boys education, and often boys who were at high risk; some of what they have to say may be applicable only to their time, place, and circumstance. I've tried to draw out the more universal principles.
16. John Paul II, "Message to Brother John Johnston."

That's the first part of the pedagogical genius of de La Salle: if the teachers are unformed, malformed, and deformed, it is very unlikely you are going to get the kind of education you want. This was the case in the lifetime of Jean-Baptiste de La Salle. The Bishop of Toul, in 1686, lamented the teachers of his day and said that schoolmasters were "gamblers, drunkards, libertines, ignorant, and brutal." They spent "their days in taverns playing cards, and are engaged to fiddle in places of pleasure and at the village festivals. In church they are not modestly dressed, and instead of applying themselves to ecclesiastical chant, they sing during the offices whatever comes into their heads." What do you think the results will be from Catholic teachers who lack a sense of the sacred, are not well-formed, are not living virtuous lives, and are too caught up in worldly pleasures? You're not going to get the kind of students that you hope for. Adrien Bourdoise (1583–1655), a contemporary of de La Salle, a French educator and theologian, put it like this: "We ought not to be astonished if we see so few of the children educated at the schools live like good Christians. That a school may become useful to Christianity, it must have masters who labor as apostles, and not as mercenaries." Are the teachers in our schools apostles or mercenaries? You can tell who's just looking for a job in education, compared to who is driven by the Catholic vision of the human person and the role of education.

This is the crisis situation in which Jean Baptiste de La Salle finds himself. His correction, his course out of it, begins with properly identifying the framework and purpose of education. John Paul II puts it like this: "[de La Salle's] insight remains fundamental today, for it underscores how education presupposes, on the one hand, the transmission of human and Christian values and, on the other, the witness of adults who show young people what a happy and balanced life is."[17] Notice what John Paul is saying: there are two things

17. John Paul II, "Message to Brother John Johnston."

happening in optimal education. Number one, there is a transmission of human and Christian values, and number two, there is a personal witness of a happy Christian life. You are not just *telling* them, as in number one, you are not just *transmitting* information and values; you are also *demonstrating* them by your life. This is a common theme in the educational pedagogies of both these saints. We focus too little on *how* we are presenting the things we present.

We can present things better following de La Salle's vision of what education is all about. "God our Savior . . . desires all men to be saved and to come to the knowledge of the truth" (1 Tim 2:3–4). That is, of course, from St. Paul: that education is tied to salvation. And in de La Salle's words: "God is so good that having created us, he wills that all of us come to the knowledge of the truth. This truth is God and what God has desired to reveal to us through Jesus Christ, through the holy Apostles, and through his Church. This is why God wills all people to be instructed, so that their minds may be enlightened by the light of faith."[18]

Now, that might seem basic, but notice what he has done. If this point is true—if God desires all men to be saved and come to the knowledge of the truth—a second thing follows: everyone ought to be educated, everyone ought to be instructed. I think we take that for granted today, but at the time it was revolutionary. Not only was education limited to boys, it was also limited to boys within certain social classes. But de La Salle said that cannot be the case if you understand the Christian vision of what education is about. Suddenly we have this sense that education is not just career prep, it is not college prep—it is heaven prep. Whoever we want to see in heaven, we ought to take the trouble of making sure they are well formed. That is a different way of understanding the discipline we all care about.

18. Jean-Baptiste de La Salle, *Meditations for the Time of Retreat,* trans. Richard Arnandez (Lasallian Publications, 1994), 432.

Something else follows from this: "We cannot be instructed in the mysteries of our holy religion," he said, "unless we have the good fortune to hear about them, and we cannot have this advantage unless someone preaches the word of God."[19] St. Paul, in Romans 10, famously says that "every one who calls upon the name of the Lord will be saved." But then he asks, "But how are men to call upon him in whom they have not believed? And how are they to believe in him of whom they have never heard? And how are they to hear without a preacher?" (Rom 10:13–14). If we take this seriously, there is a need for preachers—and de La Salle would say teachers, instructors. I want to return to the vision of Pius XI because I think it is the same vision. Pius says it is "in the lives of the numerous Saints, whom the Church, and she alone, produces" that we find "perfectly realized the purpose of Christian education, and who have in every way ennobled and benefited human society."[20]

Education is, in its fullest sense, about the formation of saints. This is both for their good, for their eternal salvation, and also for the good of the whole Church and world, because we are all enriched when one of us becomes the saint we are meant to be. That is what education is about. If your school is churning out saints, that is good for the students, it is good for society, it is good for the Church, it is good in every measurable form.

That's the idea, so how do we get there? Remember the twofold pedagogical mission that John Paul II identifies in de La Salle: "On the one hand, the transmission of human and Christian values and, on the other, the witness of adults who show young people what a happy and balanced life is."[21] De La Salle, drawing on St. Paul's imagery, says that we are "ambassadors of Christ." Further, he says, "Since you are ambassadors and ministers of Jesus Christ in the work that

19. De La Salle, *Meditations*, 432.
20. Pius XI, *Divini Illius Magistri*, 99.
21. John Paul II, "Message to Brother John Johnston."

you do, you must act as representing Jesus Christ. He wants your disciples to see him in you and to receive your instructions as if he were instructing them."[22] I love this life that he wants us to lead in the classroom; he wants us to do it in such a way that someone learning from you feels as though they are learning directly from Christ. Is that a tall order in education? I daresay it is. They, the students, must be convinced that your instructions are the truth of Jesus Christ, that he is speaking with your mouth, that it is only in his name that you teach, and that he has given you authority over them. We can identify three ways to get to this essential goal.

1. Become a Saint

I know this is obvious, but it is indispensable, because if you are not living as a saint, you cannot be the ambassador for Christ you are made to be. The moral lives of our teachers matter for their effectiveness as teachers. That should not be the kind of thing I have to tell people in the world of Catholic education, but there are numerous counterexamples of this, where we say, "Oh, that's their personal life. It doesn't matter if they believe Catholic doctrine. It doesn't matter if they're leading moral lives." According to de La Salle, it does.

This is not simply about what you are teaching, but how you're teaching it. I love this particular example he gives about what to do if rowdy students are disruptive when you are beginning class with prayer. He is dealing with young boys, but you can find some version of this at every age. What do you do if you are at home? The same situation happens in both atmospheres. What do you do? Do you stop, correct your kids and say, "Quiet down, we're praying." That would be the *tell* approach. De La Salle is firmly in the *show* approach. He actually gives instructions to his teachers to "speak neither to any particular student nor to them all in general during

22. Jean-Baptiste de La Salle, *Meditations for the Time of Retreat.*

prayers, either to reprimand them or for any other reason."[23] For no reason are you to stop the prayer and allow it to be interrupted. It is a fascinating point, because he is saying you should *show* them how to pray. Do not stop to tell them to quiet down and yell at them while you are speaking to God and having a pious moment. Show them what piety looks like. And he says if you need to correct them at all, defer it to another time and don't do it during prayer. Let this be a sacred space, not a time for your scolding.

That is simple, profound wisdom. He is saying you need to *show* them this more than you need to lecture them about it. Often, we find those two things at loggerheads. You're in the middle of praying and one kid decides to start telling you about their day and you're like, "no, seriously, stop." Even with young kids, we need to model *showing* them what it looks like to pray. And then later, if the situation requires it, you can have the conversation correcting them, and you should only reprimand them in particularly extreme situations. You have to exercise patience. You have to live virtuously to teach well. That is the first thing: become a saint.

2. *See Christ in Your Students*

In de La Salle's words, your students "must also be convinced that they are a letter that Jesus Christ dictates to you."[24] They are not going to see Christ the teacher in you until they know that you see Christ in them. If you approach them as if encountering Jesus Christ, they are more likely to see Christ in you.

Here I should give a little bit of biography about de La Salle. He was born into an upper-class French family, at a time when class was an extremely rigid world. His relatives were the founders of the Moet and Chandon winery, known for Champagne. That's the world in

---

23. Jean-Baptiste de La Salle, *The Conduct of the Christian Schools,* trans. F. de La Fontainerie and Richard Arnandez (Lasallian Publications, 1996).
24. Jean-Baptiste de La Salle, *Meditations for the Time of Retreat.*

which he was born. As a young man, he did not just say, "I'm going to give my life to the poor to teach them." Instead, he was an ordinary, comfortable, diocesan priest, who, through a whole series of events, was encouraged to help a new school dedicated to the poor. He said, "prior to this, I had never given them [the boys] a thought."[25] He agreed to help, thinking it would be a small task. He said, "I had thought that the care which I took of the schools and of the teachers would only be external, something which would not involve me any further than to provide for their subsistence and to see to it that they carried out their duties with piety and assiduity."[26] In other words, he thought he could just write a check—in modern terms. But then he found that no, they actually needed a place to stay: the teachers ended up staying in his house, and he was horrified by this. He said, "Indeed, if I had ever thought that the care I was taking of the schoolmasters out of pure charity would have made it my duty to live with them, I would have dropped the whole project. For since, naturally speaking, I considered the men I was obliged to employ in the schools at the beginning as inferior to my valet, the mere thought I would have to live with them would have been insupportable to me."[27] Despite his class, he is saying this in a spirit of self-reproach. He did not just have to grow to see Christ in the *students*, he had to grow to see Christ in the *teachers*, who were from a different social stratum than him. This is something he knows is easier said than done; seeing Christ in the teachers is something he had to be very intentional about.

3. *Keep in Mind the Day of Judgment*

This leads to the third point that helps to take the first two seriously. It's *memento mori*: remember your death, remember that you will be

---

25. Jean-Baptiste de La Salle, *Memoir on the Beginnings*, quoted in Jean-Baptiste Blain, *The Life of John Baptist de La Salle (Book One)* (Lasallian Publications, 2000), 79.
26. De La Salle, *Memoir on the Beginnings*, quoted in Blain, *Life*, 77.
27. De La Salle, *Memoir on the Beginnings*, quoted in Blain, *Life*, 80.

judged. Jesus foretells the separation of the sheep and the goats in the last day, saying that how we treat the least of these, even in the context of Catholic education, will determine our eternal salvation or damnation. De La Salle cautions that "there will be nothing on which God will examine them [educators] and by which God will judge them more severely" than on how well or how poorly they've instructed the students in their care—particularly in Catholic and catechetical formation.[28] That's a little alarming. There's not just a final exam in your religion class for your kids; there's a final exam for you as well—it just happens when you die. God can say, "How well or poorly did you look after those I put in your care?" That is a good incentive not to be a mercenary; if you know you'll be eternally judged, you should truly be an apostle.

Formation of Students

This leads to another question: if it is so important to form them, how do I do that? De La Salle gives us four ways.

1. Prepare Your Material to Present Carefully and Clearly

This is, admittedly, a time-consuming task. De La Salle wants his teachers to prepare not *only* the questions, but also what he calls sub-questions: the follow-up questions and the model answers. He says you should prepare them so that they are short, sensible, accurate, and suited to the intelligence of the average student, not just the best and the brightest.

De La Salle was revolutionary for using vernacular Bibles and teaching in the vernacular at the time when instruction—even outside of religious disciplines—was often given in Latin because it was a "gentlemanly" language. But he wanted education for everyone—and so he had education in French. He also knew that his own

28. De La Salle, *The Conduct of Christian Schools*, 109.

schoolmasters were not necessarily fluent in Latin. In a letter to one of the brothers, he gives instructions to buy a copy of the New Testament in French. He says, "please do not buy a Latin one or claim to know Latin," humorously telling his teacher that he can still go to heaven without pretending to read Latin.[29]

2. *Encourage the Students*

De La Salle encourages us not to be the strict and remote disciplinarian. Be there as a voice of encouragement. Show the mercy and love of God in the classroom. We will go into more detail when we look at Don Bosco.

3. *Reward Well*

There are two groups of students de La Salle tells you to reward. First, those who have been the best behaved and most attentive, and second, "sometimes even to the more ignorant who have made the greatest effort to learn well."[30] This is counterintuitive, because he doesn't say give rewards to the highest scoring students, but instead to those who are the best behaved, the most attentive, and those trying the hardest.

Modern educational theory talks about two types of praise. There's "innate ability praise," and there's "effort praise." Some fascinating studies have been done about this. In one, they had fourth graders take a test, and they praised group A one way and group B the other way. Afterwards, they gave them a choice between the type of follow-up test they could take. The group who had been praised for how smart they were wanted to take easy tests so they could keep acing them and looking smart. Group B, who had been praised for their effort, wanted to take harder tests so they could show how hard

29. Jean-Baptiste de La Salle, *The Conduct of the Christian Schools*, 109.
30. Jean-Baptiste de La Salle, *The Conduct of the Christian Schools*, 109.

they were willing to work. The way we give praise actually impacts the kind of performance and vision of the human person we impart. Jean-Baptiste de La Salle is on the side of "effort praise," not "innate ability praise." Our Lord is, too: in the parable of the talents, one person gets five, another gets two, and another gets one. He praises them for how well they utilize the gifts they've been given, not how many gifts they were born with. It's an important distinction. Make sure you are encouraging effort rather than simply innate giftedness.

4. Keep Your Heart Open

Good teachers, de La Salle says, "will employ various other similar means, which prudence and charity will enable them to find, to encourage students to learn the catechism more readily and to retain it more easily."[31] In other words, use prudence and charity to find all the things de La Salle did not think to talk about ahead of time. Do not just settle into your curriculum and switch on autopilot.

Don Bosco and the Two "Systems" of Education

St. John Bosco (1815–1888) is "the exemplary educator" (Pope Francis) and "the perennial force of the educational apostolate" (St. John Paul II). He describes two different systems of education: the first is what he calls the "repressive" system or approach and the second is the "preventive" system or approach.

The Repressive System

In brief, to understand the repressive system, picture, using popular imagination, nuns with rulers. That's the repressive system. You lay down the law, wait for someone to screw up, and then pounce and make an example of them. The idea is, if you do this enough, they will learn not to make mistakes anymore. The advantage of this sys-

31. Jean-Baptiste de La Salle, *The Conduct of the Christian Schools*, 109.

tem is that it's pretty easy. The disadvantage is something that Bosco points out, and it is something I had never thought of before. The perverse reality is that it actually works best the less time you spend with the children.

Let me give you a few examples you might be familiar with. There are three lines that are signs you are using the repressive system—whether you know it or not. The first is if you are constantly saying, "I'm not their friend, I'm their parent, I'm their teacher, I'm their—" whatever it is. If you're striving to prove you're not friends with them, that's a red flag.

That's not the only sign: it could also be if you use "go to the principal's office" as an ominous kind of threat—or at home: "Wait until your father gets home." Notice that it only works if the principal or the father is emotionally distant; if the kids are looking *forward* to dad coming home, it is no longer very threatening. The situation is the same if they love their principal. I was doing Catholic formation at a school in a small town in Kansas. It was an extremely small town, and the kids loved the principal. They would go to the principal's office when they had free periods—just spending time in the office. You can't say, "Go to the principal's office" as a threat there, because they love it.

The repressive system works by creating emotional distance. It works if there's a barrier, and without that, it is not effective. In fact, Bosco points out that it does not work well with kids *anyway*. He admits that it is easier and less demanding of the adults involved, and he also admits that in an adult institution, like an army, it might actually work fine. But he's dealing with young boys, and he says it does not work; all it does is breed resentment.

One of the reasons it fails is because of what, in modern terms, we would call an underdeveloped prefrontal cortex. When young people "act out," it's not because they have carefully deliberated and said, "I'm going to violate the rules. I accept the consequences, whatever they may be." By the time they give any thought to the consequences, they have already done the thing. A repressive system that acts as if they're *deliberating* on their bad choices is not an effective deterrent because they are not acting in a deliberative sort of way.

About the repressive system, Bosco says, it "can stop a disorder, but only with difficulty can it improve offenders."[32] You might scare someone into compliance, but you are not changing their heart.

The Preventive System

Instead, Bosco advocates for what he calls the "preventive system." It is built on three pillars: "reason," "religion," and what he calls "loving-kindness." The first two are self-explanatory: faith and religion should be at work in your educational system. "Loving-kindness" is taking seriously what St. Paul says about charity in 1 Corinthians 13, that charity is "patient," it is "kind," it "bears all things," it "helps all things," it "endures all things" (1 Cor 13:4, 7). Bosco's point is, if your model of education does not look and sound like that, it is not Christian education. If you do not love your kids with Christian charity, a charity that is patient, is helpful, and endures all things, you are not doing for them what you should. Even if you have Plato, Aristotle, and Aquinas, if you do not have charity, you are a clanging cymbal. Charity is far more important than the curriculum.

That is the preventive system at its heart, but how does it work? It begins the same way as the repressive system: make the rules known and supervise vigilantly. But you are not just waiting for errors to come up so you can pounce on them. Instead, you are foreseeing the problems that might come and you are getting "in the mix" with the kids. You are conversing with them and guiding them. In his words, you are to be people "who like loving fathers will converse

32. Giovanni Bosco, *The Preventive System in the Education if the Young*, in *Writing and Testimonies of Don Bosco on Education and Schooling*, ed. José Manuel Prellezo, *Salesian Sources 1. Don Bosco and His Work. Collected Works* (Kristu Jyoti Publications, 2017), 490.

with them, act as guides in every event, counsel them and lovingly correct them, which is as much as to say, will put the students into a situation where they cannot do wrong."[33] Help get them away from trouble before they get into it.

This entails a lot more work than the repressive system. When you are exhausted, the preventive does not sound good, because in the mysterious design of Providence, kids have a lot more energy than adults do. But, nevertheless, this is the more effective way.

One of the radical things about Bosco's system was that he did not want punishment. He forbids all forms of violent punishment: corporal punishment, pulling the kids by the ear, anything that inflicts physical pain on the boys. At the time, this was radical and revolutionary. He explained several ways of avoiding the need for any kind of punishment, because even outside of violent punishment, he tried "to do without even mild punishments."[34] And when children *are* to be punished, you deliberately take the child aside and either punish them or rebuke them discreetly and quietly. You do not make an example of them and humiliate them in front of the class.

So how do we avoid disciplinary situations in the first place? The preventive system gives several ways.

1. Give Plenty of Outlets for Play

This, if anything, is specifically focused on Bosco's young boys. "Let them burn off some energy," we might say. Bosco says they need to have "ample liberty to jump, run, [and] make a din as much as they please." But he also encouraged "gymnastics, music, declamation (of poems, etc.), theatricals, hikes." He says these "are very effective methods for getting discipline; they favor good living and good health."[35] If they

33. Bosco, *The Preventive System*, 490.

34. Bosco, *The Preventive System*, 490.

35. Bosco, *The Preventive System*, 492.

have an outlet to get some of that excess energy out, they will be better behaved: this is self-explanatory.

2. *Give Plenty of Spiritual Outlets*

Bosco said this at a time when many Catholic writers were discouraging the laity from going to Communion frequently. Nevertheless, he asserted that "frequent Confession, frequent Communion, [and] daily Mass are the pillars that ought to support an educational edifice."[36] But here he parts ways with St. Ignatius—who would have these be mandatory—and instead says, "never require the youngsters to go to the Holy Sacraments, but just encourage them, and offer them every opportunity to make good use of them."[37] It is a privilege, not an obligation. This is not a burden they will come to resent; it is an opportunity for them to grow in sacramental grace.

3. *Nip Problems in the Bud*

We have already seen that he is convinced that most problems are caused by what he describes as "youthful fickleness which in a moment can forget the rules of discipline and the punishments they threaten."[38] You could have the death penalty for acting out and you are still going to have kids who do it—because they're kids. But if you are there to lovingly guide them in the moment, you do not have to worry about a punishment afterwards. You can help them see their behavior *in the moment*, because that's what they're living in.

4. *No Particular (Exclusive) Friendships*

Here I want to give a word of caution. Both the Christian Brothers and the Salesians of Don Bosco have run into problems in subse-

36. Bosco, *The Preventive System*, 492.
37. Bosco, *The Preventive System*, 492.
38. Bosco, *The Preventive System*, 490.

quent centuries because they have not followed their founders' pedagogy closely enough. One of the tragic consequences of the perversion of Don Bosco's approach is the sexual abuse scandals in Salesian schools. It is a testament to the wisdom, prudence, and foresight of Jean-Baptiste de La Salle and Don Bosco that they both forbid what they call "exclusive friendships." You are to be friendly, you are to be warm—but you're not to be buddy-buddy with particular students.

Jean-Baptiste de La Salle tells the "administration" to watch new teachers and encourage them not to show preference for some students over others. There are many reasons for that being problematic. If teachers have clear favorites, that is a pedagogical problem, but Don Bosco seems to have had even a sense of the *moral* risk. He said to "try to avoid like the plague every kind of (morbid) affection or exclusive friendship with the pupils," and he warns that "the wrongdoing of just one person can compromise an educational Institute"—foresight we would have done well to listen to.[39] Remember that in being warm and loving, you are being charitable, but you are not their peer. There is an appropriate boundary. You are loving and warm to all of them, not just picking out personal favorites and trying to make exclusive friendships.

5. *The Key: Throw Yourself into the Mess*

In 1884, Don Bosco relayed a spiritual vision he had in a dream. If you know anything about Don Bosco, he constantly was having these incredible dreams, and in this one, he saw a former student of his, Valfré, and Valfré contrasts the early Salesian students with the later ones. He says that "closeness leads to love and love brings confidence. It is this that opens hearts and the young people express everything without fear to the teachers, to the assistants and to the

39. Bosco, *The Preventive System*, 491.

superiors."[40] If you create an atmosphere of fear, you are going to get a group of students who are really good at hiding things from you. If you create an atmosphere of love, you will break down those walls.

Remember, the repressive system works best with walls, walls of terror that separate principals from students and fathers from children. Bosco's approach is about tearing those walls down as much as possible, allowing the openness necessary for the students to open up. In Valfré's words, "[The students] become frank both in the confessional and out of it, and they will do everything they are asked by one whom they know loves them."[41] He goes on to stress what he calls "the best thing," which is "that the youngsters should not only be loved, but that they themselves should know that they are loved."[42] In this dream, Valfré says the earlier boys played, had fun, were open, went to the sacraments, and pursued their vocation, but the later ones were colder, more distant, and having side conversations. What's been missing? It's not that the educators loved them less; it's that the teachers weren't getting into the games. In times of physical activity, the boys were playing in one place, and the teachers are over talking to each other on the side.

That's the failure. They need to jump in. I think this is an incredible point; you should jump into the midst of what they're doing. Here's how Valfré puts it: "By being loved in the things they like, through taking part in their youthful interests, they are led to see love in those things which they find less attractive, such as discipline, study and self-denial, and so learn to do these things too with love." Get involved in their silly and stupid games. That is the radical approach for which John Bosco advocates.

---

40. John Bosco, *Letter from Rome*, 1884, in *The Gospel of Don Bosco*, trans. P. Laws (Salesian Society, 1884), https://www.sdb.org/en/GC28/Documents/Homilies_Addresses/Letter_from_Rome_1884__The_Gospel_of_Don_Bosco.

41. Bosco, *Letter from Rome*, 1884.

42. Bosco, *Letter from Rome*, 1884.

It is the antithesis of the surly standing on the side with the ruler, waiting to put the dunce cap on the student who is erring. It offers an approach of radical love and of a Christian kind of intimacy.

Being Ambassadors of Christ and of Hope

I want to close by drawing our attention to a way in which we misunderstand education. I say this frequently, particularly in the context of homeschooling. Paragraph 2223 of the Catechism is quoted often, that "Parents have the first responsibility for the education of their children."[43] If you think the paragraph stops there, you're forgiven, because that is all that often gets quoted. If we leave it at that, this seems to mean "Homeschooling vs. Parochial vs. Private vs. Classical vs. fill in the blank."

However, that is not the thrust of this paragraph. It is talking about the need for you as a parent, or an educator, by extension, to be "an ambassador of Christ," in the words of de La Salle, and to "jump into the mess" with your kids. The Catechism goes on to say that parents "bear witness to this responsibility first by creating a home where tenderness, forgiveness, respect, fidelity, and disinterested service are the rule." It's not primarily about Plato and Aristotle versus John Dewey; it's about Christ. You need to have an apprenticeship, you need to have self-denial, sound judgment, and self-mastery. If you cannot say no to yourself, you'll never teach those skills to kids. The Catechism makes the radical and shocking statement that "Parents have a grave responsibility to give good example to their children. By knowing how to acknowledge their own failings to their children, parents will be better able to guide and correct them."[44] Being an educator of children involves a radical vulnerability

43. *Catechism of the Catholic Church*, 2nd ed. (Vatican Publishing House, 2000), §2223.

44. CCC §2223.

where you admit your failings to them. This is the antithesis of the repressive method.

That is how we are to be true educators, imitating de La Salle and Bosco. Whether you serve in homeschooling, elementary schools, high schools, or colleges, you must be a witness of Christ, an ambassador of Christ, not just in what you teach, but in who you are, how you carry yourself, and, in a special way, how you show love to your students, so they both feel loved and know that you are someone deeply committed to loving and serving them.

15 John Henry Newman

Paul Shrimpton

St. John Henry Newman once commented, "Now from first to last, education, in this large sense of the word, has been my line."[1] This remark identifies one of the recurring strands of his life; it also says something about what he meant by "education." The qualification "in this large sense of the word" indicates that Newman had a very broad conception of "education" and that he resisted the tendency to reduce its meaning and narrow its scope. Then, as now, there was a common mistake of viewing education as the imparting of knowledge rather than the training of the mind, the acquisition of habits, and character formation. Nor did Newman consider education as something confined to its more formal moments or institutional settings: for him, education takes place not just in the classroom and lecture hall, but in semi-formal activities such as sport, music-making, journalism, drama and debating, and even in the informal moments of relaxation and amusement, such as meals and parties.

According to conventional wisdom, a successful educator is someone who excels at teaching children, adolescents, or adults, or else at inspiring or organizing others to do so. What is unusual about Newman the educator is that over a seventy-five-year period he dealt with every age group, instructing them both individually—in person and by letter—and collectively—in tutorial classes, lecture halls, the schoolroom, and the pulpit. The range of his contributions to the organization of teaching and learning is equally impressive.

1. Journal entry, January 21, 1863, *John Henry Newman: Autobiographical Writings*, ed. H. Tristram (Sheed & Ward, 1956), 259.

He reorganized and oversaw parish schools; played a leading part in the nineteenth-century revival of Oxford University; was the founding president of a Catholic university in Ireland; and co-founded the first Catholic public school in England. But it is for his written legacy that Newman is best known as an educator, principally *The Idea of a University* (1873), which is widely regarded as "the single most important treatise in the English language on the nature and meaning of higher education."[2]

It is not a simple task to summarize such a busy and productive life and to do justice to such a range of accomplishments; nor is it easy to illustrate how intellectual genius and down-to-earth practicality combined in one and the same person. By focusing on his literary output, and overlooking the man of action, it is all too easy to gain a distorted impression of Newman the educator. Not a few have been hypnotized by the brilliance of his prose and the force of his rhetoric, only to conclude that the *Idea of a University* is ultimately an unworkable ideal.[3] Their mistake comes from ignoring the broader picture: that Newman was using the lectures (that form the first half of the *Idea*) for a specific purpose—to rally support for a new university in a complex political situation. Other writings from Newman's time in Dublin fill out and complement the themes developed in the *Idea*;[4] and actual practice at the Catholic Univer-

2. Sheldon Rothblatt, "An Oxonian 'Idea' of a University: J. H. Newman and 'Well-being,'" *The History of the University of Oxford*, vol. vi, ed. M. G. Brock and M. C. Curthoys (Clarendon Press, 1997), 287.

3. For a good example of this, see Roy Jenkins, "Newman and the Idea of a University," *Newman: A Man for Our Time*, ed. D. Brown (SPCK, 1990), 155.

4. Newman composed twenty "university sketches" for the *Catholic University Gazette* in 1854, historical snapshots in which he tells the tale of the organic growth and development of the university. Though these essays are far less well known than the Dublin lectures, Newman scholars have argued that they are vital for a full understanding of Newman's educational views. They were published together as *Office and Work of Universities* (with an alternative subtitle, *University Teaching, Considered in a Series of Historical Sketches*) in 1856, then as the *Rise and Progress of*

sity illustrates how his erudite lectures could be translated into workable routines, even in adverse circumstances. Any reader of Newman's educational writings does well to remember that he was immersed in the *practice* of education all his life, and that his thinking derives from constant exposure to learning environments as well as from reflection on how best to shape education to match man's deepest needs.

A final introductory point. Newman is a highly original thinker who grappled with many problems that we face today. As Pope Benedict pointed out at his beatification, Newman had a profoundly modern sensibility;[5] he lived in *our* times, post-Enlightenment times when Christian institutions and indeed the very structure and ruling ideas of society were being challenged by non-believers. Newman was the first Christian thinker in the English-speaking world to confront these secularizing tendencies,[6] not just to defend Christian institutions but to explain why the alternatives were seriously deficient. That is why it is important to listen to him.

Schoolboy and Student, Fellow and Tutor

Newman's lifelong stress on the role of personal influence in education can be traced back to his formative days at his school in London, where he was befriended by the headmaster and deeply influenced by the sermons, conversations, and reading advice of the senior Classics master. Newman excelled in his studies and partic-

---

Universities in 1872, and finally they came to form the first and major part of *Historical Sketches*, vol. iii (1872), 1–251.

5. Pope Benedict spoke of the "modernity of his existence, . . . his great culture, . . . and his constant quest for the truth" as the three elements which give Newman "an exceptional greatness for our time" and make him "a figure of Doctor of the Church for us." *Benedict XVI and Blessed John Henry Newman: The State Visit 2010: The Official Record* (CTS, 2010), 45.

6. Christopher Dawson, "Newman and the Sword of the Spirit," in *The Sword of the Spirit* (Sands, 1944), 1.

ipated enthusiastically in school life, acting in Latin plays, taking part in debates, and editing several school magazines. Going up to Trinity College Oxford at the age of 16, Newman continued to pursue a wide range of interests, despite studying for two degrees at the same time, Classics and Mathematics. He entered himself for university prizes, studied manuals and tried experiments in chemistry, joined a music club (playing first violin in quartets by Haydn and Mozart), and co-founded a book society. With a close friend he composed and published a verse romance and started the second ever student-run magazine at Oxford. He also took on his first (voluntary) educational assignment: the tutoring—by post—of his five younger siblings.

After winning one of the coveted fellowships at Oriel College, the leading college in Oxford, Newman received Anglican orders and was appointed curate of a nearby working-class parish, where he threw himself into parish work. Two years later he was appointed a college tutor and, after weighing up his options and praying for light, decided to pursue his "care of souls" in education rather that in parish or even missionary work. He justified his decision on the grounds that the tutorship was a *spiritual* office, and one way of fulfilling his Anglican ordination vows. The point was that the extant statutes gave the tutor moral and religious as well as academic oversight over his tutees; though the system had fallen into neglect, Newman sought to revive it. Along with the other Oriel tutors he tightened up the admissions system, introduced written work into termly college exams—the University followed suit two years later—and made changes to the lecture system to favor serious students.[7] Together with two of the tutors, Newman offered the more deserving pupils as much time and attention as the best private coaches,

7. K. C. Turpin, "The Ascendancy of Oriel," in Brock and Curthoys, *History of the University of Oxford* vi, 188–89. The University introduced written exams in 1830, two years after Oriel.

thus eliminating the need and expense of the duplication; in doing so, the Oriel tutors provided "the germ of the modern tutorial system,"[8] which, along with the college system, forms part of the "crown jewels" of Oxford.

Newman considered that secular education should, if conducted properly, be "a pastoral cure"; he held that "a Tutor was not a mere academical Policeman, or Constable, but a moral and religious guardian of the youths committed to him." By finding extra time for the more worthy undergraduates, Newman "cultivated relations, not only of intimacy, but of friendship, and almost of equality . . . seeking their society in outdoor exercise, on evenings, and in Vacation."[9] The interest he showed was contagious, one tutee describing him as "an elder and affectionate brother."[10] However, the Provost of Oriel became uneasy with what he saw as the "proselytizing" influence of his tutors, and in 1830 refused to assign them any more students.

What seemed like a disaster, turned out to be a blessing. Released from his teaching duties, Newman had more time for his reading of the Church Fathers of the first millennium and became involved in a national battle to preserve the religious character of the university against secularizing reformers. He soon became the leader of the Oxford Movement, a revival of the Church of England that sought to revitalize the national church and shake it out of its complacency. The followers of the Movement sought to justify, preserve, and revive traditional Catholic doctrines and thereby to reverse many of the changes made at the Reformation; though they were determined to infuse a religious

---

8. M. G. Brock, "The Oxford of Peel and Gladstone, 1800–1833," in Brock and Curthoys, *History of the University of Oxford* vi, 61.

9. Memoir, June 13, 1874, *Autobiographical Writings*, 90–91.

10. Thomas Mozley, *Reminiscences: Chiefly of Oriel College and the Oxford Movement*, vol. i (Longmans, Green & Co., 1882), 181. Mozley became Newman's brother-in-law when he married his sister Harriet.

spirit into education, they were deeply intellectual and in no sense of a mind to turn Oxford into a simple seminary.[11] This applied above all to Newman, and it helps to explain why he was widely regarded as "the greatest force both morally and intellectually in the University."[12] Searching for the true successor of the primitive or early Church led Newman into the Catholic Church in October 1845.

Newman's Dublin Discourses

Newman was sent to Rome to prepare for ordination and returned as an Oratorian priest with a commission to establish the first Oratory of St. Philip Neri in England, at Birmingham. In 1851 he was invited by the Irish hierarchy to become the founding president of a Catholic university in Ireland. To prepare his Irish co-religionists for the new university, Newman composed his famous lectures on education which are endlessly cited, especially by those who take a "high" view of a university education and see Newman as the most inspiring advocate of a liberal education. Many today see in the *Idea* an attractive alternative to the shapeless, uninspiring outlook of so many contemporary universities, which increasingly function as performance-oriented, heavily bureaucratic organizations committed to a narrowly economic conception of "human excellence." Just as Newman battled against destructive trends within education in his own day, so others fight in our own times against the loss of vision of the modern university. In attempting to recover a sense of purpose, several modern critiques of the university use the *Idea* as a key

11. For an account of these battles, see P. B. Nockles, "Lost Causes and . . . Impossible Loyalties: The Oxford Movement and the University," in Brock and Curthoys, *History of the University of Oxford* vi, 195–267.
12. W. C. Lake, *Memorials of William Charles Lake, Dean of Durham* (E. Arnold, 1901), 41.

point of reference,[13] and some use Newman as the pivotal figure in their analysis.[14]

In the lectures, Newman argues that knowledge can be pursued either with a view to the cultivation of the intellect, or for more immediate practical purposes. The cultivation of the intellect, Newman explains, is a good in itself, and constitutes the primary aim of a university. While all academic disciplines tend to the cultivation of the intellect, some are particularly suited to fostering this aim, and a university should concentrate above all on these subjects. For Newman, the essence of a university is to teach people how to think; in doing so it will be indirectly preparing students for the professions and other occupations.

But I will stop there. The *Idea* is easy to acquire and can be read with one of its many commentaries. I wish to dwell on something different: about Newman the educational practitioner, the man of action. I speak not just as a historian of education but as someone who has been immersed in the practice of education for nearly forty years, teaching at an academic school in the center of Oxford, Catholic in origin but Anglican since the Reformation. I am interested in how theory and practice complement each other in the life and work of John Henry Newman.

---

13. Examples include: Duke Maskell and Ian Robinson, *The New Idea of a University* (Haven Books, 2001); Gordon Graham, *Universities: The Recovery of an Idea* (Imprint Academic, 2002); Stefan Collini, *What Are Universities for?* (Penguin, 2012); Mike Higton, *A Theology of Higher Education* (Oxford University Press, 2012); and Alasdair MacIntyre, *God, Philosophy, Universities* (Continuum, 2009).

14. Newman is the pivotal figure in Jaroslav Pelikan, *The Idea of the University: A Re-Examination* (Yale University Press, 1992); and in Sheldon Rothblatt, *The Modern University and Its Discontents: The Fate of Newman's Legacies in Britain and America* (Cambridge University Press, 1997).

Newman's Pastoral Idea of the University

Though the *Idea* is usually quoted for its purple passages on intellectual formation, it does contain a few glimpses of his pastoral vision. A champion of education outside the lecture hall, Newman recognizes that wherever students are gathered,

> they are sure to learn one from another, even if there be no one to teach them; the conversation of all is a series of lectures to each, and they gain for themselves new ideas and views, fresh matter of thought, and distinct principles for judging and acting, day by day.

Besides "mutual education," Newman was convinced that half the education a student receives derives from the self-perpetuating traditions of the place of learning. He attributes great importance in an educational institution to the *genius loci*, or "spirit of the place"; it constitutes "a sort of self-education . . . which imbues and forms, more or less, and one by one, every individual who is successively brought under its shadow." For Newman this "ethical atmosphere" amounts to "a real teaching."[15]

Surveying the university landscape in the 1850s and assessing the strengths and weaknesses of the various systems across Europe, Newman concludes that "a University seated and living in Colleges, would be a perfect institution, as possessing excellences of opposite kinds."[16]

---

15. *Idea of a University* (Longmans, 1873), 146–47.

16. *Historical Sketches* iii, 229. Newman was not the first to make this claim. The Scottish philosopher Sir William Hamilton had argued previously that "the statutory combination of the Professorial and Tutorial systems . . . is implied in the constitution of a perfect university." However, this statement was qualified by the assertion that "A tutorial system in subordination to a professorial we regard as affording *the condition of an absolutely perfect University*." Hamilton, "On the State of the English Universities, with more especial reference to Oxford," 1831, *Discussions on Philosophy and Literature, Education and University Reform* (Longmans, 1853), 417, 448.

This meant combining the professorial (i.e., lecture) system and the tutorial system. Newman was acutely aware of the deficiencies of a system relying entirely on the lecture and insisted on individual or small-group tuition as a counterbalance. In Newman's view, the college and university have complementary roles. He argues that the purpose of the college (or its equivalent) is to stretch the "strict idea" of a university—what is essential to its "being"—into "well-being" and fullness of life.[17] Taking "influence" and "system" as the two great principles governing the conduct of human affairs, Newman regards the university as the proper sphere of action for *influence*, the college for *discipline*. Certainly, the university needs the steadying hand of system. In his view, neither college nor university was complete without the other. In a Catholic university, the university would teach the faith, the college would help students *live* the faith.[18]

Newman knew from personal experience the perennial dangers and hardships that students are exposed to when living away from home, and the need for a second home, a hall of residence or "dorm" which could provide paternal oversight, discipline, and order. When setting up the Catholic University, he oversaw the provision of these collegiate houses for those not living at home. Each residence was to have its own private chapel and chaplain, resident tutors, and up to twenty students, presided over by a dean. Since the university was only partly residential, Newman grappled with the problem of how to extend collegiate living to those living at home or with relatives. He sought to attach the "externs" to the collegiate houses, stipulating their presence there for the working hours of the day, so that that

17. Rothblatt, "An Oxonian 'Idea' of a University," 293.

18. The complementarity is developed in several of his university sketches: "Discipline and Influence," "Influence: Athenian Schools," "Discipline: Macedonian and Roman Schools," "The Strengths and Weaknesses of Universities: Abelard," "Colleges the Corrective of Universities: Oxford," and "Abuses of the Colleges: Oxford." These can be found with a commentary in the critical edition *The Rise and Progress of Universities and Benedictine Essays*, ed. M. K. Tillman (Gracewing, 2001).

they might benefit from some aspects of collegiate living rather than simply attending lectures. He also wanted them to benefit from collegiate teaching, as he regarded the tutors—not the lecturers—as the engine of the university.

The tutors were to be two or three years older than their pupils, "half companions, half advisers . . . thrown together with them in their amusements and recreations . . . gaining their confidence from their almost parity of age."[19] As well as conferring academic benefits, tutors would be able to exert "those personal influences, which are of the highest importance in the formation and tone of character."[20] Newman explains that the tutor's work was,

> more of influence than of instruction. But at the same time influence is gained *through* the reputation of scholarship etc, and the very duty which comes on a Tutor is to do that which the pupil cannot do for himself, e.g. to explain difficulties in the works read in lecture, and to give aid in the higher classics, or to cram for examinations.[21]

No stranger to the student scene, Newman saw that tutors needed to anticipate in many of their tutees "little love of study and no habit of application, and, even in the case of the diligent, backwardness," and to make adjustments accordingly. The reason he laid such emphasis on the idea of a college tutor was that he saw in it,

> that union of intellectual and moral influence, the separation of which is the evil of the age. Men are accustomed to go to the

---

19. Report for the Year 1854–55, *My Campaign in Ireland, Part 1: Catholic University Reports and Other Papers*, ed. Paul Shrimpton (Gracewing, 2021), 41.
20. Report read to the Thurles Committee, 12 November 1851, *My Campaign*, 84–85.
21. Newman to T. W. Allies, November 6, 1857, *Letters and Diaries of John Henry Newman*, 32 vols, ed. C. S. Dessain et al. (T. Nelson, 1961–72; Clarendon Press, 1973–2008), vol. xviii, 164.

> Church for religious training, but to the world for the cultivation both of their hard reason and their susceptible imagination. A Catholic University will but half remedy this evil, if it aims only at professorial, not at private teaching. Where is the private teaching, there will be the real influence.[22]

In proposing guidelines for dealing with students "in that most dangerous and least docile time of life, when they are no longer boys, but not yet men," Newman laid down the guiding principle that "the young for the most part cannot be driven, but, on the other hand, are open to persuasion and to the influence of kindness and personal attachment." He saw university residence as "a period of training" linking boyhood and adulthood, designed "to introduce and to launch the young man into the world." This was an enormously important office, because "nothing is more perilous to the soul than the sudden transition from restraint to liberty." Consequently, it was both a duty and a privilege for the authorities to lead the young men,

> to the arms of a kind mother, an Alma Mater, who inspires affection while she whispers truth; who enlists imagination, taste, and ambition on the side of duty; who seeks to impress hearts with noble and heavenly maxims at the age when they are most susceptible, and to win and subdue them when they are most impetuous and self-willed.

This being the case, Newman thought university discipline should be characterized by "a certain tenderness, or even indulgence on the one hand, and an anxious, vigilant, importunate attention on the other."[23]

These words are not the polished phrases of a distant administrator, but of a university president who had to deal with disciplinary matters personally when he found himself without a vice-president. Besides, it should be emphasized that virtually every

---

22. "Scheme of Rules and Regulations," April 1856, *My Campaign*, 117, 120.
23. *My Campaign*, 114–17.

aspect of the Catholic University came into being through Newman's hands. Apart from overseeing academic affairs, the appointment of staff, the financial administration, the launching of new faculties and schools, devising statutes, writing rules and regulations, editing the weekly *Catholic University Gazette*, delivering lectures each term and preaching sermons, Newman gave priority to the pastoral needs of the students and his dealings with the academic staff. Despite all the managerial burdens he shouldered, he led the way by turning the president's residence into a collegiate house, taking on the duties of dean, chaplain, and tutor, alongside those of university president—and all this while continuing to act as Provost of the Birmingham Oratory, which meant crossing back and forth across the Irish Sea. While he could easily have distanced himself from the residences and the problems they threw up, Newman wished to deal with individuals rather than retreat into academic and administrative isolation. The vigilance he exerted over his charges—which can be seen in his correspondence—reflected his conviction that the university undertook a grave responsibility of oversight for those who entered its doors; it acted as a surrogate parent to the students, "an Alma Mater, knowing her children one by one, not a foundry, or a mint, or a treadmill."[24] Such was his estimation of the pastoral burden of establishing a university that he wondered if it were possible to make the university into a personal diocese, either with himself or the Archbishop of Dublin as its bishop.[25]

---

24. *Idea of a University*, 144–45.

25. Newman to Stanton, March 12, 1854, *Letters and Diaries* xxxii, 84. Although it is unclear how such a structure would have fitted into the canon law then in force (as the United Kingdom was regarded as mission territory, where the ordinary prescriptions of canon law did not fully apply), the 1983 *Code of Canon Law* makes provision for just such a "personal diocese" in canon 372, taking up the idea in the Second Vatican Council decree on the ministry and life of priests (*Presbyterorum Ordinis*, 10b); the idea of a "personal parish" specifically for pastoral care at universities is mentioned in canons 518 and 813.

Founding and Overseeing the Oratory School

Newman ran the Catholic University for four years. Just as he was making preparations to leave, he became involved with a different, though equally significant, educational foundation, this time in Birmingham, England. The Oratory School opened in May 1859 and over three decades—a third of Newman's long life—it was nurtured and formed by him. The school was a remarkable foundation in a number of ways, both within the Catholic system and on the national stage. The impulse for the foundation came from converts from the Oxford Movement who were unimpressed with the boarding education available to Catholics. What they wanted for their sons was an English public school—a Catholic one, but a real one. (I should emphasize that by "public school" in the English sense, as opposed to the North American sense of government-funded, I mean one of the elite fee-paying boarding schools like Eton, characterized by the wide liberty given to the boys and by the delegation of power through the prefect system, in complete contrast to the strictly run Catholic seminary schools of the time.) Besides creating the first Catholic public school, Newman was a pioneer within the Catholic system in forming the first *lay* boarding school in England; and on the national scene in the way he collaborated with parents in setting up the school. The Oratory School was a joint project with his convert friends: they raised the funds, they gathered the pupils, and in collaboration with him they appointed the teaching staff. Only the headmaster was a priest; the other teachers were laymen. Women were appointed as "dames" to oversee the younger boys outside school hours, responsible for their comfort and well-being and overseeing their acquisition of good habits and virtues. All of the staff were converts. These and other characteristics caused alarm among the English bishops and the school became the target of calumny, gossip, and general opposition for more than a decade.

What guided Newman's actions were several principles he had enunciated as an Anglican clergyman. In a sermon, the twenty-four-year-old deacon had urged that,

> When then it is said, the Church is the mother of saints, the instructress and guardian of all Christians, by Church is meant not the clergy only, but all who are concerned in the work of education with the clergy at their head—the clergy are not the only ministers—in one sense all parents and [school]masters are ministers of the household of God—and it is of these all together as forming one body, though with many distinct parts and offices that the text speaks.[26]

In another sermon he maintained that "the clergy are not to be considered as controlling education in their own right, but as representatives and instruments of the general body of Christians for whose good God has appointed them to the office of superintendence."[27] This is a remarkable insight for the time, when, in both Church of England as well as Catholic circles, education was generally considered the preserve of clerics, not just in its organization and control but in its implementation. But Newman went further. He urged that "parents should consider that from the earliest infancy of their children they are their natural guardians and instructors; that sending to school is merely an accidental circumstance, and but a part of education." And he went on to question the action of parents who think "they have done all that can be required of good and wise parents," when they have sent their children to school at the proper age.[28] This abiding conception of the educational task—that parents were the

26. "The Communion of Saints," preached December 11, 1825, *John Henry Newman: Sermons, 1824–1843*, vol. iv, ed. F. J. McGrath (Oxford University Press, 2011), 36.
27. "On General Education as Connected with the Church and Religion," preached on August 19, 1827, *Newman: Sermons, 1824–1843* v, 426–27.
28. "On Some Popular Mistakes as to the Object of Education," preached on January 8, 1826, *Newman: Sermons, 1824–1843* v, 369, 372.

primary educators of their children—was to guide him in all his dealings with the laity.

The Catholic schools were run either by the secular clergy or by the religious orders, and the education given was generally suited to those aspiring to the priesthood or religious life. What Newman's convert friends wanted was a purely *lay* school; they were concerned that the high moral standards at the colleges—which they recognized as important—were "apparently purchased at the expense of many valuable qualities of manliness, energy and readiness to face the world."[29] Their desire for a greater stress on the natural or human virtues met with Newman's full approval, and the statement in his draft manifesto that the Oratory School was intended "for youths whose duties are to lie in the world"[30] incorporated this concern and signaled an important shift in emphasis. This stress on "facing the world" can also be seen in the advice Newman gave to boys who thought they might have a priestly vocation, for he invariably urged them to be patient and avoid narrowing their options too early. His attitude shows that he regarded preparation for "the world" on same footing as preparation for the priesthood, as one calling for serious and appropriate training.[31] Whether leaving for further study or for the world of work, the Oratory School boys were prepared for life and trained to hold their own in a Protestant society.

The fact that the Oratory School was the result of parental initiative reflected Newman's conviction that a school's main task is not to replace but to assist parents in their duty to care for and educate their

---

29. John Simeon to Newman, April 30, 1857, *Letters and Diaries* xviii, 17.

30. Draft school manifesto (November 1858), Birmingham Oratory Archive. This statement supplies a *positive* definition of the laity, whereas it was usual to define the laity in a negative way before the Second Vatican Council. This is just one example of Newman's formulation of a "theology of the laity" *avant la lettre.*

31. The number of leavers going into the priesthood—twenty-three in Newman's own time—vindicated, besides, his belief that a curriculum consisting mainly of secular studies would not deter those truly called to Holy Orders.

children. Though not explicitly stated in school documents, this conviction showed itself in practice by shaping the school's attitude to the boys and their parents. When the leading promoter (and co-founder) told Newman that the school had been a great success for his sons, Newman replied that it could only take a "due portion of credit . . . seeing the patterns and guidance they have at home"[32]—in other words, a school had to build on the education received in the family.

To make his idea of partnership with parents come about, Newman sent them reports about their sons twice a year—a very unusual practice at the time. Besides writing reports, he personally undertook the task of dealing with parental demands, a task which kept him busy in term and out. His highly-educated convert friends badgered him about the curriculum, teaching methods, textbooks—even the boys' pronunciation of Latin. When parents visited the Oratory or passed through Birmingham, and particularly when they came to drop off or collect their sons at the beginning and end of term, Newman used the opportunity to speak to them at length. This degree of parental contact was unknown elsewhere, either at the Protestant public schools or at the Catholic colleges.

In December 1861, halfway through the third academic year, the school suffered a crisis that almost destroyed it. By then Newman had lost control to the Oratorian headmaster, Fr. Nicholas Darnell, and his teaching staff who, in their haste to match the best Protestant schools, swept aside the human and spiritual counterweights that Newman had put in place. After a disagreement with Newman about the role of the dames, they resigned en masse in the expectation that Newman would have no choice but to accept their demands. But Newman stood firm. His closest friends and cofounders rallied round him, and together they rescued the situation. Newman's right-hand man at the Oratory stepped in as headmaster, and over the next ten years he and Newman re-formed the school between them. This

32. Newman to Edward Bellasis, September 4, 1865, *Letters and Diaries* xxii, 42.

episode is a salutary warning about adopting or copying non-Catholic educational models. We can learn from Newman about the need to ensure that the Catholic element permeates and underpins the whole enterprise, rather than being merely bolted on.

At this juncture, I must point out that, although the name of Newman is evoked approvingly nowadays, he was at the time *persona non grata* in ecclesiastical circles; Church leaders in England and Rome struggled to make sense of his writings and suspected them of heresy; he was treated as someone who had not become fully Catholic and suspected of introducing Protestant ideas and practices into the Church. Newman spent much of his life as a Catholic in obscurity on the edge of the institutional Church, and though the cloud of suspicion was lifted in 1879, when the new pope Leo XIII created him a cardinal, his isolation from mainstream Catholic life and practice meant that his foundations had little influence on others.

One effect of the Darnell mutiny was that Newman's involvement in the school was much closer thereafter. He was now able to mold the school along lines which reflected his lifelong insistence on the pastoral role of the educator. A theme Newman repeatedly emphasized to parents was the need for patience with their sons. He calmed their eagerness for quick gains, insisting that the phases of growing up be respected and that irritating but passing habits be overlooked: boys could not be forced like plants. Another expression of his pastoral concern was the introduction of "characters" after the end-of-term exams. At these individual interviews, the headmaster would read out an account of the boy's academic progress and behavior, then Newman would give a few words of encouragement or approval—or, if necessary, a telling-off. (He established a similar practice of individual interviews at the Catholic University.[33]) Newman attached great

33. Newman copied and adapted this custom from Oriel. These brief, end-of-term interviews, which are known as "collections," still take place in Oxford colleges today and are usually chaired by the head of the college.

importance to hearing the termly "characters," refusing to depute the task to others. Nor was he satisfied with a mere acquaintance with the boys; he aimed to know them well and even to make their personal friendship—and this in spite of the age gap, for he was fifty-eight when the school began. A clue to his ability to relate to boys comes from Oscar Browning, an educational reformer at Eton and King's College Cambridge. Browning stayed overnight at the Oratory in 1866 and was struck by "Newman's marvelous copiousness of language and abundant fluency, also with his use of harmless worldly slang, that he might not appear priggish or monkish."[34]

Unlike the students in Dublin, who held Newman in great awe, the youngsters at the Oratory School generally regarded him with affection. One pupil described "Jack" or "old Jack"—as Newman was rather irreverently known—as a gentle, understanding, and approachable figure for whom nothing was too trivial. Thus, when the editorial of the *Weekly Wasp* (a school magazine run entirely by boys) criticized the lack of school facilities, Newman saw to it that their grievances were met. In chapel the younger boys found him softly spoken and given to long quotations from Scripture, but they were held spellbound by his readings from the Bible, and at times his silvery voice moved them to tears.

As one might expect, Newman attempted to impart a truly liberal education. The school, he felt, ought to make good scholars out of the boys, and he declared to one parent, "it is not simply our aim, but our passion to do so."[35] From the advice he gave, it is clear he considered there was no substitute for hard work. Yet he was *equally* insistent, particularly with parents, that boys needed down-time. He also ensured that sporting enthusiasms were respected. For example, he would rearrange the afternoon timetable in summer, to allow for

34. Oscar Browning, *Memories of Sixty Years at Eton, Cambridge and Elsewhere* (John Lane, 1910), 269.

35. Newman to John Simeon, August 22, 1864, *Letters and Diaries* xxi, 205.

longer cricket matches. Organized games coexisted with a large variety of other outdoor pursuits; and extra-curricular activities such as music, journalism, debating, and acting thrived. Newman himself oversaw the production of the annual Latin play, and he sometimes joined boys in their music recitals, playing second violin.

Newman's arrangements for religious training and instruction are interesting, bearing in mind that the Oratory School was a lay school. Before breakfast, the boys said their prayers and attended Mass; at the end of morning lessons, they prayed the Angelus; after tea there was optional Rosary; and at night there were joint prayers followed by a reading from a spiritual classic. In Holy Week all the boys made a three-day retreat. The school had two spiritual directors, whose main duty was to hear the boys' confessions. The boys learnt their catechism thoroughly and tested each other in pairs every week, in the presence of Newman or the headmaster; and there were instructions and sermons for the whole school. Newman himself gave the catechetical lectures to the older boys, and he carefully marked and annotated the essays they were required to write afterwards. And, in order to stimulate their piety, he involved the boys in devotions throughout the liturgical year, such as Stations of the Cross in Lent, devotions to Mary in May, and an annual Corpus Christi procession.

Both in Dublin and Birmingham, Newman's schemes for religious education are impressively ambitious. But what was distinctive about them? As regards teachers, Newman relied heavily on laymen. This reliance on the laity for religious instruction can be traced back to a sermon in 1827, when he maintains that, "It seems indeed to be a fundamental mistake in a system of education, when the instructors of youth in general knowledge are not also their religious instructors."[36] As regards *what* should be taught and how much, Newman observes that, "as the mind is enlarged and cultivated generally, it is

---

36. "On General Education as Connected with the Church and Religion," preached on August 19, 1827, *Newman: Sermons, 1824–1843* v, 203.

capable, or rather is desirous and has need, of fuller religious information." Therefore, there was an obligation to feed these minds with divine truth as they gained in appetite and capacity for knowledge. Newman divided the syllabus for religious teaching into sacred history, Biblical literature, and Christian theology. Church history should cover the early spread of Christianity, the Christological controversies and heresies, the Fathers and their works, the religious orders, the Crusades, what the Church has done for learning and science, and its "great eras and its course to this day." Scriptural knowledge would take in the canon of Scripture, its history, the Jewish canon, and the Protestant Bible, as well as "the languages of Scripture, the contents of its separate books, their authors, and their versions."[37]

As for theology proper, Newman preferred to confine coverage to a broad knowledge of doctrinal subjects as contained in catechisms of the Church and in those religious topics which the *lay* faithful write about—"and are thought praiseworthy" in so doing. By this he means "Christian knowledge in what may be called its secular aspect, as it is practically useful in the intercourse of life and in general conversation." The University needed to realize that their students were going out into a world not of professed Catholics, but of "inveterate, often bitter, commonly contemptuous Protestants," who had been versed in the doctrines and arguments of Protestantism. (Substitute "militant atheist" or "scornful secularist" for "contemptuous Protestant" and it sounds remarkably up to date.) Students needed to know how to answer questions commonly asked of Catholics: whether the celibacy of the clergy was a matter of faith or Church discipline; whether, and in what sense, Catholics consider Protestants to be heretics; whether Catholics deny the reality of natural virtue, and what worth they assign to it.[38]

37. Newman to the dean of the arts faculty, June 1856, *My Campaign*, 161–62.

38. Newman to the dean of the arts faculty, June 1856, *My Campaign*, 162–64. When quoting from this letter (which had become 'General religious knowledge'

In his first sermon at the Catholic University, Newman argued against compartmentalized thinking and living, what could be called "religious schizophrenia," and pressed instead for a "connected view"[39] and coherent lifestyle:

> I wish the same spots and the same individuals to be at once oracles of philosophy and shrines of devotion. It will not satisfy me, what satisfies so many, to have two independent systems, intellectual and religious, going at once side by side, by a sort of division of labor, and only accidentally brought together. It will not satisfy me, if religion is here, and science there, and young men converse with science all day, and lodge with religion in the evening. It is not touching the evil . . . if young men eat and drink and sleep in one place, and think in another: I want the same roof to contain both the intellectual and moral discipline. . . . I want the intellectual layman to be religious, and the devout ecclesiastic to be intellectual.[40]

Newman's plea is a manifestation of his integrated approach to theology, which he combined with spirituality and morality, as against an over-intellectualized theology.[41] Though greatly admired

---

in the *Idea*) in a letter to *The Rambler* (July 1859) about "Lay students in theology," Newman adds a quotation from the theologian Victor du Buck that he received from Richard Simpson: "My opinion is, which many others share, that at present laymen of a certain rank have more need of knowing *dogmatic* theology, ecclesiastical history, and canon law, than priests. The reason is, that in lay company the deepest and most difficult problems in those subjects are discussed. This is seldom done when any priest is present. Moreover, in your country, laymen have better opportunities than priests to correct a thousand false notions of Protestants." *Letters and Diaries* xix, 546–47.

39. *Idea of a University*, 134.

40. "Intellect, the Instrument of Religious Training," preached in June 1856, *Sermons Preached on Various Occasions* (1857; Longmans, 1908), 13.

41. See Keith Beaumont, "The Connection Between Theology, Spirituality and Morality," *A Guide to John Henry Newman: His Life and Thought*, ed. Juan Vélez (The Catholic University of America Press, 2022), 393–413.

for his illuminating explanations of *fides quae* (the truths of the Faith), his most original contribution consists above all in his exploration of *fides qua* (the faith by which we believe), in describing faith as a personal encounter, involving more than reason. Unhappy with practices where knowledge of faith overrides the relational dimension, where faith is reduced to an intellectual acceptance of abstract propositions, with a tendency to impoverish the vital and nourishing dimension of faith that precedes and sustains all knowledge, Newman provides a timely counterbalance. He broadens the understanding of the experience of faith by illustrating the personal aspects, from the strong but indefinable impression of dogma in the soul, to the awakening of intelligence and imagination, to the mobilization of the powers of will and affections that shape a unique encounter, relationship, and communion with God.[42]

Newman's educational activity and prayer life were also impressively integrated. At the age of sixteen he composed several long prayers which show that he was acutely conscious of his debt of gratitude to those who had nurtured him.[43] In one he thanked and praised God for his "kind and affectionate parents" and for "having given me abilities, and provided me with excellent Tutors who have encouraged them."[44] In another, he praises God for having given him "friends and benefactors who have taken care of my education and instruction."[45] In a sermon to the Oriel undergraduates, he spoke of

42. This paragraph draws heavily on Cardinal Marc Ouellet's paper on "The Significance of St. John Henry Newman for Catholic Theology" at a symposium in the Vatican the day before Newman's canonization. See *Lead Kindly Light: Essays for Ian Ker*, ed. P. Shrimpton (Gracewing, 2022), 55–58.

43. In a prayer dated 1828 he writes, "I praise Thee for . . . the blessing of a good education; for the gifts of mind Thou hast entrusted to me, and the means of their cultivation." V. F. Blehl, *Pilgrim Journey: John Henry Newman 1801–1845* (Burns & Oates, 2001), 425.

44. Prayer dated April 1817 (two months before taking up residence at Trinity College Oxford), Blehl, 405, 407.

45. Prayer dated November 1817, Blehl, 410.

his responsibility for their welfare: "Account of us as thinking much and deeply of your eternal interests, as watching over your souls as those who must give account."[46] What did this translate into as regards his prayer? As a private tutor and a college tutor, Newman prayed for his students once a week. Within a few years he began composing huge prayer lists, which included the names not just of friends but of colleagues and tutees. His prayer list for 1839 contains over two hundred names and is heavily thumbed.[47] As well as praying for individuals, his prayer intentions were grouped in categories which were allotted to different days of the week, with names listed under headings.[48]

Concluding Thoughts

One feature which is common to all Newman's ventures is that in Christianizing education he was careful not to distort it. Rather than over-stress the Christian dimension, he respected the inner autonomy of education; he understood the connaturality of education and religion, recognizing that "Knowledge is one thing, virtue is another."[49] His harmonious synthesis of the secular and religious in education—"to fit men for this world while it trained them for another"[50]—explains why he is so admired. Nevertheless, Newman recognized the ultimate supremacy of holiness over intellectual attainment. This is evident from his words of consolation to the mother of a boy who died just five years after leaving the Oratory School: "what was your mission . . . except to bring him to heaven?

46. Sermon preached on April 15, 1827, *Newman: Sermons, 1824–1843*, vol. i, ed. P. Murray (Clarendon Press, 1991), 341.
47. Ten pages of prayer lists can be found at the Birmingham Oratory in the file A.10.4.
48. Wilfrid Ward, *The Life of John Henry, Cardinal Newman* (Longmans, Green & Co., 1912), vol. ii, 361–64.
49. *Idea of a University*, 120.
50. *Historical Sketches* iii, 152.

That was your very work, not to gain him a long life and a happy one, but to educate him for his God."[51]

Whether at school or university, Newman's influence derived from dealing with the young separately or in small groups, rather than from addressing them *en masse*. Indeed, his mind instinctively recoiled from an identical treatment of individuals, for he felt that "An academical system without the personal influence of teachers upon pupils, is an arctic winter."[52] While his educational insights and reforms were both wide-ranging and ahead of his time, his contribution to education cannot be measured simply in terms of new arrangements, but by a variety of indirect means. His sensitivity to both the aspirations and the foibles of adolescents and young men enabled him to pitch his demands with success. Newman's original contribution to the ever-present dilemma of an authentic Christian presence in the world is reflected in the down-to-earth training for the challenges and duties of life. The principles that guided him owe much to his understanding of the condition of lay Christians and their need for an education suited to their state. Newman anticipated some of the key teachings of the Second Vatican Council on the laity and their role in the Church. A key idea informing his idea of the Church is that of "*pastorum et fidelium conspiratio*,"[53] literally, a breathing together of clergy and laity, which suggests a dynamic relationship—or organic cooperation—between the faithful and their pastors.

If Newman's university and school appear strangely familiar to modern eyes, it is because his insights into the truth about the human condition enabled him to anticipate a future age. And yet, when we see in contemporary education the effects of educational

51. Newman to Mrs. F. R. Ward, September 22, 1866, *Letters and Diaries* xxii, 292.
52. *Historical Sketches* iii, 74.
53. *On Consulting the Faithful in Matters of Doctrine* (1859), ed. J. Coulson (Rowman & Littlefield, 1961), 104.

policies pursued in the name of "efficiency" and "good management," and the intellectual poverty resulting from production-line learning, we would do well to heed Newman's shrewd observation that while the world is "content with setting right the surface of things," the Church aims "at regenerating the very depths of the heart."[54]

In the last three pontificates, this Christian humanist was declared first Venerable, then Blessed, and latterly Saint John Henry. My hope is that in the next he will be declared a Doctor of the Church. I wonder if Doctor of Education would be a suitable epithet?

54. *Idea of a University*, 203.

16 Magisterial Teaching

Arthur Hippler

At the opening of Aldous Huxley's *Brave New World*, infants are being conditioned to dislike, even fear, books. In Ray Bradbury's *Fahrenheit 451*, "firemen" have the task of burning books. But in Walter Miller's *A Canticle for Leibowitz*, a group of monks in post-apocalyptic America toil to preserve the remnants of learning for a future time. The genesis of *A Canticle for Leibowitz* was the author's experience of being part of the bombing crew that destroyed the sixth-century Benedictine monastery of Monte Cassino during the Second World War. Miller converted from atheism to the Catholic faith shortly after the war, and published *A Canticle for Leibowitz* in 1959.

Is it an accident that Miller imagined a future in which learning was preserved by the Church? Is it an accident that the secular dystopias of Huxley and Bradbury destroy books and replace learning with propaganda and entertainment? In his apostolic constitution on higher education, John Paul II memorably declared that the modern university was born from "the heart of the Church."[1] While the first institutions of higher learning were founded in the pre-Christian world—Plato's Academy and Aristotle's Lyceum—the university as an institution which embraced the range of human knowledge is truly an offspring of the Church. Indeed, the very idea that education should be available as widely as possible was unknown in the pagan world, and long remained so even through the time of the early Church.

1. John Paul II, *Ex Corde Ecclesia* [Apostolic Constitution], The Holy See, August 15, 1990, §1, https://www.vatican.va/content/john-paul-ii/en/apost_constitutions/documents/hf_jp-ii_apc_15081990_ex-corde-ecclesiae.html.

Pius XI, summing up this change, wrote that "in the far-off middle ages when there were so many (some have even said too many) monasteries, convents, churches, collegiate churches, cathedral chapters, etc., there was attached to each a home of study, of teaching, of Christian education. To these we must add all the universities, spread over every country and always by the initiative and under the protection of the Holy See and the Church."[2] This is a history that remains largely unknown to many educators, even Catholic ones.

After the Protestant Reformation, schools changed confessions but remained religious; e.g., English schools and universities became Anglican, schools in northern Germany and Scandinavia became Lutheran. But the disunity in belief eroded the confidence that educated people had in theology as a body of knowledge. By the mid-nineteenth century, schools began to secularize. For example, the University of London was founded in 1826 as the first secular university in England. (Both Cambridge and Oxford required students to be members of the Church of England to earn degrees). Newman's defense of theology as a body of knowledge in *The Idea of a University* was a response to this development. Newman rightly understood that making theology "optional" within education changed its purpose in an essential way.

When the popes first began to address this secularization, they focused more on its moral and spiritual effects than on the intellectual ones. Their language is very strong. Leo XIII in his commemoration of St. Peter Canisius declares: "To organize teaching in such a way as to remove it from all contact with religion is therefore to corrupt the very seeds of beauty and honor in the soul. It is to prepare, not defenders of the nation, but a plague and a scourge for the

2. Pius XI, *Divini Illius Magistri* [Encyclical Letter], The Holy See, December 31, 1929), §25, https://www.vatican.va/content/pius-xi/en/encyclicals/documents/hf_p-xi_enc_31121929_divini-illius-magistri.html.

human race."[3] Reflecting on the causes of the First World War, Pius XI pointed out that "the school forcibly deprived of the right to teach anything about God or His law could not but fail in its efforts to really educate, that is, to lead children to the practice of virtue, for the school lacked the fundamental principles which underlie the possession of a knowledge of God and the means necessary to strengthen the will in its efforts toward good and in its avoidance of sin."[4] These statements sound harsh to us, but that is only because we often do not connect the problems with modern education to its secular principles.

While retaining their worries about the failure of modern schools to provide moral and religious formation, later pontiffs began to address the intellectual and academic effects of this secularization. By the reign of Pius XII, science and technology clearly started to take precedence in schools over theology, philosophy, and the humanities. Pius XII warned students of the risk that, if they immersed themselves too strongly in the "material elements" of science, they might "lose" or diminish the sense of Christian culture, so rich in values of truth and wisdom and saturated with what ancient times had of eternal worth."[5]

Elsewhere, Pius XII made clear that this is not only for the sake of supporting moral and theological virtues, but also for intellectual ones: "This literature [of the humanities] is very suitable for training young people's minds in order that they may think and speak in a

---

3. Leo XII, *Militantis Ecclesiae* [Encyclical Letter], The Holy See, August 1, 1897, §17, https://www.vatican.va/content/leo-xiii/en/encyclicals/documents/hf_l-xiii_enc_01081897_militantis-ecclesiae.html.

4. Pius XI, *Ubi arcano Dei consilio* [Encyclical Letter], The Holy See, December 23, 1922, §30, https://www.vatican.va/content/pius-xi/en/encyclicals/documents/hf_p-xi_enc_19221223_ubi-arcano-dei-consilio.html.

5. Pius XII, "Allocution to Roman Students," The Holy See, January 30, 1949, n. 494, in Catholic Church, E. M. Bornet, and Abbaye Saint-Pierre de Solesmes, *Education*. trans. Aldo Rebeschini (Pauline Editions, 1960).

logical, clear manner, avoiding a useless excess of words and also for procuring other excellent qualities proper to the well-formed man."[6] Against the growing trend of seeing Latin and history as useless and impractical, Pius XII insisted that these disciplines are essential to education, because, among others, they provide "certain ideas and certain information, certain habits of thought, a certain mental discipline, the sense of measure and intellectual harmony—in short, a wide and deep training in fundamentals."[7]

Just before the convocation of the Second Vatican Ecumenical Council, Pope John XXIII lamented the shift in education toward an exclusive focus on the sciences, renovating learning so that students could be "immersed as much as possible in computations, in calculations, in the making of machines." John XXIII worried that, deprived of studies that "nourish and adorn the mind," young people would exist "like manufactured machines, cold, hard and devoid of love."[8]

This background helps us understand that the remarks on education and culture made by the Second Vatican Council flow from concerns articulated before the council, and reflect a coherent rejection of the modern secular approach to education. "The Constitution of the Church in the Modern World" (*Gaudium et spes*) reaffirms the intellectual goals of education, saying, "When man gives himself to the various disciplines of philosophy, history and of mathematical and natural science, and when he cultivates the arts, he can do very much to elevate the human family to a more sublime understanding of truth, goodness, and beauty, and to the formation of considered

6. Pius XII, "Allocution to Professors of Discalced Carmelites," The Holy See, September 23, 1951, n. 575, https://www.vatican.va/content/pius-xii/la/speeches/1951/documents/hf_p-xii_spe_19510923_carmelitani-scalzi.html.
7. Pius XII, "Allocution to Students of State Secondary Schools in Rome," The Holy See, March 24, 1957, n. 805, in Bornet et al., *Education*.
8. John XXIII, "Allocution to First International Congress of Ciceronian Studies," The Holy See, April 7, 1959, n. 852, in Bornet et al., *Education*.

opinions which have universal value."[9] By contrast, the Council Fathers warned of those who "unduly transgressing the limits of the positive sciences, contend that everything can be explained by this kind of scientific reasoning alone, or by contrast, they altogether disallow that there is any absolute truth."[10]

For many years, these general observations and criticisms did not have an articulated application to Catholic schools. The conciliar document on education *Gravissimum educationis* addressed education on a very general level but offered no subject-specific direction. In 1988, the Congregation for Catholic Education, in response to discussions that took place during the Second Extraordinary General Assembly of the Synod of Bishops (1985), published *The Religious Dimension of Education in a Catholic School.* This document does provide subject-specific direction in light of the council and continues to be extraordinarily helpful to us today.

In *The Religious Dimension of Education in a Catholic School,* (hereafter *RDECS*) guidelines are given for four academic areas: 1) religion, 2) science, 3) history, and 4) other "humanities" (philosophy, art, literature).

Religion

In *The Idea of a University,* Newman insisted that theology was a genuine body of knowledge, just as other bodies of knowledge in the university. Even when students are given the starting points of theology as part of catechesis, the course cannot be "easy." The tendency for decades, however, has been to make the religion class the least academically challenging part of the core curriculum. Although some schools avoided the fads and fashions in religion that gutted

9. Second Vatican Council, *Gaudium et spes* [Pastoral Constitution], The Holy See, December 7, 1965, §57, https://www.vatican.va/archive/hist_councils/ii_vatican_council/documents/vat-ii_const_19651207_gaudium-et-spes_en.html.
10. *Gaudium et spes,* §19.

the academic content for "projects" and "activities," religion texts were considerably lighter on content than science or history. In the typical Catholic school, religion courses are often the easiest, certainly never the hardest class in the school. While everyone recognizes that a school's Catholic identity requires religious education, there tends to be little reflection on the comparative difficulty of religious instruction to that of other subjects.

In response to this trend, *RDECS* insists that a Catholic secondary school "give special attention to the 'challenges' that human culture poses for faith. Students will be helped to attain that synthesis of faith and culture which is necessary for faith to be mature."[11] There is no way to address those challenges in an "easy" course. It should therefore be expected that the religion class should be required to have "the same systematic demands and the same rigor" as other classes, as is stated in the *General Directory for Catechesis* (1997), promulgated by the Congregation for the Clergy. Elaborating on this point from *RDECS*, the *General Directory* explained that religious instruction "must present the Christian message and the Christian event with the same seriousness and the same depth with which other disciplines present their knowledge. It should not be an accessory alongside of these disciplines, but rather it should engage in a necessary inter-disciplinary dialogue."[12]

Many Catholic educators struggle with this directive, because they think of the content of a religion class as fundamentally a matter of "faith," while the secular courses offer "knowledge." But

---

11. Congregation for Catholic Education, "The Religious Dimension of Education in a Catholic School," The Holy See, April 7, 1988, §52, https://www.vatican.va/roman_curia/congregations/ccatheduc/documents/rc_con_ccatheduc_doc_19880407_catholic-school_en.html, accessed November 12, 2024.

12. Congregation for Clergy, "General Directory for Catechesis," The Holy See, April 17, 1998, 73§5, https://www.vatican.va/roman_curia/congregations/cclergy/documents/rc_con_ccatheduc_doc_17041998_directory-for-catechesis_en.html, accessed November 12, 2024.

Christian teaching can be an invitation to non-believers, just as the explanations and the responses that are made to non-believers can be illuminating for believers. Hence, "religious instruction cannot help but strengthen the faith of a believing student, just as catechesis cannot help but increase one's knowledge of the Christian message."[13] The rational account one gives for faith provides an important "common ground" for believers and unbelievers alike.

The distinction that *RDECS* makes between "catechesis" and "religious instruction" helps us to see that, in both cases, students are being offered a form of "knowledge" based on cooperation between faith and reason. What a believing Christian learns in a religion class is "catechesis": "catechesis presupposes that the hearer is receiving the Christian message as a salvific reality."[14] What a non-believer receives is "religious instruction," that is, an explanation of what the Churches teaches, which does not presuppose acceptance of Church authority. Both believers and non-believers are therefore poorly served by intellectually undemanding religion courses that seem to offer little to the challenges posed by the larger culture.

Science

The engagement with the larger culture cannot be the sole responsibility of the religion faculty. It is the responsibility of all teachers in a Catholic school, albeit in various ways and to varying degrees. It is perhaps no surprise that *RDECS* first raises the distinctive task of science instructors, who are exhorted to "help their students to understand that positive science, and the technology allied to it, is a part of the universe created by God."[15]

What is the task of the science teacher in the Catholic school? The teacher is often called upon to correct the limitations of science

13. "General Directory for Catechesis," §69.
14. "Religious Dimension of Education," §68.
15. "Religious Dimension of Education," §54.

textbooks. To take one example, the *Catechism of the Catholic Church* teaches that "the eternal God gave a beginning to all that exists outside of himself; he alone is Creator. . . . The totality of what exists . . . depends on the One who gives it being."[16] From this, the *Catechism* denounces *materialism* as an error, which "reject[s] any transcendent origin for the world, but see[s] it as merely the interplay of matter that has always existed."[17] And yet, secular science textbooks used in Catholic schools are overwhelmingly materialistic in their account. They virtually equate "materialism" with "the scientific method." Students learn in their religion class that God is the creator of all, but then this basic principle is systematically denied in their science textbooks. Who better to correct this error than the teacher in the room?

The same problem occurs in science texts' treatment of the human person. *RDECS* condemns the "fragmented and insufficient curriculum" in which science does not "complement" religious knowledge of the human person, but contradicts it. Here as before, the teacher must provide what is missing for the students: "Teachers dealing with areas such as anthropology, biology, psychology, sociology and philosophy all have the opportunity to present a complete picture of the human person, including the religious dimension. Students should be helped to see the human person as a living creature having both a physical and a spiritual nature."[18] Students learn in a religion class that man is defined by the possession of a rational soul, that is, with a mind and will that allows him to know, to choose, and to love: "the human individual possesses the dignity of a person, who is not just something, but someone."[19] Students then learn from their science texts that either man has no soul, or that the religious notion of "soul" explains nothing in one's lived human experience.

16. CCC no. 290.
17. CCC no. 285.
18. "Religious Dimension of Education," §55.
19. CCC no. 357.

Indeed, the science textbooks treat human origins entirely in terms of the body, implicitly or sometimes explicitly denying a soul. Man, in their account, is merely a more advanced primate who has evolved by chance. He is not a being who is "made to the image and likeness of God" as part of a providential plan. The *Catechism* teaches that "The unity of soul and body is so profound that one has to consider the soul to be the 'form' of the body: i.e., it is because of its spiritual soul that the body made of matter becomes a living, human body; spirit and matter, in man, are not two natures united, but rather their union forms a single nature."[20] As a logical consequence, "The Church teaches that every spiritual soul is created immediately by God—it is not 'produced' by the parents—and also that it is immortal." This is why the Church allows for an evolutionary development in the human body, but cannot allow a similar development in the human soul: "for the Catholic faith obliges us to hold that souls are immediately created by God."[21]

The general challenge for science instruction within our Catholic schools can be summed up by the observation in *Gaudium et spes* that "today's progress in science and technology can foster a certain exclusive emphasis on observable data, and an agnosticism about everything else. For the methods of investigation which these sciences use can be wrongly considered as the supreme rule of seeking the whole truth."[22] The Council Fathers declared that, while the sciences have their own principles that must be respected, the autonomy of the sciences does not mean that they are divorced from the creator: "Without the Creator, the creature becomes unintelligible."[23] "Unintelligible" should not be taken as a form of hyperbole.

---

20. CCC no. 365.

21. Pius XII, *Humani generis* [Encyclical Letter], The Holy See, August 12, 1950, §36, https://www.vatican.va/content/pius-xii/en/encyclicals/documents/hf_p-xii_enc_12081950_humani-generis.html.

22. *Gaudium et spes*, §57.

23. *Gaudium et spes*, §36.

While having their own principles, natural things are not, ultimately, sufficient to explain themselves. We do not live in a universe governed "by chance, blind fate, anonymous necessity" but rather "by a transcendent, intelligent and good Being called 'God.'"[24]

Philosophy and the "Humanities"

In a time that has seen the development of the STEM school, the "humanities" courses can appear only necessary to give the rudiments of literacy and a veneer of culture. But *RDECS* insists that the "increased attention given to science and technology must not lead to a neglect of the humanities: philosophy, history, literature and art."[25] For, in addition to the theoretical and practical knowledge that comes from the sciences, students still need an "understanding of all that is implied in the concept of 'person': intelligence and will, freedom and feelings, the capacity to be an active and creative agent; a being endowed with both rights and duties, capable of interpersonal relationships, called to a specific mission in the world."[26] This is not exclusively or even primarily the task of religion courses. History, literature, and philosophy each in their own way help students understand human nature and the distinctive dignity of human life. This is one among many reasons why they are called "humanities."

The Second Vatican Council was alarmed at the way that "the denial of God or of religion" had influenced "literature, the arts, the interpretation of the humanities and of history and civil laws themselves."[27] While the scientific method yields impressive discoveries, its focus on experimentation and controlled experimentation prevents it from answering questions "about the place and role of man in the universe, about the meaning of its individual and collective

24. CCC no. 284.
25. "Religious Dimension of Education," §60.
26. "Religious Dimension of Education," §55.
27. *Gaudium et spes*, §7.

strivings, and about the ultimate destiny of reality and of humanity."[28] The Council exhorted modern men to seek "wisdom": "The intellectual nature of the human person is perfected by wisdom and needs to be, for wisdom gently attracts the mind of man to a quest and a love for what is true and good. Steeped in wisdom, Man passes through visible realities to those which are unseen."[29] "Wisdom" is not just another way of saying "theology"; as the Council notes elsewhere,[30] the patrimony of philosophic and literary reflection offers wisdom too.

The Catholic school therefore should not emphasize science to the detriment of other forms of "knowing." Indeed, it should help students see that one can reason about human nature and the universe in which he lives in other ways than the scientific method. The most evident way of seeing this is moral knowledge: "In the depths of his conscience, man detects a law which he does not impose upon himself, but which holds him to obedience. Always summoning him to love good and avoid evil, the voice of conscience when necessary speaks to his heart: do this, shun that."[31] The moral law (or "natural law") is known to all. As the *Catechism* observes, it is evident in its basic moral commands, which one finds in all cultures throughout history.[32]

Sadly, for many of our Catholic young people, all they know is moral disagreement and confusion. No one teaches them what cultures share in common, but rather how they are all different and "diverse." As *RDECS* notes, "Concepts such as truth, beauty and goodness have become so vague today that young people do not know where to turn to find help" (9). Having no formation in the moral law, they turn instead to purely worldly goals. They often live "in a one dimensional universe in which the only criterion is practical

28. *Gaudium et spes*, §3.

29. *Gaudium et spes*, §15.

30. *Gaudium et spes*, §44, 56

31. *Gaudium et spes*, §16.

32. CCC nos. 1956–1958. See *Gaudium et spes*, 10§3.

utility and the only value is economic and technological progress."[33] While STEM programs can contribute to our physical well-being, courses in the humanities should contribute to understanding the nature and purpose of human life. The exploration of cultures and the study of literature, for example, can bring to light the essential goods of human life: bravery, self-control, justice, judgment, love, friendship, and ultimately wisdom.

History

The Catholic identity of a school does not demand that it teach history with an emphasis on "Church history" or a revisionist "pro-Catholic" version of secular history. Certainly, these might be more desirable than history texts that either ignore or denigrate the Church, which is too often the case. But *RDECS* does not call for merely "partisan" history that ignores or minimizes the moral failings of Catholics and other Christians.

Rather, it exhorts teachers in a Catholic school to consider history as a means for understanding human nature, and its supernatural possibilities. History is not, as many modern history texts would have it, a narrative in which cultures proceed from religion and other forms of "superstition" to science and enlightenment. Rather, it is a "drama of human grandeur and human misery," a "monumental struggle" between "the good and the evil that is within each individual."[34] Just the previous year before *RDECS* was published, John Paul II had emphasized this principle in his encyclical "On Social Concern": "history is not simply a fixed progression towards what is better, but rather an event of freedom, and even a struggle between freedoms that are in mutual conflict, that is, according to the well-known expression of St. Augustine, a conflict between two loves: the love of God to the point of disregarding self, and the love of self to the point

33. "Religious Dimension of Education," §10.
34. "Religious Dimension of Education," §58.

of disregarding God."[35] Human history is rightly defined by man's supernatural goal, which he can freely accept or freely reject.

This struggle is not resolved as the result of advances in technological innovation, economic development, and government reform. As *Gaudium et spes* made clear, "man is split within himself. As a result, all of human life, whether individual or collective, shows itself to be a dramatic struggle between good and evil, between light and darkness. Indeed, man finds that by himself he is incapable of battling the assaults of evil successfully, so that everyone feels as though he is bound by chains."[36] One does not have to accept a doctrine of "original sin" to see that the human problem is not solved by "technical" inventions, by having the "right" people in power, or better schools and public institutions, for "the disturbances which so frequently occur in the social order" ultimately "flow from man's pride and selfishness."[37]

At the same time, the study of history in a Catholic school should allow for hope: "When they are ready to appreciate it, students can be invited to reflect on the fact that this human struggle takes place within the divine history of universal salvation. At this moment, the religious dimension of history begins to shine forth in all its luminous grandeur."[38] The "progressive" view of history always looks toward some heaven on earth, and is profoundly disappointed when it never comes. Indeed, many political projects in the name of "progress" have made life a hell on earth.

For its part, Christian belief and practice have given rise to real social progress, despite the sinful behavior of Christians. As part of

---

35. John Paul II, *Sollicitudo rei socialis* [Encyclical Letter], The Holy See, December 3, 1987, §27, https://www.vatican.va/content/john-paul-ii/en/encyclicals/documents/hf_jp-ii_enc_30121987_sollicitudo-rei-socialis.html. See John Paul II, *Familiaris consortio*, [Apostolic Exhortation], The Holy See, §6, https://www.vatican.va/content/john-paul-ii/en/apost_exhortations/documents/hf_jp-ii_exh_19811122_familiaris-consortio.html.

36. *Gaudium et spes*, §13.

37. *Gaudium et spes*, 25§3.

38. "Religious Dimension of Education," §59.

his argument that Catholic social teaching is not merely a "theory" but a "basis for action," John Paul II cites the historical record: "Through the power of the Gospel, down the centuries monks tilled the land, men and women Religious founded hospitals and shelters for the poor, Confraternities as well as individual men and women of all states of life devoted themselves to the needy and to those on the margins of society, convinced as they were that Christ's words 'as you did it to one of the least of these my brethren, you did it to me' (Mt 25:40) were not intended to remain a pious wish, but were meant to become a concrete life commitment."[39] Indeed, learning about these forms of genuine progress can provide a reasonable optimism for students and "help to offset the disgust that comes from learning about the darker side of human history."[40] Catholic school students would be ill served if they graduated ignorant of the concrete ways in which the Gospel has improved human life.

Literature

Literature, like history, has its way of helping students understand their own humanity. The Second Vatican Council noted the contribution of "literature and the arts" for the way in which they "strive to make known the proper nature of man, his problems and his experiences in trying to know and perfect both himself and the world."[41] Our lived experience can often be very narrow, but the broader range of experience that literature makes possible can help the student to see true human potential for good and evil, nobility and wickedness.

There is always the temptation to give students stories primarily from their own culture and time, but the stories from faraway places

---

39. John Paul II, *Centesimus annus* [Encyclical Letter], The Holy See, May 1, 1991, §57, https://www.vatican.va/content/john-paul-ii/en/encyclicals/documents/hf_jp-ii_enc_01051991_centesimus-annus.html.

40. "Religious Dimension of Education," §59.

41. *Gaudium et spes*, 62§2.

and the remote past provide greater opportunities for seeing our shared humanity. In great literature such as Homer's *Odyssey*, Shakespeare's *Romeo and Juliet*, and Dostoevsky's *Crime and Punishment*, one sees "the struggles of societies, of families, and of individuals" that "spring from the depths of the human heart, revealing its lights and its shadows, its hope and its despair."[42]

The trend of secular education has been to turn literature into "consciousness raising" and other forms of political indoctrination. To be sure, politics is a part of literature. But students are denied the true greatness of literature if it is seen primarily through a "pacifist" or "feminist" or "multiculturalist" lens. More important than political categories are the character "types" that manifest the moral and spiritual dimension of human life. To see the world through the eyes of an Antigone or MacBeth broadens the students' ability to see the consequences of moral choices. C. S. Lewis put it best when he wrote "in reading great literature I become a thousand men and yet remain myself. Like the night sky in the Greek poem, I see with a myriad eyes, but it is still I who see. Here, as in worship, in love, in moral action, and in knowing, I transcend myself; and am never more myself than when I do."[43]

Within a Catholic school, literature courses should also allow students to encounter stories with a spiritual dimension. Even pre-Christian and non-Christian literature can do this to some extent, for "in every human culture, art and literature have been closely linked to religious beliefs."[44] But of course there is no substitute for exposure to classics informed by a Christian perspective: "The artistic and literary patrimony of Christianity is vast and gives visible testimony to a faith that has been handed down through centuries."[45]

---

42. "Religious Dimension of Education," §61.
43. C. S. Lewis, *An Experiment in Criticism* (Cambridge University Press, 1961), 141.
44. "Religious Dimension of Education," §60.
45. "Religious Dimension of Education," §60.

Conclusion

The story of education in the modern world is the story of the revolution against the classical learning that developed in the ancient world and was "Christianized" by the Church during the Dark and Middle Ages. While the Church would not oppose "science" and "knowledge," the secular spirit of the modern world has sought to emphasize science in a way that marginalizes theology and the philosophical disciplines that supported and defended it. The magisterium of the twentieth century did not defend that educational tradition merely because it was "old." Rather, the popes and the council fathers of Vatican II insisted that this was an intellectual patrimony which no new scientific formation could replace.

The students today who enter the Catholic school are asking the same questions that men have always asked, because they are "human questions": "What is man? What is the meaning, the aim of our life? What is moral good, what is sin? Whence suffering and what purpose does it serve? Which is the road to true happiness? What are death, judgment, and retribution after death? What, finally, is that ultimate inexpressible mystery which encompasses our existence: whence do we come, and where are we going?"[46] These are questions that the scientific disciplines cannot answer, because they are not scientific questions. Indeed, they are questions "of another order, which goes beyond the proper domain of the natural sciences."[47] The Catholic school has the obligation, especially in the face of the aggressive secularism of the modern world, to form minds and hearts in the truths that not only dispose us to a complete human life on earth but also the supernatural life of beatitude to which God calls all men.

46. Second Vatican Council, *Nostra aetate* [Declaration], The Holy See, October 28, 1965, 1§3, https://www.vatican.va/archive/hist_councils/ii_vatican_council/documents/vat-ii_decl_19651028_nostra-aetate_en.html.

47. CCC no. 284.

Bibliography

Church Documents

All texts available at Vatican.va unless otherwise noted.

Benedict XVI and Blessed John Henry Newman: The State Visit 2010: The Official Record. CTS, 2010.

Benedict XVI. "Address to Commemorate the 40th Anniversary of the Dogmatic Constitution of Divine Revelation, *Dei Verbum*." September 16, 2005.

Benedict XVI. "Boethius and Cassiodorus." General Audience, Pope Paul VI Audience Hall. March 12, 2008.

Benedict XVI. *Deus caritas est.* Encyclical Letter. December 25, 2005.

Benedict XVI. "Faith, Reason and the University: Memories and Reflections." University of Regensburg. September 12, 2006.

Benedict XVI. "Meeting with Representatives from the World of Culture." Address. September 12, 2008.

Benedict XVI. Opening Discourse for the Synod of Bishops on Scripture. October 6, 2008.

Benedict XVI. "Presentation to the Diocese of Rome of the 'Letter on the Urgent Task of Education.'" February 23, 2008.

Catechism of the Catholic Church. 2nd ed. Vatican Publishing House, 2000.

Catechism of the Council of Trent. Translated by John McHugh, OP, and Charles Callan, OP. Marian Publications, 1976.

Congregation for Catholic Education. "The Religious Dimension of Education in a Catholic School." April 7, 1988.

Congregation for Clergy. "General Directory for Catechesis." April 17, 1998.

John Paul II. *Centesimus annus*. Encyclical Letter. May 1, 1991.

John Paul II. *Ex corde Ecclesia*. Apostolic Constitution. August 15, 1990.

John Paul II. *Fides et ratio*. Encyclical Letter. September 14, 1998.

John Paul II. "General Address on May 23, 2001."

John Paul II, "Message to Brother John Johnston." May 2, 2000.

John Paul II. *Sollicitudo rei socialis*. Encyclical Letter. December 3, 1987.

John XXIII. "Allocution to First International Congress of Ciceronian Studies." April 7, 1959.

Leo XII. *Militantis Ecclesiae*. Encyclical Letter. August 1, 1897.

Paul VI. *Lumen Ecclesiae*. Apostolic Letter. November 20, 1974.

Pius XI. *Divini Illius Magistri*. Encyclical Letter on Christian Education. December 31, 1929.

Pius XI. *Ubi arcano Dei consilio*. Encyclical Letter. December 23, 1922.

Pius XII. "Allocution to Professors of Discalced Carmelites." September 23, 1951.

Pius XII. "Allocution to Roman Students." January 30, 1949. In Catholic Church, E. M. Bornet, and Abbaye Saint-Pierre de Solesmes. *Education*. Translated by Aldo Rebeschini. Pauline Editions, 1960.

Pius XII. "Allocution to Students of State Secondary Schools in Rome." March 24, 1957 in Catholic Church, Bornet, and de Solesmes, *Education*, 1960.

Pius XII. *Humani generis*. Encyclical Letter. August 12, 1950.

Second Vatican Council. *Dei Verbum*. Dogmatic Constitution on Divine Revelation. November 18, 1965.

Second Vatican Council. *Gaudium et spes*. Pastoral Constitution. December 7, 1965.

Second Vatican Council. *Nostra aetate*. Declaration. October 28, 1965.

Primary and Secondary Sources

Adler, Eric. *The Battle of the Classics: How a Nineteenth-Century Debate Can Save the Humanities Today*. Oxford University Press, 2020.

Alcuin of York. *Versus de Sanctis Eboracensis Ecclesiae*, vv.1535–1557. James Catalogue of Western Manuscripts. Trinity College. https://mss-cat.trin.cam.ac.uk/Manuscript/O.2.26.

Alcuin of York and Charlemagne. *The Rhetoric of Alcuin & Charlemagne*. Translated by Wilbur Samuel Howell. Russell & Russell, 1965.

Aristotle. *The Eudemian Ethics*. Translated by Anthony Kenny. Oxford University Press, 2011.

Aristotle. *The Politics*. Translated by T. A. Sinclair and Trevor J. Saunders. Penguin Books, 1992.

Arnold, Matthew. *Culture & Anarchy and Friendship's Garland*. The MacMillian Company, 1924.

Augustine, Saint. *City of God*. Translated by Marcus Dods. Modern Library, 2000.

Augustine, Saint. *Confessions*. Translated with an introduction and notes by Henry Chadwick. Oxford University Press, 1991.

Augustine. *Confessions*. Translated by Frank J. Sheed. Hackett, 2006.

Augustine, *Confessions*. Translated by Thomas Williams. Hackett Publications, 2019.

Augustine. *On Christian Doctrine*. In *Nicene and Post-Nicene Fathers, First Series*, vol. 2. Translated by James Shaw, edited by

Philip Schaff. Buffalo, NY: Christian Literature Publishing Co., 1887.

Augustine. *On Christian Doctrine.* Translated by J. F. Shaw. Dover Publications, 2009.

Augustine. *St. Augustine's Cassiciacum Dialogues,* 4 vol. *Against the Academics, On the Happy Life, On Order,* and *Soliloquies.* Translated by Michael Foley. Yale University Press, 2019, 2020.

Babcock, William S. "The Human and the Angelic Fall: Will and Moral Agency in Augustine's *City of God.*" In *Augustine: From Rhetor to Theologian,* edited by Joanne McWilliam. Wilfrid Laurier University Press, 1992.

Balthasar, Hans Urs von. *The Glory of the Lord,* vol 1. Ignatius Press, 1998.

Barker, Ernest. *The Political Thought of Plato and Aristotle.* Dover, 1959.

Barnish, S. J. B. "The Work of Cassiodorus After His Conversion." *Latomus* 48, no. 1 (1989): 157–87.

Barrett, Helen M. *Boethius: Some Aspects of His Times and Work.* Russell and Russell, 1965.

Basil of Caesaria. "Address to Young Men on the Right Use of Greek Learning." In *Essays on the Study and Use of Poetry by Plutarch and Basil the Great,* edited by Frederick Morgan Padelford. Henry Holt and Company, 1902.

Beaumont, Keith. "The Connection Between Theology, Spirituality and Morality." *A Guide to John Henry Newman: His Life and Thought,* edited by Juan Vélez. The Catholic University of America Press, 2022.

Bedouelle, Guy, OP. *St. Dominic: The Grace of the Word.* Ignatius Press, 1987.

Benedict, Saint. *RB 1980: The Rule of Benedict in English.* Edited by Timothy Fry. Liturgical Press, 1981.

Benson, Joshua C. "Bonaventure's *De reductione artium ad theologiam* and Its Early Reception as an Inaugural Sermon." *American Catholic Philosophical Quarterly* 85, no. 1 (2011): 7–24.

Benson, Joshua C. "Identifying the Literary Genre of the *De reductione artium ad theologiam*: Bonaventure's Inaugural Lecture at Paris." *Franciscan Studies* 67 (2009): 149–78.

Bergsma, John, and Brant Pitre. *A Catholic Introduction to the Bible.* Vol. 1: *The Old Testament.* Ignatius Press, 2018.

Berquist, Marcus R. "Learning and Discipleship." *The Aquinas Review* 6, no. 1 (1999): 1–51.

Bertucio, Brett. "The Monastic Turn: 400–1150." In *A History of Western Philosophy of Education in the Middle Ages and Renaissance*, edited by Kevin H. Gary. Bloomsbury Academic, 2021.

Bertucio, Brett. "*Paideia* as *Metanoia*: Transformative Insights from the Monastic Tradition." *Philosophy of Education* 71 (2015): 509–17.

Blain, Jean-Baptiste. *The Life of John Baptist de La Salle. Book One.* Lasallian Publications, 2000.

Blair, Peter Hunter. *The World of Bede.* Cambridge University Press, 1990.

Blehl, V. F. *Pilgrim Journey: John Henry Newman 1801–1845.* Burns & Oates, 2001.

Boethius. *The Consolation of Philosophy.* Translated and edited by Richard Green. Macmillan Publishing Company, 1962.

Boethius. *The Consolation of Philosophy.* Translated by V. E. Watts. Penguin Books, 1969.

Boethius. *The Consolation of Philosophy.* Translated with an introduction and notes by P. G. Walsh. Oxford University Press, 1999.

Boethius. *The Consolation of Philosophy.* Translated and edited by Scott Goins and Barbara Wyman. Ignatius Critical Editions. Ignatius Press, 2011.

Bonaventure. *De Reductione Artium et Theologian.* Translated by Sister Emma T. Healey. In *Works of Saint Bonaventure I.* Saint Bonaventure University, 1955.

Bonaventure. *On the Reduction of the Arts to Theology,* The Works of Saint Bonaventure, vol. 1. Translated with an introduction by Zachary Hayes, OFM. The Franciscan Institute, 1996.

Bonelli, Raphael, R. E. Dew, H. G. Koenig, D. H. Rosmarin, and Sasan Vasegh. "Religious and Spiritual Factors in Depression: Review and Integration of the Research." *Depression and Research Treatment* (2012). https://www.hindawi.com/journals/drt/2012/962860/.

Bosco, John. *Letter from Rome,* 1884. In *The Gospel of Don Bosco.* Translated by P. Laws. Salesian Society, 1884. https://www.sdb.org/en/GC28/Documents/Homilies_Addresses/Letter_from_Rome_1884__The_Gospel_of_Don_Bosco.

Bosco, Giovanni. *The Preventive System in the Education of the Young.* In *Writing and Testimonies of Don Bosco on Education and Schooling,* edited by José Manuel Prellezo, *Salesian Sources 1. Don Bosco and His Work. Collected Works.* Kristu Jyoti Publications, 2017.

Browning, Oscar. *Memories of Sixty Years at Eton, Cambridge and Elsewhere.* John Lane, 1910.

Brown, G. F. *Alcuin of York.* E. S. Gorham, 1908.

Bultmann, Rudolf. *New Testament and Mythology and Other Basic Writings.* Fortress Press, 1984.

Caldecott, Stratford. *Beauty in the World: Rethinking the Foundations of Education.* Angelico Press, 2012.

Carruthers, Mary. *The Book of Memory: A Study of Memory in Medieval Culture*, 2nd ed. Cambridge University Press, 2008.

Cassiodorus. *Explanation of the Psalms* [*Expositio Psalmorum*]. Edited by W. J. Burghardt, T. C. Lawler, and P. G. Walsh. Paulist Press, 1990.

Cassiodorus. *Variae*. Edited by S. J. B. Barnish. Liverpool University Press, 1992.

Cassiodorus. *Institutes of Divine and Secular Learning and On the Soul*. Translated by James W. Halporn. Liverpool University Press, 2004.

Chadwick, Henry. *The Consolations of Music, Logic, Theology, and Philosophy*. Clarendon Press, 1981.

Cicero. *Brutus—Orator*. Translated by G. I. Hendrickson and H. M. Hubbell. Loeb Classic Library 342. Harvard University Press, 1962.

Clark, Kevin, and Ravi Scott Jain. *The Liberal Arts Tradition: A Philosophy of Christian Classical Education*, 3rd ed. Classical Academic Press, 2021.

Colby, Charles W. *Selections from the Sources of English History*. New York: Longmans, Green & Co., 1899.

Collini, Stefan. *What Are Universities for?* Penguin, 2012.

Coolman, Boyd Taylor. "*Pulchrum esse*: The Beauty of Scripture, the Beauty of the Soul, and the Art of Exegesis in Hugh of St. Victor." *Traditio* 58 (2003): 175–200.

Coolman, Boyd Taylor. *The Theology of Hugh of St. Victor: An Interpretation*. Cambridge University Press, 2010.

Coulter, Dale M. *Per visibilia ad invisibilia: Theological Method in Richard of St. Victor*. Bibliotheca Victorina XIX. Brepols, 2006.

Courcelle, Pierre. *Connais-toi toi-même; de Socrate à saint Bernard [Know Thyself: From Socrates to St. Bernard]*. Études Augustiniennes, 1974–75.

Crabbe, Anna. "Literary Design in the *De consolatione philosophiae*." In *Boethius: His Life, Thought and Influence*, edited by Margaret T. Gibson. Basil Blackwell, 1981.

Crenshaw, James. *Education in Ancient Israel: Across the Deadening Silence*. Doubleday, 1998.

Dawson, Christopher. "The Study of Christian Culture." *Thought: Fordham University Quarterly* 35, no. 4 (1960): 485–93. www.catholicculture.org/culture/library/view.cfm?id=650.

Dawson, Christopher. *The Sword of the Spirit*. Sands, 1944.

Dawson, Christopher. *Understanding Europe*. The Catholic University of America Press, 2009.

De Ghellinck, Joseph. "La table des matières de la première edition des oeuvres de Hugues de Saint-Victor." *Recherches de sciences religieuses* I (1910): 270–89, 385–96.

De Koninck, Charles. *The Hollow Universe*. University of Notre Dame Press, 1960.

de La Salle, Jean-Baptiste. *Meditations for the Time of Retreat*. Translated by Richard Arnandez. Lasallian Publications, 1994.

de La Salle, Jean-Baptiste. *The Conduct of the Christian Schools*. Translated by F. de La Fontainerie and Richard Arnandez. Lasallian Publications, 1996.

Dervic, Kanita, M. A. Oquendo, M. F. Grunebaum, Steve Ellis, A. K. Burke, and J. J. Mann. "Religious Affiliation and Suicide Attempts." *The American Journal of Psychiatry* 161, no. 12 (December 2004): 2303–8. https://ajp.psychiatryonline.org/doi/full/10.1176/appi.ajp.161.12.2303.

Dewey, John. *The School and Society*. Southern Illinois University Press, 1980.

Drane, Augusta Theodosia. *Christian Schools and Scholars*. G. E. Stechert and Co., 1910.

Dulles, Avery Cardinal. *The Catholicity of the Church*. Clarendon Press, 1987.

Einhard. *The Life of Charlemagne*. Translated by David Ganz. Penguin Books, 2008.

Einhard. *The Life of Charlemagne*. Translated by Lewis Thorpe. Penguin Books, 1969.

Einhard. *Vita Karoli* [Life of Charlemagne]. In *Charlemagne's Courtier: The Complete Einhard*. Translated by Paul Edward Dutton. Broadview Press, 1998.

Eliot, T. S. *The Rock: A Pageant Play*. Harcourt, Brace and Co. 1934.

Farrell, Allan. *The Jesuit Ratio Studiorum of 1599*. Conference of Major Superiors of Jesuits, 1970.

Farrell, Allan P., SJ. *The Jesuit Code of Liberal Education: Development and Scope of the Ratio Studiorum*. Bruce, 1938. https://archive.org/details/jesuitcodeofliteoooounse.

Farey, Caroline, Waltraud Linnig, and Sr. M. Johannah Paruch, FSGM, eds. *The Pedagogy of God: Its Centrality in Catechesis and Catechist Formation*. Emmaus Road, 2011.

Feiss, Hugh, OSB. "Hugh of St. Victor: *On the Three Days*." In *Trinity and Creation*, edited by Boyd Taylor Coolman and Dale M. Coulter. New City Press, 2011.

Feiss, Hugh, OSB. "Hugh of St. Victor, *Soliloquy on the Betrothal-Gift of the Soul*." In *On Love*, edited by Hugh Feiss. Victorine Texts in Translation 2. New City Press, 2012.

Feiss, Hugh. *Writings on the Spiritual Life*, edited by Christopher P. Evans. Victorine Texts in Translation 4. New City Press, 2013.

Fleteren, Frederick van. "*Acies mentis*." In *Augustine Through the Ages: An Encyclopedia*, edited by Allan Fitzgerald and John Cavadini. Eerdmans, 1999.

Fortin, Ernest. "Reflections on the Proper Way to Read Augustine the Theologian." *Augustinian Studies* 2 (1971): 253–72.

Ganz, David. "Einhard's Charlemagne: The Characterization of Greatness." In *Charlemagne: Empire and Society*, edited by Joanna Story. Manchester University Press, 2005.

Gilson, Étienne. *History of Christian Philosophy in the Middle Ages*. Random House, 1955.

Giszczak, Mark. *Wisdom of Solomon, Catholic Commentary on Sacred Scripture*. Baker Academic, 2024.

Graham, Gordon. *Universities: The Recovery of an Idea*. Imprint Academic, 2002.

Gregory the Great. *Life of Benedict*. Translated by Hilary Costello and Eoin de Bhaldraithe, with commentary by Adalbert de Vogüé. St. Bede's Publications, 1993.

Hamilton, Sir William. "On the State of the English Universities, with more especial reference to Oxford." 1831. In *Discussions on Philosophy and Literature, Education and University Reform*. Longmans, 1853.

Hammer, Jacob. "Cassiodorus, the Saviour of Western Civilization." *Bulletin of the Polish Institute of Arts and Sciences in America* 3, no. 2 (1945): 369–84.

Hammond, Jay. "Dating Bonaventure's Inception as Regent Master." *Franciscan Studies* 67 (2009): 179–226.

Hawking, Stephen. *The Grand Design*. Bantam, 2010.

Higton, Mike. *A Theology of Higher Education*. Oxford University Press, 2012.

Hinkle, Adrian. *Pedagogical Theory of the Hebrew Bible: An Application of Educational Theory to Biblical Texts.* Wipf & Stock, 2016.

Hofer, Andrew, OP. "Frequent Communion for the Greater Glory of God: Thomas Aquinas and Ignatius of Loyola." In *Ignatius of Loyola and Thomas Aquinas: A Jesuit Ressourcement,* edited by Justin M. Anderson, Matthew Levering, and Aaron Pidel, SJ. The Catholic University of America Press, 2024.

Holder-Egger, Oswold, ed. *Monumenta Germaniae Historica* 32. Hannoverae: Impensis Bibliopolii Hahniani, 1905–1913.

Horace. *Epistles of Horace.* Translated by David Ferry. Farrar, Straus, and Giroux, 2001.

Hösle, Vittorio. *The Philosophical Dialogue: A Poetics and a Hermeneutics.* Translated by Steven Rendall. University of Notre Dame Press, 2012.

Hugh of St. Victor. *Ark of Noah.* In *Hugh of Saint-Victor: Selected Spiritual Writings.* Translated by a Religious of CSMV. Harper and Row, 1962.

Hugh of St. Victor. *Didascalicon of Hugh of St. Victor: A Medieval Guide to the Arts.* Translated by Jerome Taylor. Columbia University Press, 1991.

Hugh of St. Victor. *Hugh of Saint-Victor on the Sacraments of the Christian Faith.* Translated by Roy Deferrari. Wipf & Stock, 2007.

Hugh of St. Victor. *Interpretation of Scripture: Practice,* edited by Frans van Liere and Franklin T. Harkins. Victorine Texts in Translation 6. New City Press, 2016.

Hume, David. *Dialogues Concerning Natural Religion.* Doubleday, 1974.

Ignatius of Loyola. *The Autobiography.* Edited by J. F. X. O'Conor, SJ. Benzinger Brothers, 1900.

Jenkins, Roy. "Newman and the Idea of a University." *Newman: A Man for Our Time*. Edited by D. Brown. SPCK, 1990.

Jerome, St. "Letter 107." In *Nicene and Post-Nicene Fathers, Second Series*, vol. 6. ed. Philip Schaff and Henry Wace. Translated by W. H. Fremantle, G. Lewis, and W. G. Martley. Buffalo, NY: Christian Literature Publishing Co., 1893.

Koenig, Harold. "Research on Religion, Spirituality and Mental Health: A Review." *Canadian Journal of Psychiatry* 54, no. 5 (2009): 283–91. https://journals.sagepub.com/doi/pdf/10.1177/070674370905400502.

Kraut, Richard. *Aristotle*. Oxford University Press, 2002.

Lake, W. C. *Memorials of William Charles Lake, Dean of Durham*. E. Arnold, 1901.

LeClercq, W. Jean. *Love of Learning and the Desire for God*. Translated by Catherine Misrahi. Fordham University Press, 1961.

Lehman, Jeffrey S. *Socratic Conversation: Bringing the Dialogues of Plato and the Socratic Tradition into Today's Classroom*. Classical Academic Press, 2021.

Lerer, Seth. *Boethius and Dialogue: Literary Method in The Consolation of Philosophy*. Princeton University Press, 1985.

Lewis, C. S. *The Abolition of Man*. Oxford University Press, 1943.

Lewis, C. S. *An Experiment in Criticism*. Cambridge University Press, 1961.

Liber Pontificalis. Translated by Raymond Davis. Liverpool University Press, 2009.

Lonergan, Bernard. *Method in Theology*, vol. 14 of *The Collected Works of Bernard Lonergan*, edited by Frederick Crowe and Robert Doran. University of Toronto Press, 1990.

MacIntyre, Alasdair. *God, Philosophy, Universities*. Continuum, 2009.

MacIntyre, Alasdair. *Whose Justice? Which Rationality?* University of Notre Dame Press, 1988.

Marenbon, John. *Boethius*. Oxford University Press, 2003.

Maritain, Jacques. *Art and Scholasticism and the Frontiers of Poetry*. Translated by Joseph W. Evans. University of Notre Dame Press, 1974.

Masi, Michael. *Boethian Number Theory: A Translation of the De Institutione Arithmetica*. Editions Rodopi B. V., 1983.

Maskell, Duke, and Ian Robinson. *The New Idea of a University*. Haven Books, 2001.

McMahon, Robert. *Understanding the Medieval Meditative Ascent: Augustine, Anselm, Boethius, and Dante*. The Catholic University of America Press, 2006.

Meyvaert, Paul. "Bede, Cassiodorus, and the Codex Amiatinus." *Speculum* 71, no. 4 (1996): 827–83.

Michael, William C., OP. "Against Dorothy Sayers." Classical Liberal Arts Academy. 2009. https://classicalliberalarts.com/blog/against-dorothy-sayers-2009/.

Monk of St. Gall. *The Life of Charlemagne*. Translated by Lewis Thorpe. Penguin Books, 1969.

Mozley, Thomas. *Reminiscences: Chiefly of Oriel College and the Oxford Movement*, vol. i. Longmans, Green & Co., 1882.

Newman, John Henry. *A Benedictine Education: The Mission of Saint Benedict & The Benedictine Schools*. Edited by Christopher Fisher. Cluny Press, 2020.

Newman, John Henry. *An Essay in Aid of Grammar of Assent*. New York: Longmans, Green & Co., 1903. The National Institute of Newman Studies, www.newmanreader.org.

Newman, John Henry. *An Essay on the Development of Christian Doctrine*. London: James Toovey, 1845.

Newman, John Henry. *The Idea of a University* (1873). Longmans, Green & Co., 1907.

Newman, John Henry. *Historical Sketches*, vol. iii (1872). Longmans, Green & Co., 1909.

Newman, John Henry. *John Henry Newman: Autobiographical Writings*. Edited by H. Tristram. Sheed & Ward, 1956.

Newman, John Henry. *John Henry Newman: Sermons, 1824–1843*, vol. iv. Edited by F. J. McGrath. Oxford University Press, 2011.

Newman, John Henry. *Letters and Diaries of John Henry Newman*, 32 vols. Edited by C. S. Dessain et al. T. Nelson, 1961–72. Clarendon Press, 1973–2008.

Newman, John Henry. *Meditations and Devotions*. Edited by Rev. W. P. Neville. Longmans, Green & Co., 1907.

Newman, John Henry. *My Campaign in Ireland, Part 1: Catholic University Reports and Other Papers*. Edited by Paul Shrimpton. Gracewing, 2021.

Newman, John Henry. *Newman: Sermons, 1824–1843*, vol. i. Edited by P. Murray. Clarendon Press, 1991.

Newman, John Henry. *On Consulting the Faithful in Matters of Doctrine* (1859). Edited by J. Coulson. Rowman & Littlefield, 1961.

Newman, John Henry. *The Rise and Progress of Universities and Benedictine Essays*. Edited by M. K. Tillman. Gracewing, 2001.

Newman, John Henry. *Sermons Preached on Various Occasions* (1857). Longmans, 1908.

Nockles, P. B. "Lost Causes and . . . Impossible Loyalties: The Oxford Movement and the University." In *The History of the University of Oxford*, vol. vi, edited by M. G. Brock and M. C. Curthoys. Clarendon Press, 1997.

Ockham, William of. *Opera Theologica*, 10 vols. St. Bonaventure Press, 1967–86.

O'Daly, Gerard. *The Poetry of Boethius*. Duckworth, 1991.

O'Donnell, J. J. *Cassiodorus*. University of California Press, 1979.

Olson, Paul A. *The Journey to Wisdom: Self-Education in Patristic and Medieval Literature*. University of Nebraska Press, 1995.

Ouellet, Marc. "The Significance of St. John Henry Newman for Catholic Theology." In *Lead Kindly Light: Essays for Ian Ker*, edited by Paul Shrimpton. Gracewing, 2022.

Padelford, Morgan. *Essays on the Study and Use of Poetry by Plutarch and Basil the Great*. Yale University Press, 1902.

Page, Rolph Barlow. "The Letters of Alcuin." PhD diss., Columbia University, 1909.

Page, Rolph Barlow. *The Letters of Alcuin*. The Forest Press, 1909.

Patch, Howard Rollin. *The Tradition of Boethius: A Study of His Importance in Medieval Culture*. Russell & Russell, 1935.

Pelikan, Jaroslav. *The Idea of the University: A Re-Examination*. Yale University Press, 1992.

Petrovich, Douglas. *The World's Oldest Alphabet: Hebrew as the Language of the Proto-Consonantal Script*. Hendrickson Academic, 2017.

Pieper, Josef. *Leisure, the Basis of Culture*. Ignatius, 2009.

Pieper, Josef. *Only the Lover Sings: Art and Contemplation*. Ignatius Press, 1990.

Plato. *Complete Works*. Edited by John M. Cooper. Hackett, 1997.

Plato. *Plato in Twelve Volumes*, vol. 9. Translated by W. R. M. Lamb. Harvard University Press, 1925.

Polanyi, Michael. *The Tacit Dimension*. Doubleday, 1966.

Ratzinger, Joseph. *Joseph Ratzinger Gesammelte Schriften* (JRGS) vol. 3/1. Herder, 2020.

Reiss, Edmund. *Boethius*. Twayne Publishers, 1982.

Rorem, Paul. *Hugh of Saint Victor*. Oxford, 2009.

Rothblatt, Sheldon. "An Oxonian 'Idea' of a University: J. H. Newman and 'Well-being.'" *The History of the University of Oxford*, vol. vi. Edited by M. G. Brock and M. C. Curthoys. Clarendon Press, 1997.

Rothblatt, Sheldon. *The Modern University and Its Discontents: The Fate of Newman's Legacies in Britain and America*. Cambridge University Press, 1997.

Rudolph, Conrad. "'First I Find the Center Point': Reading the Text of Hugh of Saint Victor's *The Mystic Ark*." *Transactions of the American Philosophical Society* 94, no. 4 (2004).

Ryle, Gilbert. "Knowing How and Knowing That." *Proceedings of the Aristotelian Society* 46 (1945–46): 1–16.

Salzmann, A. B. "The Holy Spirit and the Life of the Christian According to Hugh of St. Victor: Dator et Donum, Cordis Omne Bonum." PhD diss., Boston College, 2015.

Salzmann, Andrew Benjamin. "Hugh of St. Victor." In *A Companion to Medieval Christian Humanism*, edited by John P. Bequette. Brill, 2016.

Salzmann, Andrew Benjamin. "A Trinitarian Introduction to Hugh of St. Victor's Exegesis." In *Victorine Restoration: Essays on Hugh of St Victor, Richard of St Victor, and Thomas Gallus*, edited by Robert J. Porwoll and David Allison Orsbon. Cursor Mundi 39. Brepols, 2021.

Sayers, Dorothy. *The Lost Tools of Learning*. GLH Publishing, 2017.

Scarry, Elaine. "The Well-Rounded Sphere: The Metaphysical Structure of the *Consolation of Philosophy*." In *Essays in the*

Numerical Criticism of Medieval Literature, edited by Caroline D. Eckhardt. Bucknell University Press, 1980.

Schindler, D. C. *Plato's Critique of Impure Reason*. The Catholic University of America Press, 2008.

Scruton, Roger. *An Intelligent Person's Guide to Modern Culture*. St. Augustine's Press, 2000.

Sicard, Patrice. *Iter Victorinum: La tradition manuscrite des œuvres de Hugues et de Richard de Saint-Victor; Répertoire complémentaire et études, avec un index cumulatif des manuscrits des œuvres de Hugues et de Richard de Saint-Victor*. Bibliotheca Victorina 24. Brepols, 2015.

Sillem, Dom Aelred. "St. Benedict." In *Benedict's Disciples*, edited by D. H. Farmer. Fowler Wright Books Ltd., 1980.

Slattery, William J. *Heroism and Genius*. Ignatius Press, 2017.

Spijker, Ineke van't. "*Non quaerat extra se, qui haec propter se facta credit*: Hugh of Saint-Victor's Pedagogy." In *Omnium expetendorum prima est sapientia: Studies on Victorine Thought and Influence*, edited by Wanda Bajor, Michal Buraczewski, Marcin Jan Janecki, and Dominique Poirel. Bibliotheca Victorina 29. Turnhout, 2021.

Smith, Randall. *Aquinas, Bonaventure and the Scholastic Culture of Medieval Paris: Preaching, Prologues, and Biblical Commentary*. Cambridge University Press, 2020.

Smith, Randall. *Bonaventure's Journey of the Soul into God: Context and Commentary*. Cambridge University Press, 2024.

Spaemann, Robert. *Persons: The Difference Between 'Someone' and 'Something.'* Oxford Studies in Theological Ethics. Oxford University Press, 2006.

Spitzer, Robert J., SJ. *Challenges of the Modern World*. Sophia Institute for Teachers, 2022.

Spitzer, Robert J., SJ. *Christ, Science, and Reason: What We Can Know About Jesus, Mary, and Miracles*. Ignatius Press, 2024.

Spitzer, Robert J., SJ. *Christ Versus Satan in our Daily Lives*. Ignatius, 2020.

Spitzer, Robert J., SJ. *Escape from Evil's Darkness*. Ignatius Press, 2021.

Spitzer, Robert J., SJ. *The Four Levels of Happiness*. Sophia Institute Press, 2024.

Spitzer, Robert J., SJ. *Healing the Culture*. Ignatius Press, 2000.

Spitzer, Robert J., SJ. *The Moral Wisdom of the Catholic Church*. Ignatius Press, 2022.

Spitzer, Robert J., SJ. *New Proofs for the Existence of God*. Eerdmans, 2010.

Spitzer, Robert J., SJ. *Science at the Doorstep to God*. Ignatius, 2023.

Spitzer, Robert J., SJ. *Science, Reason, and Faith: Discovering the Bible*. OSV Press, 2023.

Spitzer, Robert J., SJ. *The Spirit of Leadership*. Executive Excellence, 2000.

Spitzer, Robert J., SJ. *Ten Universal Principles*. Ignatius Press, 2011.

Spitzer, Robert J., and James Sinclair. "Fine-Tuning and Indications of Transcendent Intelligence." In *Theism and Atheism: Opposing Arguments in Philosophy*, edited by Joseph Koterski, SJ, and Graham Oppy. Macmillan Reference, 2019.

Strunk, William, and E. B. White. *The Elements of Style*. Pearson, 1999.

Strunk, William, Jr. *Elements of Style Workbook*. Tip-Top Education, 2018.

Taylor, Charles. *Sources of the Self*. Harvard University Press, 1989.

Taylor, Jerome. *Origin and Early Life of Hugh of St. Victor: An Evaluation of the Tradition*. Texts and Studies in the History of Mediaeval Education 5. University of Notre Dame Press, 1957.

Thomas Aquinas. *Academic Sermons*. The Catholic University of America Press, 2012.

Thomas Aquinas. *De Veritate*. Vol. 2: Questions 10–20. Translated by James V. McGlynn, SJ. Henry Regnery Company, 1953.

Thomas Aquinas. *The Divisions and Methods of the Sciences*. Translated by Armand Maurer. Pontifical Institute of Mediaeval Studies, 1986.

Thomas Aquinas. *Opera Omnia Sancti Thomae Aquinatis*. Musurgia, 1948.

Thomas Aquinas. *Summa Theologica*. Translated by English Dominican Province. Benzinger Bros., 1948.

Twu, Krista Sue-Lo. "This Is Comforting? Boethius's *Consolation of Philosophy*, Rhetoric, Dialectic, and 'Unicum Illud Inter Homines Deumque Commercium.'" In *New Directions in Boethian Studies*, edited by Noel Harold Kaylor, Jr. and Philip Edward Phillips. Studies in Medieval Culture Series 45. Western Michigan University Press, 2007.

Uhlfelder, Myra L. *The Consolation of Philosophy as Cosmic Image*. Medieval and Renaissance Texts and Studies 474. Arizona Center for Medieval and Renaissance Studies, 2018.

Virchow, Rudolf. *Cellular Pathology as Based upon Physiological and Pathological Histology*. Translated by Frank Chance. London: John Churchill, 1860.

Ward, Wilfrid. *The Life of John Henry, Cardinal Newman*. Longmans, Green & Co., 1912.

West, Andrew. *Alcuin and the Rise of the Christian Schools*. New York: Charles Scribner's Sons, 1892. Reprint 1912.

Weisheipl, James A., OP. "Classification of the Sciences in Medieval Thought." *Mediaeval Studies* 27 (1965): 54–90.

Wilde, Oscar. *Complete Works*. HarperCollins, 1989.

Wilson, Douglas. *The Case for Classical Christian Education*. Crossway, 2003.

Wilson, James Matthew. *The Vision of the Soul: Truth, Goodness, and Beauty in the Western Tradition*. The Catholic University of America Press, 2017.

Yeats, W. B. "The Second Coming." *Poetry Foundation*, https://www.poetryfoundation.org/poems/43290/the-second-coming.

Zinn, Grover. "*Historia fundamentum est*: The Role of History in the Contemplative Life According to Hugh of St. Victor." In *Contemporary Reflections on the Medieval Christian Tradition: Essays in Honor of Ray C. Petry*, edited by G. H. Shriver. Duke University Press, 1974.

Zuckert, Catherine H. *Plato's Philosophers: The Coherence of the Dialogues*. University of Chicago Press, 2012.

Author Biographies

David P. Deavel is Associate Professor of Theology at the University of St. Thomas in Houston, Texas. He holds a PhD from Fordham, is a winner of the Acton Institute's Novak Award, is a former Lincoln Fellow at the Claremont Institute, and is a Senior Contributor at The Imaginative Conservative. With Jessica Hooten Wilson he edited *Solzhenitsyn and American Culture: The Russian Soul in the West* (Notre Dame, 2020).

Erik Z. D. Ellis is Assistant Professor, Education and Classical Learning at the University of Dallas. He earned a BA in the University Scholars Program at Baylor University with major concentrations in Greek and Latin and a minor concentration in History. He stayed at Baylor to earn an MA in History, and upon graduation, worked as a teacher for five years. He then received master's and doctoral degrees at the University of Notre Dame's Classics Department and Medieval Institute, and then taught Latin, Greek, and Literature courses at the Universidad de los Andes (Chile) before returning to the US. As a researcher, Dr. Ellis focuses his efforts on tenth-century Byzantium and sixteenth-century Northern Europe, spending much time with Constantine Porphyrogennitos, Thomas More, Erasmus, and Juan Luis Vives, although he often allows himself to be distracted by J. R. R. Tolkien and C. S. Lewis. He is enthusiastic about sacred choral music, visiting remote places, and speaking classical and modern foreign languages.

Edward Feser is Professor of Philosophy at Pasadena City College. He is the author of many academic articles and books, including *Aquinas*, *Scholastic Metaphysics*, and *Aristotle's Revenge: The Metaphysical Foundations of Physical and Biological Science*.

Michael P. Foley is a Catholic theologian, a Professor of Patristics in the Great Texts Program at Baylor University, and the author of over 400 articles and sixteen books ranging from the writings of St. Augustine of Hippo to Catholic food and drink. He also serves on the board of Adeodatus.

Josef Froula is a 1992 graduate of Thomas Aquinas College. He went on to teach at an all-boys prep school for five years. Then, for over twenty years, he taught the liberal arts and theology at two seminaries: The Legion of Christ College of Humanities and Holy Apostles College and Seminary. He has earned graduate degrees in literature, theology, and education. In 2018 he accepted a position as a tutor at Thomas Aquinas College and now teaches at the campus in Northfield, MA. The title of his doctoral dissertation is "St. Thomas on the Nature and Purpose of Education: The Importance of Aristotelian-Thomistic Principles for Educational Leaders."

Joe Heschmeyer, a Kansas City native, is a staff apologist for Catholic Answers. A popular author, speaker, blogger, and podcaster, he joined the apostolate in March 2021 after three years as an instructor at Holy Family School of Faith in Overland Park, Kansas. While at School of Faith, Joe focused primarily on formation for the Kansas City Archdiocese's elementary and high school teachers. He also spent a year helping to manage the Catholic Spiritual Mentorship program. Prior to his work at Holy Family, he discerned the priesthood from 2012–17 for the Archdiocese of Kansas City. During that time, he earned both a bachelor's degree in philosophy from Kenrick-Glennon Seminary in St. Louis and a degree in sacred theology (STB) from Rome's Pontifical North American College. A regular contributor to Catholic Answers Live, Catholic Answers Focus, and Catholic Answers Magazine (print and online) even before joining the apostolate, Joe has blogged at his own "Shameless

Popery" website and co-hosted a weekly show called "The Catholic Podcast." To date, he has authored three books, including Pope Peter for Catholic Answers Press. A former practicing attorney in Washington, DC, Joe received his Juris Doctor degree from Georgetown University in 2010 after earning a bachelor's degree in history from Topeka's Washburn University.

Arthur Hippler is Chairman of the Religion Department at Providence Academy, where he has taught since 2006. He also teaches as an Adjunct Professor in St. Paul School of Divinity at the University of St. Thomas and as an instructor in the Harry Flynn Catechetical Institute for the Archdiocese of St. Paul-Minneapolis. A graduate of Thomas Aquinas College in California, he received his Doctorate in Philosophy from Boston College. He is the author of two books on Catholic social teaching and two iBooks on C. S. Lewis. He is married with five children.

Jeffrey S. Lehman is co-founder and Dean of Fellows at the Boethius Institute. He earned a BA in Biblical Literature and Philosophy from Taylor University, an MA in Philosophy of Religion and Ethics from Biola University, and an MA and PhD in Philosophy from the University of Dallas. He is the founder and President of the Arts of Liberty Project, a Founding Fellow of the Center for Thomas More Studies, and he has served on the teaching faculty at Biola University, Thomas Aquinas College, Hillsdale College, and the University of Dallas, where he received the Haggerty Award for Excellence in Teaching. While at the University of Dallas, he also served as director of the Classical Education Graduate Program and executive director of the St. Ambrose Center for Catholic Liberal Education. He has several publications on a wide array of authors, including *Augustine: Rejoicing in the Truth* and *Socratic Conversation: Bringing the Dialogues of Plato* and the *Socratic Tradition into Today's Classroom*. Since the fall of 2023, as Professor of Philosophy and

Theology he is building and directing a new MA program in Catholic Education at the Augustine Institute's Graduate School of Theology (St. Louis, MO).

Alex E. Lessard, editor, studied theology as an undergraduate at the University of St. Thomas (MN) with Don Briel, the founder of the Catholic Studies movement, who introduced him to the writings of St. John Henry Newman and to the breadth and depth of Catholic literature. He took his doctorate in systematic theology at Boston College with Fr. Matthew Lamb. He teaches theology at Rosary College and is the director of intellectual formation at the Santiago Catholic Trade School. Having co-founded St. Monica Academy, an independent Catholic school in Pasadena in 2001, he and his wife, Angela, now support the renewal of Catholic Liberal Education and Culture through their nonprofit, Adeodatus. Alex is Executive Co-Director of The Cornerstone Forum, founded by Gil Bailie to bring René Girard's anthropological contribution to human self-understanding into fruitful dialogue with the theological tradition exemplified by Joseph Ratzinger. He is a Fellow of the Boethius Institute; serves on the Thomas Aquinas College Board of Regents; on the Wyoming Catholic College Presidential Advisory Council; on the board of the Cantwell Foundation, a nonprofit supporting Los Angeles Catholic Arts & Culture; as theological advisor to Gaudent Angeli, an apostolate promoting renewed devotion to St. Vibiana, the patroness of the Archdiocese of Los Angeles; and is Executive Board Secretary of the Newman Club of Los Angeles, a lay Catholic literary organization founded in 1899 under the inspiration of Bishop George Montgomery—less than a decade after Newman's death—with an uninterrupted series of monthly meetings over the subsequent 126 years. He is a perpetual member of the Fellowship of Catholic Scholars and a Knight of Columbus at St. Therese Carmelite Church in Alhambra, CA. Alex & Angela have nine children and nine grandchildren.

Richard Meloche is the President of the Alcuin Institute for Catholic Culture in the Diocese of Tulsa & Eastern Oklahoma. He earned his initial degrees in philosophy and theology from the University of Western Ontario, and his PhD in Systematic Theology from Ave Maria University in Naples, FL.

Andrew Salzmann is the director of the Sheridan Center for Classical Studies at Benedictine College and Assistant Professor of Theology. Originally from Wisconsin, he writes on Augustine and the Augustinian tradition, with particular attention to anthropology and pneumatology. He did his graduate work at Yale Divinity School (MAR, 2007) and Boston College (PhD, 2015). At Benedictine, Dr. Salzmann teaches Christ and the Trinity, Christianity & World Religions, and American Catholic History, among other courses. In addition, he assists with deacon formation for the Archdiocese of Kansas City (Anthropology, Christology, Mariology) and serves as a subject matter expert in religion for the University of Foreign Military and Cultural Studies at Ft. Leavenworth.

Paul Shrimpton is a graduate of Balliol College, Oxford, and has taught at Magdalen College School, Oxford for nearly forty years. He has given many talks and lectures on Newman and education, and is the author of *A Catholic Eton? Newman's Oratory School* (2005) and *The 'Making of Men': The Idea and Reality of Newman's University in Oxford and Dublin* (2015). He has also written about the influence of Newman on the students of the White Rose resistance in Nazi Germany in Conscience before Conformity (2018). Recently he brought out two volumes of Newman's unpublished university papers, *My Campaign in Ireland*, Parts I & II, both of which are critical editions, as well as editing a festschrift for the leading Newman scholar Ian Ker.

Randall B. Smith is a Full Professor with tenure at the University of St. Thomas in Houston, Texas. He also teaches regularly in the University's interdisciplinary Honors Program. He earned his BA in Chemistry at Cornell College where he studied the history and philosophy of science, earned an MA in Theology at the University of Dallas, and an MMS and a PhD at the University of Notre Dame. He has served as the President of CatholicThinkers.com (previously known as the International Catholic University) since 2014, and has served on the board of the Fellowship of Catholic Scholars since 2019.

Fr. Robert J. Spitzer, SJ, is a Jesuit, and is currently the President of the Magis Center of Reason and Faith (www.magiscenter.com) and the Spitzer Center for Ethical Leadership (www.spitzercenter.org). He is the host of a weekly international EWTN television program—Father Spitzer's Universe. Fr. Spitzer was President of Gonzaga University from 1998 to 2009. He serves on multiple boards including as board chair for Reell Precision Manufacturing, which has plants and offices in the US, Europe, and Asia and the board of trustees at the University of Mary and Catholic Eldercare.

R. Jared Staudt, editor, serves as Director of Content for Exodus 90. He also teaches for Rosary College, Catholic International University, and the Institute of Catholic Culture. He earned his BA and MA in Catholic Studies at the University of St. Thomas in St. Paul, MN and his PhD in Systematic Theology from Ave Maria University in Florida. He is author of *Words Made Flesh: The Sacramental Mission of Catholic Education* (Catholic Education Press); *The Primacy of God: The Virtue of Religion in Catholic Theology* (Emmaus Academic); and *Restoring Humanity: Essays on the Evangelization of Culture* (Divine Providence Press). He and his wife Anne have six children and he is a Benedictine oblate. Jared also serves on the board of Adeodatus.

Michael Waldstein is Professor of New Testament at Franciscan University (2019–) and Senior Faculty Fellow at the St. Paul Center for Biblical Theology (2018–2019). He holds a BA from Thomas Aquinas College (1977), a PhD in Philosophy from the University of Dallas (1981), an SSL summa cum laude from the Pontifical Biblical Institute in Rome (1984), and a ThD in New Testament and Christian Origins from Harvard University (1990). From 1988 to 1996 he was assistant professor of New Testament at the University of Notre Dame, where he received tenure in 1996. From 1996 to 2006 he served as the founding president of the International Theological Institute in Gaming, Austria, and as the St. Francis of Assisi Chair of New Testament (to 2008). From 2008 to 2017 he was Max Seckler Chair of Theology at Ave Maria University. He served as a member of the Pontifical Council for the Family (2003–2009), the Board of Trustees of the University of Eichstätt, Germany (2007–2011), and as an Ordinary Academician of the Pontifical Academy of St. Thomas Aquinas, Rome (2011–).

James Matthew Wilson is the Cullen Foundation Chair in English Literature and the founding director of the MFA program in Creative Writing at the University of Saint Thomas. The author of eleven books, his most recent book of poems, *The Strangeness of the Good*, won the poetry book of the year award from the Catholic Media Awards. The Dallas Institute of Humanities awarded him the Hiett Prize in 2017. He serves as poet-in-residence of the Benedict XVI Institute, editor of Colosseum Books, and poetry editor of *Modern Age* magazine.

Index

Also in the Adeodatus Series on Catholic Education & Culture

Words Made Flesh: The Sacramental Mission of Catholic Education, by R. Jared Staudt. Foreword by Patrick Reilly

Also from Catholic Education Press

A Brief Quadrivium and *Teaching the Quadrivium: A Guide for Instructors,* by Peter Ulrickson

Shared Mission: Religious Education in the Catholic Tradition, Revised Edition, by Leonardo Franchi. Preface by Gerhard Cardinal Müller

Thomas Shields and the Renewal of Catholic Education, by Leonardo Franchi. Foreword by Mary Pat Donoghue

From The Catholic University of America Press

Renewing Catholic Schools: How to Regain a Catholic Vision in a Secular Age, by Institute for Catholic Liberal Education. Edited by R. Jared Staudt. Foreword by Most Rev. Samuel J. Aquila

Renewing the Mind: A Reader in the Philosophy of Catholic Education. Edited by Ryan N. S. Topping

A Reason Open to God: On Universities, Education, and Culture, by Pope Benedict XVI. Foreword by John H. Garvey

What We Hold in Trust: Rediscovering the Purpose of Catholic Higher Education, by Don J. Briel, Kenneth E. Goodpaster, and Michael J. Naughton. Foreword by Dennis Holtschneider, CM

The Vision of the Soul: Truth, Goodness, and Beauty in the Western Tradition, by James Matthew Wilson

A Guide to John Henry Newman: His Life and Thought. Edited by Juan R. Vélez

A Brief Life of Thomas Aquinas: The Theologian in His Context, by Jean-Pierre Torrell, OP